The GAO: The Quest for Accountability in American Government

Frederick C. Mosher

The underlying theme of this book—the first thorough work on the General Accounting Office to be published since 1939—is the GAO as a tool of accountability in government. The first part of the book is essentially a biography of the institution. The second part describes and analyzes the institution, discussing such topics as the constitutional and managerial questions that grow out of the GAO's semi-independent status, the various roles it performs, and its relationships with Congress, the executive branch, and outside institutions, both public and private.

The performance of the GAO has been a vital component of the development of governance in the United States. As Professor Mosher focuses on the agency, he inevitably sheds light as well on a number of other topics of concern to scholars of American government: separation of powers, the changing nature and structure of Congress, legislative oversight, intergovernmental relations, and public-private relationships in a complex democratic society.

About the Author

Frederick C. Mosher, Doherty Professor in the Woodrow Wilson Department of Government and Foreign Affairs at the University of Virginia, has also been a professor in the Department of Political Science, University of California at Berkeley. He received the Louis Brownlow Memorial Book Prize for his book *Democracy and the Public Service.*

THE GAO

Other Titles of Interest

THE GAO: THE QUEST FOR ACCOUNTABILITY IN AMERICAN GOVERNMENT

Frederick C. Mosher

Published in cooperation with the
National Academy of Public Administration

Westview Press / Boulder, Colorado

Published in 1979 in the United States of America by
  Westview Press, Inc.
  5500 Central Avenue
  Boulder, Colorado 80301
  Frederick A. Praeger, Publisher

Library of Congress Cataloging in Publication Data
Mosher, Frederick C.
  The GAO.
  Bibliography: p.
  1. United States. General Accounting Office—History. 2. Finance, Public—United
  States—Accounting—History. I. Title.
HJ9802.M68   353.007'232   78-27105
ISBN 0-89158-458-7
ISBN 0-89158-459-5 pbk.

Printed and bound in the United States of America

For
Edith

CONTENTS

Part 2
Emerging Roles of the GAO

FIGURES AND TABLES

FOREWORD

During the winter of 1976-1977, Comptroller General of the United States Elmer B. Staats requested the cooperation and assistance of the National Academy of Public Administration (NAPA) in the preparation of a study of the General Accounting Office (GAO). The study was to consist of a history and description of the development of the office. Recognizing the great importance of the GAO as the principal agency charged with the task of assuring accountability in government, the academy responded positively to the Comptroller General's initiative. A key consideration in this response was the awareness that, despite the importance of the GAO role and the increasing attention accorded it in the popular media, the agency is one of the least understood organizations in the federal government.

In accordance with its normal practice in the conduct of its studies, NAPA designated a panel of distinguished citizens, representing a variety of experiences and professional perspectives, to guide, advise on, and generally superintend the project. The panel was actively engaged in shaping the study, taking a particular interest in assuring its accuracy, scholarly integrity, objectivity, and balance. Panel members reviewed and criticized the several drafts of the study in seeking to assure its optimum value in the literature of public administration.

On behalf of the trustees of the academy, I want to take this occasion to express our great appreciation to the members of the panel who devoted so much of their time and energy to the guidance of this study. Its value has been greatly enhanced by their continuing involvement and commitment. Particular recognition should be accorded the role of Wayne L. Thompson, senior vice-president of Dayton Hudson Corporation, who served as panel chairman.

One of the principal contributions of the panel was its recommendation that the study include a collection of case studies illustrating the ways in which the GAO carries out specific tasks. This collection of case studies was undertaken jointly with the main history, resulting in a pair of companion volumes. The general book, entitled *The GAO: The Quest for Accountability in*

American Government, was written by Frederick C. Mosher, Doherty Professor, Department of Government and Foreign Affairs, University of Virginia. The case study collection was edited by Erasmus H. Kloman, senior research associate of NAPA working in close collaboration with Mosher.

As director of the study, Mosher brought to the undertaking his extraordinary knowledge of public administration, his incisive insight, and his ability to present a complex array of information in a clear and readable text. We are also indebted to Kloman for assembling and editing the case studies, while also serving as secretary to the panel. Finally, the overall project was facilitated in all respects by Jeffrey L. Jacobs, the GAO staff assistant on the project, who provided invaluable support.

George H. Esser
Executive Director
National Academy of
Public Administration

MEMBERS OF THE ADVISORY PANEL

Richard Bolling, U.S. Representative, Missouri

William G. Colman, consultant and former Executive Director, Advisory Commission on Intergovernmental Relations

Martha W. Griffiths, attorney and former Congresswoman

Charles G. Hitch, President, Resources for the Future, Inc.

Charles F. Luce, Chairman, Consolidated Edison Co. of New York, Inc.

Charles McC. Mathias, Jr., U.S. Senator, Maryland

Robert K. Mautz, Partner, Ernst and Ernst

Arthur S. Miller, Professor, National Law Center, The George Washington University

Don K. Price, Professor and former Dean, John F. Kennedy School of Government, Harvard University

Wayne E. Thompson, Senior Vice President, Dayton Hudson Corp.

PREFACE

When Comptroller General Elmer B. Staats first suggested the project of which this book is the major product, he had in mind a straightforward descriptive history of the General Accounting Office (GAO) from its beginnings to the present day. Its purpose would be to set forth for interested segments of the public the evolutionary processes through which that organization has been transformed to its current posture and responsibilities. As the reader will recognize, the changes in the organization particularly since World War II have been enormous; a person familiar with it thirty years ago would hardly recognize it today. It was my suggestion that the historical treatment would be more valuable if to it were added a more intensive analysis of the roles of the GAO in American government and society today. This was agreed, and the resultant volume is consequently divided into two interdependent parts: a history, and an analysis of the current situation.

Like other established organizations, the GAO has an institutional personality of its own. But the most interesting and challenging aspects of its work involve its interdependence with its environment. Its external relationships comprise a highly complex system of variegated and shifting transactions with the Congress, the executive branch, state and local governments, foreign governments and international organizations, and a great variety of organizations and individuals in the private sector. Particularly in recent years, the potential sweep of the GAO's concerns has become almost as broad as that of the federal government itself. I have found this study particularly revealing of how our system of government works, what it does, and the problems attending its decisions and actions. The GAO is, among other things, a picture window on a moving vehicle traversing a rapidly changing landscape. I very much hope that this document will contribute as much to the understanding of American government as it does to the understanding of the GAO.

It was agreed from the beginning that this study should be expository, not evaluative. It is intended neither as a panegyric nor a condemnation. I have tried to the best of my ability to avoid the introduction of any biases (though I recognize, as should the reader, that complete objectivity is impossible, given that an author must select the facts, events, and views on which he reports, and that this selection process itself involves subjective judgments). The GAO is, like most other sizable governmental agencies, controversial. Its methods, reports, recommendations, and indeed its very survival have been objects of criticism, both in the past and the present. I have endeavored to identify and define the basic issues and to provide the arguments on every side, documented as far as possible. But this book contains no recommendation on the part of its author.

The study would not have been possible without the support and encouragement of the GAO. It was conducted under the auspices of the National Academy of Public Administration and specifically with the guidance of the ten-member panel that the Academy designated. I sought and received information and advice from a great many GAO employees, and a very few of its leaders were asked to read and criticize all or selected parts of the manuscript—this was intended to avoid errors of fact, interpretation, and emphasis. As agreed at the outset, no pressure was brought to bear, and there was no censorship.

The methods employed in the study were not different from those of historians on the one hand and of the more traditional political scientists on the other. My colleague, Jeffrey L. Jacobs, and I relied in the first place on the literature of others—books, articles, and speeches about the ancient and recent past and about the present. We scoured, read, or at least glanced through thousands of pages of official documents—congressional acts, bills, reports, and hearings; executive orders and other documents; reports of official study commissions; court decisions; GAO reports; testimony; and other relevant official materials. We read a great many internal GAO documents, attended a variety of GAO meetings, and conducted unstructured interviews with more than one hundred persons, some of them on two or more occasions. These included members and staff of Congress, officials and employees of the GAO, current and past, representatives of executive agencies, representatives of nonfederal groups interested in the GAO, academics, and others. We organized and conducted a number of meetings on our own, directed at eliciting the views of others about the GAO, most of which lasted several hours. They included separate meetings with congressional staff members, representatives of various executive agencies, representatives of nonfederal organizations concerned with the GAO, leading staff members of the Congressional Research Service, and senior staff of the Brookings Institution. Finally, we conducted or reviewed a number of studies of GAO audits and investigations in a variety of subject matter areas. Some of these are described in the companion work, *Cases in Accountability: The Work of the GAO,* edited by Erasmus H. Kloman.

In works of this kind, which are descriptive of past history as well as of current developments, it is necessary to determine a cutoff date. On a number of the succeeding pages, the phrase "at the time of this writing" or its equivalent is inserted. The time of writing may be considered to be July 1, 1978. Some relevant subsequent developments that occurred before the book went to press are included. Unless otherwise noted, the years referred to in the text are fiscal years, not calendar years.

The panel that the National Academy of Public Administration designated for this study was the most valuable group of this kind with which I have ever worked. It was wise, dedicated, and frank. Most of its members attended most of its five meetings, and their advice and criticisms greatly contributed to the balance and insight of this volume, to the extent that those qualities are present.

This work has depended heavily upon the people who inhabit or have inhabited the GAO, from Comptroller General Staats and Deputy Comptroller General Keller on down. I have never associated with a group more friendly, more courteous, and more helpful than those in the GAO. They have led me to, and provided me with, more information and more guidance than an outsider could reasonably expect. It is impracticable to list all of their names and titles, even if I could. But I think it appropriate that I link my name with theirs in that our goals are consonant: to contribute to the improvement of American government.

I am indebted also to a large number of people outside of the GAO who have contributed to this volume. To list them all would likewise be impracticable, but their information, experiences, and insights were invaluable.

Of all those who aided in this project, the most important were my immediate assistants. First among them was Jeffrey L. Jacobs, who worked with me during most of the project's duration. He was more collaborator than assistant, for we worked together, dividing tasks between one another. He knew where the information was and could dig it out; he wrote a great many of the statements that formed the basis for the draft. Second was Mary E. Amburgey, our secretary, who arranged our meetings and interviews and managed our files. She also typed—and endlessly retyped—our drafts.

In a book dedicated to the principle of accountability it would be redundant for the author to proclaim or admit his responsibility. Rather

would I say simply that I am indebted to all those who have helped me
and that I have done my best.

Frederick C. Mosher
Doherty Professor
Government and Foreign Affairs
University of Virginia
Charlottesville, Virginia

THE GAO

INTRODUCTION

In 1789, Benjamin Franklin wrote: "Our Constitution is in actual operation; everything appears to promise that it will last; but in this world nothing is certain but death and taxes."[1] Very probably, most Americans then and since then would agree that "death and taxes" are not only inevitable but almost equally undesirable. There has been resistance to taxation from the beginning of civilization; it has given rise to rebellions and wars, including the American Revolution. As this is written[2] the United States is in the midst of what is widely described as a "tax revolt," sparked by an initiative to reduce property taxes in California that was passed by a two-to-one majority of Golden State voters. Subsequent public opinion polls indicated that the California sentiment is echoed in all of the other states. The drive to reduce taxes or at least to minimize their increase has been reflected in statements of the President of the United States, many congressmen, state governors, state legislators, county commissioners, and city mayors and council members.

The other side of taxes is expenditures, a topic conveniently avoided in the California initiative. But there also appears to be a strong undercurrent of opinion that public expenditures are inefficiently administered, ineffective, or downright fraudulent. A general distrust of government and the way it spends the taxpayers' money is no more novel in American life than is the distaste for taxes. Discontent and frustration about public spending have ebbed and flowed throughout the course of our history. They are at a high, perhaps still rising, tide today. This recent disenchantment probably reflects not only what many perceive as the increasing tax "bite" but also the pinch of continuing inflation and the disillusionment growing out of the Vietnam War and Watergate. Whatever the source, the products have been renewed demands for more frugality and efficiency in public spending and the holding of governmental institutions and officials more accountable for their actions.

This Volume

This book concerns accountability and, more specifically, one of the institutions initially set up primarily for the purpose of assuring accountability for governmental performance. It is a history and analysis of the Comptroller General of the United States and the General Accounting Office (GAO) over which he presides.[3] Its aim is to enhance understanding of the nature of the GAO as an institution, its role in the American system of government, how it "got this way," and the directions in which it is moving. The GAO's major products are hundreds of reports and decisions as well as testimony before Congress that deal with an enormous variety of facets of American government and society. Most of its reports are available to the public at small cost, and some are picked up by the media and given wide circulation. Yet works about the GAO itself as an institution of American government have been relatively rare and have not enjoyed a wide readership; much of what has been written about it is out of date, often based upon a book written forty years ago,[4] or is simply mistaken.

The GAO's activities today go considerably beyond accountability as the word has been traditionally understood. According to its own leadership, its primary mission is to increase the effectiveness with which the government is meeting its growing responsibilities and to help in bringing about improvements. Among those familiar with the organization, most would assent to this view of the GAO's purpose. Even though there may be disagreement as to how that purpose should be given effect, few among them would question that the GAO is an important element in the national government and that its importance is growing.

In many respects, the GAO is unique: as an organization of the national government; in comparison with organizations of other American governments; and in contrast to institutions of other national governments in the world. Some organizations in American state and local governments and in other national governments are approaching or emulating it, but none is a true parallel. It differs too in many significant ways from accounting firms in the private sector, which at one time it endeavored to imitate.

The uniqueness of the GAO stems in part from its legal and official status in the U.S. government. It is an arm of the Congress, from which it receives its powers, responsibilities, and resources. But it is also independent, even of Congress, in the exercise of some of its powers and in its choice of the majority of its projects and the conduct of virtually all of them. This independence, which the GAO treasures, is enhanced by the nature of the appointment and tenure of its top leaders. The Comptroller General and the Deputy Comptroller General are both—like many other high federal officials— appointed by the President with the consent of the Senate; but unlike most other officials except judges, they have long terms (of fifteen years) and are almost unremovable. Although most of the GAO's work concerns the executive branch, it is not responsible to it.[5] Its potential scope is almost as broad as that of the government itself.

Another reason for studying the GAO is that remarkable changes have transformed it since the closing months of World War II. Established in 1921,[6] its functions and modes of operating remained essentially unchanged for almost a quarter century. But since that time, it has changed so completely in most respects as to be almost unrecognizable from its early description. This may be the major reason why the general perception of the GAO today so differs from the reality. The process of change in this agency—including the difficulties, resistances, sources, and strategies—is an interesting story itself. But it is also a matter of immediate concern, and not to scholars alone. For the GAO is still changing today, and the direction in which it moves in the future will affect the welfare of the American people and their government.

The book is divided into two parts. Part 1 deals with the evolution of the GAO, beginning with the English heritage and continuing to the time of writing. The first chapter treats the antecedents of the GAO from the American Revolution and before to the GAO's establishment in 1921. The second concerns the events and forces leading to the Budget and Accounting Act in 1921, which created the GAO and the position of Comptroller General as well as the Bureau of the Budget. The two chapters thus overlap in time. The rest of the chapters of part 1 deal with the GAO itself during three periods of time from 1921 to the present—the "first," "second," and "third" GAO, respectively. The first GAO began in 1921 and ended roughly at the conclusion of World War II; the second carried on from 1945 to about 1966; and the third began in 1966 and continues to the time of this writing. This division into time periods is significant because, as will become apparent in the pages that follow, each succeeding phase of the GAO's development reflected major changes in roles, activities, goals, and modes of operating, changes that rendered each "new" GAO in fact quite different from the one that preceded it. The phases also reflect the impact of the changing leaders, the Comptrollers General themselves: John Raymond McCarl, the first incumbent, whose influence was a dominant factor until the close of World War II (chapter 3); Lindsay Warren, who presided over the major turnabout after that war (chapter 4); Joseph Campbell, who followed through and somewhat modified the Warren initiatives (chapter 5); and Elmer Staats, who directed another set of thrusts that began in 1966 and are still moving the organization as this is written (chapters 6 and 7). The changes from one GAO to another were not sudden; they did not occur in a single year. Many of them had some antecedents in the preceding period: the processes of change may therefore be properly described as evolutionary. But the cumulative products of those changes were so substantial as to warrant depicting them as organizational revolutions, with profound impact upon the GAO's roles in American government.

Part 2 concerns the current GAO—its roles, relationships, and problems.

It is introduced with a discussion of the somewhat reciprocal themes and problems of accountability and independence. Chapter 8 has to do with the GAO's posture in American government. The succeeding chapters treat the GAO in its relations with Congress (chapter 9) and with the executive branch and institutions outside the federal government (chapter 10). Chapter 11 discusses the internal practices, problems, and trends in the organization that are in some part consequences of the changes in the ways in which its officers and staff perceive its mission.

It is not the intention of this volume to recommend changes in the GAO's role or functions. Rather, the issues surrounding the role of the GAO will be raised and discussed, and the pros and cons of the GAO's activities will be analyzed.

At its first meeting, the oversight panel of the National Academy of Public Administration recommended that a series of case descriptions of various GAO studies be developed to illustrate the nature, depth, and variety of its work, as well as the origins and impact of the studies. In consequence, a series of about thirty brief cases about GAO "audits" have been prepared. These studies have been directed and edited by Erasmus H. Kloman of the NAPA staff. They have been published as a companion volume to this one under the title *Cases in Accountability: The Work of the GAO* (Westview Press, 1979). Where appropriate, individual cases are referred to in this volume for purposes of illustration. Conversely, some of the individual cases refer to sections of this volume to provide the case reader relevant background and rationale.

The Deceptions of Semantics and Etymology

There are imperfections and pitfalls in every language, including English. The reader of this book should be warned of two particular kinds of difficulties. One is the "institutional fallacy," whereby an agglomeration of individuals and groups is considered as a single entity. That is, a group of people or an organization are treated as a "person." An extreme example in American government is the use of the word *Congress* as though it were a unified body, as in the expression "the General Accounting Office is an agent of Congress." Congress is in fact rarely a unified body, and then mostly on ceremonial occasions. It consists of two houses, vastly different from each other in respect to their powers, practices, and leadership. Each of its houses has a majority and minority party, and each is a collection of committees and subcommittees, more than 300 in all. There are 535 individual members, each with his distinctive views, experience, influence, and constituency. Further, on significant issues, members of Congress form blocs and coalitions, the compositions of which are constantly changing. Finally, a major part of the work of the members of Congress and its committees is actually performed by the more than 18,000 staff personnel—more than triple the number of employees in the GAO.

Another example of the institutional fallacy is the use of the term *executive,* or *executive branch,* as if it were a single entity. The executive branch is a vast array of diverse agencies that are differently related to the President, to Congress, to the public, and to each other. A similar example is the common use of the term *bureaucracy* to describe all of the personnel who work in the executive branch or all of its career personnel. In fact, the federal government includes hundreds of bureaucracies, most of them significantly different from most of the others.

Another example is the use of titles of agencies or organizations as though they were representative of unified entities, like the Department of State or the Veterans Administration or the General Accounting Office. Large organizations are made up of progressively smaller organizations that in turn are made up of individual people. In some, there may be a high degree of organizational identification and loyalty and of homogeneity of perspective and background. But it should be borne in mind that there is usually a considerable diversity within a large organization: of knowledge, skills, attitudes, and conflicts.

In the interest of literary convenience, in this volume collectivities are frequently referred to as single entities—as in most other works of this kind— so let the reader be forewarned. It would be awkward, if not impossible, to differentiate the institution from its membership and still maintain comprehensibility in the writing.

A second difficulty arises from the perseverance of titles and of words even after their meaning and the understanding of their meaning has vastly changed. In this volume, the problem applies particularly to the language most relevant to the work of the General Accounting Office. The organization's own title remains as it was established in 1921. Yet the agency has no significant responsibility for maintaining the accounts of the U.S government. Since 1950 this task has been legally the duty of individual departments and agencies and, for the government as a whole, of the Treasury Department. The GAO does prescribe general standards for governmental accounting, and it advises on, criticizes, and approves or disapproves agency accounting systems, proposed or in place. However, these constitute a rather small fraction of its work. There is another rather little-used meaning of accounting: calling to account or holding account- able.[7] Such a construction, which is more nearly descriptive of the GAO's present responsibilities, supports the occasional description of the Comp- troller General as the "chief accounting officer of the government,"[8] meaning approximately "the officer who holds other officers accountable." It is interesting in this connection that the so-called public accounting firms are not public in the sense of being governmental and they are not engaged in accounting; their basic work in the past and present is to attest to reports on accounts kept by others.

The derivation of the title of the Comptroller General of the United States, adapted from the British comptroller and auditor general, is a source of a good deal of disagreement among etymologists.[9] Like many other English words, it grew from Latin roots through French usage to English (and American) meanings with some variations and mistakes along the way. Its origin was probably the Latin *contra* (against) and *rotula* (roll),[10] itself derived from *rota* (wheel). In the old French, *contra* became *contre* and *rotulus* became *rolle;* the words combined, *contre-rolle*, literally meaning "roll checked against," were used to describe the function of an officer (controller) who used a *contre-rolle* to check the documents of a treasurer or other person charged with accounts. In the sixteenth century, the title *comptroller* appeared in English documents. Most of the current dictionaries consider this a mistaken translation of the French term, based on the idea that the first syllable derived from the French *compt* (count or account). The title *comptroller*, it seems now generally agreed, stems from the same origins as *controller*, but experienced a spelling detour in medieval Britain.[11] For several centuries it retained the connotations of checking on the records of other officers and of dealing primarily or solely with finances. The title *controller*, on the other hand, developed in a broader sense—like the word *control*—to encompass financial management and even management generally. Probably because of this extension of scope the spelling of *controller* is preferred by most financial managers in American business and is also used in several governmental enterprises.[12] It is interesting in this connection that there is within the GAO and under the Comptroller General a controller, who superintends the GAO's own financial activities.

The responsibilities of a *comptroller* expanded more slowly and sporadically from checking the financial transactions of others to taking charge of the accounts and later of superintending financial affairs in general. This mix of the checking and managerial functions was reflected in the establishment and development of the American comptroller of the treasury, the Comptroller General's immediate predecessor; the comptroller of the currency in the Treasury Department, and later in some other agencies, notably all of the military departments in 1949. The association of comptrollers with finance and with accounting seems to have been quite generally accepted—at least until quite recently. But the mix between the checking function and that of financial management has for some time been debated—not least in connection with the responsibilities of the Comptroller General of the United States.

A further problem attends the continuing use of the words *audit* and *auditors*. Audit derives from the Latin *audire,* meaning literally to hear. It was originally used in the financial sense to describe hearings by kings or noblemen or landlords of the financial transactions of their subordinates who were entrusted with the collection or expenditure of money. These were normally associated with financial matters and with the idea of the accountability of one individual to another. In Britain and the United States, principles and practices of auditing developed in the eighteenth and nineteenth centuries in private business, and auditing became a recognized profession, or subprofession of accounting, around the beginning of the twentieth century. As a profession, it did not really reach government and especially the federal government until many years after that. As will appear in later chapters, the greatest and growing proportion of GAO work is not auditing in its historic sense; however, the word and much of the methodology associated with auditing in private business linger on. Most GAO projects and reports, whatever their content, are referred to as audits, and the bulk of its professional personnel are frequently referred to as auditors. The majority of them were initially educated in accounting, which in university programs includes courses in commercial auditing, and an impressive proportion of them are licensed as certified public accountants (CPAs). While there is still a substantial financial component in much of their work, it is at least probable that a considerable number of people, including some in the executive branch and in the Congress, do not fully understand the GAO definitions of audits and auditors.

Bibliographical Note

The Mansfield book, *The Comptroller General: A Study in the Law and Practice of Financial Administration* (Yale University Press, 1939), was published as a limited edition and was never reprinted. It is now a "rare book," copies of which are hard to find except in some public and university libraries and on the bookshelves of a few scholars and government officials. Written by a young political scientist who has since distinguished himself as one of the nation's foremost scholars in that field, the work is a thorough, penetrating, readable, and harsh critique of the GAO before World War II—the organization described in this current study as the "first GAO."

Before the Mansfield work, there were two relevant studies of the GAO produced by the Institute for Government Research, both published in 1927 by the Johns Hopkins Press. One was by W. F. Willoughby, *The Legal Status and Functions of the General Accounting Office;* the other was by Darrell Hevener Smith, *The General Accounting Office, Its History, Activities and Organization.* The Brownlow Committee in 1937 and later the first Hoover Commission in 1949 discussed and made recommendations about the GAO. Joseph P. Harris included a chapter and a few other sections on this subject in his *Congressional Control of Administration* (Brookings Institution, 1964). Two recent books focused primarily on the GAO have been Richard E. Brown, *The GAO:*

Untapped Source of Congressional Power (University of Tennessee Press, 1970), which has to do primarily with the GAO's relations with the Tennessee Valley Authority, and *The Government Contractor and the General Accounting Office* (Machinery and Allied Products Institute and Council for Technological Advancement, 1966).

A brief general history and a number of articles on the development of particular aspects and functions appeared in *The GAO Review* in its fiftieth anniversary edition (summer 1971). There have been a number of unpublished manuscripts about the GAO, including Joseph Pois, *Watchdog on the Potomac: A Study of the Comptroller General of the United States* (January 1971), and several doctoral dissertations and masters theses. The Comptrollers General, particularly Elmer B. Staats, have produced an imposing number of monographs, articles, and speeches. Most of these seem not to have reached the authors of more general books about American government, the Congress, public administration, accounting, public law, and other fields to which the GAO's work would appear relevant. A cursory examination of texts in these subjects indicates that, with a very few exceptions, the GAO either goes unmentioned or is accorded the skimpiest of descriptions (some of which are inaccurate).

Probably the best sources on the practical aspects of the GAO's development and operations are official documents: its own reports and the hearings and reports of congressional committees. Many of these are referred to in the text that follows. Of a more general nature, the GAO has published two series of lectures by a variety of distinguished speakers. The first, entitled *Improving Management for More Effective Government* (Government Printing Office, 1971), contains lectures delivered to commemorate the GAO's fiftieth anniversary in July 1971. The second, entitled *Evaluating Governmental Performance: Changes and Challenges for GAO* (Government Printing Office, 1975), was a series delivered periodically between 1973 and 1975.

Perhaps the two most provocative volumes dealing with underlying theoretic problems relevant to the GAO contained a number of papers written by scholars as well as practitioners in Great Britain and the United States. The first of these was *The Dilemma of Accountability in Modern Government: Independence versus Control*, edited by Bruce L. R. Smith and D. C. Hague (St. Martin's Press, 1971); and the second was *The New Political Economy: The Public Use of the Private Sector*, edited by Bruce L. R. Smith (Wiley, 1975). Both of these volumes, as well as a third one that focused on the British experience, were sponsored by the Carnegie Corporation of America.

Notes

1. Benjamin Franklin, letter to M. Leroy, 1789.

2. As previously noted, the time of writing is July 1, 1978.

3. The GAO is in fact, if not in title, the office of the Comptroller General, who directs and has responsibility for it. In the interest of literary convenience, that office will usually be referred to in this book simply as the GAO except where the Comptroller General is immediately or personally involved.

4. Harvey C. Mansfield, Sr., *The Comptroller General: A Study in the Law and Practice of Financial Administration* (New Haven, Conn.: Yale University Press, 1939).

5. For some processes in its internal management, including personnel and supply, it operates under the jurisdiction of other agencies, like the Civil Service Commission.

6. By the Budget and Accounting Act, P.L. 67-13.

7. For example, *The Random House Dictionary of the English Language* (1967) lists this meaning twelfth in its definitions of "account."

8. As in Justice Holtzoff's opinion in 1964, quoted in chapter 8.

9. For an interesting discussion of the derivation of *comptrollers* and *controllers*, terms that are pronounced the same and that most dictionaries treat as synonyms, see Hugh J. Jackson, "The Growth of the Controllership Function" in *Controllership in Modern Management*, ed. Thornton F. Bradshaw and Charles C. Hull (New York: Macmillan, 1936), pp. 21-23.

10. Some dictionaries trace the Latin origin to *computare* (compute).

11. One leading authority describes *comptroller* as a "word that has remarkably little reason for existence. In meaning it differs not at all from the more modern *controller*." William and Mary Morris, *Morris Dictionary of Word and Phrase Origins* (New York: Harper and Row, 1977), p. 147.

12. Including, for example, the Federal Reserve System, the Commodity Credit Corporation, the Federal Deposit Insurance Corporation, the U.S. Postal Service, the Veterans Administration, and most recently the Department of Energy.

PART ONE

THE
EVOLUTION OF
THE GENERAL
ACCOUNTING OFFICE

Chronology of Significant Events

1688   British Parliament institutes legislative system of appropriations

1789   Congress establishes the office of comptroller of the treasury within the newly created U.S. Treasury Department and authorizes the development of a system for issuing and auditing appropriations warrants

1817   Congress centralizes all federal audit and claim functions in the Treasury Department

1894   The Dockery Act, enacted by Congress following the Dockery-Cockrell Commission, provides for complete control of accounting and auditing functions by the comptroller of the treasury and for a revised federal financial system

1912   President Taft recommends the executive budget system as proposed by his Commission on Economy and Efficiency

1917   Proposed legislation on the executive budget system is introduced in Congress

1920   Each house of Congress establishes a select committee on budget and approves a bill creating a budget agency for the President and an accounting office independent of the executive branch. President Wilson vetoes the legislation because of a constitutional objection to the provision which provides for congressional removal of the accounting office head, the Comptroller General

1921   President Harding signs the Budget and Accounting Act of 1921, creating the General Accounting Office and the Bureau of the

Budget, and names J. R. McCarl to fill the fifteen-year term of the new position of Comptroller General. The General Accounting Office (GAO), under McCarl's direction, inherits 1,700 employees from the Treasury Department to begin its operations

1923   President Harding submits a reorganization plan to Congress recommending that GAO's functions be transferred back to the Treasury Department

1932   President Hoover recommends that GAO's executive functions be transferred to the Bureau of the Budget

1936   As McCarl completes his statutory term as Comptroller General, GAO consists of 4,400 employees in five divisions (Audit, Claims, Accounting and Bookkeeping, Post Office, and Records)

1937   President Roosevelt's Committee on Administrative Management (the Brownlow Committee) recommends that GAO's executive functions be transferred to the Treasury Department and that GAO be confined to postaudit activities

1939   At the behest of Representative Lindsay Warren, President Roosevelt agrees with Congress to exclude GAO from legislation on presidential reorganization authority

1940   Roosevelt nominates Lindsay Warren as Comptroller General

1942   GAO establishes War Contract Project Audit Section to provide site audits at the plants of war contractors

1945   Congress describes GAO as part of the legislative branch in the Reorganization Act of 1945. Following congressional enactment of the Government Corporation Control Act in the same year, GAO begins to conduct commercial-type audits of government-owned corporations and to hire professional accountants

1946   The size of GAO's staff reaches an all-time high of 14,900 because of workload demands from the wartime emergency

1947   GAO seeks to improve government accounting systems by forming its Accounting Systems Division and by entering into the Joint Accounting Improvement Program with the Treasury Department and Bureau of the Budget

1949   The first Hoover Commission recommends that GAO's executive functions be transferred to an accountant general in the Treasury Department and that GAO only handle postaudit functions. GAO begins the expansion of its "comprehensive audits" from government-owned corporations to all departments and agencies of the federal government, causing the abolishment of the longtime GAO functions of bookkeeping and voucher examination

1950   Congress enacts the first major revision of the 1921 act, the Budget and Accounting Procedures Act of 1950, which assigns primary responsibility in accounting and internal auditing to government agencies and in standard-setting and legislative monitoring to GAO

1951   GAO occupies its present headquarters at 441 G Street, N.W.

1952   GAO establishes its first overseas offices at congressional request

1954   Following Lindsay Warren's resignation, President Eisenhower nominates Joseph Campbell as Comptroller General, the first certified public accountant to head the General Accounting Office

1955   The second Hoover Commission proposes no significant alteration in the role and functions of GAO. GAO audits of contractor overpayments and management deficiencies begin to reach newspaper headlines

1962   Congress passes the Truth in Negotiations Act, which aids GAO's continued audit of irregularities in the costs of defense contracts

1965   House Government Operations Committee, under Representative Chet Holifield, opens hearings on GAO audits of defense contractors and criticizes a variety of GAO audit practices: attempting to secure voluntary refunds from contractors; seeking excessive publicity from audit reports; identifying individuals by name in reports to Congress and the Justice Department before giving time for response; and saturating Congress with reports on similar subjects. Campbell resigns as Comptroller General due to ill health, and GAO employment reaches a postwar low of 4,100

1966   President Johnson nominates longtime Deputy Budget Bureau Director Elmer B. Staats as Comptroller General

1967   GAO begins to hire nonaccountants for its professional staff. An amendment to the Economic Opportunity Act marks the first major GAO program evaluation study from a congressional request

1969   GAO begins to monitor cost overruns on major weapons acquisitions

1970   Congress passes the Legislative Reorganization Act, calling upon GAO to perform cost-benefit analyses of federal programs and to assist in the development of standard budget terminology

1972   GAO assumes responsibility for monitoring presidential campaign contributions

1974   GAO begins new initiatives in energy policy and program analysis and terminates its campaign finance functions with the creation of the Federal Election Commission. Congress enacts the Congressional Budget and Impoundment Control Act, providing GAO with authority to act upon the presidential impoundment of funds and with additional responsibilities in program evaluation

1975   Under the Impoundment Act, GAO sues President Ford and Budget Director Lynn to release impounded housing funds (suit is ultimately dismissed as the President releases funds)

1977   Congressional requests make up 35 percent of GAO's workload, and GAO's staff reaches a total of 5,100

1

THE ANTECEDENTS

Article 1
  Section 1   *All legislative powers herein granted shall be vested in a Congress of the United States, which shall consist of a Senate and House of Representatives.*

  Section 8   *The Congress Shall have Power to lay and collect Taxes, Duties, Imposts and Excises, to pay the Debts and provide for the Common Defense and General Welfare of the United States . . .;*

                          To borrow Money on the credit of the United States . . .;

                          To make all Laws which shall be necessary and proper for carrying into Execution the foregoing Powers, and all other Powers vested by this Constitution in the Government of the United States, or in any Department or Officer thereof.

  Section 9   *No Money shall be drawn from the Treasury, but in Consequence of Appropriations made by Law; and a regular Statement and Account of the Receipts and Expenditures of all public Money shall be published from time to time.*

Article II
  Section 1   *The executive Power shall be vested in a President of the United States of America.*

  Section 2   *. . . he [the President] shall nominate, and by and with the Advice and Consent of the Senate, shall appoint . . . all other Officers of the United States, whose Appointments are not herein otherwise provided for, and which shall be established by Law. . . .*

  Section 3   *. . . he [the President] shall take Care that the Laws be faithfully executed. . . .*

                          —The Constitution of the United States, 1787

Preconstitutional Experience

The activities of fiscal accounting and auditing and the concepts of control and accountability are probably about as old as government itself. Aristotle wrote knowledgeably about them in his *Politics.* The General Accounting Office as established in 1921 by the Budget and Accounting Act embodied no very new idea in social affairs. Indeed, the executive budget provided in the second title of the act was far newer, both in relation to its American setting and to the development of budgeting in the Western world.[1] In medieval struggles toward nationalism and then democracy, the ratification and later the control of finances were the central focus. Attention was first directed to taxation and borrowing; somewhat later, to the legitimation of expenditures through appropriations; then to the propriety and legality of actual expenditures and revenues; still later, to the planning and authorization of expenditures and revenues through budgets. To its designers, the GAO represented a culmination of an extended history in the third direction above: toward assurance of the propriety and legality of financial transactions.

Great Britain, parent country to all thirteen American colonies, provided the nearest thing to a model for financial administration for the colonies and later the American states and the United States. But aside from some very general principles, which enjoyed widely varying degrees of acceptance at the time of the American Revolution and Constitution, the model was a confusing and evolving one. Indeed, some of its features were abhorrent to our own founding fathers and in fact were major reasons that the Revolution was fought. "For generations the fundamental changes in British government, indeed the entire saga of the nation's constitutional history, have been interpreted largely in terms of the struggle for money."[2] Perhaps it would be more accurate to say the "struggle for the control of money." The history of the British treasury, its various lord treasurers, and the exchequer from the time of William the Conqueror is a long and devious one, punctuated by personal and institutional struggles for power and influence, court and later bureaucratic intrigue, scandals, contests over finances, and civil wars, including the American Revolution itself.

With the aid of about 800 years of hindsight, one can generalize on the underlying directions of the sporadic British experiences, even though some of them may have been less clear at the time of drafting of the U.S. Constitution. The earliest manifestation was the growing demand that the supply of funds to the executive, the Crown, be provided only on the authorization of the nobility, later the Parliament, and ultimately the lower house, the Commons. The principle that "taxation without representation is tyranny" was well established long before the revolt of the American colonies. Legislative control over the destination of funds through the appropriation process had a less firm and ancient foundation. Though there are occasional references to instances of appropriations of funds to specific purposes as early as the fourteenth century, a fairly regular system of appropriation by the Parliament was not begun until 1688. But for many decades thereafter, the terms of appropriations were so loose as to provide little legislative direction as to how the Crown should apply its funds. In some years in the eighteenth century, the voting of appropriations was completely neglected. At the time of the revolt of the American colonies, though there was a recognized principle against expenditures without appropriations, its practice was embryonic and usually ineffective.

Real legislative control over the king's financial business, however, could not rest on revenues and appropriations alone. It required some check on how the Crown actually raised, allocated, and applied the funds, especially when the Crown and the Parliament were at loggerheads. The idea of a more or less systematic audit of revenues and expenditures was medieval in its origins and for many centuries was associated with the ancient exchequer in Britain. The methods of accounting and subsequent auditing became notoriously antiquated and inefficient by the eighteenth century, and they were completely dominated by the Crown. "Until the nineteenth century parliament had no control over them and wished none."[3]

It was not until after the American Revolution that the British Parliament began its drive toward more systematic control of the workings of the financial system through its Civil Establishment Act of 1782, sponsored by Edmund Burke. It resulted in a series of inquiries and reforms that culminated about the time of the American Civil War in a system of parliamentary control over finance, largely independent of the Crown, enacted in the Exchequer and Audit Control Act of 1866. Those reforms included the establishment of an office of comptroller and auditor general, accountable to the Parliament, and a permanent Public Accounts Committee of the Parliament to receive and review his reports and accounts. It was during that period—roughly the first two thirds of the nineteenth century—that cabinet government as we now know it matured, and with it the system of budgeting. Until the Reform Act of 1832, it could hardly be said realistically that the members of the House of Commons were accountable to the people.

At the time of the formation of the American republic, many of the fears as well as the ideals from the British experience were well ingrained among the leaders of the colonies: fear of executive power, faith in legislative control of finance; fear of peculation of officials, faith in independent review (audit) of financial transactions; and fear of personal avarice and greed, faith in law. Most of all, these leaders believed that control of government rested first of all in the control of the purse and that such control should be exercised by representatives duly elected by and accountable to the people.

But British experience was still very incomplete and a good deal less than satisfactory. The Americans, who were pursuing a new and unique scheme of self-government—though it rested on many of the same objectives as those of the British reformers—had to strike out for themselves in uncharted territories of financial management and control.

As in England, much of the dissension in the prerevolutionary colonies arose from the growing demand for popular control over finance, especially against royal governors exercising the prerogatives of the English king: the raising of revenues, the allocation of those revenues through appropriations, and the accountability for the propriety and legality of their use. Most of the original state constitutions, adopted during the Revolutionary War, provided a variety of means to guard against gubernatorial or other executive domination of controls over public funds. Among these were legislative appointment of state treasurers and committees to audit their accounts; preaudit and postaudit[4] of expenditures by legislatures; and requirements that no public funds could be spent unless authorized by warrants signed or countersigned by designated representatives of the legislatures. These all reflected the dominant importance then attached to public finances. They also reflected the prevailing distrust of officials who were not themselves legislators. Legislators were perceived as the true representatives of the "people"—or, rather, that portion of the people who were allowed to vote. Finally, they reflected a distrust of individuals exercising sole power over the use of public monies, even when those individuals were also legislators. Thus they preferred to rely upon collegial bodies, councils, and boards, whose members would police the conduct of each other; or upon dividing financial work among different officers so that one would be in the position of checking on others. There was, they hoped, safety in numbers.

The views built upon the colonial and early state experiences and the British heritage were clearly expressed in the variety of devices tried by Congress, beginning almost immediately after the outbreak of the Revolutionary War, in the preconstitutional government of the united colonies and later the United States. First was the appointment by the Continental Congress in July 1775 of two treasurers, responsible for the handling of funds. This arrangement was not wholly satisfactory, and Congress two months later established a Committee of Accounts to "examine and report" upon all claims or accounts against the government before payment—the beginning of the preaudit. In 1776, a number of new committees and offices were established, some to be abolished or replaced within a few months. Then, in 1778, Congress established offices of comptroller, auditor, treasurer, and six commissioners of accounts, all to operate under the supervision of a Treasury Board, actually a standing committee of Congress. This board and its 1779 successor, the Board of

Treasury, which included three outside members appointed by Congress as well as three congressmen, came under increasingly severe criticism in 1780 for mismanagement and incompetence, and there developed growing pressure to establish a single, unified head of financial affairs. Among those reported in favor of such an organization were Alexander Hamilton, John Jay, Robert Morris, and George Washington. In 1781, Congress accordingly established the Office of the Superintendent of Finance and appointed to it Robert Morris. Later in the year, it abolished the Board of Treasury and replaced the other old offices with a comptroller, a treasurer, a register, auditors, and clerks—almost exactly the pattern to be followed later in the establishment of the Treasury Department.

After the end of the war, however, Morris and his office too came under attack, though apparently for reasons opposite to those addressed against the old Board of Treasury. He was too vigorous and severe in his efforts to reduce expenditures and reform the financial affairs of the government. Losing much of his support, he ultimately resigned in 1784. Congress then reverted to a new three-man Board of Treasury, appointed by Congress and with powers identical to those of the Office of the Superintendent of Finance. After its appointment in 1785, the board continued to manage the nation's financial affairs until Hamilton became secretary of the treasury in 1789.

Although the framers of the Constitution leaned on financial management precedents derived from their English and colonial experiences, it is likely that they were influenced to some extent by the French. Well before Columbus's discovery of America, in the early fourteenth century the French Estates General (Etats Généraux) had directed their attention primarily to the levying of taxes by the king. There were three "estates" that represented the dominating groups—certainly not the masses—in the medieval French culture: the nobility, the clergy, and the commons (later labelled the bourgeoisie). Representatives of these groups were occasionally assembled to authorize taxes recommended by the monarchy. For several hundred years, they met an average of only five or six times per century, and there was in fact a lapse of 175 years between their meetings of 1614 and 1789. Nonetheless, through the Estates General, the French established the notion that "no tax shall be imposed on the people without convening the Etats Généraux and without having obtained their consent in conformity with the liberties and privileges of the kingdom."[5] This idea of popular consent for taxes is said to have been "engraved in the conscience of the public,"[6] but the "public" as represented by the three estates was a small minority of the population. In practice the doctrine seems to have been breached more often than practiced, except when the monarch was in real financial and political trouble.

The last convening of the Estates General in 1789 was called by Louis XVI on demand of his parliament because of the near bankruptcy of his regime.

This was the beginning of the French Revolution. It is interesting that the meeting occurred during the same spring that George Washington was first inaugurated as President of the United States. Thereafter, in many ways, the French, American, and British struggles reflected a similar objective: to "reconcile strong administration with popular control—to establish strong leadership and to safeguard democracy";[7] but the subsequent experiences and institutional managements of the three nations differed widely.

The Constitution and Its Early Implementation

The framers of the Constitution in 1787 apparently felt that the nature of financial administration and audit in the new government was either guided adequately by the broader pronouncements of the document or could more appropriately be determined by the new government once it was in place; or both. In any case, there was no explicit instruction as to who should do what with respect to assuring that appropriations would be, or had been, expended in accordance with the law. In fact, the subjects of audit and accountability and the tribulations, described above, during the preconstitutional period were not extensively discussed at the Philadelphia convention.[8] However, the idea of legislative control of the purse and of financial management became a warm issue in the closing days of the convention. The Report of the Committee of Detail enumerated as one of the powers of Congress "To appoint a Treasurer by ballot." A motion to strike the clause was defeated six states to four on the argument, as expressed by George Mason, that "it might be considered to whom the money would belong; if to the people, the legislature representing the people ought to appoint the keepers of it." It therefore remained in the draft of the Constitution that was referred to the Committee of Style, and it remained in the draft as reported by that committee. Another motion to strike the clause was introduced on the very last day of the convention, and, following a spirited debate, it carried by a vote of eight states to three. Thus did a majority of the framers implicitly opt to consider the superintendence of financial matters, along with other executive powers, a responsibility of the executive.

The subjects of fiscal audit and accountability were not explored in much depth in the many papers for and against the new Constitution during the crucial debates in the several states. Alexander Hamilton, in the seventy-second of the *Federalist Papers,* made it clear that in his opinion financial management should be treated within the general framework of separation of powers like other governmental activities. He wrote:

> The administration of government, in its largest sense, comprehends all the operations of the body politic, whether legislative, executive, or judiciary; but

in its most usual and perhaps in its most precise signification, it is limited to executive details, and falls peculiarly within the province of the executive department. The actual conduct of foreign negotiations, *the preparatory plans of finance, the application and disbursement of the public money in conformity to the general appropriations of the legislature,* the arrangement of the army and navy, the directions of the operations of war—these and other matters of a like nature, constitute what seems to be most properly understood by the administration of government. The persons, therefore, to whose immediate management these different matters are committed ought to be considered as the assistants or deputies to derive their offices from his [the President's] appointment, at least from his nomination, and ought to be subject to his superintendence. (Emphasis added.)[9]

Hamilton, apparently without dissent from other supporters of the Constitution, lumped financial management with other executive responsibilities.

By and large, the opponents of the Constitution, the so-called Anti-Federalists, directed their criticisms to larger matters in the area of finance: states' rights, direct taxation by the federal government, the handling of federal and state debts, and so on. There was little comment on the internal distribution of powers with respect to financial management and accountability.

Yet the Constitution made it almost inevitable that there would be an immediate confrontation on a number of issues in this area. As every school girl or boy is taught, the Constitution was built on the central premise that there be a clean division among the executive, legislative, and judicial branches, a division that was in some respects accentuated by the authorized instances of conjunction and sharing (like presidential messages to Congress, senatorial confirmation of the more important appointments, the veto power, the treaty power, and others). The separation of powers flew in the face of the hard-earned and long-recognized special legislative concern and responsibility in the areas of finance and the conviction that control of finances by legislators directly answerable to the electorate is a central tenet of democratic government.

Early in the first session of the First Congress under the Constitution (in 1789), the confrontation began. It is not yet ended. It started from the initial proposal to establish three departments in the executive branch: the Foreign Affairs (later changed to State), War, and Treasury departments. The basic, indeed the crucial, issue concerned the power of the President to remove the heads of those departments in the absence of any specific instruction on the matter in the Constitution. Congressman James Madison introduced resolutions to the effect that they were "to be removable by the President." Thus was begun the first "great debate" of the

U.S. Congress on the meaning of the Constitution. In the minds of those first congressmen, the question had significance far beyond the question of removing one or another officer; it was central to the unity, the responsibility, and the governing authority of the President on the one hand, and to the loyalty, responsiveness, and discipline of his subordinates on the other.[10]

Four constructions of the Constitution with respect to removal were presented, each of which was advocated by a minority of the members of Congress:

1. That the Constitution provided only for removal by impeachment, and that therefore, by strict legal construction, this was the exclusive method of removal;
2. That the Constitution provided that all but inferior officers be appointed by the President by and with the advice and consent of the Senate, that the power to remove is an incident of the power to appoint, and that therefore removal could only be effected by the President with consent of the Senate;
3. That Congress was granted the powers of creating the offices and of making laws necessary to their execution, and therefore, by implication, of determining by law the tenure and the mode of removal of officers appointed to them;
4. That the Constitution made it clear that the execution of the laws rested in the President; that the requirement of senatorial approval of appointments was an explicit qualification of that power which did not extend to removals; and therefore that the Constitution itself granted unqualified power of removals to the President.

There was spirited debate in both houses of Congress on these alternatives, and it now seems clear that no one of them commanded majority support in either house. But through an astute series of maneuvers, the language originally introduced by Madison—that the secretaries be removable by the President—was eliminated and another expression was added in connection with succession to office during vacancies, alluding to vacancies "whenever the said principal officer shall be removed from office by the President of the United States." This change clearly was intended to convey that the presidential power of removal without senatorial consent was established in the Constitution and that Congress had no option in the matter (alternative 4 above). During the course of the debate, Madison himself changed his position from the third to the fourth alternative. About a century and a third later, the Supreme Court affirmed the fourth alternative in the case of *Myers v. United States.*[11]

The language with respect to removal as finally enacted was identical in the three separate acts that established the Departments of Foreign Affairs, War, and Treasury. But it is significant, and probably a reflection of deliberate parliamentary strategy, that the provision was introduced and later enacted initially in connection with the Department of Foreign Affairs, secondly with the Department of War, and finally with the Department of Treasury. The case was strongest in foreign affairs and defense, for which the Constitution recognized presidential initiative; and it was weakest in financial management, about which the Constitution was at least equivocal as to the division of powers. This was reflected in the Senate's response to the three House bills, all of which contained the same language with respect to removal. It acceded to the removal provisions for both the Departments of Foreign Affairs and War, but it at first refused to go along with respect to the Department of Treasury. After a conference on the question, neither side yielded. But eventually the Senate split in a ten-ten tie, which was broken by the Vice President in favor of presidential removal. Thus was it presumably established that the secretary of treasury should, like the other secretaries, hold office only at the pleasure of the President.

On two other questions the unified authority and responsibility of the President in respect to financial management were upheld. Both were considered, argued, and disposed of before the vote establishing the Treasury Department. The first was a proposal for a plural executive for the Treasury: a Board of Treasury of three commissioners to superintend the government's finances. This proposal, modeled on the experience during the prior decade, was defeated following a spirited debate.

The second concerned the tenure of the comptroller, an office provided in the Treasury bill and the great-grandparent of the modern Comptroller General. Among the duties of the comptroller was that of judging and deciding upon financial claims between the government and individual citizens. Madison proposed that, because the responsibilities of the office were in part judicial rather than executive in nature, it should be treated differently from purely executive offices; appointments to it should be made for a fixed term unless the incumbent were sooner removed by the President. Madison's proposal would not in any way have diminished the power of the President to remove the comptroller at his pleasure. It would have provided that he could be periodically reappointed subject to reconfirmation of the Senate. His intent was that the comptroller be "dependent upon" the entire government, not the President alone: the President through the removal power; the Senate through the power to consent, or not consent, to his continuance after every term of years; the House through the impeachment powers; and the judiciary, through its rulings on appeals of his judgments. The most telling argument against the proposal was that, far from making the office independent and therefore impartial, it would subject it to more subordination than any other office. A variety of objections were raised to

Madison's proposal, and he withdrew it the following day. But his argument about the quasi-judicial character of the position and its impact upon the removal power provided support, a century and a half later, for limiting the President's removal power over regulatory commissioners and for the long-term tenure of the Comptroller General as provided in the act establishing that office in 1921.

In almost all other respects, the act creating the Department of Treasury differed from those founding the Departments of Foreign Affairs (State Department) and War, and virtually all of the differences implied greater congressional control of finances than of international relations and defense. In the first place, the latter departments were defined as "executive departments"; the Treasury Department was defined merely as a "department." This distinction suggests that the first Congress viewed foreign affairs and defense as instruments of presidential powers enunciated in the Constitution, whereas public finances grew out of powers not allocated by the Constitution to the President, but more directly instrumental to the revenue, appropriation, and borrowing powers of Congress. In the cases of both the Departments of Foreign Affairs and War, the secretaries were designated "principal officers"; the secretary of the treasury was deemed "head of the department."

The secretaries of foreign affairs and war both were directed to "perform and execute such duties as shall from time to time be enjoined on or entrusted to him by the President of the United States." Not so for the secretary of the treasury. Aside from its references to appointment and to replacement in the event of removal (see above), the Act to Establish the Treasury Department makes no mention whatever of the President. The secretary of the treausry is directed to prepare a variety of reports, estimates, and plans on financial matters to the houses of Congress without any reference to the President. He is directed to superintend all aspects of financial management: revenues, including estimates and collections; expenditures and control thereof; sales of lands; accounts and audits; and debt.

Unlike the acts establishing the other departments, which required only the appointment of chief clerks, the Treasury Act established a number of subordinate officers and prescribed in some detail their duties: the comptroller to superintend the accounts, countersign warrants drawn by the secretary, review the auditor's accounts, and perform other duties; the treasurer to receive, keep, and disburse funds; the auditor to receive, examine, and certify all accounts; and the register to maintain the records of all accounts. These offices and their responsibilities were obviously a direct inheritance from the Confederation. They were also to provide the foundations of the federal financial system, most of which would persist for more than a century and a half.[12]

The Constitution, the early debates, and the laws of 1789 raised the questions and provided very tentative answers about financial accountability in a system wherein executive, legislative, and judicial powers are largely separated. The Treasury Act of 1789 reflected the equivocal posture of the First Congress. While the act provided a single head with appointment and removal provisions precisely like the secretaries of other departments, the detailed provisions as to internal organization and as to powers and responsibilities clearly placed it in a uniquely close relationship with Congress, suggesting that it should operate as an arm of Congress as well as of the President.

The Financial System in the Early Years

The first secretary of the treasury (1789-1795), Alexander Hamilton, is probably best remembered for his broad financial and commercial innovations, his report on manufactures, his initiative in the establishment of a national bank, his insistence on restoring the credit of the United States and of the individual states through the assumption of debts, and like achievements. He is also remembered for his drive, ambition, and stubbornness, which were reflected in his growing acrimony with Jefferson, Adams, and others in the administration and Congress. More significant for purposes of this study was his development of a system for financial administration and control, built on the framework of the Treasury Act of 1789. Since many of the central features of that system, though modified during the succeeding decades, survived up to and beyond the establishment of the Comptroller General and the General Accounting Office in 1921, it is worth briefly summarizing some of them here.

First was the system of warrants governing the issuance of funds by the U.S. Treasury, which became the cornerstone of federal financial management. The 1789 act required that the secretary grant "all warrants for moneys to be issued from the Treasury, in pursuance of appropriations by law" (Sec. 2). It further provided that all such warrants be countersigned by the comptroller (Sec. 3). Further, the treasurer was directed to "disburse the same [moneys] upon warrants drawn by the Secretary of the Treasury, countersigned by the Comptroller, recorded by the Register, and not otherwise" (Sec. 4).[13] The primary basis of payments and accounts was warrants, and the basis of warrants was appropriations and other legislation. The actions of the register and the treasurer were solely ministerial, involving no discretion. Those of the comptroller, according to Hamilton, were discretionary only as to legality, not as to wisdom. He wrote:

> The Secretary and Comptroller, in granting warrants upon the Treasury, are both answerable for their legality. In this respect, the Comptroller is a check upon the Secretary. With regard to the expediency of an advance, in my

opinion, the right of judging is exclusively with the head of the department. The Comptroller has no voice in this matter.[14]

A second major feature of financial management in the early years was a high degree of centralized control in the Department of Treasury, based again upon the original act and furthered in a variety of directions by Hamilton. In addition to the centralization inherent in the warrant system, payments could only be made or approved and accounts settled following an audit by the Treasury Department's auditor and its review by the comptroller. Indeed, for some years, the Treasury Department served as accountant and purchasing agent (as well as auditor and treasurer) for some other agencies, notably the War Department. Even during the Hamilton years there began a considerable movement away from centralized control in the Treasury Department. Very probably, the stringency of Treasury Department controls through warrants and audits retarded the development of management-related accounting in the line departments for a good deal longer than a century.

A third element of the early financial system was the carefully designed device of dividing responsibilities among a number of different officers, each positioned to check upon the others. The comptroller checked on the warrants signed by the secretary and upon the accounts reviewed and certified by the auditor; the register kept his own set of accounts. The treasurer could not dispense any funds unless they were appropriately approved by the others. Theft or misuse of funds within the Treasury Department headquarters was difficult in the absence of massive collusion and conspiracy among most or all of them. But the costs of the system were considerable. They included long delays in settling and paying bills, and duplications in accounting near the points of decision making. To a considerable extent, accounting and auditing were made obstacles rather than instruments of public management.

A fourth feature of the early financial system may be termed the rule of specificity. Every transaction, every voucher had to be reviewed by the auditor and later the comptroller to assure that it was beyond criticism in form and substance.[15] The predictable consequence was paperwork and delay. Very probably, the process also resulted in hesitancy and timidity in administrative decisions by responsible line officials.

A final and perhaps most significant observation about financial management in those first years is that it was largely independent of either the executive or Congress. Except on major economic issues, President Washington refrained from involvement in matters of internal finance. Despite a number of tries, Congress failed to provide a committee to receive and examine the Treasury Department reports about the financial accounts. For other reasons, though related, Hamilton was persuaded to resign as secretary of the treasury after six years. But the fundamental elements of the financial system, based on the 1789 act and effected by Hamilton relatively independent of either the chief executive or Congress, were firmly embedded. It appears too that the office of comptroller enjoyed a considerable degree of independence as well as status within the Treasury Department. As measured by salary, the original comptroller was outranked in the executive branch only by the President, the Vice President, and the three department secretaries. (Later, during the nineteenth century, this ranking would slip to the level of bureau chiefs.) The second comptroller, Oliver Wolcott, appointed in 1791, had been the first auditor, and he later succeeded Hamilton as secretary of the treasury in 1795 and served ably in that post until retiring in 1800. He was the only person in history to advance to the secretaryship from the office of comptroller, and he was very nearly the only "career" professional in the field of financial management ever to occupy the post. Hamilton described the requirements of the office to President Washington in the strongest terms:

> It is of the greatest importance to the proper conducting of the business of the Treasury Department that the Comptroller should be a man of the following description: of strong sense, of clear discernment, sound judgment, inde-fatigable industry, firmness, and prompt decision of temper; possessing a comprehensive knowledge of accounts, and of course of good principles.[16]

Yet, almost from the start, the financial system differed in significant respects from what was apparently envisaged by the framers of the Treasury Act and from some of the central features described above.[17] In the first place, Congress did not at first even try to control the use of its appropriated funds except in the very broadest terms. The first appropriation bill in 1789, which covered the entire government, was one paragraph long, and its "items" were four in number: the civil list, the Department of War, pensions to invalids, and costs to discharge warrants issued by the Confederation's Board of Treasury.[18] This of course left enormous discretion in the actual allocation of funds to the executive and particularly the Treasury Department, which issued the warrants and audited the accounts. More specific itemization as to the objects of expenditure developed in succeeding years, but Hamilton construed the items as estimates, not limits; he regarded only the four total sums as limiting. This issue as to the legal authority of itemization became one of the major issues between Hamilton and the faction in Congress that was coalescing, with the leadership of Jefferson, into the Republican Party. After Jefferson's accession to the presidency in 1801, a detailed system of itemization was instituted—a system that, despite some exceptions and lapses, was to persist for the following century and a half. But the universal applicability of itemization was not established until the last day of Jefferson's administration in 1809 when Congress enacted a bill providing that "the sums appropriated by law for each branch of expenditure in the several departments shall be solely applied to the objects for which they are respectively appropriated, and to no other."[19]

It was apparently the intent of Congress in 1789 that accounts of the various departments be examined and settled by the auditor and the comptroller prior to actual payment, a practice instituted and maintained under the Confederation. Hamilton almost immediately modified the system with respect to some kinds of payments, especially those that were made overseas or far from Washington. In such instances, Hamilton began the practice of authorizing advances, made on requisition, to the heads of departments, who assumed responsibility for applying the funds and submitting accounts of funds already expended back to the Treasury Department's auditor and then the comptroller for review and final settlement. The examination of such transactions became in effect a postaudit rather than a preaudit. The further practice developed around 1808 of designating disbursing officers in the various departments to whom advances for payments would be made and who would be held accountable for their proper usage and would be bonded to protect the government against defalcations. This was at first an extralegal practice, as was that of making advances to private contractors and suppliers. Disbursing officers were not legally recognized by statute until 1823,[20] but their use grew rapidly and inevitably. A century after the founding, 90 percent of all payments were out of advances to disbursing officers. One writer described disbursing officers in these terms: "their origin was illegitimate, their growth rapid and irregular, their fees enormous, their services indispensable."[21]

The development of disbursing officers involved some degree of decentralization away from the Treasury Department. But soon after the nation's founding, other more overt steps in that direction had been taken by Congress, partly to curb Hamilton's dominance in public finance. An act of 1792[22] established an accountant in the War Department with power to settle most of that department's accounts, subject to review by the comptroller. The secretary of war was authorized to issue warrants against his appropriations that, after being countersigned by his accountant, authorized the treasurer directly to disburse funds. Similar provisions were included in the act setting up the Department of the Navy in 1798.[23] During the same decade, the postmaster general was empowered to apply postal revenues directly to operating expenses and to make initial settlement of the accounts of his deputies.[24] In this manner three of the largest agencies gained substantial autonomy in the management of their own finances within the first decade following passage of the Treasury Act of 1789.

These agencies, as well as others in the federal establishment, soon undertook a detailed examination and control of their own accounts in what came to be known as administrative review. The consequence of these various developments was a system of quadruple bookkeeping and auditing of many federal expenditures; first, by the departmental officials, then by the disbursing officers, third by the treasurer's auditor, and finally by the comptroller. This procedure prior to the final settlement of accounts was obviously cumbersome, duplicatory, slow, and irreconcilable. With the growing transactions of government, these problems became more and more painful, and the whole system virtually collapsed during the War of 1812. Meanwhile the powers and the esteem of the secretary of the treasury and of the comptroller declined from their earlier preeminence. The latter's auditing of accounts, coming after the detailed examinations of three other groups, became increasingly perfunctory as the need for it declined.

The Act of 1817

In the administrative and financial confusion following the War of 1812 and in view particularly of the long and growing backlogs in settling financial accounts, the Senate directed the secretaries of the four departments jointly to study and make recommendations on executive organization and procedures. It is interesting that in this study and the report that it produced, the first general study on administrative organization since the Constitution, the President played no part, though he submitted it to the Senate as a matter of protocol. The report was apparently prepared by William H. Crawford, then secretary of the treasury, but was signed by the other three secretaries.[25] Some of its proposals, including particularly one to establish a new Home Department, gained little support in Congress. But its recommendations about financial management, organization, and accountability provided the groundwork for basic legislation in 1817, the act "to provide for the prompt settlement of public accounts."[26] Faced with the alternatives of placing basic responsibility for settling accounts in the several agencies or reverting to the original idea of concentrating this responsibility in the Treasury Department, the secretaries' report, and the ensuing legislation, opted for the latter. The act abolished the office of accountant in both the War and Navy Departments and provided that "all claims and demands whatever . . . in which the United States are concerned, either as debtors or as creditors, shall be settled and adjusted in the Treasury Department." Thus a partial recentralization in the Treasury Department was effected.

In certain other respects, the Act of 1817 was quite different from the original plans of the First Congress. In the interest of expediting financial reviews and settlements, the work of the comptroller was divided by the establishment of a second comptroller with responsibilities to handle the accounts of the War and Navy departments, for which the duties of the first comptroller had become largely formal. To the original auditor were added four new auditors, each with comparable duties but with different departmental jurisdictions. The first auditor audited accounts in the Treasury Department itself and some of the accounts in other civil departments; the second and third auditors handled War Department accounts; the fourth auditor handled Navy Department accounts; and the fifth auditor handled accounts of the State Department, Indian Affairs, and, temporarily, the Post Office. Later, in 1836, a sixth auditor was added to audit postal accounts. And in 1849 Congress established a commissioner of customs to whom were transferred the powers of the first comptroller in that field—he thus became in effect a third comptroller.

The net effect of the 1817 act was to recentralize in the Treasury Department some of the financial management and auditing functions that it had lost in the early years, but at the same time to reallocate among a considerable number of different comptrollers and auditors within the department the responsibilities that had been formerly centered in two. In the process, the position of register of the treasury was reduced to the status of a figurehead and became a patronage plum.

There were a number of changes in organization and practices in the years following the Act of 1817, especially during and following the near chaos of the Civil War. Most significant during this period was an act in 1868 that emphatically affirmed the finality of the decisions of the Treasury Department accounting officers: "Such balances, when stated by the auditor and properly certified by the comptroller . . . shall be taken and considered as final and conclusive upon the executive branch of the government, and be subject to revision only by Congress or the proper courts."[27] But the central features of the system laid down in 1817 persisted through nearly the next eighty years.

The Dockery Act of 1894

During the three decades following the Civil War, there were conducted a series of studies of the federal administration, all directed to retrenchment of costs, greater efficiency of operations, and the elimination of backlogs in work and in financial transactions. They included the investigations of the Patterson Committee of 1869-1871,[28] the Boutwell Committee of 1875-1876,[29] the Cockrell Committee of 1887-1889,[30] and the Dockery-Cockrell Commission of 1893-1895.[31]

In addition to sharing the same general purposes, these four bodies were similar in some other significant respects. All were set up by and reported back to one or both houses of Congress without reference to the President. All thus implicitly assumed that the supervision of the management of the business of the executive departments was a congressional rather than an executive responsibility. All were a response to a feeling of the legislators, reinforced by complaints from their constituents, that many or most executive operations were inefficient, wasteful, slow, and sometimes corrupt. All were composed exclusively of congressmen, most of whom were lawyers by profession with little or no managerial experience. For the most part, they directed their attentions to fairly low level clerical, bookkeeping, and service operations selected on the basis of complaints or suspicions of mismanagement. They paid little attention to what later came to be recognized as principles of administrative responsibility and hierarchy, and none undertook broad studies of administrative organization or budgeting or personnel (except to urge that salaries be kept as low as possible). The systematic study of administrative management was not yet born.

The first three of these bodies, especially the Cockrell Committee, made recommendations on a number of ad hoc matters, some of which were acted upon by the departments and a few of which contributed to legislation. But they had rather fleeting impact upon the general conduct of the departments. Not so the fourth, the Dockery-Cockrell Commission. It was the only one authorized to hire consultants, and it engaged the services of three outstanding accountants from private business in what was perhaps the first federal recognition of the fledgling profession of accounting.[32] As the commission intended and as the nature of its consultants reflected, its concentration was upon expediting and simplifying the business practices in the various departments with emphasis upon their financial management, accounting, and auditing. In its two years of operation it produced twenty-nine reports, many of which resulted in new legislation dealing with such diverse matters as the procedures and accounts of the Post Office, the operations of the General Land Office, the handling of public surveys, record keeping and paperwork generally, and the business processes of the War Department.

By far the most important and most lasting of the commission's achievements was its fundamental revision of organization and processes of accounting and auditing in the Treasury Department, most of which were embodied in the Dockery Act of 1894.[33] That act provided the first basic changes in the financial systems within the Treasury Department and its relations with other departments since the Act of 1817; and many of the powers and practices it instituted were transferred with little change to the Comptroller General when the General Accounting Office was established more than a quarter of a century later in 1921. It combined the functions of the two comptrollers and the commissioner of customs into a single comptroller of the treasury as in the original act of 1789. "His main duty was to provide a uniform construction of the appropriation laws, conclusive upon all the departments.''[34] He was required to render advance opinions on the legality of payments on request either of the disbursing officers or the heads of departments, and he was authorized to prescribe "the forms of keeping and rendering all public accounts," except postal accounts. He was relieved of the onerous routine of re-reviewing all accounts after they had been checked by the auditors, but was placed in an appellate capacity with regard to exceptions or questions raised by the departments, other claimants, or auditors. His decision on these matters was final for all departments of the executive branch. The offices of six auditors were left intact, but their responsibilities—and probably also their prestige—were enhanced and their respective jurisdictions were clarified on a strictly departmental basis. Separate auditors were designated for the Departments of War, Navy, Treasury, Interior, and Post Office. The sixth auditor was given responsibility for the State and other departments. Bookkeeping within the Treasury Department was further centralized in a Division of Bookkeeping and Warrants, and through a great many other technical and procedural changes the whole financial system was simplified and expedited.

The Dockery-Cockrell Commission, by its very existence, its report, and the laws that it produced, reaffirmed congressional preeminence with regard to the modes of federal financial management. On the other hand, the Dockery Act "retained administrative accountability in the executive branch. The Commission never considered establishing a legislative audit."[35]

Presidential Initiatives: The Keep Commission and the Taft Commission

With regard to administrative reorganization and management, President Theodore Roosevelt took a view diametrically opposite to the congressional position, which had been tacitly accepted by most of his predecessors. More nearly in keeping with Alexander Hamilton's emphasis upon "energy in the executive," he urged that the President be granted and exert authority to reorganize and improve the administration of the departments. Early in his first (and only) elected term, he established, without congressional sanction, a Commission on Department Methods, better known by its chairman's name as the Keep Commission.[36] The composition and nature of the commission were altogether unique. It consisted of five departmental officials of high but subcabinet rank, and it depended almost entirely upon other personnel in the administration for its subcommittees (task forces) and staff assistance.[37] During the four years of its existence, 1905 to 1909, it conducted a wide-ranging series of investigations and produced an impressive number of recommendations and reports. Many of its proposals that could be implemented through executive action were carried out. But those that required legislative action fell on deaf ears in a Congress suspicious of executive intrusion on its turf. Many of the commission's ideas were pioneering and modern—more so than those of any other group since the Constitutional Convention—and a good many were put into practice in later years.[38]

Like the committees that had preceded it, the Keep Commission concentrated a good deal of its effort on financial management and accounting. Here its achievements were less spectacular than those of the Dockery-Cockrell Commission because of the reluctance of Congress to take action. Its major accomplishments in this area were the institution of double-entry bookkeeping in the Treasury Department and the introduction of cost accounting in federal agencies. The commission published a brief handbook on cost keeping for the edification of departments and agencies.

Beyond its individual recommendations, the Keep Commission experience was significant in at least four ways. First, it was the initial attempt to apply to the federal government the practices and principles of administrative and management analysis that were then burgeoning in private industry and that later became widely known as scientific management. Second, it was, in effect, a declaration for the first time in a century of presidential responsibility for administration, including financial management. Third, it demonstrated that there was within the executive branch an abundance of human resources capable of careful investigation into virtually the full gamut of administrative problems, and able and willing to produce objective, imaginative, and constructive recommendations. Finally, it showed that the President could not "go it alone." The unwillingness of Congress to provide the commission more than the most penurious financial support and to act on its legislative recommendations indicated that Congress was as reluctant to accept executive proposals on management problems as it has often been since then.

President Taft shared Roosevelt's interest in improving administration and his belief in presidential responsibilities in this regard. He asked Congress to establish and fund a Commission on Economy and Efficiency to be appointed by the President. Rather than relying totally upon officials within the government, he appointed some insiders and some outsiders, all experts in public administration, public law, or finance.[39] The commission was established in 1909, but many of its most important reports (and Taft's proposed legislation to give them effect) were not issued until the waning days of the Taft administration in 1912 and 1913. His successor, President Wilson, himself a political scientist and vigorous enthusiast of presidential leadership, was sympathetic with many of them, but they had a rather low priority on his agenda for the New Freedom and later the prosecution of World War I. Congress largely ignored the most important recommendations, and they languished until near the end of Wilson's second term.

Like some of their predecessors, the twenty reports of the Taft Commission ranged widely over the governmental spectrum, with much of their attention directed to financial matters. For example, the commission recommended that the six auditors in the Treasury Department be consolidated in a single auditor of the treasury, but no action was taken. It endorsed the concept of presidential responsibility for administration and recommended provision for presidential initiative in regard to reorganization, and this too failed. Most significant of all, and in the long run its major landmark, was its proposal to establish an executive budget system in which the President would be responsible for reviewing and consolidating the estimates of the various agencies into a single budget recommendation to Congress. Such a budget would serve not only as a financial tool for the development and execution of appropriations, but also as an instrument for recommending policies and programs. Although it took nearly a decade to mature, this proposal was the seed that grew and eventually blossomed as the Budget and Accounting Act of 1921.

The Comptrollers and the Auditors

From 1789 to 1921, the fulcrums of internal control of the federal financial system were the secretary of the treasury, one, two, or three comptrollers of the treasury, and one to six auditors. From the outset, the office of secretary of the treasury was a political position, though several of the secretaries had through prior experience gained a good deal of knowledge and skill in financial matters. Some exerted potent influence upon public policy through the President or Congress, but only a few of them subsequently advanced to higher political office.[40]

There is little evidence that either the comptrollers or the auditors significantly affected policy. And after the first few years, they do not appear to have commanded exceptional prestige or stature in the government. Their potential power in public administration, however, was considerable though mostly negative. They could disallow payments already made, and in some cases prevent them before they were made. Their judgments as to the legality of financial transactions under the laws and appropriations were final for most of the executive branch. They could and did settle claims of the government against debtors and of claimants against the government. Although they were all appointed by the President with the consent of the Senate and were removable by him, they apparently operated with some independence of the secretary of the treasury, of the President, and indeed of Congress. On the other hand, the historical evidence suggests that they were reluctant to pursue issues that would bring about open confrontations with the heads of departments or the President (as did their immediate successor, the first Comptroller General). Their work largely concerned the detail of vouchers and ledger accounts. It was technical, legal, financial, and laborious, and as such was of rather little interest to Congress. That body established no regular and continuing procedures to receive, examine, and act upon its reports—as had the British in the mid-nineteenth century—and congressional attention was at most sporadic.

The evidence about the political nature of the post of comptroller (and, in the years between 1817 and 1894, the first and second comptrollers) is not conclusive. A number of incoming Presidents appointed new comptrollers (and second comptrollers) during the early months after their inauguration, and in most instances in which there was a change in party, there was a change in comptrollers, presumably in keeping with the political affiliation of the President. On the other hand, a few survived presidential turnovers and served relatively extended terms.[41] The average tenure of comptrollers and second comptrollers in the 132 years between the founding of the government and the Budget and Accounting Act was about five-and-one-half years. Clearly, these offices were not generally political sinecures (as the offices of register of the treasury and treasurer became). It would appear too that the position of comptroller gained stature and stability through the Dockery Act of 1894. Between its passage and the creation of the Comptroller General in 1921 there were only four comptrollers.

It is interesting that very few of the comptrollers were versed, experienced, or accredited as accountants or as financial auditors. The great majority were lawyers, a small fraction of whom had had some prior experience in financial management. Of course, through most of that history, accounting enjoyed little recognition as a profession; and a legal background was a pervasive characteristic of political officers, both elective and appointive. But it suggests that the Presidents who appointed them and the Senates that confirmed them regarded the position of comptroller as predominantly legal in its nature: the interpretation of law against financial transactions.

It is significant too that a substantial majority of the comptrollers (though not the second comptrollers in the mid-nineteenth century) had prior experience in Congress. In fact, for most of this period, congressional experience (and congressional connections?) seemed almost a prerequisite for the appointment. Thus did Presidents acknowledge a somewhat special relationship between the function of auditing and the legislature. The relationship and the tradition would persist in appointments to the office of Comptroller General for almost thirty years after the Budget and Accounting Act of 1921.

The auditors were likewise appointed by the President with senatorial confirmation, and the available evidence suggests that their appointments and tenure were—or became—at least as susceptible to political considerations as those of the comptrollers. The last comptroller of the treasury testified in 1919: "It is customary for them to resign with the beginning of another administration and to secure men in harmony with the administration."[42] Five of the six auditors at that time had been appointed by the incumbent President Wilson. They had a greater variety of backgrounds than the comptrollers. Of the six, two had been lawyers, one a secretary to a senator, one a banker, one a newspaperman, and one a career public servant in the Post Office. In response to a question as to whether these auditors had prior experience as accountants or auditors, Warwick at the same hearing responded: "I have not known of any in my experience who was appointed with those qualifications."

The Heritage to 1921: A Recapitulation

The system of financial accountability and control as it had evolved to the time of passage of the Budget and Accounting Act in 1921 was in most respects compatible with the intention of the framers of the Treasury Act of 1789. It was designed basically to assure that all financial transactions be carried out in strict conformance with congressional intent as expressed in laws and appropriations and that they be conducted without fraud or peculation. The system reflected a continuing distrust of individual persons in the handling of public funds and a heavy reliance upon law and legalism. For these purposes, it provided multiple reviews within the executive branch, including a final, exhaustive check in the Treasury Department. It did not distinguish the large from the small or the important from the unimportant. All transactions were to be reviewed for legality, propriety, and accuracy with complete meticulousness.

The system provided for ultimate control, both before and after the fact of spending or receiving, in the Treasury Department. By carefully spelling out the titles and powers and limitations of individual offices of that department, it endeavored to assure some degree of independence in the monitoring of public finances; but it continued to recognize the presidential executive power by making all of these offices subject to presidential removal. It is interesting that, after the debates of the First Congress about the removal power, there was no serious proposal to make the comptroller(s) directly accountable to Congress until the second decade of the twentieth century.[43]

Perhaps the most significant departure from the intentions of the founders in 1789 was the practice, initiated by Alexander Hamilton, of advancing funds to officers in the various agencies with powers to spend prior to audit. Ultimately, this meant that the great bulk of federal expenditures would be audited in the Treasury Department after payment (postaudit) rather than before (preaudit). It did not, however, lessen the Treasury Department's power to review and settle accounts, to disallow expenditures it considered illegal or improper, and to demand reimbursement to the government. And it is unlikely that the framers of the original Treasury Act anticipated that appropriations would be made in itemized detail, a practice instituted and legalized early in the nineteenth century and enforced in Treasury Department and GAO practices and reviews for about a century and a half thereafter.

In the light of subsequent developments in the GAO, it may be useful to emphasize certain features of the old system and particularly that part of it involving audit:

- it was concerned almost exclusively with legality, accuracy, and regularity; it seldom raised questions as to the efficiency, wisdom, or effectiveness of expenditures;
- it was detailed, extending to the review to the penny of individual vouchers and other financial papers;
- it was duplicative; most transactions were reviewed at least three times—by the disbursing officer, by his agency (administrative examination), and by the Treasury Department auditor; this meant, among other things, the maintenance of duplicating (but usually irreconcilable) accounting records;
- it was highly centralized in both organizational and geographical senses; though there were significant exceptions, most accounts, with their supporting documents, had to be reviewed by one of the auditors in the Treasury Department and had therefore to be transmitted to Washington;
- it was unprofessional; almost none of the comptrollers or auditors or their staffs had prior training or experience in accounting or auditing; apart from a scattering of lawyers at the top, the bulk of the staffs were low-level clerks, educated to read, write, count, and add;
- the Treasury Department review and decision on questionable items were legally final upon the executive branch, though subsequent recourse to Congress and the courts was possible.

But the central legacy from the Treasury Department's comptrollers and auditors was disagreement, and consequent ambiguity, as to their role and power in the American polity. To what extent and in what ways were they independent, responsible to the executive (secretary of the treasury and President), or responsible to Congress? Which of their functions were executive, which legislative, and which judicial? The early decisions of 1787 and 1789 seemed to lean toward executive responsibility, though with qualifications. Subsequent developments suggested growing congressional control, not only of finances but of the federal administration generally. With Theodore Roosevelt, the pendulum started to swing toward the presidency. In certain respects, the accounting officers' independence from either branch was legally strengthened by the Acts of 1817, 1868, and 1894.

But politically, their continuance in office depended upon presidential pleasure, and the record (discussed in the next chapter) suggests that they were seldom eager to challenge the President or his department and agency heads on politically important or sensitive issues. In these regards, the situation precedent to the Budget and Accounting Act of 1921 was uncertain and equivocal.

Notes

1. The Budget and Accounting Act (P.L. 67-13) signed into law by President Warren G. Harding on June 10, 1921, created the Bureau of the Budget (Title II), and the Comptroller General and the General Accounting Office (Title III); it remains the basic charter to this day. See chapter 2.

2. Hugh Heclo and Aaron Wildavsky, *The Private Government of Public Money: Community and Policy Inside British Politics* (London and Basingstoke: Macmillan, 1974), p. xiii.

3. Basil Chubb, *The Control of Public Expenditure: Financial Committees of the House of Commons* (London: Oxford University Press, 1952), p. 12.

4. The distinction between preaudit and postaudit used here and later in this volume refers to examination of a financial transaction before or after, respectively, funds have actually been paid.

5. *The Etats Généraux of 1483*, as quoted in René Stourm, *The Budget* (New York: D. Appleton and Co. for the Institute for Government Research, 1917), p. 31.

6. Ibid., p. 31n. Stourm was quoting Georges Picot, *Histoire des Etats Généraux*.

7. Charles A. Beard in his Introduction to Stourm, *The Budget*, p. ix.

8. This account of the proceedings in the convention is summarized from James Hart, *The American Presidency in Action, 1789: A Study in Constitutional History* (New York: Macmillan, 1948), pp. 215-16.

9. *The Federalist Papers* (New York: Mentor Books, 1961), pp. 435-36.

10. Most modern students would agree to this proposition in principle. In actuality, both the strength of presidential direction and the degree of appointee loyalty have, almost from the start, been severely modified by the practice of referring to senatorial courtesy in the making of many appointments in the executive branch.

11. 272 U.S. 52 (1926).

12. There is some evidence that Alexander Hamilton, who was to become and probably expected to become secretary of the treasury, played a major part in framing the Treasury bill. President James Monroe three decades later is reported to have told his cabinet that Hamilton wrote the act. See Leonard D. White, *The Federalists* (New York: Macmillan, 1948), p. 118n.

13. 1 Stat. 12, September 2, 1789.

14. Hamilton, *Works*, 4:271, as quoted in White, *The Federalists*, p. 337.

15. White, *The Federalists*, p. 344.

16. As quoted from Hamilton, *Works*, 10:82, in White, *The Federalists*, p. 345.

17. The major points of difference that are here summarized are drawn from Harvey C. Mansfield, Sr., *The Comptroller General: A Study in the Law and Practice of Financial Administration* (New Haven, Conn.: Yale University Press, 1939), pp. 31-46.

18. 1 Stat. 95, September 29, 1789.

19. 2 Stat. 535, March 3, 1809.

20. 3 Stat. 723, July 31, 1823.

21. Quoted from E. I. Renick, "Control of National Expenditures," *Political Science Quarterly* 248 (1891):250; in Mansfield, *The Comptroller General: A Study in the Law and Practice of Financial Administration* (New Haven, Conn.: Yale University Press, 1939), p. 40.

22. 1 Stat. 279, May 8, 1792.

23. 1 Stat. 610, July 16, 1798.

24. 1 Stat. 733, March 2, 1799.

25. *American State Papers: Miscellaneous*, 2:396-99 (December 6, 1816).

26. 3 Stat. 366, March 3, 1817.

27. 15 Stat. 54, March 30, 1868.

28. The Joint Select Committee on Retrenchment, chaired by Senator James W. Patterson.

29. A special Senate committee chaired by Senator George S. Boutwell.

30. A special Senate committee "to inquire into and examine the methods and work in the Executive Departments," chaired by Senator Francis M. Cockrell.

31. A Joint Commission to Inquire into the Laws Organizing the Executive Departments, chaired by Representative Alexander M. Dockery of its House members, and by Senator Cockrell of its Senate members. When the whole commission met together, Dockery served as chairman.

32. They were Joseph W. Reinhart, Charles W. Haskins, and Elijah W. Sells, all of whom had extensive experience in modernizing accounting systems and financial organization, particularly in railroads. Haskins and Sells later joined forces to establish the firm that continues today as one of the "big eight" of public accounting firms.

33. 28 Stat. 162, pp. 205-11. Much of what follows is summarized from Oscar Kraines, the "The Dockery-Cockrell Commission, 1893-1895," *Western Political Quarterly* 7, no. 3 (September 1954):417-62; and Harvey C. Mansfield, Sr., "Reorganizing the Federal Executive Branch: The Limits of Institutionalization," *Law and Contemporary Problems* (summer 1970):461-95.

34. Mansfield, *The Comptroller General*, p. 62.

35. Kraines, "Dockery-Cockrell Commission," p. 440.

36. Much of what follows is drawn from the thorough account by Kraines, "The President Versus Congress: The Keep Commission, 1905-09: First Comprehensive Presidential Inquiry Into Administration," *The Western Political Quarterly* 23, no. 1 (March 1970):440.

37. The members of the Commission were: Charles H. Keep, assistant secretary of the treasury (chairman); James R. Garfield, commissioner of the Bureau of Corporations in the Department of Commerce and Labor; Frank H. Hitchcock, first assistant postmaster general; Lawrence O. Murray, assistant secretary of commerce and labor; and Gifford Pinchot, chief of the Forest Service in the Department of Agriculture.

38. Among the proposals of the commission and its subcommittees that were acted upon many years later were position classification and salary standardization; a retirement system for federal employees; an official gazette, ultimately the *Federal Register*; the coordination of federal statistics; units for systems and methods analysis in the various departments; a central purchasing agency for common supplies; and lump sum appropriations.

39. The commission was chaired by Frederick A. Cleveland, a leading budgetary exponent and the director of the New York Bureau of Municipal Research; its other members were Harvey S. Chase, a certified public accountant from Boston; Frank J. Goodnow, political scientist and a prominent leader in administrative law; W. W. Warwick, the associate justice of the Supreme Court of the Canal Zone and later, the comptroller of the treasury; W. F. Willoughby, then assistant director of the census and later the first director of the Institute for Government Research. M. O. Chase, the auditor for the Post Office, served as secretary and later as a member of the commission.

40. Three later became chief justices, and at least one became a senator.

41. For example, Joseph Anderson, appointed by President Madison in 1815, continued as comptroller and then as first comptroller until 1836. And Robert Tracewell, appointed by President McKinley in 1897, held the post until he was replaced by President Wilson in 1913.

42. U.S. Congress, House, Select Committee on the Budget, *Hearings*, 66th Cong., 1st sess., 1919, p. 239.

43. The first such proposal to come to our attention was contained in the 1911 annual report of Comptroller of the Treasury Robert Tracewell, who concluded his argument favoring independence of his office by stating: "the accounting officers of the government should be directly responsible to Congress, and to Congress alone, for their official actions in interpreting its laws and in the stating of accounts thereunder." Quoted in W. F. Willoughby, *The Legal Status and Functions of the General Accounting Office of the National Government* (Baltimore: Johns Hopkins Press, 1927), p. 5.

2

THE BUDGET AND ACCOUNTING ACT OF 1921

All government—indeed, every human benefit and enjoyment, every virtue and every prudent act— is founded on compromise and barter.

—Edmund Burke,
*Second Speech on Conciliation
with America,* 1775

This Act (the Budget and Accounting Act of 1921) is probably the greatest landmark of our administrative history except for the Constitution itself.

—Herbert Emmerich,
*Federal Organization and
Administrative Management,* 1971

The Context

Despite the almost ceaseless cacophony that has been heard through much of American history about governmental extravagance and waste, there was actually rather little financial pressure on the national government until recent decades except during the years of, and soon following, major wars. It is probably no accident that most of our legislative reform acts in the financial field were passed a few years after the deficits and confusion of major wars: the Constitution and the Treasury Act of 1789 following the Revolution; the Acts of 1817 and 1868 following the War of 1812 and the Civil War respectively; and the Budget and Accounting Act of 1921 following World War I.[1] In between the wars, the revenues usually comfortably matched expenditures and sometimes produced embarrassing surpluses. This may explain in part the long delay in developing anything like a modern budget system until after the grinding experience of World War I.

Another contributing factor was the fact that the major revenue producers for the national government—the customs—were not visible to those who really paid them. The income tax, which had been used during and after the Civil War, before being declared unconstitutional, was revived after passage

43

of the Sixteenth Amendment in 1913 and was employed increasingly during and after World War I to meet the geometrically increased expenditures of the war and the period following it. The income tax is of course visible; it is personal; and it is sometimes painful. It stripped the disguise off the customs and brought home to the citizenry the costs of national government.

Another element was that, apart from wars and the operations of the Post Office, which was in the main self-sustaining, the national government did little that cost very much—in relation to the economy as a whole or to governmental costs generally. During the first decade of the twentieth century, federal expenditures were between 2 and 3 percent of the gross national product and about 30 percent of total public expenditures. About half was for, or related to, national defense. The federal portion began to rise during Wilson's first term with its New Freedom programs, including the beginnings of major grants-in-aid—in dollars, not land. It of course mushroomed with World War I.

Again excepting the conduct of wars, by far the largest share of American government was local—about 60 percent of all public expenditures. The states ran a poor third—less than 10 percent. The administrative reform movement, which got underway after the turn of the century in government as a corollary to scientific management in private business, had as its first target the cities. In the second decade of the century, it moved up to the states. Though earlier efforts were made at the national level, as described in the preceding chapter, its first real breakthrough there was the Act of 1921, discussed in this chapter. The themes of administrative reform at all levels were similar: economy, efficiency, honesty, control, and accountability. Its tools were also comparable: strong central executive leadership; reorganization along rational and hierarchical lines; merit and specialization of personnel; planning; the executive budget; and an independent audit. The executive budget was perceived as pivotal because it was instrumental to most of the others. The logic of integrating the budget into a single system and document developed and executed under a chief executive was in part a negative reaction to the alleged extravagance, imbalance, and corruption associated with fragmentation among semiindependent agencies, legislative committees, and political bosses.

The Budget and Accounting Act of 1921 was thus a product of a larger reform movement. To a considerable extent, it was modeled upon ideas and developments at other levels of government; and it was stimulated and pushed by persons many of whom drew their ideas and arguments from experience at other levels.

The Movement for Budget Reform

The Taft Commission (discussed in chapter 1) and President Taft himself had given the initial kickoff to a national budget system, but several factors inhibited any immediate legislative action on their recommendations. The Democratically controlled House of 1912 was not sympathetic to what it perceived to be encroachment on its spending prerogatives by the Republican President, Taft. In addition, the opposition to Taft of Theodore Roosevelt and others within his own party gave rise to serious doubts on the likelihood of his reelection and contributed to his "lame duck" loss of influence. Finally, the success of Taft's own effort in reducing (and eventually eliminating) the national deficit lessened the urgency for reforming the government's financial administration.

In July 1912, the month after the commission recommendations urging adoption of a national budget were transmitted to Congress, Taft attempted to introduce this reform by administrative fiat.[2] For the following fiscal year, he ordered each department head to prepare summaries of estimates in accordance with the commission recommendations: namely, that all estimates be described and analyzed

1. by each organizational unit,
2. for each class of work to be done,
3. by character of expenditure (current expense, capital outlay, fixed charge, and so on), and
4. by appropriation authority (permanent legislation, annual appropriation, and so on).

In addition, each department would provide its traditional budgetary material for inclusion in the "Book of Estimates," the standard transmittal to Congress.

Since Taft had vetoed several annual appropriations bills, Congress was still considering the level of expenditures for the fiscal year in progress. In August, one month later, Congress attached a clause to one of these bills requiring departmental heads to submit estimates in the form and at the time required by law and at no other time and in no other form. The confusion that resulted in the various executive agencies caused Taft to write each member of his cabinet on September 9, instructing them to follow the orders both of the President and Congress.

Neither house of Congress was anxious to receive Taft's budget or message, particularly after his defeat in the November election. The budget and message were submitted to Congress on February 26, 1913, and ignored. The form and content of Taft's budget were endorsed by newspaper editorials and local chambers of commerce around the country. But President Wilson, though an avowed believer in budget reform, felt that other, more substantive programs on his agenda deserved the whole of his political capital and gave it no push. The idea of a national budget system was relegated to a "back burner" for several years, and President Taft was no doubt correct in his complaint in 1916 that "dust is accumulating on the Commission's reports."[3]

Meanwhile, however, the movement for an integrated executive budget system was gathering momentum in the cities and the states and among students and reformers of government, many of whom were the same people. As early as 1906, the New York Bureau of Municipal Research had recommended an executive budget for New York City. In succeeding years the idea spread to more than a hundred other cities, partly through infiltration of bureau staff, and a large number of cities adopted it. In 1916, the National Municipal League, a highly reputed citizen reform organization, issued its second Model City Charter, which had been drafted by a distinguished committee including a number of highly regarded political scientists.[4] One of its central features was an executive budget to be prepared and transmitted to the city council by the city manager. Another feature was an independent audit to be conducted by a state officer when authorized by state law or otherwise "by qualified public accountants, selected by the council."[5] It is unlikely that any document of that era had as much influence upon the structure and operations of city government as that of the Model City Charter.

The states were not far behind. Between 1909 and World War I, reorganization proposals in Oregon, Massachusetts, Illinois, Wisconsin, New York, and other states included integrated budget systems, usually under the direction of governors and with expenditures subject to postaudit by officials elected by the people or, less commonly, designated by the legislatures. In either case, the premise was an audit independent of the executive branch. The state reform movement was capped in 1921 by a Model State Constitution, likewise produced by the National Municipal League.[6] In addition to an executive budget, reinforced by the power of item veto by the governor, that document proposed that the state legislatures appoint an auditor of their own choosing to examine the accounts of the executive branch, to conduct a continuous postaudit, and to report regularly to the legislative body. The model constitution specifically excepted from the legislative auditor's jurisdiction the keeping of accounts, which it deemed to be the sole province of the governor's accounting office or comptroller.

The pressure for reorganization and especially the executive budget in the cities and states, and their apparent success in some jurisdictions, gave rise to renewed interest at the national level. Such interest was spurred by some of the civic groups and the media across the country. It was further encouraged by the studies and publications of professional research organizations, notably the New York Bureau of Municipal Research, headed by Frederick A. Cleveland, and the Institute for Government Research, established in 1916 under its first director, W. F. Willoughby, which subsequently formed the nucleus of the Brookings Institution. Both Cleveland and Willoughby had been members of the Taft Commission. In 1917, Willoughby's group published five studies of budget systems, including comparative studies of British and Canadian practices and analyses of various budgetary proposals, as well as an English translation of a general treatise on budgeting.[7] Later, in 1919, an ad hoc citizen group under the leadership of Cleveland painstakingly studied and reported on the goals and mechanics of budget laws enacted in forty-four states between 1911 and 1919.[8] Both sets of reports contributed to the national legislation that was in the offing.

In the campaign of 1916, both major parties pledged their support for budgetary reform, but the Republican endorsement was the more specific and enthusiastic. President Wilson's state of the union message in December of 1917 only went so far as to reiterate the Democrats' promise to establish a single committee in the House of Representatives with authority over appropriations as a "practicable step towards a budget system."[9] In the same year, Congressman Medill McCormick (R., Ill.), encouraged by the apparent success of budgetary reform in his home state, introduced legislation for a national budget system. But action in this area was foreclosed for more than two years by American entry into World War I.

Congressional Consideration and Passage, 1919-1920

Following the war, the great increases in the costs and range of services by the federal government, coupled with the burden of servicing the vastly enlarged war debt, rekindled popular and political concern about public economy. Measures to reduce government expenditures, including a unified budget system and an effective audit, moved to the top of the domestic agenda. In the 1918 elections the Republicans, who had been the more enthusiastic sponsors of budget reform, won majorities in both houses of Congress. The time appeared to be right.

The Institute for Government Research and other advocates for change intensified their campaign for budget reform during the first session of the Sixty-sixth Congress in 1919. Particularly effective tools employed by the reformers were the budgeting tracts produced by the institute and personal visits to influential congressmen by institute chairman Robert S. Brookings.[10] Partly in response to these efforts, both houses established Select Committees on the Budget. The Senate acted first, on July 14, creating such a committee under the chairmanship of Senator Medill McCormick (R., Ill.), who had moved from the House to the Senate. The House followed suit on July 31, and Congressman James W. Good (R., Iowa), who was to become the principal leader in the cause, was named chairman. One of Good's first actions was to enlist the assistance of Willoughby in planning hearings and in drafting a budget and auditing bill. This bill (H.R. 1201), as introduced by Good, was only one of five different bills introduced in the House on the subject, but it became the principal focus of subsequent deliberations and actions.

Public attention was captured by the House Committee's hearings, held from September 22 to October 4, 1919.[11] On the first day of those hearings, former President William Howard Taft wrote in the *Washington Post*, "Congress has nothing before it of more importance than the proposal for a national budget system." Most of the forty-seven witnesses who testified in the committee's hearings in 1919, recruited mainly by Willoughby and Brookings, did not question the general desirability of either a budget or an independent audit. With regard to preparation of the budget, however, there was a good deal of differing opinion on several matters: whether the executive budget agency should report directly to the President or should be under the secretary of the treasury; whether congressional actions to increase budget proposals should be forbidden or impeded;[12] whether representatives of the executive branch should be permitted to defend their estimates before the houses of Congress; and others. There was apparently no serious attention given to the possibility of a presidential veto of individual items in appropriation bills, although this power had been included in the budgetary reorganizations of several states. These issues, which are abundantly discussed elsewhere, were ultimately resolved by placing the Bureau of the Budget in the Treasury Department but under the direction of the President; providing no limits on the actions Congress might take on presidential proposals; not authorizing executive lieutenants to defend their budgets before the two houses; and, of course, not providing an item veto.

With regard to the audit provisions of the budget bills, most of the witnesses who testified on the subject[13] favored an independent audit, but there was a good deal of disagreement about the specifics. A crucial issue was the locus of the auditing function in the government. Secretary of the Treasury Carter Glass vigorously opposed moving the responsibility from his department, while his nominal subordinate, Comptroller of the Treasury W. W. Warwick, urged independent status.[14] The prevailing sentiment among other witnesses and the congressmen themselves favored independence from the Treasury Department and the executive branch as a whole. The hearings elicited a number of grievances against executive interference in the past. Good, for example, related one instance of political influence on auditing and used it in subsequent House debates:

> I think it was under the administration of President Cleveland that the President desired to use a certain appropriation for a given purpose, and was told by his Comptroller of the Treasury, who happened to be a little independent of this system, that he could not do it. But the President insisted and finally said, "I must have that fund, and if I can not change the opinion of

my comptroller, I can change my comptroller." With less independence all comptrollers, no matter to which political party they owe allegiance, have been forced to face the same practical situation.[15]

Good was joined in this cause by Congressman William E. Andrews (R., Neb.), who had served as the auditor for the Treasury Department for eighteen years before resuming his seat in Congress. In testimony before the committee, Andrews spoke of the "executive domination" of the auditors:

> It is true, as proved by my observation, that we will never have an efficient accounting system until they are removed from the administrative control of the government. So long as they remain where they are now, they are more or less under an influence that will bias judgment. . . .[16]

Most of those who testified on the subject as well as most of the congressmen on the committee seemed agreed that responsibility to Congress should supersede "bias" for the executive. They felt that legislative power over the purse should be restored through the new office of auditor. As expressed by Congressman Henry W. Temple (R., Pa.):

> It seems to me that the whole plan gets back to the scheme of the Constitution of the United States. It restores something of the power that Congress formerly had and ought to have, but which in practice has been largely taken over by the Executive.[17]

Many congressmen, probably most, viewed the independent audit as the "quid pro quo" for instituting an executive budget. Good himself envisioned the auditing department as a counterweight to the proposed bureau of the budget:

> Then comes this separate and distinct office, semijudicial in character, which determines whether or not expenditures made are legal, and then audits the account. That department is intended as a check against extravagance. That department is intended to have a reflex influence upon the bureau of the budget. The bureau will know at all times that that department is watching it, and that for every appropriation that is made there will have to be a legitimate use.[18]

The Good Committee was influenced to a considerable extent by the British experience and, in lesser degree, by that of other countries. The title it chose for the comptroller general was an American adaptation of the British comptroller and auditor general. The demand for an extended or indefinite term of office also reflected British practice, as did the special reporting relationship of the new office to the Congress. In testimony before the committee, Swagar Sherley, who had been chairman of the House Committee on Appropriations, dwelt on the need for independence of an auditor answerable only to Congress by citing the British system: "This was the one great reform that Gladstone brought about in the parliamentary procedure of England, the creation of an independent audit, and the most feared man there is the man who has the power to pass upon the legality and rightfulness and wisdom of expenditure on the part of the government."[19] This view, shared by other congressmen and witnesses, was expressed repeatedly throughout the hearings and debate on the bill.

In one significant respect, the proposed provisions for the American comptroller general differed basically from the British model. The comptroller and auditor general of Britain did not have authority to disallow payments and finally settle accounts; he only audited and reported to Parliament.[20] The American comptroller of the treasury had such authority, and under the proposed legislation it would simply be transferred to the new comptroller general who could exercise it independently of either the executive or legislative branches. This discrepancy apparently resulted from a misunderstanding or a deliberate ignoring of the British practice on the part of some of the legislators and witnesses.[21]

A few witnesses presented dissenting opinions on this question. One of these was Samuel McCune Lindsay, who had collaborated with Willoughby on a treatise about the English budgeting system and who testified as vice-chairman of the National Budget Committee, a public interest group. Another, John T. Pratt, chairman of that group, explained in the hearings that: "auditing, which is merely a question of bookkeeping, following the vouchers and seeing that the receipts and books are properly kept, is quite distinct from interpretation of the law when it comes to the expenditure of money."[22] In the British system the accounts are examined by the comptroller and auditor general for the express purpose of supplying the House of Commons with the means of maintaining its constitutional control over appropriations. Final settlement of accounts and interpretation of laws remained the province of the legislature. The proposal by Good (and Willoughby) would vest both functions in the new position, and would leave that individual with almost total discretionary power in the settlement of accounts.

For these reasons, Pratt and others pressed Congress to consider formation of a Public Accounts Committee, or other congressional expenditure committees, to oversee the work of the comptroller general: "I would appoint an auditor general who would look into the accounts purely from an accountant's standpoint, to see that the vouchers were properly executed, etc., and I would have those committees . . . report annually to the Congress."[23] Congressman Martin B. Madden apparently understood the dissenters' argument. He stated on the House floor:

If I have my way, when this legislation is completed, I shall propose the creation of a great committee of the House, to be known as the committee on expenditures, consisting of the best men in the House—because it is to be a great committee if it is created—to whom this auditor and comptroller general may report from day to day, and through that medium supply the House of Representatives and the Senate with such information as to what is being done with the money appropriated as to keep the Congress advised in connection with every step taken.[24]

The idea of an independent auditor responsible primarily to Congress raised a variety of other questions in a governmental system based upon the separation of powers. How should the principal officer be appointed, for what term, and subject to whose removal powers? Through what formal process should his responsibilities to Congress be expressed? What powers should he have to enforce his findings? Or should he merely audit and report to Congress? Who in Congress would receive and act on his reports?

The committee did not really face up to all these questions, but it nonetheless agreed on a bill, H.R. 9783, and reported it to the House. The bill, based primarily upon Good's original proposal, would create an independent accounting department under the direction of a comptroller general and an assistant comptroller general, both appointed by the President with senatorial consent. Both of those officers would serve for life or until the mandatory retirement age of seventy. They would assume all the powers and duties of the comptroller and the auditors of the Treasury Department. In addition, if not indeed primarily, the bill provided an integrated executive budget to be prepared by a bureau of the budget under the direction of, and in the office of, the President.

The bill provoked an extended discussion and many questions but little dissent on the floor of the House. It passed the House on October 21, 1919, by a vote of 285 to 3. However, the Senate was so preoccupied with the Treaty of Versailles and the League of Nations that it failed to take the subject up before its fall adjournment.

Despite being partially incapacitated by a stroke in September 1919, President Wilson soon became fully involved in the movement for national budget and auditing reform. In his state of the union address to the second session of the Sixty-sixth Congress on December 2, he urged immediate passage of national budget legislation as well as the adoption of improved appropriations procedures by the Congress. Regarding the nature of auditing and the work of the comptroller of the treasury, Wilson said:

Another and not less important aspect of the problem is the ascertainment of the economy and efficiency with which the moneys appropriated are expended. Under existing law the only audit is for the purpose of ascertaining whether expenditures have been lawfully made within the appropriations. No one is authorized or equipped to ascertain whether the money has been spent wisely, economically and effectively. The auditors should be highly trained officials with permanent tenure in the Treasury Department, free of obligations to or motives of consideration for this or any subsequent administration, and authorized and empowered to examine into and make reports upon the methods employed and the results obtained by the executive departments of the Government. Their reports should be made to the Congress and to the Secretary of the Treasury.

Within a month, under the leadership of Senator McCormick, the Senate Select Committee on the Budget held five days of hearings in December 1919 and January 1920 on H.R. 9783. Once again, the committee chairman specifically requested the assistance of the Institute for Government Research and W. F. Willoughby in developing a workable piece of legislation. In actuality, the Senate struck out all of the provisions of the House bill and substituted McCormick's budget measure for it.

McCormick and the majority of the Senate committee had a number of differences with the proposals passed by the House. They favored a budget formulated by a unit under the secretary of the treasury, not under the immediate direction of the President. They also favored a term of office for the comptroller general limited to seven years, and they preferred that the audit group, instead of being called the "accounting department," bear the title of "general accounting office" to emphasize its separation from the executive departments.

Like the Good Committee, the Senate committee heard from a variety of witnesses who urged the separation of the audit and settlement functions, with a new committee established to correspond to the Public Accounts Committee of the British House of Commons. Ogden L. Mills of the National Tax Association testified:

> that a joint committee from each chamber shall be appointed to follow the expenditures of the executive departments and the money granted by Congress, with the power and duty to examine, review, and criticize every item of expenditure made, and to report to Congress annually, and at such other times as Congress, or any committee thereof, may demand.[25]

Like their House counterparts, the senators chose to disregard such advice.

Furthermore, the Senate committee sought a complete overhaul of the government's accounting and bookkeeping apparatus. The House provisions served to consolidate the powers and authority exercised by separate offices within the Treasury Department, and to transfer them to the new, independent organization. The Senate committee favored extending its powers to encompass supervision of the financial activities of the operating departments and agencies, including those of the nonfinancial agencies:

collecting, disbursing, bookkeeping, and related matters.

The Senate report that subsequently accompanied the bill to conference stated:

> Since the auditing and accounting functions are scattered among seven offices, there is little coordination of effort among the Treasury accounting officers. The House bill would correct this particular defect. But this is probably the least important of the defects of the present arrangement. If new provisions are to be made for the accounting establishment of the United States at this or any other time, they should accomplish a concentration of authority over all Federal accounting activities. They should confer upon a single official the power to prescribe and to supervise departmental methods of bookkeeping and of examining claims and accounts of fiscal officers. . . . The Committee bill, however, goes further and confers upon the general accounting office the authority and power to prescribe and to supervise the methods employed in the administrative examination of accounts and claims; and to exercise in general a control over all the accounting procedures of the Government.[26]

In other words, the success of a uniform independent audit depended on the existence of a unified system of accounting; to guarantee the success of the former, the Senate provided the comptroller general with authority to prescribe and enforce the latter. This resulted in the extension of the comptroller general's authority to develop and supervise the methods of accounting in the departments and the methods employed by them in the administrative examination of accounts.

Willoughby wrote to the Trustees of the Institute for Government Research on March 1, 1920, and reported his progress in working with the Senate committee stating: "It (the Senate Committee on the Budget) permitted him (Willoughby) practically to rewrite the bill with the result that . . . in some respects it is a superior bill to the House bill." A version of H.R. 9783 incorporating such provisions passed the Senate without a recorded vote on May 1, 1920.

The Senate and House versions of the bill went to conference and, in accord with custom, the proposal that emerged represented a compromise of their differences. The Senate version on the question of accounting control was substantially adopted. Authority and responsibility for the budget were vested in the President, but the bureau of the budget was lodged in the Treasury Department. The Senate's title for the general accounting office was retained. In the provisions for the offices of comptroller general and assistant comptroller. general, the conference committee agreed on provisions midway between the House and Senate versions. Both offices would be filled by presidential appointment with Senate consent; they would each enjoy a fixed fifteen-year term; and neither could be removed except by impeachment or by concurrent resolution of both houses of

Congress, which does not require presidential signature. This last provision would within a few days become the critical issue. The bill, so modified, passed both houses of Congress without a record vote and was sent to the President on June 2, 1920.

The Wilson Veto, 1920

As indicated earlier, President Wilson was an avowed advocate of budget reform. He had used his veto power sparingly, and there was apparently little anticipation in Congress that he might veto the budget bill. But he believed in this case that the removal provisions violated the constitutional prerogatives of the President, and on June 4, two days after he received it and the day before scheduled adjournment of Congress, he vetoed it and returned it to Congress. In his veto message, he wrote:

> I do this with the greatest regret. I am in entire sympathy with the object of this bill and would gladly approve it but for the fact that I regard one of the provisions contained in section 303 as unconstitutional.

He went on to state:

> The effect of this provision is to prevent the removal of these officers for any cause except either by impeachment or by concurrent resolution of Congress. It has, I think, always been the accepted construction of the Constitution that the power to appoint officers of this kind carries with it as an incident the power to remove. I am convinced that the Congress is without constitutional power to limit the appointing officer and its incident, the power of removal.

It is relevant to note that the Wilson veto occurred six years before the Supreme Court ruled in favor of the President's power to remove executive officers without consent of the Senate.[27] But that ruling was later qualified in the case of regulatory commissioners in 1935.[28] There has been no court test of the President's power to remove a comptroller general to the time of this writing.

Wilson's veto message was transmitted immediately to the floor of the House so that the offending provision could be removed before the adjournment of the Sixty-sixth Congress, scheduled for the next day. Read to the entire House shortly before midnight, the veto message met with a less than enthusiastic response. Congressman Good immediately denounced the President's action:

> I regret more than I can express that the President has thought it necessary to veto the Budget bill. I cannot arrive at any conclusion other than that the legal advice he has received as to the constitutional powers of Congress in this

respect is, indeed, faulty. In creating the General Accounting Office and providing for the Comptroller General and Assistant Comptroller General the committee was guided by a single thought; that was, that these two officers should be placed upon a plane somewhat comparable to the position occupied by a Federal judge. . . . I think it may be stated as a general rule that the power given to the President to appoint an officer carries with it the inherent power of removal unless that inherent right or incidental right is taken away by the statute itself; and that is what this Congress intended to do, to take from the President the incidental right of removal and to provide the circumstances and the method of removal.[29]

In spite of Congressman Good's rhetoric and the fact that Republicans in the House were joined by several influential Democrats, the vote to override Wilson's veto fell short of the needed two-thirds, 178-103. Even with only one day remaining in the congressional session, Good would not admit defeat. On Saturday, June 5, 1920, he introduced a new bill (H.R. 14441), identical to the vetoed bill in all provisions except for the appointment and removal of the comptroller general. Good's bill vested those functions in the Supreme Court, without the advice or consent of the Senate. Much to Good's dismay, the House leaders would not accept his revision. Instead, they reverted to the original provision on appointment and simply deleted the section on removal. So revised, the bill passed the House, but was resisted in the Senate and did not reach a vote there before adjournment.

Enactment, 1921

In the spring of 1921, the Sixty-seventh Congress convened, with budget reform high on its agenda—again. The reelection of the Republican majority in Congress, as well as the presidential victory of the ticket of Warren G. Harding and Calvin Coolidge, assured the prompt introduction and passage of budget legislation. The Senate passed the new bill, S. 1084, on April 26, without a recorded vote, and the House concurred, by a vote of 335 to 3, on May 4. In response to Wilson's veto, the only major change from the legislation of the previous year concerned the removal of the comptroller general and the assistant comptroller general; they were made removable at any time for cause by joint (rather than concurrent) resolution of Congress, which requires presidential approval. This action made it somewhat more difficult to remove the comptroller general, but it very probably was irrelevant to Wilson's argument about constitutionality.

During the floor debate in the House on the consideration of the budget act, Congressman Robert Luce (R. Mass.) reintroduced an amendment that had met defeat earlier. The original legislation had empowered the comptroller general to investigate "all matters relating to the receipt and disbursement of public funds," but did not explicitly indicate the legislative intent that his investigations extend to extravagance, duplication, and inefficiency in executive departments.

To remedy this situation, Luce proposed that the word "application" be appended to "receipt and disbursement":

> It is in this particular section that we can make this clear. The section was worded, I fear, in a way that might have led some occupant of this office to imagine that his functions were purely clerical; that is, the functions implied by the word "accountant." The words used have the savor of the bookkeeper, of the cashier, of the treasurer, not of the investigator of the way money is spent, not of the man who goes out and looks for trouble, not of the man who attempts of his own initiative to find places to save money. Therefore I make the suggestion that we add to the words of the cashier and the treasurer and the accountant, namely, "receipt and disbursement," the word "application." If there ever was presented on this floor a single word of amendment which might have a wider extent of usefulness to the people, it has not come to my knowledge.[30]

Congressman Luce's plea convinced Good and the other House members, and his word, "application," was included in the bill as reported out of conference and passed in the Senate on May 26 and in the House on May 27.

President Harding, who is not especially celebrated as a governmental reformer, on June 20, 1921, signed the bill as amended into the law, known to this day as the "Budget and Accounting Act of 1921."[31] Robert S. Brookings wrote to his fellow Institute of Government trustees on February 12, 1920: "It is not going too far to say that the efforts now being made for budgetary reform are largely the results of the work of the Institute and the latter has certainly been the one body relied upon by both Houses of Congress in considering the matter."

Concluding Observations

The origin and the primary stimulus of the movement that ultimately produced the Budget and Accounting Act was the executive budget, not the independent audit. Scholars and professionals at the time wrote of a "budget system" of several steps, the first of which was budget preparation and the last was auditing of expenditures and receipts.[32] For legislators, including those in Congress, the last step was at least as important as the first for it provided a counterbalance to the enhanced executive power of reviewing, consolidating, and amending the estimates of the agencies; it offered some assurance of legislative control of the purse. But most of the popular support and debate centered on the executive budget; the audit was viewed as an appendage that rode "piggyback" on the rest of the package. Thus, from the time that the budget bill was first given serious consideration, its Title II, which provided for the budget process and the Bureau of the Budget, attracted far more attention than did its Title III, which provided for the audit and the General Accounting Office.

The relative deemphasis upon the potential importance of the Comptroller General even after the act was passed was deplored by some observers. For example, William H. Allen, an early advocate of budget reform and a witness before the Good Committee, wrote early in 1923:

> The opportunities of the comptroller general to serve the United States where it now most urgently needs help are greater than those of any other elected or appointed public officer, not excluding the president and his cabinet. A comptroller general who lives up to his opportunities can do more to make the president's budget director efficient, to make congress and its committees and our voters efficient than any other single officer.[33]

Allen may have overstated the case. But, in spite of the wrangling about the GAO for many years thereafter, it is probably true that until very recently the literature about American government has seriously downplayed, where it has not totally ignored, the role and the potential of that organization.

In fact, the role described in the act went considerably beyond that customarily associated with the auditing of public agencies. Indeed it goes beyond that provided in the British system and the roles then being pushed and adopted in some state and local governments, which were to some extent used as models. This is partly because Congress simply transferred to the Comptroller General the powers previously vested in the comptroller and auditors of the Treasury Department, some of which partook more of current control of financial administration than of auditing.[34] To these Congress added some of its own, such as the supervision of agency accounting systems.

Harvey C. Mansfield, Sr., probably spoke for a majority of American political scientists and many professional accountants in 1939 when he criticized the assumption of these functions by the GAO as an invasion of executive prerogatives.[35] He described the Budget and Accounting Act, particularly its Title III on the Comptroller General, as the product of "almost masterly inattention to draftmanship," partly because of its alleged inconsistency and ambiguity.[36] On the other hand, it has stood the test of time and of enormous change—like the Constitution of the United States. In spite of fundamental changes in other legislation affecting the GAO and in the operations of the office, most of the provisions of Title III remain unscathed fifty-seven years later as its basic charter.

Addendum: Basic Features of the Budget and Accounting Act

In comparison with much congressional legislation, the Budget and

Accounting Act of 1921 was deceptively simple and direct. Following a brief *Title I—Definitions*, it provided, in *Title II—The Budget*, that the President transmit to Congress on the first day of each regular session an annual budget including estimates of expenditures, appropriations, receipts, debt, and borrowing along with accompanying information about the current and past year, and other supporting data and, as required during the year, supplemental or deficiency estimates. It forbade agencies to submit any separate requests for increases except on request of Congress. To prepare such estimates and materials, it established a Bureau of the Budget in the Treasury Department;[37] but it was to be headed by a director and assistant director appointed by, and responsible to, the President. Each agency was to submit its estimates to the bureau in such manner as the President might prescribe, and for this purpose was to designate its own budget officer.

The basic provisions of Title III on the General Accounting Office read as follows:

> *Sec. 301.* There is created an establishment of the Government to be known as the General Accounting Office, which shall be independent of the executive departments and under the control and direction of the Comptroller General of the United States. The offices of Comptroller of the Treasury and Assistant Comptroller of the Treasury are abolished, to take effect July 1, 1921. All other offices and employees of the office of the Comptroller of the Treasury shall become officers and employees in the General Accounting Office at their grades and salaries on July 1, 1921, and all books, records, documents, papers, furniture, office equipment and other property of the office of the Comptroller of the Treasury shall become the property of the General Accounting Office. The Comptroller General is authorized to adopt a seal for the General Accounting Office.
>
> *Sec. 302.* There shall be in the General Accounting Office a Comptroller General of the United States and an Assistant Comptroller General of the United States, who shall be appointed by the President with the advice and consent of the Senate, and shall receive salaries of $10,000 and $7,500 a year, respectively. The Assistant Comptroller shall perform such duties as may be assigned to him by the Comptroller General, and during the absence or incapacity of the Comptroller General, or during a vacancy in that office, shall act as Comptroller General.
>
> *Sec. 303.* Except as hereinafter provided in this section, the Comptroller General and the Assistant Comptroller General shall hold office for fifteen years. The Comptroller General shall not be eligible for reappointment. The Comptroller General or the Assistant Comptroller General may be removed at any time by joint resolution of Congress after notice and hearing, when, in the judgment of Congress, the Comptroller General or Assistant Comptroller General has become permanently incapacitated or has been inefficient, or guilty of neglect of duty, or of malfeasance in office, or of any felony or conduct involving moral turpitude, and for no other cause and in no other manner

except by impeachment. Any Comptroller General or Assistant Comptroller General removed in the manner herein provided shall be ineligible for reappointment to that office. When a Comptroller General or Assistant Comptroller General attains the age of seventy years, he shall be retired from his office.

Sec. 304. All powers and duties now conferred or imposed by law upon the Comptroller of the Treasury or the six auditors of the Treasury Department, and the duties of the Division of Bookkeeping and Warrants of the Office of the Secretary of the Treasury relating to keeping the personal ledger accounts of disbursing and collecting officers, shall, so far as not inconsistent with this Act, be vested in and imposed upon the General Accounting Office and be exercised without direction from any other officer. The balances certified by the Comptroller General shall be final and conclusive upon the executive branch of the Government. The revision by the Comptroller General of settlements made by the six auditors shall be discontinued, except as to settlements made before July 1, 1921.

The administrative examination of the accounts and vouchers of the Postal Service now imposed by law upon the Auditor for the Post Office Department shall be performed on and after July 1, 1921, by a bureau in the Post Office Department to be known as the Bureau of Accounts, which is hereby established for that purpose.

Sec. 305. Section 236 of the Revised Statutes is amended to read as follows:

Sec. 236. "All claims and demands whatever by the Government of the United States or against it, and all accounts whatever in which the Government of the United States is concerned, either as debtor or creditor, shall be settled and adjusted in the General Accounting Office."

Sec. 306. All laws relating generally to the administration of the departments and establishments shall, so far as applicable, govern the General Accounting Office. Copies of any books, records, papers, or documents, and transcripts from the books and proceedings of the General Accounting Office, when certified by the Comptroller General or the Assistant Comptroller General under its seal, shall be admitted as evidence with the same effect as the copies and transcripts referred to in sections 882 and 886 of the Revised Statutes.

Sec. 307. The Comptroller General may provide for the payment of accounts or claims adjusted and settled in the General Accounting Office, through disbursing officers of the several departments and establishments, instead of by warrant.

Sec. 308. The duties now appertaining to the Divison of Public Moneys of the Office of the Secretary of the Treasury, so far as they relate to the covering of revenues and repayments into the Treasury, the issue of duplicate checks and warrants, and the certification of outstanding liabilities for payment, shall be performed by the Division of Bookkeeping and Warrants of the Office of the Secretary of the Treasury.

Sec. 309. The Comptroller General shall prescribe the forms, systems, and procedure for administrative appropriation and fund accounting in the several departments and establishments, and for the administrative examination of fiscal officers' accounts and claims against the United States.

Sec. 310. The offices of the six auditors shall be abolished, to take effect July 1, 1921. All other officers and employees of these offices except as otherwise provided herein shall become officers and employees of the General Accounting Office at their grades and salaries on July 1, 1921. All books, records, documents, papers, furniture, office equipment, and other property of these offices, and of the Division of Bookkeeping and Warrants, so far as they relate to the work of such division transferred by section 304, shall become the property of the General Accounting Office. The General Accounting Office shall occupy temporarily the rooms now occupied by the office of the Comptroller of the Treasury and the six auditors.

Sec. 311. (a) The Comptroller General shall appoint, remove, and fix the compensation of such attorneys and other employees in the general Accounting Office as may from time to time be provided for by law.

(b) All such appointments, except to positions carrying a salary at a rate of more than $5,000 a year, shall be made in accordance with the civil-service laws and regulations.

(c) No person appointed by the Comptroller General shall be paid a salary of more than $6,000 a year, and not more than four persons shall be paid a salary at a rate of more than $5,000 a year.

(d) All officers and employees of the General Accounting Office, whether transferred thereto or appointed by the Comptroller General, shall perform such duties as may be assigned to them by him.

(e) All official acts performed by such officers or employees specially designated therefor by the Comptroller General shall have the same force and effect as though performed by the Comptroller General in person.

(f) The Comptroller General shall make such rules and regulations as may be necessary for carrying on the work of the General Accounting Office, including rules and regulations concerning the admission of attorneys to practice before such office.

Sec. 312. (a) The Comptroller General shall investigate, at the seat of government or elsewhere, all matters relating to the receipt, disbursement, and application of public funds, and shall make to the President when requested by him, and to Congress at the beginning of each regular session, a report in writing of the work of the General Accounting Office, containing recommendations concerning the legislation he may deem necessary to facilitate the prompt and accurate rendition and settlement of accounts and concerning such other matters relating to the receipt, disbursement, and application of public funds as he may think advisable. In such regular report, or in special reports at any time when Congress is in session, he shall make recommendations looking to greater economy or efficiency in public expenditures.

(b) He shall make such investigations and reports as shall be ordered by either House of Congress or by any committee of either House having jurisdiction over revenue, appropriations, or expenditures. The Comptroller General shall also, at the request of any such committee, direct assistants from his office to furnish the committee such aid and information as it may request.

(c) The Comptroller General shall specially report to Congress every expenditure or contract made by any department or establishment in any year in violation of law.

(d) He shall submit to Congress reports upon the adequacy and effectiveness of the administrative examination of accounts and claims in the respective departments and establishments and upon the adequacy and effectiveness of departmental inspection of the offices and accounts of fiscal officers.

(e) He shall furnish such information relating to expenditures and accounting to the Bureau of the Budget as it may request from time to time.

Sec. 313. All departments and establishments shall furnish to the Comptroller General such information regarding the powers, duties, activities, organization, financial transactions, and methods of business of their respective offices as he may from time to time require of them; and the Comptroller General, or any of his assistants or employees, when duly authorized by him, shall, for the purpose of securing such information, have access to and the right to examine any books, documents, papers, or records of any such department or establishment. The authority contained in this section shall not be applicable to expenditures made under the provisions of section 291 of the Revised Statutes.

Sec. 314. The Civil Service Commission shall establish an eligible register for accountants for the General Accounting Office, and the examinations of applicants for entrance upon such register shall be based upon questions approved by the Comptroller General.

Approved, June 10, 1921.

Notes

1. As will appear in subsequent chapters, the pattern has continued to the present day. The only significant exception during the nineteenth century was the Dockery Act of 1894.

2. Much of this discussion is excerpted from Frederick A. Cleveland and Arthur E. Buck, *The Budget and Responsible Government* (New York: Macmillan, 1920), pp. 82-90.

3. William Howard Taft, *Our Chief Magistrate and His Powers* (1916), pp. 64-65.

4. Committee on Municipal Program of the National Municipal League, *A Model City Charter and Municipal Home Rule* (Philadelphia, 1916).

5. Ibid., p. 45.

6. Committee on State Government of the National Municipal League, *A Model State Constitution* (New York, 1921).

7. The studies were H. G. Villard and W. W. Willoughby, *The Canadian Budget System*; W. F. Willoughby, *The Movement for Budgetary Reform in the United States*; W. F. Willoughby, *The Problem of a National Budget*; W. F. Willoughby, W. W. Willoughby, and Samuel McCune Lindsay, *The System*

of *Financial Administration in Great Britain*; and René Stourm, *The Budget*, translated by T. Plazinski.

8. Cleveland and Buck, *The Budget*.

9. James D. Richardson, ed., *A Compilation of the Messages and Papers of the Presidents*, 17:8405, as quoted in Louis Fisher, *Presidential Spending Power* (Princeton, N.J.: Princeton University Press, 1975), p. 32.

10. A successful St. Louis businessman, Brookings was well regarded among congressmen by virtue of his wartime investigation of price fixing in American industry.

11. U.S. Congress, House, Select Committee on the Budget of the House of Representatives, *National Budget System*, 66th Cong., 1st Sess., September 22–October 4, 1919.

12. Specifically endorsed by several witnesses including former President Taft, former Secretary of War Henry L. Stimson, and Secretary of the Treasury Carter Glass.

13. Several declined comment on auditing. They included then Assistant Secretary of the Navy Franklin D. Roosevelt, one of the few administration spokesmen.

14. Warwick has been credited by at least one writer with authorship of this part of the bill. Harvey C. Mansfield wrote in 1939 that this section of "the bill was drawn in his office." *The Comptroller General*, p. 68.

15. *Congressional Record*, May 3, 1921, p. 982.

16. U.S. Congress, House, Select Committee on the Budget, *Hearings*, 66th Cong., 1st Sess., 1919, p. 367. Andrews also referred to the collaboration between Comptroller Warwick and Congressman Good in working out the details of the auditing provisions of the act; as quoted in Lucius Wilmerding, *The Spending Power* (New Haven, Conn.: Yale University Press, 1943), p. 257.

17. *Congressional Record*, October 20, 1919, p. 7636.

18. *Congressional Record*, October 21, 1919, p. 7719.

19. *Hearings*, p. 396.

20. This point is developed in a more thorough fashion in Wilmerding, *The Spending Power*, and in Mansfield, *The Comptroller General*. See particularly his section on "The Pseudo-Solution," pp. 250-83.

21. Although Willoughby, the third witness, acknowledged it in his testimony when he said: "It struck me as rather remarkable that the controller and auditor general had no power of final decision regarding expenditures such as our controller has. His functions come after the expenditure is made." *Hearings*, p. 64.

22. *Hearings*, p. 141.

23. *Hearings*, p. 132-33.

24. *Congressional Record* as quoted in Wilmerding, *The Spending Power*, p. 287.

25. As quoted in Wilmerding, *The Spending Power*, p. 287.

26. U.S. Congress, Senate Report no. 524.

27. Myers v. United States, 272 U.S. 52 (1926).

28. Humphrey's Executor v. United States, 295, U.S. 602 (1935).

29. *Congressional Record,* June 4, 1920, p. 8610.

30. *Congressional Record,* May 5, 1921, p. 1090.

31. A summary of the act as it was passed is provided in the Addendum to this chapter.

32. For example, W. F. Willoughby described the budget cycle as consisting of formulation by the executive, legislative consideration, and independent audit (*Hearings*, p. 70). Later writers would add execution, including control, before the audit, and attribute it to the executive.

33. William H. Allen, "The U.S. Comptroller General and His Opportunities," *National Municipal Review* (February 1923); pp. 58-61.

34. These are discussed in the following chapter. They included, for example: countersigning of warrants before appropriated funds could be spent; issuing advance rulings binding upon the executive branch; reviewing and maintaining accounts of disbursing officers; disallowing payments already made; and settling claims for or against the government.

35. Mansfield, *The Comptroller General*, especially in the Introduction.

36. Ibid., p. 67.

37. The Bureau of the Budget was subsequently moved to the Executive Office of the President (in 1939). Still later its name was changed to Office of Management and Budget (in 1970).

3

THE FIRST GAO: VOUCHER CHECKING AND LEGAL COMPLIANCE, 1921-1945

An institution is the lengthened shadow of one man.
—Ralph Waldo Emerson, *Self-Reliance,* 1841

Whoever desires to found a state and give it laws, must start with assuming that all men are bad and ever ready to display their vicious nature, whenever they may find occasion for it.
—Niccolo Machiavelli, *Discourse Upon the First Ten Books of Livy,* 1519

In the first fifty-seven years after the Budget and Accounting Act was passed, there were only five Comptrollers General. Except for one,[1] all held the post for a decade or longer, and each impressed upon the nature and conduct of the GAO his unique values, his view of the world and his office, his character, and his personality. The length and security of the term enabled the top man to shape and reshape the organization to an extent unusual for public officials.

The period discussed in this chapter covers three totally different eras in the evolution of American society, economy, and government. The first—roughly the decade of the 1920s—was one of limited government, and particularly of limited national government. It was ushered in with President Harding's 1920 campaign plea for a "return to normalcy" and was typified by President Coolidge's confident and simple statement that the "business of government is business." In relation to the society in general and Congress in particular, the stance of the Presidents was passive until the last years of President Hoover's term in the early 1930s.

The second era was the decade of the great depression and the New Deal—roughly the 1930s. It was a period of aggressive federal intervention in the society and the economy, of social invention and experimentation, and of unprecedented growth of federal responsibilities, size, and scope. The third era—roughly 1940 through 1945—encompassed the preparation for and conduct of World War II, when under federal leadership most of the efforts of the nation were directed to military victory.

The major part of the chapter treats the formulation, development, and crystallization of the GAO during the 1920s and early 1930s. As federal business spiralled upward geometrically during the New Deal and again during the war, the staff of the GAO also grew. But it is true and even remarkable that the organization's basic posture, self-image, and modus operandi changed little during the New Deal and the war periods despite the enormous changes that were going on around it.

The Beginnings

On July 1, 1921, the General Accounting Office inherited all "powers and duties" of the comptroller and of the six auditors in the Treasury Department as well as those relating to the accounts of the disbursing and collecting officers previously performed by the Treasury Department's Division of Bookkeeping and Warrants. It also received all the personnel (other than the comptroller and assistant comptroller of the treasury, whose offices were abolished), together with the associated "books, records, documents, papers, furniture, office equipment, and other property."[2]

To the traditional powers were added a very few others, the most significant of which were to "prescribe the forms, systems, and procedure for administrative appropriation and fund accounting in the several departments and establishments" (Sec. 307) and to "investigate, at the seat of government or elsewhere, all matters relating to the receipt, disbursement, and *application* of public funds . . ." (Sec. 312; emphasis added). Of course, the GAO also inherited the practices and procedures built up over the previous 132 years on the basis of the original Treasury Act of 1789 as it had been modified and extended by the acts of 1817, 1867, 1894, and others.

In the main, then, the GAO appeared to be the product of a simple transfer of powers, duties, and resources from the Treasury Department to a new agency. But in three significant respects the change was fundamental. First of these was the position of the GAO in the total governmental system, which was decidedly different from that of the office of the Comptroller of the Treasury but still somewhat equivocal. It would be "independent of the executive departments," but not entirely of the executive branch. Its head, the Comptroller General (together with his assistant) would be appointed by the President with senatorial consent for a fifteen-year term, but the President could not remove him. Removal required congressional initiative, but under such conditions and procedures that his security in office for a decade and a half was very nearly absolute. Nowhere in the act was there a clear statement that the GAO was a congressional agency. On the other hand, its independence was fortified by the expressions that its major powers and duties "be exercised without direction from any other officer" (Sec. 304) and that the Comptroller General's determinations "shall be final and conclusive upon the executive branch of the government" (Sec. 304). In fact, the first Comptroller General construed his freedom to be a step beyond the act. In his *Annual Report* for 1926, he alleged that his agency was "free from executive or *judicial* control and responsible only to the Congress . . ." (emphasis added). Yet two other passages in the act seemed to qualify the office's independence. One (Sec. 306) provided that: "All laws relating generally to the administration of the departments and establishments, shall, so far as applicable, govern the General Accounting Office." Among many other things, this was interpreted to mean that GAO was subject to the civil service system and the regular executive budget system, both of which operate mainly under the direction of the President.[3] The other (Sec. 312) required that the Comptroller General "make to the President when requested by him, and to Congress at the beginning of each regular session, a report in writing" of the GAO's work. Other paragraphs of the same section of the act called upon him to respond to requests for information and reports from Congress, to report to Congress any violations of law, and to report on the financial systems of the various executive agencies. Finally, and still further confusing as to his independence, was a requirement that he provide information "relating to expenditures and accounting to the Bureau of the Budget as it may request from time to time" (also Sec. 312).

A second significant change from what had gone before was the virtually unqualified power of the Comptroller General in the internal management of the GAO, and this power was in no sense equivocal. Indeed, so broad a grant of power to the head of a governmental agency could have had few precedents in American history. The act provided only one other officer, the Assistant Comptroller General, appointed and removable under the same conditions as the Comptroller General and likewise for a fifteen-year term though not necessarily concurrent with the latter. But the assistant should perform only "such duties as may be assigned to him by the Comptroller General" (Sec. 302) (which were sometimes either trivial or totally absent); and he should serve as Comptroller General in the latter's absence or incapacity. All other offices previously established by law were abolished. The Comptroller General could organize the GAO as he pleased, establish or refuse to establish field offices as he wished, deploy his personnel and other resources, and, perhaps most important, interpret his legal powers with little fear of appeal to higher authorities. Indeed, some parts of the act suggested that there was no higher authority.

The third major change was in the person of the Comptroller General in contrast to the many comptrollers that he succeeded. The first Comptroller General, and the only one to the time of this writing to serve out his fifteen-year term, was J. Raymond McCarl, appointed by President Harding in 1921 and in office until the last year of President Franklin D. Roosevelt's first term in 1936. McCarl had been a young lawyer from McCook, Nebraska, who had become interested in politics as a progressive Republican. He came to Washington as secretary to Senator George Norris, and then in both 1918 and 1920 served as Executive Secretary to the Republican Congressional Campaign Committee. It was widely expected that the first appointee to the new post of Comptroller General would be W. W. Warwick, the last comptroller of the treasury, who is credited by some as principal author of the GAO provisions of the Budget and Accounting Act and the initiator of the idea of the fifteen-year term. But Warwick's ambition for the post was aborted by the Wilson veto. It is reported[4] that McCarl advised President Harding for and against a number of potential candidates for the job and finally accepted it himself. Harding was faithful to the precedents of most of his predecessors in their appointments of comptrollers of the treasury; McCarl was a lawyer, a not very prominent politician of the President's party, and was closely associated with Congress (though not himself a member or former member). Like most of the comptrollers, he brought little or no experience in or knowledge of administration, the workings of large organizations, accounting, or auditing.

But Harding could hardly have anticipated the nature of the man in the job, for McCarl was sui generis, and he would become for many years one of the most controversial figures in Washington. Admirers and critics would probably agree on some descriptive adjectives: he was strong willed, stubborn, unafraid, independent, righteous (or self-righteous?), legalistic, contentious, ambitious, and humorless. His supporters, particularly in the press, would hail him as a bastion of the law, the principal protector of the public purse, a high saint of honesty, economy, and efficiency, and the ultimate savior against political and bureaucratic miscreants, liars, and thieves. One of his journalistic admirers described him as "the only official in Washington who obeys the law."[5] His opponents, who included a good number of administrative officials of both political parties, would label him a ruthless zealot, a despot, a would-be czar, a nitpicker, an empire builder with insatiable personal ambition, an ideologue whose judgments were governed by political bias, and a manufacturer of red tape and delay that obstructed the timely and efficient conduct of public business.

Regardless of one's views concerning the performance of J. Raymond McCarl, there can be no doubt that he had tremendous influence upon the nature and the evolution of GAO. His influence extended well beyond his fifteen-year term. For although the severity and the aggressiveness of the GAO associated with him declined after his retirement in 1936, the essential elements of his administration pervaded the GAO for nearly half of the organization's life span to the time of this writing. The GAO image—associated primarily with the first Comptroller General—remains to a very substantial extent intact in the minds of those who know of the existence of the GAO but not very much of its current operations. That image is perhaps the principal source of misunderstanding about the organization today.

The Organization

McCarl in 1921 took command of an army of about 1,700 employees, almost all of them clerks. Before the end of his first full year, he had added to that total several hundred persons by assuming most of the personnel and responsibilities of the comptroller of the Post Office Department. Thereafter, for more than a decade, the staff hovered in the neighborhood of 2,000. It more than doubled during the New Deal period, and grew to nearly 15,000 in World War II. Until 1934 all except McCarl and the Assistant Comptroller General—for the first decade, Lurtin R. Ginn[6]—were in the classified civil service. The great bulk of McCarl's army were "privates," clerks in the lowest salary brackets. The average annual salary of the office as a whole in 1921 was less than $1,600—unusually low even in comparison with other government agencies.[7] Following the Classification Act of 1923, salaries gradually rose, but the average did not reach $1,800 until 1927 and was still under $2,000 in 1937. McCarl's army had very few officers. In addition to the Comptroller General and Assistant Comptroller General, there were only four with salaries of $5,000 or more in 1922. This number grew to 12 in 1928, 22 in 1932, and 33 in 1937. These upper-level hires were drawn increasingly from the ranks of attorneys, and lawyers more and more assumed the role of the elite leadership profession of the GAO. The trend persisted through World War II, and it was not seriously challenged until the postwar years when professional accountants began to assume greater influence.

The organization structure that McCarl inherited was of the "clientele" type; that is, each division would handle virtually all the work for a given department or agency of the government, like the old six auditors of the Treasury Department. The original pattern included a Division of Law, immediately under the supervision of the Comptroller General, and separate divisions for the Treasury, War, Navy, Interior, Post Office, and State (and other) departments. Probably in the interests of centralizing control from the top and of standardizing procedures, McCarl moved in the direction of a functional structure in which the primary divisions would be based upon the kinds of activities and responsibilities exercised regardless of the departments from which the work emanated. During his first two years, he consolidated the audit and claims work of the War and Navy departments into a Military Division and that of most of the other departments into a Civil Division. He established a Transportation Division to handle all audits and claims in connection with transportation; a Check Accounting Division to receive and have custody of cancelled checks and to adjust the bank balances of fiscal agents; an Investigation Section with a variety of responsibilities; and a Bookkeeping Section to keep track of and check

registers, warrants against appropriations accounts, disbursing officers'
accounts, and other papers. Later (in December 1923) was established a
Claims Division to take over the claims work of the Civil and Military
divisons. Still later (in 1926) he merged the Military and Civil divisions into
a single Audit Division and combined the claims and transportation work in
a single Claims Division.

Among the original divisions, the only ones to survive the transfer from
clientele (or departmental) to functional structure were the Division of Law
(which became the Office of General Counsel in 1928 and so remains at the
time of this writing) and the Post Office Department Division. The legal
work of course was handled across the departmental board from the outset.
The Post Office was unique in that, following an extraordinary agreement
by the postmaster general with the Comptroller General in 1923, the latter
took over almost all of the accounting as well as the auditing of postal
accounts.[8] Thereafter, for twenty-seven years, the postal division of the GAO
handled virtually all aspects of postal accounts and audits, virtually free of
direction or guidance from the Post Office.

Except for the special arrangements made for the Post Office, the GAO
remained organized primarily according to function for nearly a half
century. Its structure in 1936 consisted of the following:[9]

Division	*Employees*
Office of the Comptroller General, including budget and finance, personnel, physical maintenance, General Counsel, legislative relations, and Office of Investigations	461
Records Division, which handled the flow of work and maintained the files of settled claims and accounts and of debts	1,250
Audit Division, which checked and either certified or initiated exceptions on accounts and supporting documents of the various departments, other than Post Office	1,384
Claims Division, which handled claims for and against the United States, including particularly those associated with transportation	408
Accounting and Bookkeeping Division, which kept the books on appropriations and warrants, countersigned warrants, settled accounts, and considered replies to exceptions arising from the postaudits, among a variety of other duties	344

Internally, the GAO was highly centralized and disciplined. Organization was tightly structured with severe respect for hierarchy, lines of
command, and multiple internal reviews and checks. The old GAO was a
model of the authoritarian type of organization characterized by Douglas
McGregor as "Theory X."[10] McCarl himself is reputed to have been a strict
disciplinarian. Some of the surviving old-timers recall that he required the
ringing of bells to mark the time when employees were to sit down and begin
their work, when they were to go to lunch, when they were to resume work,
and when they could go home. There was little opportunity for most GAO
employees to have contact with people outside the organization except
through formal written communication; mainly they worked at their desks
midst "the clickety-clack of typewriters and the busy hum of clerical
workers."[11]

From its beginning, the GAO's functioning was significantly conditioned
by its office accommodations. McCarl and his immediate staff began by
utilizing the space in the Treasury Building previously occupied by the office
of the comptroller of the treasury. Most of the remainder of his staff and the
mass of fiscal records already accumulated were housed in a number of
federal and rented buildings nearby in downtown Washington. Beginning
with his first annual report in 1922, McCarl complained of the difficulties of
managing and reorganizing his agency and preserving its irreplaceable
records because it was scattered in so many different buildings. His repeated
demand for a single GAO building, stated in most of his own and his
successors' annual reports to Congress, was not satisfied until long after his
death with the completion of the present GAO building in 1951. But he had
at least partial solace when in 1926 the central offices of the GAO were
transferred to the old Pension Building, which occupied most of the block
bounded by Fourth, Fifth, F, and G streets, N.W., in Washington. The
Pension Building, which became a symbol of the original GAO, had been
completed in 1882 to accommodate the processing of pensions for war
veterans. It was and remains an enormous architectural oddity, sometimes
referred to as "Meigs' Old Brick Barn,"[12] one of the largest brick buildings in
the world and, as an office building, one containing possibly the highest
proportion of wasted cubic footage in the world. Beside providing the
headquarters of the GAO for about a quarter of a century, its principal claim
to fame is as the site of inaugural balls, beginning with Presidents Cleveland,

Harrison, McKinley, Theodore Roosevelt, and Taft, and more recently Nixon and Carter. But the "Old Brick Barn" could not accommodate the GAO's entire army of 2,000, which would later grow seven-fold. Most of the troops were scattered in various buildings in downtown Washington.

Work of the First GAO

The GAO of the 1920s, 1930s, and war years of the 1940s can be best described as a prodigious paper mill and an enormous warehouse of paper. Most of its paper was received from the departments and agencies of the government, and sometimes from private citizens, normally on forms and according to procedures prescribed by law and by the Comptroller General. On receipt of these documents, the GAO recorded and checked them, sometimes returned or otherwise responded to them, and stored them.

The principal categories of papers and the GAO activities associated with them are sketched below. The second, third, and ninth of these are discussed in greater depth in succeeding paragraphs.

1. The GAO reviewed *requisitions* from the various agencies and disbursing officers for advances of funds; if approved, these were forwarded to the Treasury Department, which drew up *warrants* that were signed by the secretary and then countersigned by the Comptroller General. The warrants were a legal authorization to spend, receive, borrow, or transfer government money. For the most part, the signature and countersignature have been considered nondiscretionary acts assuring only that the money was legally available for the purposes sought, although McCarl did not accept this ministerial interpretation.[13] Other kinds of warrants were used for the receipt of funds, for transfers, for public debt transactions, and so forth, and they numbered in the thousands every year. From the time of Alexander Hamilton until the 1950s, the warrants remained the foundation of the federal financial system.

2. The Comptroller General inherited the power and duty from the comptroller of the treasury to render *advance decisions* on payment questions raised by heads of departments or disbursing officers as well as by its own auditors. These were limited in number before 1921 to an average of about 250 per year. Under McCarl, their use mushroomed to several thousand per year as agencies sought to protect themselves from future disallowances. The decisions now comprise an ever-growing library of volumes that constitute much of the bible and verse of legal and financial officers throughout the government.

3. The central and best known of the GAO's responsibilities was the *audit of expenditure vouchers*[14] (mostly after they had been paid) and the *settlement of accounts*—primarily those of the various disbursing officers scattered around the government—which were required to be submitted periodically along

with all their supporting documents. The GAO's checking of individual vouchers was intended to assure that the money was authorized and available, the payment was lawful in every respect, the proper procedures had been followed, and no fraud or other irregularity was involved. If any objections were raised, notices of exception were issued to the responsible officers, and unless satisfactory explanation could be made the payments were disallowed. This meant that either the payee or the officer responsible for the payment must make up the amount to the government. In the event that the disallowance was not satisfied, the GAO could refer the case to the Department of Justice for legal action.

4. Another activity, which was neither required nor prohibited in law, was the *preaudit of vouchers* by the GAO prior to payment. McCarl was an enthusiastic supporter of preauditing on the grounds that it would prevent disallowances and all their accompanying inconveniences in advance, and he urged the departments to use it. But few of them did, and with some significant exceptions (transportation bills, some commodity payments, and other transactions in a scattering of agencies) the postaudit continued as the predominant practice.

5. In addition to its auditing of vouchers, the GAO received and reviewed government *contracts* and audited payments based on them.

6. It also received copies of *cancelled checks* written against government accounts, reconciled them with the depositary balances of the fiscal agents in the various agencies and filed them.

7. It reviewed and decided upon *claims* both for and against the government, and its decisions were final for all agencies in the executive branch. Private parties could appeal GAO decisions to the Court of Claims (or take their claims there in the first instance if they chose), and there was often recourse to Congress and sometimes to the general court system. The GAO set up a process also to *collect payments* due the government.

8. On January 1, 1923, the Comptroller General ordered the departments and agencies to transmit the *transportation bills* of common carriers for direct settlement by the GAO and payment by means of Treasury Department warrants.[15] The War and Navy departments refused, and the attorney general denied that the GAO had the power to order such a procedure.[16] But this centralized preaudit of transportation vouchers became the prevailing practice in the government and one to which the GAO for many years assigned many (about 400) people.

9. One of the objectives of the 1921 law was to bring about the improvement of accounting methods throughout the government, and the primary responsibility for this was lodged in the GAO. It was empowered to *prescribe and standardize accounting forms and procedures* in the several agencies and to inspect and correct the practices in the various fiscal offices. For these and related purposes, a small investigation section was organized in 1922

and later considerably expanded.

10. A very large part of the GAO's time was devoted to *maintaining records* and copies of all the variegated categories of forms and other papers associated with the above responsibilities.

11. The GAO was called upon to make *reports and recommendations* to Congress and, on request, to the President and the Bureau of the Budget. In the main, it appears that it preferred to act on its own authority. Its annual reports to Congress were largely records of its own work and its problems with the agencies, sprinkled with recommendations for legislation, usually to enlarge its scope and authority and often introduced by a statement about the philosophy and objectives of the organization.

12. In addition to the above general activities, the GAO continued from 1923 on to maintain as well as audit virtually all the *central accounts of the Post Office.*

The volume of documents handled for these various purposes was simply staggering, as indicated in Table 1. Of the activities enumerated above, three of the most important in their impact upon the administrative operations of the government were: advance decisions and other rulings; the audit and settlement of accounts; and the prescription of agency accounting forms and systems. With respect to all three, the determinations of the GAO were presumed to be final and binding on the executive branch.

Advance Decisions and Rulings

The Comptroller General was—and is—called upon to interpret the meaning and the limitations of appropriations and other statutes and court decisions, as well as some of his own previous regulations in their application to individual cases or classes of cases. A great many, probably most, of these instances dealt with relatively minor and technical matters without severe impact upon public policy and the general conduct of governmental business. Some concerned one-time questions, unlikely to recur. But others were of considerable importance and had a long-range impact upon many agencies and programs. An example of these was the issue as to whether an executive agency could assign and defray the salary and expenses of employees in education or training courses when such expenditures were not explicitly authorized by law. The landmark decision on the question had been made in the negative by the comptroller of the treasury in 1910 on the grounds that "all appropriations must be used for the specific purpose for which made and not otherwise" and that "it is presumed that the officers and employees of the Government when appointed and employed have the necessary education to perform the duties for which they were appointed or employed."[17]

That early decision survived for nearly half a century through a succession of appeals on training cases. After World War II and the Korean conflict,

TABLE 1

Indicators of GAO Workload, 1932 and 1939

	1932	1939
Reports issued on inspections and investigations	1,200	700
Reports to Congress, President, Bureau of the Budget	346	227
Replies to miscellaneous congressional inquiries	3,660	2,900
Legal decisions	7,100	8,200
Approved accounting forms	200	357
Vouchers audited	N/A	14,000,000
Vouchers preaudited	350,000	538,000
Appropriation and limitation accounts maintained	N/A	65,000
Accountable officers' accounts maintained	29,000	N/A
Other accounts maintained	N/A	238,000
Treasury warrants countersigned	24,000	57,000
Requests for disbursing funds approved	N/A	13,000
Claims settled	284,000	445,000
Transportation claims settled	225,000	305,000
Contracts examined	227,000	993,000
Checks reconciled	33,000,000	152,100,000
Postal accounts audited	174,000	263,000
Postal money orders audited	191,000,000	248,000,000

Source: Annual Report of the Comptroller General, 1932 and 1939.

conditions and needs had changed sufficiently to induce the Comptroller General to modify the ruling to permit expenditures for particular training when it (1) was special in nature and for a period of limited duration, (2) was essential to carry out the purpose for which the appropriation was made, and (3) was not of a type that the employee would normally be expected to furnish at his own expense.[18] The decision as to whether any given training program satisfied these criteria would of course be made by the Comptroller General, not the agency. Subsequently, he determined that "limited duration" meant normally not more than two weeks. The net effect of these GAO decisions was to virtually prohibit governmentally supported training programs of substantial length except for certain categories that had specific statutory authorization (such as the Foreign Service and the military), until Congress passed the Government Employees Training Act of 1958.[19]

Examples of other GAO rulings of lasting impact include:

- If advertisement for purchases omits any factor considered by the Comptroller General to be an essential competitive factor, none of the bids received can be accepted. (8 C.G. 649.)
- The desire to match equipment on hand does not warrant purchase without competition. (8 C.G. 649.)
- The lowest responsible bid meeting specifications must be accepted, and, when any other than the lowest bid is accepted, a detailed statement of reasons must be submitted to the General Accounting Office. (4 C.G. 254.)
- Leasing of premises for use of governmental agencies must be after advertising and competition. (14 C.G. 769.)
- Commercial purchase of brushes is illegal without a showing that the federal penitentiary was unable to furnish such brushes; the law does not contain any provision exempting purchases on account of emergencies. (14 C.G. 271.)
- All claims of common carriers must be transmitted to the General Accounting Office for settlement before payment. (Regulation—January 1, 1923.)
- Treatment of the walls and ceilings of a public building with sound-deadening felt is not an item of repair or preservation but an improvement and is not payable from an appropriation for repairs and preservation of public buildings. (2 C.G. 301.)[20]

Some of the Comptroller General's rulings concerned questions of general management and were only indirectly related to the legality and propriety of payments. Thus in 1933, he responded to a series of questions of the secretary of the treasury as to the effect of an executive order reorganizing the Bureaus of Industrial Alcohol and Internal Revenue. In 1935, he advised the Public Works Administration on three alternative methods of operating housing projects: by lease, by direct governmental maintenance, or by management contracts. In the same year, he rendered an opinion to the Department of Agriculture on the framing of contracts for milk purchases.[21] In a celebrated early case (1924) McCarl ruled that a married woman employee of the government must appear on the payroll in her husband's name and could not enroll under her maiden surname. This must have been primarily a matter of his judgment as to social mores and common law since there was no federal law on the books forbidding the use of the maiden name. He wrote: "A wife might reside apart from her husband, but as long as she remains his lawful wife she has but one legal domicil and that is the domicil of her husband. So it is with the name. She may have an assumed name, but she has but one legal name." This ruling was later qualified in 1939 when the Comptroller General ruled that a married woman could use her maiden surname when she "continued its use after her marriage for practically all purposes, and the administrative office desires the continued use of her maiden name on the payrolls."[22] It was finally reversed during International Women's Year, 1975, in response to the growing recognition of women's rights and of a number of intervening court decisions. The Comptroller General then ruled "that a married woman has the right to be designated on agency payroll records by her maiden name if she desires to do so." In the same decision, he authorized the use of the prefix *Ms.* if the employee wished it.[23]

Audits and Settlements

Probably the best remembered feature of the first GAO was its receipt and review of the disbursing officers' accounts with their accompanying vouchers and supporting documents. This abundance of papers was shipped into GAO offices in Washington from all over the country and, indeed, from all over the world. Often carloads of these documents stood in the freight yards as backlogs, awaiting their turns for attention by the GAO clerks. Relatively few of them, usually 5 percent or less, consisted of unpaid vouchers to be preaudited prior to payment. The rest were the records of and documentation for transactions already completed by disbursing officers in the various agencies in Washington and in the field. They would each be checked for authority in appropriation and statute, for availability of funds in the warrants issued to individual disbursing officers, for accuracy and correctness in computation, for conformance with the GAO's prescribed procedures and forms, and for any other possible irregularity. The accounts and vouchers related to virtually all of the administrative activities of the executive agencies, other than corporations. Their variety was nearly limitless. In volume, the accounts of disbursing and other fiscal officers that were reviewed ran in the tens of thousands, and the vouchers numbered in the millions.

When the auditors could find no flaw in an account, they would clear, certify, and thus settle it. A payment of doubtful legality could be referred to the GAO counsel for advice or, if necessary, a new ruling. If they found any other irregularity, exception would be taken, and the matter would be referred back to the disbursing officer or agency for correction, explanation, or further documentation. Unless the response was satisfactory, there might be further correspondence, sometimes over several months and years. If the exception was still not resolved to the satisfaction of the GAO, the payment would be disallowed, and the agency officer responsible for the payment would be personally liable to reimburse the government, either from its recipient or, failing that, from the officer himself.

There is rather little documentation as to how much of the public money was actually saved through this slow and complex procedure, and the reports of the Comptroller General are not of much help. For the fiscal year 1934-1935, Mansfield reports that the GAO questioned less than $11 of each $1,000 disbursed and that of this all but one dollar had been cleared by 1937—about 1/10 of 1 percent.[24]

In retrospect, it is not difficult to ridicule the first GAO and its practices. A few old timers may recall its effort to disallow the purchase of a prize mule by the Tennessee Valley Authority (TVA) for its agricultural demonstration program because such an expenditure was not specifically authorized in the law. Some who remember the first GAO recall its memorandum to the Department of the Interior questioning how a bureau of that department would use a camera it had purchased. The response was a pencilled notation: "To take pictures, you damned fool." It was initialled by Harold L. Ickes.

But for a good many others, GAO audits were neither trivial nor amusing. Disbursing and certifying officers for governmental programs had to be concerned with how the GAO would interpret the statutory powers of their agencies. Purchasing officers were concerned with GAO interpretations of what they could purchase and of proper purchasing procedures. Administrators of emergency programs facing sudden and unexpected contingencies were compelled to anticipate possible challenges when they were not specifically covered in statutory law. Official travelers had to prove that they traveled by the cheapest route or justify in detail any departures therefrom on grounds of official business.[25] Arguments in defense of any deviations from legally prescribed rules had to be made in writing to clerks sitting at desks in Washington, almost none of whom had any experience in the operational or managerial aspects of government.

In sum, the settlements of accounts and the audits by the first GAO undoubtedly contributed to the strict enforcement of law and regulation. They prevented or at least discouraged minor transgressions of propriety. On the other hand, they undoubtedly added to the procedural requirements and delays. It is curious and perhaps symbolic that the individual sets of accounts and their supporting documents were customarily encased in packages bound, as in ancient British practice, in strips of red tape.

Prescription of Accounting Forms and Procedures

In the first year of the GAO, the Comptroller General set up a small investigations staff to make spot inspections of agencies and their bookkeeping systems and to develop standard systems and forms for agency accounting and financial reporting. Among its first jobs was the auditing of the Emergency Fleet Corporation; several years later it was involved in the audit of the TVA; later, according to the Comptroller General's annual reports, it conducted investigations of accounting practices in a number of agencies.

It is difficult today to assess the work of the GAO in this field because the documentation that exists is conflicting. Some reports suggest that the GAO was helpful in bringing some order and uniformity to a chaotic and primitive accounting situation; others that it lacked the technical expertise for the job, which it largely botched; still others, that it prescribed forms and procedures geared to reconciling agency systems with GAO accounts, which meant that they were of little use for purposes of agency management or to the Treasury Department or the Bureau of the Budget.

The GAO's first major attempt to standardize and modernize federal accounting practices was its issuance in 1926 of Circular 27, which provided a statement of procedures and a chart of accounts to be followed by all agencies. In 1943, Circular 27 was succeeded and somewhat revised by the Comptroller General's General Regulations 100, which at least technically remained in effect until it was officially killed in 1959. One writer describes Circular 27 as "important because it marked the development of a new concept for installation in one system of the cost (or accrual) basis of accounting alongside accounting for appropriation funds in Federal Government agencies."[26] The same author, however, reported that General Regulations 100—and presumably its predecessor, Circular 27—"were not generally accepted nor the prescribed system installed by many of the agencies."[27] Other writers are less generous about General Regulations 100, suggesting that the system it prescribed was impossibly complex, that it was virtually useless for managerial or control purposes, and that it was more an obstruction than an aid in the development of useful federal accounting systems.[28]

Studies of government accounting practices made after the era of the first GAO, such as those by the two Hoover Commissions and their task forces, indicate that federal accounting was still amateur, of little use to management, duplicative, unintegrated, and bogged down in excessive procedure and red tape. The forms and procedures prescribed by the GAO may have served the GAO's purposes. But there is little evidence that the GAO provided effective leadership in the reform and modernization of accounting for the government as a whole.

GAO Conflicts within the Government

The positions of auditors are not designed to foster friendship and popularity among those who are audited, even under the best circumstances. Auditing entails, among other things, finding fault with the work of others, and the more faults that can be identified the more defensible is the work of the auditors. There is thus a positive incentive to find fault. For those who are audited, the independent auditor is an inconvenience and a threat—a necessary one perhaps, but still one who should be treated at arm's length and with caution.

In the case of the GAO, this posture was exacerbated by the many other powers it possessed by law and upon which it built—powers that are not usually coupled with auditing. It could force the perpetrators of the faults it discovered to repay the costs of their mistakes or misdeeds, even when they were made in good faith. It could command the methods and forms whereby accounts were maintained and the procedures whereby they were submitted to it. It could interpret the meaning of the law and indeed make some "laws" of its own. Under the leadership of the first Comptroller General and for a good many years thereafter, it exercised these powers with unrelenting vigor. Further, most of its decisions were final and binding upon the agencies and their accountable officers. There was no effective appeal to an agency head or even to the President. And although the GAO was reputedly responsible to Congress, it seldom reported to it on questions of substance and rarely recommended legislation except that which would give it a new building or enlarge and tighten its own control. Of course, the agencies could, and not infrequently did, appeal to Congress for legislation to alleviate particularly onerous decisions or, in a few cases, to escape GAO jurisdiction entirely,[29] and for private bills to relieve officials charged with heavy disallowances. But such recourse was clearly inexpedient for thousands of the judgments that the GAO rendered every year. McCarl respected and obeyed legislation duly passed by Congress and signed by the President (though subject to his own interpretation), and he abided by decisions of the Supreme Court. But he regarded the decisions of lower courts, when they ran counter to his own determinations, as only advisory.[30]

Conflicts of the GAO with the spending and revenue-collecting agencies in the executive branch and with the regulatory commissions were endemic and sometimes bitter. As indicated earlier, the great majority of items to which the GAO initially took exception in its audit were subsequently resolved to the agencies' satisfaction. But those that were ultimately disallowed, together with the thousands of GAO rulings, provided ample grounds for dispute and grievance. The GAO complained repeatedly about the tardiness of the submittals of accounts by disbursing and accounting officers, and the agencies in turn complained about GAO backlogs and consequent delays, sometimes extending several years, in settling accounts.

The New Deal, with its many new programs and agencies and its vast increases in federal expenditures, added ideological fuel to the flames. McCarl bitterly opposed the unprecedented costs, their accompanying budget deficits, and the enormous borrowing. In 1936, a few months after his retirement and a few weeks before the presidential elections of that year, he wrote two blistering articles in the *Saturday Evening Post* that attacked the President and his brain trust for an alleged betrayal of the American people, and the Congress for going along with the President's program.[31] As Comptroller General he had been able to observe but not stem the tide toward what he felt would be the destruction of the treasury, the economy, and the republic.

The Attorney General

In addition to the endemic controversies between the GAO and the executive agencies in general, there were some of a more specific kind: those involving respectively the attorney general, the Treasury Department, and the government corporations. With regard to the first of these, Congress through its legislation had made controversy almost inevitable. In its original act establishing the office of attorney general, it included among his duties "to give his advice and opinion upon questions of law when required by the President of the United States, or when requested by the heads of any of the departments."[32] The degree to which such opinions were intended to be final and binding upon the executive departments remains to this day moot. But as a practical matter, the heads of departments and agencies (including the comptroller when he was in the Treasury Department) accepted most opinions of the attorney general as final, subject only to reversal in the courts.

On the other hand, the Dockery Act of 1894 authorized that, on the application of disbursing officers and the heads of executive departments, "the Comptroller of the Treasury shall render his decision upon any question involving a payment to be made by them or under them, which decision . . . shall govern the Auditor and the Comptroller of the Treasury in passing upon the account containing such disbursement."[33] This authority devolved upon the Comptroller General when the office was established in 1921. For many years, the attorney general minimized the possibility of disagreement by a self-imposed rule to decline to render opinions on accounts "unless a question is very important and affects large interests of government."[34] In one case involving the disallowance of a payment by the Comptroller General, the attorney general permitted the Comptroller General to file his own brief.[35] Further, the old comptroller of the Treasury regularly asked the departments to seek opinions of the attorney general on legal questions, which he normally respected. After 1921, however, the Comptroller General, having ceased this practice, rarely accepted the opinion of the attorney general: "Indeed, no case has been found where the opinion of the Attorney General has caused a change of decision once rendered by the Comptroller General."[36]

The first conflict after the 1921 act occurred in 1922 when the secretary of war contested a regulation of the Comptroller General requiring that transportation accounts be submitted directly to the GAO for certification and warrant for payment rather than to the departmental disbursing officers. The secretary appealed to the attorney general for an opinion, and the latter rendered it in his favor, denying the Comptroller General's power to require such a procedure. Some departments abided by the Comptroller General's ruling, some by the attorney general's, resulting in considerable confusion—a situation about which the Comptroller General complained with acerbity in his *Annual Report* of 1923.[37]

The first Comptroller General made it clear that he regarded the opinions of the attorney general, like the decisions of the lower courts, only advisory to him. He wrote, in a letter to President Harding in 1923:

> I am always pleased to consider most carefully the views of any interested branch of the Government in connection with any matter before me or in support of a proper request for reconsideration of action taken, but I may not accept the opinion of any official, inclusive of the Attorney General, as controlling of my duty under the law.[38]

In the subsequent years, under McCarl and his successors, most of the sources of dispute were resolved by accommodation on one side or the other or by the play of power. The GAO could disallow payments and could threaten to refuse requisitions for further funds to disobeying certifying officers. On the other hand, it could not bring legal action to enforce or defend its findings in court except through the Department of Justice (until very recently and then only when specifically authorized by statute). The agencies could take their chances on which side to take in case of dispute. Like so many other issues of law, to this day there has been no ultimate resolution.

The Treasury Department

In a quite different field, the laws placed the Comptroller General in potential opposition with the Treasury Department. The latter organization was required to submit to the President and Congress periodic reports on the expenditures and revenues of the government, based upon reports it received from the various spending and receiving departments. But the GAO built its own summary accounts of receipts and expenditures, based upon the reports it received (and settled) from accountable officers. Initially, the foundations of both were the same: appropriations and warrants. Beyond that, they were irreconcilable.

To our knowledge, the GAO under McCarl never undertook to report to Congress the overall condition of federal finances—revenues, expenditures, and debt. In 1938, it included in its annual report such information plus a detailed statement about the experience of every appropriation and item for every agency during the year, but this detailed information was subsequently omitted. During the early years, there was almost no professional competence in accounting within the GAO. As mentioned above, beginning in 1926, the GAO sought to develop and impose a generalized accounting system. But it was not synchronized with the needs of the Treasury Department or of the Bureau of the Budget. Accounting for the GAO was basically to assure compliance with the law; for the Treasury Department, it was to keep track of appropriations, expenditures, revenues, debt, and the financial condition of the government; for the Bureau of the Budget, it was to provide information for effective management and appropriations control. During the period of the first GAO, the triad did not meet.

Just before his retirement from office, Comptroller General McCarl provoked a specific controversy with the Treasury Department by issuing a regulation requiring a totally new and different code of symbol numbers for receipt and appropriation accounts.[39] They presumably would have replaced the numerical symbols previously prescribed by the Treasury Department to classify items for the purpose of its various tabulations and reports. The new code, which filled a 700-page document, was apparently developed without Treasury Department consultation, and that department vigorously protested the GAO's jurisdiction to superimpose a new system upon or in place of the one it had developed over many years. Some agencies complied with the GAO directive and had to use both codes at the same time; some refused to comply. The consequence was persistent confusion and duplication.

During the same period, a further controversy was precipitated after the Treasury Department set up special organizations in Washington and the field to preaudit and make financial reports on the enormous numbers of payments for emergency and work relief programs. This operation, which was established in response to an executive order[40] of the President, was according to most reports amazingly successful in the latter years of the New Deal in its rapid processing of accounts, its prompt summary reports to the President and Congress, and its correction of errors almost to zero, prior to the GAO audit of disbursements.[41] The Comptroller General disapproved the operation from the outset and its very success may have added to his opposition. Following a survey of the system in 1938, the Comptroller General recommended that it be abolished on the grounds that the Treasury Department's accounting for emergency payments duplicated the work of the agencies and of the GAO.[42] The week after the GAO conclusion had been sent to Congress, Secretary of the Treasury Morgenthau, in a letter to the chairman of the House Committee on Expenditures,[43] expressed his suspicion "that the General Accounting Office seeks to thwart attempts to provide adequate administrative accounting and to tear down accounting safeguards in the executive branch . . . in order that the General Accounting Office may have sufficient grounds for complaint to prove the value of its audits."[44] Despite GAO objections, the operation continued until the relief program itself was sharply curtailed and then abandoned with the onset of World War II.

These episodes reflected a growing disenchantment of a group of Treasury Department officials in the years before the war with federal financial and accounting systems in general and a feeling that the GAO was obstructing efforts to improve and reform them. The feeling, which was no doubt reciprocated in the GAO, became a significant motivating force toward the changes that followed the war.

The Government Corporations

Beginning in 1904 with the purchase of the Panama Railroad Company, the federal government utilized the device of government corporations, wholly or partly government owned, to carry on operations of an industrial or commercial nature. In most instances, they were operations conducted for a public purpose and supported in whole or in major part from revenues derived from the sale of their own goods or services. The corporate device was utilized extensively during World War I and again during the New Deal years. One of its major purposes was to free organizations of a commercial type from the controls and restraints customarily associated with the annual appropriations process. Among other things, most of the corporations were either specifically exempted or considered exempt from the audit and settlement controls of the financial officers—the comptroller and auditors of the Treasury Department and later the Comptroller General.

The case of one of the wartime corporations, the Emergency Fleet Corporation of the U.S. Shipping Board, however, became the source of repeated dispute on the question of centralized financial control. In an early ruling of August 1917, the comptroller of the treasury declared that Congress had intended to "relieve it of accounting for the use of public moneys as such moneys are usually accounted for."[45]

In 1918, Congress passed a law requiring a Treasury Department audit of the corporation; and later, in 1922, it directed the Comptroller General to continue the audit "in accordance with the usual methods of steamship or corporation auditing."[46] The Comptroller General thereafter audited the accounts of the corporation but usually (though not always) acknowledged that he lacked authority to prescribe the procedures or to enforce his exceptions. Nonetheless, he repeatedly made exceptions and sought further legislative authority.

The freedom of the Emergency Fleet Corporation was emphatically affirmed in a 1927 Supreme Court decision in which, following a brief summary of the development of government corporations, the Court held that the

> accounts of the Fleet Corporation, like those of each of the other corporations
> named, . . . have been audited, and the control over their financial transactions
> has been exercised, in accordance with commercial practice, by the board or
> the officer charged with responsibilities of administration. Indeed, an
> important if not the chief reason for employing these incorporated agencies
> was to enable them to employ commercial methods and to conduct their
> operations with a freedom supposed to be inconsistent with accountability to
> the Treasury under its established procedure of audit and control over the
> financial transactions of the United States.[47]

In his *Annual Report* for 1928, the Comptroller General urged Congress to
require that the accounts of the corporations be made through the GAO to
Congress.[48] He reiterated this recommendation in his *Annual Report* for 1932
after Congress had established the Reconstruction Finance Corporation
independent of GAO audit.[49]

In spite of this declared freedom, two of the most contentious and
prolonged conflicts of the first GAO concerned two government
corporations: the Emergency Fleet Corporation and the Tennessee Valley
Authority. In both cases, the GAO had been directed by Congress to audit,
but not to settle, the accounts of the corporations. In both cases the
Comptroller General endeavored, not without some success, to subject the
organizations to the same procedures and voucher review typically applied
to departmental agencies. At one point he forced the TVA to send all of its
vouchers to Washington for a GAO check on threat that he would refuse
requisitions for further appropriated funds. The fight between the GAO and
the TVA became a cause célèbre in the 1930s, to the advantage of neither.[50]
It led to an investigation into the TVA by a joint congressional committee in
1938 and 1939; this was followed by negotiations between the two agencies in
1939-1941 and an agreed settlement in 1941. The agreement was embodied
in an amendment to the TVA Act in that year. The protracted GAO-TVA
dispute and its ultimate settlement probably laid the groundwork for the
Government Corporation Control Act of 1945.

The Presidents and the GAO

The vast majority of the altercations and arguments between the GAO
and other federal agencies occurred well down the hierarchy of the executive
branch. It is unlikely that very many reached the heads of the agencies,
although some of these are the most conspicuously documented; only a
handful could have found their way to the oval office of the President. Most
of the Presidents' information about the GAO must have reached them
secondhand from agency chiefs, immediate advisers, and study groups. Yet,

in the two decades between the first consideration of the Budget and Accounting Act in 1920 to 1940, four out of the five Presidents had taken or proposed major action to modify the position or the title or the powers of the GAO. The only exception was President Coolidge.[51] Wilson, the first of the five Presidents, had vetoed the original bill on the grounds of the alleged unconstitutionality of its removal provisions (see chapter 2). Presidents Harding, Hoover, and Roosevelt each proposed basic changes in the GAO as parts of larger reorganization packages.

The Harding Recommendation of 1923

Early in the Harding administration, Congress established a Joint Committee on the Reorganization of Government Departments, chaired by Walter F. Brown, who had been designated by the President. That committee invited the President and his cabinet to submit recommendations for reorganization. These were submitted in the form of a summary and a chart but without explanatory discussion or argument on February 13, 1923.[52] Harding in his letter of transmittal noted that the changes "with few exceptions . . . have the sanction of the Cabinet." The Harding proposals must have been among the most sweeping and far reaching in American history.[53] Nothing whatever resulted from them at the time, but many years later, the majority of them were adopted.

With regard to the GAO, the recommendation was clear and abrupt: "The General Accounting Office, now an independent establishment, is transferred to the Treasury Department." Thus did the same President who, less than two years earlier, had signed the bill that removed GAO functions from the Treasury Department propose a complete reversal—at least on paper. Then, in the following sentence, the President recommended that the Bureau of the Budget be removed from the Treasury Department and made an independent agency.

In spite of Harding's assurance in his transmittal, it does not appear that the GAO recommendation had much "sanction of the Cabinet." In the hearings on the various proposals the following January 1924, only one cabinet member, Secretary of the Treasury Andrew W. Mellon, spoke on the subject, and he testified vigorously that the GAO should be independent and that the Bureau of the Budget should remain in the Treasury Department. His arguments were essentially similar to the earlier ones supporting the Budget and Accounting Act. No action was taken.

Hoover's Aborted Executive Orders of 1932

President Hoover had long been an enthusiastic supporter of reorganization as a major device to achieve efficiency and economy in government. He had collaborated with the Joint Committee on the Reorganization of Government Departments under Harding and Coolidge, and as Secretary of

Commerce had substantially reorganized that department. He firmly believed that effective reorganization should be at the initiative of the President. Near the depth of the depression, he was able to persuade Congress to pass the Economy Act of June 30, 1932,[54] which authorized the President to transfer or consolidate, but not abolish, agencies by executive order. Such orders would be effective after sixty days unless vetoed in whole or in part by a simple resolution of either house of the Congress. The device was the first peace-time authorization of presidential initiative subject to congressional veto and clearly the predecessor of later reorganization plan systems that have been periodically debated and repassed up to the present day. It was motivated and justified on the arguments that reorganizations would make possible reductions in governmental expenditures, which would balance the budget and thus end the depression. Such a hopeful scenario, widely espoused in 1932, would subsequently be questioned and then abandoned by liberals and even most conservatives.

On December 9, 1932, about a month after Roosevelt's electoral victory, Hoover submitted eleven reorganization orders to Congress. One of these would have transferred from the GAO to the Bureau of the Budget "those duties and functions which are administrative or executive in character, except those relating to the primary function of auditing the Government accounts."[55] More specifically, the GAO would have lost its power to prescribe and install accounting forms and systems and to superintend the administrative examination of accounts and claims in the various agencies. Although the language is not altogether clear, it appears from Hoover's message that he intended to reduce the GAO function essentially to the postaudit of transactions and accounts already made and settled. The underlying doctrine, which would be articulated more forcefully in later years, was that the keeping of accounts and the conduct of financial operations should be an exclusively administrative responsibility and therefore under the superintendence of the President's principal managerial arm, the Bureau of the Budget.

The proposal had little chance in the interregnum between Hoover and Roosevelt. In the December 1932 hearings of the House Committee on Expenditures in the Executive Departments, the administration's only spokesman, Col. J. Clawson Roop, director of the budget, gave testimony that was neither enthusiastic nor convincing either on the GAO or on the other reorganization orders.[56] He was unable to specify what savings would result. Near the close of his testimony, he was asked by the chairman, John J. Cochran (D., Mo.), whether he did "not think it would be advisable for the one who is going to be in control of the Government to make the recommendations rather than to take the views of the outgoing President?" He responded: "Personally, I think that would be wise."[57] No one else testified on the GAO proposal, and virtually all the witnesses were hostile to

Hoover's other recommendations. On January 19, 1933, the House voted down all of the President's executive orders on reorganization on a party-line vote without any discussion of their merits.

Roosevelt, the Brownlow Committee, and Reorganization, 1937-1939

After his inauguration in 1933, President Roosevelt took no action on the GAO issue until well after his reorganization powers under the Economy Act had expired in 1935. But during his second term, Roosevelt carried on the most vigorous and most carefully reasoned and articulated attack on the "first GAO" in its history. It grew out of the *Report of the President's Committee on Administrative Management,* better known for the committee's chairman as the Brownlow Report,[58] which in turn was formed to bring some order and rationale to the chaotic administrative situation in Washington growing out of the multitude of New Deal agencies and the difficulties of coordinating their operations. The report remains perhaps the nearest thing to a "classic" of American public administration. It was recently described by a distinguished scholar as "the first comprehensive reconsideration of the Presidency and the President's control of the executive branch since 1787, and . . . probably the most important constitutional document of our time."[59]

The Committee's first—and to some extent implicit—premise was a quite literal definition of the separation of powers, especially between the legislative and executive branches. The President is, among other things, the chief administrator since the Constitution requires that he "take care that the laws be faithfully executed." He must have the powers, the resources, and the organization at his command to fulfill that responsibility. Congress is the lawmaker and it is the body to which the executive is fully accountable. Among the instruments for assuring accountability are hearings and investigations and, particularly in the fiscal realm, an independent audit. But in order that the executive may be held accountable for administration, Congress should refrain from specifying "in great detail minute requirements for the organization and operation of the administrative machinery"; once it has made an appropriation, "the responsibility for the administration of the expenditures under that appropriation is and should be solely upon the Executive."[60]

Consonant with this general philosophy, the committee made a frontal attack on many of the powers of the GAO and on the way in which they were being carried out. Affirming the position of President Hoover five years earlier, it argued that the setting up and keeping of accounts and the current control of expenditures were executive functions, indispensable to effective management. It declared that the GAO, as an independent office, should be divested of its powers to prescribe and superintend accounting forms and systems in the departments, to determine the uses of appropriations, to settle accounts and claims, to issue rulings applicable to future financial decisions, to render advance decisions, and to preaudit projected expenditures. It felt that the mixture of such activities with the independent audit function not only deprived the executive of essential tools of management but also deprived Congress of a truly independent audit since the GAO was in the position of auditing its own prior decisions. The report defined an "audit" strictly as a "postaudit":

> an examination and verification of the accounts after transactions are completed in order to discover and report to the legislative body any unauthorized, illegal, or irregular expenditures, any financial practices that are unsound, and whether the administration has faithfully discharged its responsibility.[61]

The specific recommendations of the committee were simple but emphatic:

- the powers to prescribe and supervise accounting forms and systems in the agencies should be transferred to the secretary of the treasury;
- the powers of settling and adjusting accounts and claims should be transferred to the Treasury Department;
- any dispute between the secretary of the treasury and another agency with regard to the settlement of public accounts could be referred to the attorney general by either party, and his opinion on the question of jurisdiction (but not on the merits of the case) should be final;
- the Comptroller General and Assistant Comptroller General should be renamed Auditor General and Assistant Auditor General, respectively, and the General Accounting Office should be called the General Auditing Office;
- the auditing work should be decentralized to the field and should proceed "independent of, but practically simultaneous with, disbursement,"[62] and exceptions should be promptly reported to the Treasury;
- in the event of failure of the Treasury and GAO to agree on any exception, the Auditor General should report such exception to the Congress through such committees as the Congress may designate.

On January 12, 1937, President Roosevelt transmitted the Brownlow Report to Congress with vigorous endorsement of its major proposals, including those affecting the GAO. But the proposals were then to travel a rocky road. At about the same time that the Brownlow Committee was established, the Senate created a select committee under the chairmanship of Senator Harry F. Byrd of Virginia to study and make recommendations on overlapping and extravagance in the executive branch. Byrd engaged the Brookings Institution to conduct its survey. Although there was some effort at the outset to coordinate the work of the two groups (Brownlow and Brookings), they soon went their own ways, and many of their conclusions and recommendations opposed each other. Probably their differences stemmed from disagreement on the central premise, the locus of administrative powers. As noted above, the Brownlow group held that they resided solely in the executive; Brookings stressed that the agencies were also, if not primarily, responsible to Congress, which set them up and provided their duties and their financial sustenance. Fiscal management was the central focus of disagreement. Brookings expectably came out at the opposite pole from the Brownlow Committee: the GAO should retain its existing powers and in fact should be further strengthened by adding some of those powers that had been repeatedly urged by McCarl. Despite his experience as a strong, management-oriented governor of Virginia, Byrd endorsed the Brookings position and opposed the President fundamentally on the grounds that his recommendations were not aimed at achieving economy in government but, on the contrary, would facilitate greater spending.

There was thus in Congress a substantial opposition to the Brownlow proposals, backed by a research study of a distinguished, private, nonpartisan group. Different bills incorporating modified versions of the President's reorganization plans were introduced in the two houses in both 1937 and 1938. With respect to financial administration, they were some distance apart on the mechanics but agreed on the central principle of executive control of expenditures and legislative postaudit. But though some of the bills passed one or the other house, no bill was passed. The efforts were frustrated, it is probable, partly by the fact that the bills stepped on the jurisdictional toes of so many different committees in Congress and partly because they became linked with Roosevelt's unpopular proposal to "pack" the Supreme Court, which he issued in the spring of 1937. Both the Court and the reorganization bills were branded as "dictatorship" legislation.

On April 3, 1939, following extensive congressional debate and much compromise, the President signed a rather limited and temporary Reorganization Act, the major feature of which was to permit the President to initiate reorganization plans that would become effective in sixty days unless vetoed by concurrent resolution of both houses.[63] Under the legislation, some of Roosevelt's other reorganization objectives would be achieved in subsequent months and before the act expired in two years. But the bill included a number of limitations, and it specifically excluded any reorganization plans for a number of "sensitive" agencies. Among those excluded was the GAO.[64]

It is significant that the author of the bill and one of the two who introduced it in the House was Representative Lindsay C. Warren, who would the following year become the third Comptroller General of the United States. He was an influential party to the compromises that made passage possible, including the exemption of GAO. In the ensuing emergency period of preparing for and then fighting World War II, the GAO was spared further threat of presidential aggression for almost a full decade.

Interregnum and World War II

McCarl's term as Comptroller General expired on June 30, 1936, and under the law he was not eligible for reappointment even had President Roosevelt desired it, which seems at least doubtful. Roosevelt offered the post to congressional leader Lindsay C. Warren (D., N.C.), but he turned it down, and the job devolved upon Assistant Comptroller General Richard N. Elliott, in an acting capacity.[65] Elliott, who had succeeded Lurtin Ginn in 1931 upon the latter's retirement,[66] had served seven terms as a Republican congressman from Indiana before being appointed by President Hoover. His tenure of nearly three years as Acting Comptroller General—serving a dominantly Democratic Congress, with a President actively seeking to reorganize most of his powers away, and attended by recurrent struggles with administrative agencies like the Treasury Department and the TVA— must have been a difficult one. He determined not to further rock a boat that was already in turbulent waters:

> I have conceived it a duty as Acting Comptroller General . . . to carry on the business of the office without drastic changes in the procedures that have prevailed for the past fifteen years, unless facts should make it necessary, so as not to in any way affect the freedom of action—either in matters of organization or of procedure—of a Comptroller General when appointed.[67]

The posture and the activities of the GAO in fact changed in only one noteworthy way: the form and substance of the annual report of 1938. Elliott's report was four times longer than McCarl's average report, more informative, and more detailed. But most of the increase in length was "a presentation of financial statements for all agencies of the government"[68] plus an overall calculation of expenditures, revenues, and deficit to the last penny.

The appointment of Fred H. Brown to succeed McCarl-Elliott as Comptroller General may have been part of an agreement between Congress (led in this regard by Lindsay Warren) and the President about the Reorganization Act of 1939. After the President yielded to the demand that the GAO be exempted from presidential reorganization authority, the bill passed Congress on March 30. On the same day, the Senate received

Roosevelt's nomination of Brown. On April 3, the President signed the bill into law, and on the same day, the Senate confirmed Brown. The first Democratic senator from New Hampshire in many decades, Brown had been defeated for reelection in 1938. A lawyer and one-time professional baseball player with the Boston Braves, Brown was a popular figure in the Senate as well as in his home state.

Brown had little experience for the job of Comptroller General and too little opportunity to gain it. On June 19, 1940, he resigned after fourteen months because of ill health. In his annual report for 1939, he mentioned his efforts to continue the "good work" of his predecessors. He did, however, return the report to its customary length, including the usual legislative recommendations for a GAO central building and expanded claims authority.

The Appointment of Comptroller General Lindsay Warren[69]

After Brown's departure, Elliott again acted as Comptroller General, but this time for only a few months. On his third try, Roosevelt induced Lindsay Warren to accept the post, but on Warren's one condition: that the President would not again interfere with the organization or mission of the GAO.[70] Roosevelt sent the nomination to the Senate on August 1, 1940, and on the same day that body unanimously confirmed him.[71] Warren resigned from the House on October 31, 1940, and became the third Comptroller General the following day. Three years later, Elliott reached the mandatory retirement age of seventy and Roosevelt replaced him as Assistant Comptroller General with Frank L. Yates, a career employee and attorney who had served in a variety of legal and special capacities with the Treasury comptroller and the GAO since 1919. Thus, after ten years in office and three successful presidential elections, Roosevelt finally had nominated the two top officials of the GAO.

Lindsay Carter Warren was a congressman's congressman. A native of Washington, North Carolina, he had graduated and then obtained a law degree at the University of North Carolina, begun his practice of law in 1912, became active in county and state Democratic politics, and then had been elected to Congress in 1924. He had served sixteen years without opposition as representative from North Carolina's First District. His interests and experiences in the House had been numerous and varied. He had served on or chaired a variety of committees, including the Select Committee on Government Organizations and the Committee on Expenditures in the Executive Branch. Highly reputed and well liked by his fellows, he had been twice elected speaker pro tem and chosen majority leader—a post that he filled for just two weeks before resigning to become Comptroller General. The respect and friendship for him of both representatives and senators, Democratic and Republican, persisted throughout his tenure as Comptroller General. They would serve the GAO well.

Warren reciprocated the feeling. He brought to his new post an unwavering loyalty to Congress and a fervent conviction that the GAO was and should be a servant of Congress, completely independent of the executive branch. In his reports and testimony through the years, he repeatedly referred to his organization as a congressional agency. He was proud that the number of GAO reports to Congress multiplied several times during his tenure, that it responded more quickly to more congressional inquiries, and that it loaned or detailed more of its personnel to congressional committees.

But Warren's continuing allegiance to Congress did not preclude a sympathetic understanding of the executive branch and a willingness to cooperate with it on problems of mutual concern. One such problem that faced him immediately upon his assumption of office was the impasse between the GAO and the TVA, mentioned in an earlier section. He led the GAO in its conduct of negotiations with the TVA, which resulted in a settlement and legislation in 1941 to which both sides agreed. The principal representative of the TVA in those discussions was Eric L. Kohler, then comptroller of the TVA, and it is worth mentioning that Kohler later became an ardent supporter of the GAO in its efforts to improve accounting and auditing in the government as a whole. A somewhat comparable problem was simmering at the time between the GAO and another corporation, the Commodity Credit Corporation (CCC) of the Department of Agriculture. Warren and the secretary of agriculture set up a joint committee that agreed on a solution involving a commercial type audit of the corporation's capital transactions, which was subsequently legislated.[72] These settlements, reached cooperatively, of the twenty-year-old issue of the GAO's audit of corporations led to extended studies and negotiations during the war involving a congressional committee, the GAO, the Budget Bureau and the Treasury Department; and they finally led to general legislation in 1945 (see chapter 4).

There were further early evidences of a more collaborative spirit toward the executive branch. One was the increasing number of reports sent by the GAO to the President and the Bureau of the Budget. Another was the provision of experienced GAO staff to help

> in the instruction of training classes of new personnel of the departments and establishments in order that they might become quickly qualified for procurement and administrative accounting work in the field. Representatives of the General Accounting Office have also cooperated by reviewing and aiding in the preparation of departmental instructions and regulations dealing with accounting and audit requirements.[73]

The War Years

However, even had Warren and the GAO staff been ready for it, there was too little time between his appointment and the onset of all-out war for fundamental changes in the orientation and the functions of the GAO. While it is true, as Warren wrote in his *Annual Report* for 1942,[74] that the war "affected directly or indirectly practically every branch of the work performed by the General Accounting Office," the main changes resulted from the tremendous workload increases in the traditional activities of voucher checking, settlement of accounts, claims, records, and the on-site auditing of war contracts. The size of the staff more than tripled during the war, reaching a peak of 14,904 in April 1946. Like other civilian agencies at that time, the GAO lost to military service many of its most skilled supervisors and technicians, and the quality standards for new recruits went down. Despite its greatly augmented staff, 35 million vouchers remained unaudited at the end of 1945.[75]

The mushrooming workload, coupled with the congestion in Washington and the demand for speed, particularly in military and war contract work, virtually forced a wholesale departure from McCarl's long-established practice of concentrating all activities in Washington. In 1942, the entire postal accounting and auditing operation was moved to Asheville, North Carolina, where Warren had once gone to school. In the same year, a war contract audit organization was set up to provide site audits at the plants of war contractors to provide prompt resolution of questionable payments on cost-plus-a-fixed-fee contracts.[76] For this purpose, the country was divided into five (later six) zones with audit locations established in about thirty different cities; at one time during the war, there were 276 audit locations at contractors' plants throughout the country. These were later to form the nucleus of a field audit section. In 1944, the GAO established four army audit branches and one navy audit branch in five major cities across the country. They were designed to provide a prompt auditing of expenditures made by military disbursing offices. However, no overseas offices were established, as had been the case during World War I.

By the end of World War II, the activities of the GAO, though still centered in Washington, were widely distributed across the country. However, aside from the auditing of the books of war contractors, its responsibilities and modus operandi remained substantially unchanged. Except for the legal work, GAO operations remained about as unprofessional as they had been in 1921. This lack of professionalism had not gone unnoticed among the CPAs in the private sector. As early as 1937, the American Institute of Certified Public Accountants had formed a committee on government accounting. That committee's first efforts were directed to municipal accounting, but it soon became interested in the problems of federal accounting. Its overtures to the GAO were rebuffed. Just before American entry in World War II, the committee reported:

Several efforts have been made to contact the newly appointed Comptroller General, Honorable Lindsay C. Warren, who took office on November 1, 1940, for the purpose of securing his interest in recommendations of the committee affecting his office. Unfortunately no success has attended these efforts. Contacts with some of the members of his staff have not produced any evident effect and have indicated a considerable lack of understanding of the principles which the committee has endeavored to emphasize, and of proper methods of auditing and of financial reporting.[77]

But the committee sought to widen interest in the modernization of federal accounting, and in late 1943—the middle of the war—it convened a two-day conference on that subject in which the GAO, the Bureau of the Budget, and the Treasury Department cooperated and participated. The proceedings of the conference were published and widely distributed; they were highly critical of the GAO, and very possibly they lit the fuse for the explosive changes that were to begin at the end of the war. One writer summarized the discussions at the conference in the following terms:

Following the formal papers there was extended general discussion, in which the General Accounting Office representatives found themselves frequently on the defensive. Objections were voiced to the GAO's legalistic pre-audit procedure, involving the shipping of vouchers and supporting documents to Washington, and the open-ended liabilities imposed on certifying and disbursing officers until payments had been approved; to the general absence of accrual accounting; to the lack of financial audits, of the kind common in industry, even of business-type operations of the government; to the absence of coordination and consistency in the requirements of the General Accounting Office, the Treasury Department and the Bureau of the Budget; and to the fact that the GAO made administrative determinations and then audited payments which it had already determined could properly be made.[78]

The Nature and Impact of the First GAO

The development of the GAO in its formative years was in many ways consistent with the mores of the times. The reform or improvement of government was very nearly synonomous with more effective control to assure that what was done was in exact accordance with the intent of the legislature. This meant detailed laws and items in appropriation bills and checking every financial transaction to the last penny and to the last letter of the law. It meant too that like situations and questions be handled in similar ways wherever they might arise; and this required a single central authority to interpret the laws and prescribe the rules; that is, standardization and centralization. The emphasis upon control was not confined to the GAO and its various activities. It applied equally to the budget process itself as it was conducted until the 1930s and to the development of personnel administration during the same period under the Civil Service Commission. The concept that budgeting, accounting, and personnel were tools of management and should be integrated with it was not widely accepted until the Brownlow Committee report was issued. The Budget Bureau moved toward the management orientation beginning in the late 1930s, but the commission and the GAO successfully resisted any such transformation until the close of World War II.

The posture of the GAO in the totality of government was also shaped by a very rigorous interpretation of the separation of powers between executive and Congress. Leaders of the GAO, with the support of many in Congress, insisted upon a strict separation of the former from the administrative departments and officials. Relationships between the two sides were characterized for most of the period by distance, formality, and mutual suspicion, a condition not likely to encourage collaborative efforts to improve federal financial management.

Critics of the GAO, like Presidents Hoover and Roosevelt, and the Brownlow Committee, grounded their arguments too on a strict separation of powers. They were convinced that many of the powers vested in the Comptroller General by the 1921 act were executive in nature and that his activities therefore constituted an infringement on the executive branch. The merits of this argument will be discussed later in this book. Suffice it here to observe that the heat of the debate, particularly in the late 1930s, inhibited any search for informal accommodations and cooperation.

First among the objectives of the GAO's work was to assure compliance with the letter of the law, conformance with form and procedure, accuracy of computation, and honesty. Economy and efficiency had been the watchwords of the movement that gave birth to the organization, and they were repeatedly invoked over the years by the Comptrollers General and their supporters in Congress. But "legality" is not necessarily synonomous with "wisdom" or "efficiency," and as most students of organization know, they are often not even compatible. In his annual reports, the Comptroller General customarily totaled up the savings resulting from GAO operations during the year and showed by how much they exceeded the costs of the organization itself. Some critics charged that the savings were padded by including receipts that would have been collected anyway and that the extra costs in agency bookkeeping, reporting, correspondence, and time far exceeded the savings. But the argument is a sterile one. No one will ever know how much these latter costs were nor, on the other hand, what preventive savings the GAO occasioned by its very existence and the knowledge that financial transactions would be checked. But with the main point most would now agree: the GAO's main focus was on legal compliance, not on the economy, efficiency, or effectiveness of governmental operations.

Finally, the stance of the GAO—like that of other auditing and investigative organizations—tilted heavily to the negative. Its search was for mistakes, misinterpretations, and misdeeds. Its own role in the governmental system was such that its reputation and esteem in Congress and in public, and very possibly its survival, depended on finding things wrong in the executive branch. Its basic output was criticism, sometimes anointed with ill-concealed acrimony. Even when delivering an affirmative answer to a question, its response was commonly phrased in a double negative: "This office is not required to object."[79]

Notes

1. Fred H. Brown served only fourteen months (April 1939–June 1940) before resigning because of illness.

2. Budget and Accounting Act, 42 Stat. 18 (1921), sec. 301.

3. In 1924 and again in 1929, the Comptroller General protested cuts in his budget by the President and the Bureau of the Budget, respectively. In both cases, his protest was unavailing.

4. By Harvey Mansfield, *The Comptroller General: A Study in the Law and Practice of Financial Administration* (New Haven, Conn.: Yale University Press, 1939), p. 71.

5. Herbert Corey, "A Conscience in Black," *Collier's*, November 29, 1924, p. 26. In the same article, Corey assured his readers that: "He saves millions of the taxpayers' money. . . . In consequence he is hated. Mandarins jump in the air and snap at their peacock feathers when they speak of him. He compels them—think of the odious insolence of this—to obey the law."

6. Ginn had been for many years employed in one of the auditing offices of the Treasury Department. He was appointed assistant comptroller of the treasury in 1917 and until the end of World War I supervised treasury auditing operations in Europe, which were terminated at about that time.

7. Most of the statistics and other factual data here and in succeeding paragraphs are drawn from Mansfield, *The Comptroller General*, chapter 6.

8. According to Mansfield, a new postmaster general wanted to remove the postal comptroller, whom he had inherited but was unable to dismiss outright since he had had long governmental service and was not a patronage appointee. So he negotiated with McCarl an arrangement whereby the GAO took over the bulk of the job, and the postal comptroller resigned. Mansfield, *The Comptroller General*, p. 173.

9. Ibid., p. 157 ff.

10. Douglas McGregor, *The Human Side of Enterprise* (New York: McGraw Hill, 1960).

11. This somewhat romanticized description of an operation that in most respects hardly seems romantic is quoted from May H. Wilbur, *General Accounting Office: A History* (1943) (processed), p. 43.

12. Its designer was General Montgomery C. Meigs of the Corps of Engineers.

13. In the *Annual Report of the General Accounting Office,* 1924, pp. 6-7, he wrote: "If it is the purpose and intention of the Congress that the certifying and warranting of public money should be perfunctory so far as the General Accounting Office is concerned and its duties in that respect are merely ministerial, then the accounting officers are performing useless work and should be relieved therefrom. Until it is otherwise directed by the Congress I shall feel it my duty to continue to construe such action as being performed pursuant to a useful purpose and will continue to construe that purpose to be that the approval of such matters . . . is intended as a check upon the advance and payment of public moneys and to supervise the correct application thereof."

14. A voucher is a document that describes an expense chargeable to the government and that, when properly certified by an authorized officer, is authority for payment.

15. *Annual Report,* 1923, pp. 4-5.

16. Op. Att'y Gen. 383 (1929).

17. 16 Comp. Gen. 423, January 13, 1910.

18. 34 Comp. Gen. 631, 1955.

19. P.L. 85-507, July 7, 1958.

20. These cases are synthesized from John McDiarmid, *Government Corporations and Federal Funds* (1938), pp. 2-13.

21. The cases referred to above are drawn from Mansfield, *The Comptroller General,* pp. 185-86.

22. 19 Comp. Gen. 203, August 15, 1975.

23. 55 Comp. Gen. 177, August 28, 1975.

24. Mansfield, *The Comptroller General,* p. 183.

25. For an illustration of the auditing of travel vouchers, see the case on travel vouchers in Erasmus H. Kloman, ed., *Cases in Accountability: The Work of the GAO* (Boulder, Colo.: Westview Press, 1979).

26. H. W. Bordner, "Impact of General Regulations 100 on Accounting in the Federal Government," *The Federal Accountant* (June 1962):64.

27. Ibid., p. 63.

28. Particularly Walter F. Frese, "Early History of the Joint Financial Management Program," unpublished recollections, 1974-1976.

29. Among the executive branch transactions exempted from GAO review by law or appropriation act during the 1920s and 1930s were internal revenue assessments; veterans' adjusted compensation claims; commodity benefit and conservation payments (Agriculture Department); expenditures

of the Federal Reserve System; and expenditures by the President for the executive offices. Other transactions previously exempted included those of most of the government corporations; the State Department secret fund; and Naval intelligence.

30. In the *Annual Report*, 1926, pp. 25-26, McCarl wrote: "While this office promptly examines and carefully considers the decisions of the lower courts as rendered in so far as they bear upon its problems, and applies them for accounting purposes to the extent it consistently can with its knowledge of their effect from the standpoint of Government accounting, thereby, lessening in so far as it may any variance of its decisions with those of the lower courts, if after such careful consideration of all phases involved it still concludes its position to have been correct it must in the interest of the United States adhere thereto, notwithstanding a divergence of views, pending the rendition by the Supreme Court of the United States of a decision upon the point or points involved, or an expression by the Congress through legislation."

31. The articles, both entitled "Government-Run-Everything," appeared in the *Post* issues of October 3, 1936 (pp. 8, 9, 52) and October 17, 1936 (pp. 8, 9, 70-74).

32. 1 Stat. 20, Sec. 35 (1789).

33. 28 Stat. L 207, Sec. 8 (1894).

34. Albert Langeluttig, *The Department of Justice of the United States* (Baltimore: Johns Hopkins Press, 1927), p. 159.

35. Miguel v. McCarl, 291 U.S. 442 (1934).

36. Langeluttig, *The Department of Justice*, p. 161.

37. Page 5.

38. Quoted in Langeluttig, *Department of Justice*, p. 170.

39. GAO Gen. Reg. no. 84, June 15, 1936.

40. Executive Order no. 7034, May 6, 1935.

41. It was reported that GAO suspensions of payments preaudited through this procedure amounted to less than one quarter of 1 percent of total disbursements. See Mansfield, *The Comptroller General*, p. 221.

42. Letter of the Comptroller General to the House Speaker, May 18, 1938, transmitting a "Report on Survey of the Central Treasury Accounts Office of the Office of Commissioner of Accounts and Deposits, Treasury Department."

43. May 20, 1938.

44. Quoted in Mansfield, *The Comptroller General*, p. 222.

45. 24 Comp. Gen. 118, August 16, 1917.

46. 42 Stat. 444, March 20, 1922.

47. United States ex rel., Skinner and Eddy Corporation v. McCarl, Comptroller General, October 10, 1927. The Court's decision was rendered by Justice Brandeis. The quotation is from pp. 7 and 8.

48. Pages 11-12.

49. Pages 13-18.

50. It has been thoroughly documented elsewhere. See particularly: Richard E. Brown, *The GAO: Untapped Source of Congressional Power* (Knoxville: University of Tennessee Press, 1970); Harvey C. Mansfield, *The Comptroller General*, chapter 9; and Herman C. Pritchett, *The Tennessee Valley Authority: A Study in Public Administration* (Chapel Hill: University of North Carolina Press, 1943).

51. In his annual message of December 8, 1925, "Silent Cal" Coolidge vigorously supported the GAO: "The purpose of maintaining . . . the Comptroller General is to secure economy and efficiency in government expenditure. No better method has been devised for the accomplishment of that end. These offices can not be administered in all the various details without making some errors both of fact and of judgment. But the important consideration remains that these are the instrumentalities of the Congress and that no other plan has ever been adopted which was so successful in promoting economy and efficiency. The Congress has absolute authority over the appropriations and is free to exercise its judgment, as the evidence may warrant, in increasing or decreasing budget recommendations. But it ought to resist every effort to weaken or break down this most beneficial system of supervising appropriations and expenditures. Without it all the claim of economy would be a mere pretense."

52. U.S. Congress, Senate, S. Doc. no. 302, 67th Congress, 4th Sess.

53. *Reorganization of the Executive Departments* (Washington, D.C.: U.S. Government Printing Office, 1923). Among many other things, they would have merged the War and Navy Departments into a Department of National Defense; transferred all nonmilitary functions of the army and navy to other departments; eliminated all nonfiscal functions from the Treasury; and established a new Department of Education and Welfare (which would also have included the Public Health Service).

54. 47 Stat. 413-415.

55. *Message of the President of the United States*, December 9, 1932, 72nd Cong., 2nd Sess. (Washington, D.C.: U.S. Government Printing Office, 1932).

56. *Hearings on President's Message on Consolidation of Government Agencies* (U.S. Government Printing Office, 1932).

57. Ibid., p. 25.

58. *Report of the President's Committee on Administrative Management* (Washington, D.C.: U.S. Government Printing Office, 1937). The committee consisted of Louis Brownlow, longtime political journalist, administrator of a variety of governmental institutions, adviser to Presidents, and "dean" of the public administration fraternity; Charles E. Merriam, chairman of Political Science at the University of Chicago,

Chicago councilman, national planner; and Luther Gulick, director of the Institute of Public Administration. The committee engaged a staff of twenty-six, mostly academics in political science.

59. Rowland Egger, "The Period of Crisis: 1933 to 1945," in Frederick C. Mosher, ed., *American Public Administration: Past, Present, Future* (Tuscaloosa: University of Alabama Press, 1975), p. 71.

60. *Report of the President's Committee,* pp. 49-50.

61. Ibid., p. 21.

62. Ibid., p. 25.

63. 53 Stat. 36 (1939).

64. The GAO was similarly exempted from presidential reorganization authority in the First War Powers Act of 1941 (Public Law 354, December 18, 1941) and every subsequent reorganization act, including that of 1977.

65. Warren is reported to have been offered, and to have declined, the appointment in both 1936 and 1938 before accepting Roosevelt's offer in 1940. Frank H. Weitzel, "Lindsay Carter Warren: Comptroller General of the United States, 1940-1954," *The GAO Review* (spring 1977), pp. 1-30. We have found no reference to any other offer of the job by Roosevelt before 1939.

66. At the statutory retirement age of seventy.

67. *Annual Report* of the Acting Comptroller General of the United States for the fiscal year 1937, p. iii.

68. *Annual Report,* 1938, p. ii.

69. Some of the material about Warren and about the war years is drawn from the more complete article by Frank H. Weitzel, previously cited.

70. Alfred Steinberg, "Single-Minded Skinflint," *Tax Outlook* (May 1952), pp. 12-16.

71. By another coincidence of dates, Roosevelt also nominated the former Comptroller General, Fred H. Brown, then apparently recovered, to the U.S. Tariff Commission on August 1, 1940, and he was likewise confirmed on the same day. But he served on that commission less than a year before again retiring because of illness.

72. P.L. 240, February 28, 1944.

73. *Annual Report,* 1941, pp. 89-90.

74. Page 103.

75. *Annual Report,* 1945, p. 54.

76. The War Contract Project Audit Section was established by GAO Order no. 29 on August 18, 1942. Such contracts were reinitiated for war purposes by Public Law 703, July 12, 1940.

77. John L. Carey, *The Rise of the Accounting Profession* (American Institute of Certified Public Accountants), p. 419.

78. Ibid., p. 421.

79. Quoted in Mansfield, *The Comptroller General,* p. 185.

4

THE SECOND GAO:
NEW DIRECTIONS, 1945-1954

The hole and the patch should be commensurate.
    —Thomas Jefferson, in a letter to James Madison, 1787

It is an axiom of statesmanship . . . that great changes can best be brought about under old forms.
    —Henry George, *Progress and Poverty,* 1879

The beginning of the transformation of the General Accounting Office coincided approximately with the conclusion of World War II. There were corrective and creative impulses behind the transformation, which will be discussed below. But one element, which was basically negative, was an imperative. The war and the emerging postwar responsibilities of government made it clear that no single office in Washington could provide an effective control over every expenditure and receipt or check every financial transaction. The McCarl system was doomed simply by scale—if by nothing else. In 1947, for example, the GAO:

- Maintained 100,000 appropriation and limitation accounts, 44,000 personal accounts with accountable officers, and about 270,000 other accounts;
- Countersigned 60,000 Treasury Department warrants and approved 14,000 requisitions for disbursing funds;
- Audited 93,000 accountable officers' accounts (containing 35 million vouchers), 5 million transportation vouchers, 1.5 million contracts, 260 million postal money orders, 57 million postal notes, and 26 million postal certificates;
- Settled 108,000 accountable officers' accounts, 354,000 postmasters' accounts, and 773,000 claims;
- Reconciled 490 million checks;
- Issued 1,300 reports on inspections, surveys, and special investigations, made 6,200 replies to miscellaneous inquiries from members of Congress, issued 400 reports to the President, Congress and to the Bureau of the Budget, and issued 7,400 decisions of the Comptroller General and 2,200 reports to the attorney general.[1]

There were more positive elements in the remarkable turnabout of the GAO, which occurred mainly in the years of 1945-1954. These stemmed principally from two thrusts, one concerning the audit of government corporations, the other growing from efforts, in cooperation with other agencies, to improve federal accounting systems. Both had origins prior to World War II, and they were to a considerable extent supportive of one another. Both benefited by the findings and recommendations of the first Hoover Commission in 1949. They tended to converge in 1950 and the years immediately preceding and following it and were expressed in new legislation, new practices, reorganization, and basic changes in staffing.

The GAO: "A Part of the Legislative Branch"

Precedent and probably essential to the transformation of the GAO were the good will and the support of a majority of Congress. These were abundantly assured in 1945 and 1946, first, by its legislation concerning government corporations in 1945; second, by the Reorganization Act of 1945; and, third, by the Legislative Reorganization Act of 1946.

The most explicit legislative recognition of the tie between Congress and the GAO came in the latter part of 1945 in connection with President Truman's proposal to revive for twenty-seven months the reorganization authority that had originally been voted in 1939 but had expired. Warren, testifying in behalf of the exemption of GAO from presidential reorganization authority, stated:

> During most of my public life, . . . I have been a member of the Legislative Branch. Even now, although heading a great agency, it is an agency of the Congress, and I am an agent of the Congress.[2]

Later, by way of reemphasis, he argued that the GAO "is exempted by the terms of the pending bill not because it is sacrosanct or any more angelic than the rest, but in recognition that it is the creation and agent of Congress."[3]

Congress agreed. Members of both Houses were effusive in their plaudits for the Comptroller General and the work of the GAO. Indeed, some of the minority party would have extended its powers. For example, Senator Chapman Revercomb (R., W. Va.) suggested that the GAO, being "in right close contact" with the agencies, "ought to be the one to propose reorganization plans to the Congress";[4] and Senator Homer Ferguson (R., Mich.) regretted that the GAO was able to report upon, but unable to act upon, extravagances in the government (as opposed simply to the illegality of payments).[5] In the Reorganization Act of 1945, enacted on December 20, 1945, Congress not only exempted the Comptroller General and the GAO from presidential reorganization authority but also described them as "a part of the legislative branch of the government."⁶ This was the strongest, most affirmative statutory statement of the relationship between the GAO and Congress to that date—or to the date of this writing.

During 1945 and 1946, a Joint Committee on Legislative Reorganization made a thorough investigation of congressional structure and procedures and reported out a bill, which after a number of amendments became the Legislative Reorganization Act of 1946.⁷ The GAO was not a major focus of the act, though Warren was called upon to testify and there was discussion of the value and usefulness of the GAO to Congress. The act provided that the House and Senate Committees on Expenditures in the Executive Departments (both later changed to Committees on Government Operations) "shall have the duty of . . . receiving and examining reports of the Comptroller General of the United States." A later section (206) directed the Comptroller General

> to make an expenditure analysis of each agency in the executive branch of the Government (including Government corporations), which, in the opinion of the Comptroller General, will enable Congress to determine whether public funds have been economically and efficiently administered and expended.

He was further directed to submit reports on such analyses to the appropriations, expenditures, and appropriate legislative committees of both houses. The GAO neither advocated nor opposed the provision, which was to become a source of some embarrassment to it a decade later (see chapter 5). But its passage constituted a congressional vote of confidence in the GAO as well as a directive to extend its activities beyond questions of legality to the more general area of efficient management.

Commercial Auditing of Government Corporations

The initial impetus for modernizing GAO audit practices came in by a side door: the accountability of government corporations. The problem of the corporations and their relation to the GAO dated to the early 1920s and the Comptroller General's altercations with the Emergency Fleet Corporation. Later, the Comptroller General had raised the question of GAO control over the corporations in his annual reports, particularly in 1928 and 1932, wherein he urged that it be given authority to audit them. The struggles between the GAO and the TVA during the 1930s, culminating in their "treaty" in 1940, have already been mentioned. But that agreement did not apply to the dozens of other corporations created before, during, and after the New Deal. There were at the close of World War II more than 100 government corporations, the majority totally owned by the federal government; about 40, mostly in the banking business, had mixed ownership.[8] About one quarter of the total had been established before the depression; the oldest was the Panama Railroad Company, which had been purchased by the government in 1904. More than half, including some of the most important,[9] were products of the Great Depression. The remaining sixteen were emergency agencies, created during the war. Congress had established or provided authority to establish the great majority of them, but because most of them were self-financed and not subject to the annual appropriation process, they were exempt from normal congressional control.

This weakness or absence of financial control became a significant issue during World War II. The Joint Committee on Non-Essential Federal Expenditures, chaired by Senator Harry F. Byrd (D., Va.), made an extensive two-year study of the subject in the midst of the war and reported on it to the Senate in 1944.[10] That study concluded that there was no effective control over the corporations and recommended that they be required to prepare business-type budgets to be reviewed by the Bureau of the Budget and Congress and that they be audited by the GAO.

The first product of the study was an amendment to the so-called George Bill that was designed for an entirely different purpose: to remove the Federal Loan Administrator's functions from the jurisdiction of the Secretary of Commerce, then the former Vice President, Henry A. Wallace. Senator Byrd introduced an amendment providing that the financial transactions of all government corporations be audited by the GAO "in accordance with the principles and procedures applicable to commercial corporate transactions and under such rules and regulations as may be prescribed by the Comptroller General."[11] It further provided that the audits "be conducted at the place or places where the accounts of the corporations are normally kept." The amendment and the bill were debated, passed, and signed into law in February 1945.

Later in the same year, Congress passed more comprehensive legislation to provide stronger governmental controls over the budgeting and financial operations, as well as auditing by the GAO, of government corporations. It was—and remains—the Government Corporation Control Act of 1945.[12] The George Act and the Corporation Control Act, which renewed and amplified it, provided the "foot in the door" toward the modernization of GAO auditing generally. They required commercial-type audits directed not alone to legal compliance but to the efficacy of financial management and internal controls to be performed annually rather than continuously. These audits were to be modeled upon the practices of public accounting firms in the private sector, and were to result in reports to Congress rather than arguments about, and occasional disallowances of, individual vouchers. They called for orientations and expertise entirely different from those of the traditional GAO auditors.

Comptroller General Warren, who had been an enthusiastic supporter and contributor to the legislation, moved fast to give it effect.[13] In July he established a Corporation Audits Division, completely separate from the going audit organizations. He called upon the public accounting profession, including the American Institute of Accounting, to advise on and recommend qualified personnel who had extensive experience in public accounting in the private sector, and most of his early appointees had from ten to thirty years of such experience.[14] The first director was T. Coleman Andrews, a prominent CPA of Richmond, who was senior partner of the accounting firm that bore his name. Howard W. Bordner, who had served for nine years as a supervising manager of Arthur Andersen and Co., was named the first deputy director. Dozens of other qualified CPAs were hired from outside the GAO, beginning in the fall of 1945. In addition, the new division almost immediately began a program of college recruitment of graduates from leading schools of accounting and business administration. For the first several months, the division provided a training program for new personnel (after working hours). Later this was discontinued, but for several years training was offered to its younger members toward passing the CPA examination. By 1948, the division's staff included 167 professionals, of whom 54 were CPAs; two years later, in 1950, the total had grown to 210, including 88 CPAs. Thus the Corporation Audits Division became the launching pad for the professionalization of accounting in the GAO.

The mode of operations of the new division was entirely foreign to the old GAO. It conducted its studies at the locus of the headquarters of the corporation under review, whether in Washington, the Virgin Islands, Knoxville, Tennessee, or the Panama Canal Zone. It reviewed the financial management and the internal controls of the corporations and investigated individual transactions only on items under question or on the basis of a limited sampling. It raised questions on legal compliance, but more often on the efficacy of financial and control systems and sometimes the wisdom of decisions. It had no power to disallow payments but was required to make reports to Congress on findings it considered indicative of illegality or waste or inefficiency.

It appears that from the beginning the corporation audits were conceived in broader terms than was customary for audits of private business. This was due in part to specific requirements of the Corporation Control Act, which called not alone for examinations of the financial accounts and the adequacy of internal accounting controls but also for reporting to Congress on operations and financial condition of the corporations; reports on any impairment of capital; recommendations for the return of government capital or the payment of dividends; and other information. In its first internal guidelines on policies and procedures to govern the conduct of audits, issued in October 1945, the division contemplated evaluations of the effectiveness with which the corporations were carrying out their purposes. It included the statement:

> It is necessary in all corporations to measure the costs of the activities in relation to the accomplishments, from the standpoint of justifying the activities, as well as for the purpose of showing the effectiveness with which the activity's responsibilities have been discharged.

That early document presaged the emphasis given many years later to program evaluation. It was supplemented by a number of documents in 1950, and was ultimately superseded by the development of the *Comprehensive Audit Manual* on September 1, 1952, prepared primarily by Ellsworth H. Morse, Jr.[15]

One of the first and most ambitious audits of the new Division was its ten-volume study of the Reconstruction Finance Corporation (RFC) and its subsidiary corporations, which was submitted to Congress in June 1946, replete with criticisms of the corporation's financial and other operations and decisions. The report was the occasion for congressional hearings and was enthusiastically received by the House Committee on Expenditures in the Executive Departments.[16]

A later audit of the U.S. Maritime Commission proved to be a landmark in the history of the GAO.[17] The Maritime Commission was not established as a corporation, but, pursuant to the Comptroller General's instructions, the Corporation Audits Division conducted its review in accordance with the principles applicable to commercial transactions. The report on the audit, submitted to Congress in February 1950, was also well received in Congress. The success of the audit helped convince the Comptroller General of the feasibility of site auditing of regular departments and agencies other than corporations and of the capability of the GAO staff to carry on such audits. It contributed to the decision, described later, to develop the program of comprehensive auditing for the government in general.

Some critics, including academic scholars, objected to the Corporation Control Act at the time on the grounds that subjecting the corporations to the budgeting, auditing, and other financial controls of the government would critically damage their flexibility and managerial freedom. Professor Herman Pritchett, for example, wrote a few months after the act's passage that:

> It goes far toward completing the task of eliminating the features which have made government corporations useful instruments for enterprise purposes. . . . The pattern of control imposed means that, for good or ill, American experience with autonomous public corporations is substantially at an end.[18]

Whether because of the act or not, there is no doubt that there has been much less reliance upon the corporate device, even for business-type operations, since 1945. The number of federal corporations has declined substantially, as has their relative importance in the totality of government finances.

On the other hand, Congress and the executive have invented or utilized a congeries of other types of enterprises, public and private or in the "twilight zone" between the two, to provide substantial managerial freedom and autonomy.[19] Further, they have relied increasingly upon contractual and subsidized arrangements with private businesses and not-for-profit institutions, including universities, all of which later raised even thornier problems of public accountability.[20] Audits of government corporations, which since 1975 are required only once every three years, now comprise only a small fraction of GAO work. The significance of the Corporation Audits Division really lay elsewhere. The division itself was merged in 1952 with several others to form a new Division of Audits, of which its staff provided the solid backbone. It upgraded the caliber and image of the GAO in the profession of accounting. And it was the first major step toward a new concept of the GAO's role and function in the field of auditing.

The Reform of Federal Accounting Systems

The second movement that led to revolutionizing the GAO's orientation and activities in accounting and auditing likewise stemmed, at least in considerable part, from prewar criticism and dissatisfaction in the executive branch and the conflicts arising from them. Conceptually, the critics were supported by the conviction of many in the executive agencies, and in the public administration fraternity generally, that the Comptroller General should not be both accountant and auditor—that accounting, and the functions of advance decisions, disallowing expenditures, settlements, and so forth, were properly executive responsibilities. Further, the Treasury Department complained about the duplicating nature of central accounts and the difficulty if not impossibility of instituting an integrated and modern system of accounting for the government as a whole as long as the GAO insisted on forms and procedures primarily to accommodate its own requirements. The Treasury Department and the Bureau of the Budget (BoB) joined forces in issuing a glossary of terms and instructions for reports on appropriations, obligations, apportionments, and like matters, quite unrelated to the GAO stipulations. Edward F. Bartelt, commissioner of accounts and later fiscal assistant secretary of the treasury, became for many years the leader in seeking an integrated accounting system useful for agency management, consolidated government-wide financial reporting, and the integration of budget and accounting needs. He directed the Treasury Department's system of nationwide accounting for emergency relief payments, starting in 1935, which achieved a spectacular success (see chapter 3). In 1938, he organized a committee to survey and develop plans to integrate the various accounting systems in the Treasury Department and in some agencies with a view to better serving managerial needs. Later, in 1939 and 1940, a group of Treasury Department officials were loaned to the BoB, which had just been made a part of the Executive Office of the President, to advise on how needs for financial information in connection with the budget process might best be served. This effort resulted in an executive order[21] that directed the secretary of the treasury, with the approval of the director of the budget, to establish a system of financial records and reports needed in the budget process. Part of the purpose of the order was to force, or to at least encourage, the GAO to adapt its requirements to the needs as perceived by executive agencies. Walter F. Frese, who had been prominent in many of these Treasury Department and BoB initiatives and who would later be the hub of reform efforts in the GAO, sought to enlist participation in this work on the part of GAO officials; at one point, GAO, BoB, and Treasury Department representatives planned a pilot test in a single agency.[22] But Frese was reassigned, the test did not come off, and further developments were postponed because of the war. The executive order apparently had little impact on GAO practices, but these prewar experiences had illuminated some of the problems and needs and had inaugurated the idea of a cooperative approach among the financial agencies most concerned.

According to one account, the seed that led to the transformation of the GAO was planted in the mind of Comptroller General Warren before World War II in a chance meeting on a Washington street car with Eric L. Kohler, then Comptroller of the Tennessee Valley Authority. Kohler commended to Warren's attention the recent book by Harvey C. Mansfield, Sr., on *The Comptroller General* (discussed in the Introduction above) and subsequently sent him a copy to read.[23] That book may have been the source of Warren's later initiatives. At any rate during the war and the immediate postwar months, Warren, with the encouragement of his special assistant, Frank Weitzel, became concerned about the need to improve accounting practices in the government and increasingly doubtful about the effectiveness of the GAO's auditing and other controls. Warren launched his crusade immediately after the war. In 1950 he said:

> On the day after the surrender of Japan, I called a meeting of my staff and told them the No. 1 problem in the General Accounting Office from that date was improvement of accounting in the Government. Because of the legal responsibilities and interests of the Treasury Department and the Bureau of the Budget, from the standpoint of fiscal administration in the Government, I felt it was essential to have their full participation in any such program. Because the day-to-day maintenance of accounting systems is the responsi-

bility of the various administrative agencies their cooperation was just as important.[24]

Warren's memory in 1950 may have misled him about his statement in 1945 with respect to collaboration with the executive agencies. His good friend, James E. Webb, also from North Carolina, recalls "twisting Warren's arm" about collaborating with the Treasury Department and the Bureau of the Budget after Webb became director of the budget in 1947. Webb later wrote that Warren's response to his urging was: "What you are asking me to do is to reorganize the General Accounting Office and nobody ought to be asked to do that."[25]

In any case it was a happy coincidence that Warren and John W. Snyder, secretary of the treasury, and Webb, were all congenial Democrats from the south. They were encouraged toward a collaborative approach by the Senate Committee on Expenditures in the executive departments and by trusted aides: Warren by Weitzel and others in the GAO; Snyder by Bartelt and others in the Treasury Department; Webb by Frederick Lawton, assistant director, and others in the Bureau of the Budget. The three agreed in December 1947 to collaborate in the stimulation of a Joint Accounting Improvement Program (JAIP),[26] in which all departments and agencies were to participate. The JAIP was announced in a celebrated letter from the Comptroller General to the heads of all agencies on October 20, 1948, which urged their participation in the development of accounting systems suited to their own managerial needs and tied in to an integrated government-wide accounting pattern. Leadership would be provided by the Comptroller General with the support of the secretary of the treasury and the director of the budget, and the effort would be spearheaded by a small, highly qualified GAO staff, helped as needed by staff from the Treasury Department and the BoB. The letter promised continuing review of GAO reporting requirements and assurance that its audit programs would "be developed in balanced relationship with internal control considerations."

Warren transferred some of the functions of his Office of Investigations to the new Accounting Systems Division, which would be the nucleus of the joint program. And he went outside the GAO for the director of the new division. Probably on the recommendation of Bartelt of the Treasury Department, he appointed Frese, who had previously worked in both the Treasury Department and the BoB but not in GAO. Frese in turn appointed a number of administrative and accounting professionals, many of whom had had experience in the executive branch. His total professional staff grew to about seventy.

The JAIP was an altogether unique organization created without benefit of legislation through the cooperation of leaders of one legislative and two executive agencies. It sidestepped the constitutional and organizational issue that had so long stymied effective action to improve financial management. And it constituted a dramatic reversal in the stance of the GAO. Henceforth, that organization would recognize the primary responsibility of the individual agencies to develop and operate their own accounting systems; it would provide standards, guidance, and technical assistance in that work, and it would review and approve such systems once in place. It would encourage the development of internal audit systems in the agencies and would give due weight to the requirements of financial information for internal management, for budget preparation and execution, and for the overall needs of the Treasury Department and the Bureau of the Budget.

The style of Frese, chief of the GAO's Accounting Systems Division, which provided the principal staff for the JAIP, was directly reflected in its performance. Frese liked to think of its role as that of a catalyst—not of a policeman or director or even consultant. The ideas should come up from below, not be prescribed from above. Accounting systems should center on the needs of managers who made substantive decisions, not the accounting technicians. Financial information should go to the places where it would be most useful for managerial decisions, however far down in the hierarchy. He was suspicious of uniformity and standardization, preferring systems tailored to the needs of the individual agencies. And though he disdained slogans and the technical language of some accountants (like "accrual accounting"), a favorite among his expressions was integrated programming, budgeting, accounting, and reporting.

The achievements of the JAIP in its first eight years were gradual rather than spectacular and somewhat spotty because of Frese's predilection to focus on individual agencies rather than on sweeping reforms and standards. Overall, they were impressive, possibly the most sweeping overhaul of federal financial procedures since the beginning of the republic. It is, however, difficult to attribute specific changes and actions to the JAIP as such, partly because of the participatory nature of its operations. Its contributions were expressed in legislation, directives of various kinds and at various levels, changes in operating practices, and changes in personnel policies and in the personnel themselves. In many of these, the JAIP was but one of several contributors or a catalyst among them. It might lay some claim to almost all the major changes in financial management that were made during those years, but exclusive claim to almost none of them.

The emphasis placed by the JAIP on the responsibility of the executive agencies to develop and maintain their own accounting and internal auditing systems obviously had serious implications for some of the traditional activities of the GAO—that was the other side of the coin. The JAIP could hardly succeed unless many of the old GAO requirements and procedures were modified, relaxed, or abolished. The Accounting Systems Division joined the Corporation Audits Division in its advocacy of comprehensive, on-site auditing to replace the centralized voucher checking that had for so long been the main dish in the GAO's menu.

In a lengthy memorandum of July 14, 1949, to the Comptroller General, Frese enunciated three main principles growing out of the agreed policies of the JAIP.

1. The individual operating agencies of the Government are the key points for effectuation of real control over the financial operations of the Government. Accordingly, the joint program, and the exercise of responsibilities for prescribing systems, must be directed at providing effective controls in the agencies, and, as a consequence, in the whole system of accounting in the Government. The joint program states in this respect "that the keeping of proper records and exercise of proper control at that point (i.e., in each agency) are the foundation on which the entire system of accounting and reporting in the Government must rest."

2. The consolidation and necessary integration of accounting processes for the Government as a whole will be accomplished with the proper integration of accounting processes of the individual agencies with the accounting of the Treasury Department. The "linking together" of agency and Treasury accounting systems will provide "internal controls" in the accounting for the Executive Branch as a whole and will enable the Treasury Department to develop, on the basis of its own and agency accounting results, composite financial statements for the Government as a whole.

3. The control and audit procedures of the General Accounting Office should be adjusted to the effectiveness of accounting and internal control in the agencies and in the Treasury Department. This will result in the maintenance of control by the General Accounting Office on a broader and more effective base through the prescribing of accounting systems, systems inspections, and comprehensive audits of accounting records, including those of the Treasury Department.

Frese defined the term *comprehensive audit* as "the verification of assets, liabilities, and operating results, combined with a voucher audit with power to take exceptions, aimed at the proper level, such power to be used with discretion." The memorandum went on to make a number of specific recommendations, including the abolishment of a variety of records, accounts, and ledgers in the GAO and the transfer to the Treasury Department of the function of matching and reconciling checks with checking accounts. Frese argued that his recommendations would make the GAO's control far more effective at the same time that it reduced its personnel and costs.

The potential impact of the Frese recommendations upon the whole structure and orientation of the GAO was obviously tremendous. They would turn the auditing function around, virtually abolish most of the records and controls of the large and powerful Accounting and Bookkeeping

Division, and remove the check-reconciling and some other functions. They threatened the status and the jobs of thousands of officers and employees, including a great many of the old-timers. On receipt of the memorandum, the Comptroller General sent copies to the heads of all divisions and offices for comment. The responses covered the spectrum from full approval on the part of the director of the Corporation Audits Division to the total and vituperative opposition of the chief of the Accounting and Bookkeeping Division. The latter officer described the proposals as "(1) being very definitely and unwisely revolutionary; (2) unduly extravagant in promises; (3) inaccurate in appraising and reporting upon some of our present practices and in stating accomplishments under the joint program; (4) undeveloped to an extent which leaves entirely too much to conjecture; (5) taking away from your direct supervision functions essential to the proper performance of your duties; and (6) being incapable of accomplishment under existing law."

The chief of the Audit Division generally approved with minor modification, while the chiefs of the Investigation and Reconciliation and Clearance Divisions opposed with vigor. The operations of the Postal Accounts Division were specifically exempted from Frese's memorandum, but its chief could hardly fail to see the handwriting on the wall. He argued that "the audit for accounting purposes and the audit for legal purposes are . . . separate and distinct and unrelated" and that the legality audit, which required detailed review of every transaction, should never be sacrificed. He implied that Frese's proposal would do just that—and he was certainly correct.

In spite of the contrary advice of several of his most influential lieutenants, the Comptroller General moved promptly and decisively. On October 19, 1949, he issued Administrative Order No. 70, which in general terms endorsed the bulk of Frese's auditing proposals: the comprehensive audit and the evaluation of agency systems at the site of operations. A few weeks later, on November 29, in a memorandum to the chiefs of GAO divisions and offices, he specified in greater detail the decisions he had reached, including the abandonment, as rapidly as possible, of the bulk of the central records and the operations connected with them. Most of the Frese recommendations were dealt with. Warren opened his memorandum with a statement of policies, including the adoption of the comprehensive audit "as and when it is determined to be feasible, advantageous and otherwise permissible." Most sweeping of the policies was the second:

> All operations in the General Accounting Office not essential to effective exercise of its audit and control responsibilities, in the light of the comprehensive audit policy or otherwise, and which are not specifically required by law will be eliminated as rapidly as possible.

He further mandated that the divisions submit recommendations for legislative changes needed to effectuate his policies. Warren's directives of October 19 and November 29, 1949, were probably the crucial keys in the turnabout of the GAO.

On November 29, he also designated Ted B. Westfall, then assistant director of the Corporation Audits Division, to lead a study of organization and operations of the GAO and to develop plans for its transition to the new role—under the aegis of the Accounting Systems Division. Meanwhile, Frese and others concentrated on the preparation of legislation that the general counsel had advised would be necessary to make the proposals fully effective.

The First Hoover Commission

Concurrent with many of the developments described above and very relevant to them was the work of the first Hoover Commission,[27] which reported in February 1949. Composed of representatives and appointees of the President and of both houses of Congress, equally divided between the political parties, it conducted the most exhaustive and elaborate study of the executive branch as a whole in American history to that time. Its reports, which totaled nineteen in number, were far more detailed than that of the Brownlow Committee more than a decade before, but basically consistent in philosophy and approach. The Hoover Commission instituted the practice of delegating to task forces of experts in various fields investigation, research, and the development of recommendations; seventy-eight task force studies were published. Most relevant to the GAO was the Task Force on Fiscal, Budgeting, and Accounting Activities. That task force in turn engaged the services of individual specialists or groups of specialists in particular areas. The group that concentrated on accounting was in fact the Committee on Federal Government Accounting of the American Institute of Accounting. Its chairman was T. Coleman Andrews, who had been the director of the GAO's Corporation Audits Division during its first two years. As representative of the Comptroller General, Frese attended most of the meetings of the committee, which was also assisted by Bartelt of the Treasury Department and Lawton of the BoB. All three were of course intimately associated with the Joint Accounting Program.

As one might anticipate, the report of the Andrews Committee was supportive of the efforts and proposals of the Corporation Audits and Accounting Systems divisions, both of which were well underway during the course of its deliberations. Specifically, it endorsed the focusing of accounting responsibilities on the agencies, the comprehensive rather than the voucher audit, site auditing, steps to make the accounts and reports more clearly reflect real costs (mainly through accrual accounting), and a closer relationship between the accounting and budgeting systems. These recommendations were endorsed in more general terms by the task force and later by the Hoover Commission itself.[28] They provided external support for the changes that were already underway or contemplated within the GAO from respected outside experts, administrative and political leaders, and the interested public generally.

However, the committee, the task force, and the commission became embroiled in the old organizational and constitutional issue as to executive-legislative prerogatives with respect to the superintendence of accounting and the exercise of controls over finances. Frese, with the presumed support of the leaders of the JAIP, believed that this issue could be finessed by planting firm responsibility for accounting in the operating agencies, by vesting in the GAO the responsibility for assisting in the development of accounting systems and for the establishment of accounting standards, and by the provision of cooperative leadership by the three top financial organizations: the GAO, the Treasury Department, and the BoB. He thought that Andrews, chairman of the Committee on Federal Government Accounting, had given assurance of his confidence in the JAIP approach and would not raise the organizational issue. But at its last meeting in late October of 1948,[29] which Frese did not attend, the committee adopted for its report a proposal that the direction of accounting was properly an executive responsibility, that the Comptroller General's functions should be limited strictly to auditing, and that his title should be changed to auditor general. In keeping with its professional aspirations, the committee recommended that there be a central accounting office in the Executive Office of the President to be headed by an accountant general of the United States with full authority over all accounting standards and systems and with a fifteen-year term.

The Task Force on Fiscal, Budgeting, and Accounting Activities accepted the principle but only part of the specifics of its accounting committee. It recommended an accounting service in the Treasury Department to govern federal accounting systems, headed by a career accountant general. It proposed transferring to the accountant general the various accounting and settling powers of the Comptroller General, but no change in his title.

The commission itself split in four different directions on the organizational issue. President Hoover, with a slim majority of seven of the twelve members, recommended a system substantially like that proposed by the committee. Two of the congressional members chose to retain the powers of the Comptroller General substantially intact, to strengthen the central accounts of the Treasury Department, and not to establish an accountant general. Two other members made proposals essentially consonant with those of the Brownlow Committee—transfer of all but the postaudit to the executive branch and change in title of the Comptroller General to auditor general. One, Vice Chairman Dean Acheson, expressed confidence in the joint program of the GAO, the Treasury Department, and the Bureau of the Budget, and proposed no change "under present circumstances." This view would ultimately prevail.

Obviously the dozen years that separated the Brownlow and Hoover reports had not resolved this issue. But the President, Harry S. Truman, did not this time go along with the recommendation of the Hoover Commission to alter the legal responsibilities of the GAO. Probably influenced by his budget director and treasury secretary and possibly also the Comptroller General himself, Truman made no move to establish an accountant general or an accounting service in the Treasury Department. He later gave enthusiastic support to the act that gave statutory recognition to the Joint Accounting Improvement Program and fulsome praise to Comptroller General Lindsay Warren.

Bills to carry out the Hoover Commission's proposed accounting reorganization were, however, introduced in both Houses in June 1949 by two conservative Republicans, Senator Joseph McCarthy (R., Wis.), who was becoming better known for other activities, and Representative Clare Hoffman (R., Mich.). Lindsay Warren testified vigorously against the accountant general proposal in the hearing of the Senate Committee on Government Operations, and the secretary of the treasury and the director of the budget each wrote letters opposing it. Both the Senate and House Committees on Government Operations voted unanimously against it. Thus did the commission's idea for an accountant general suffer a not very memorable—and probably a permanent—death.

In a thoughtful appraisal of the first Hoover Commission, Paul H. Appleby described the accountant general proposal as "probably a counsel of confusion as it certainly is a counsel of evasion."[30] The central problem, as Appleby saw it, was the same one that went back to 1920: that the Comptroller General exercises a basic executive function but is responsible to Congress. He attributed the failure to recommend basic change principally to "key officials in the executive branch who preferred not to raise the issue."[31] Appleby thought that the recommendations with respect to auditing were "about as constructive as possible," but he raised a question that would be echoed and debated over the succeeding years: "Yet the pretensions of the General Accounting Office . . . to deal with public management broadly on a basis of accounting expertness are readily subject to question."[32]

Financial Legislation, 1949 and 1950

Although its proposal to shift the authority over governmental accounting came to naught, other Hoover Commission recommendations in the area of financial management occasioned or contributed to profound changes in legislation and practices. Some of these grew out of its report, *Budgeting and Accounting;* others derived from task force studies and commission reports primarily directed to other subjects.

One of the first legislative products of the commission was in the latter category. The Federal Property and Administrative Services Act,[33] which became law in June 1949 only a few months after the publication of the Hoover reports, established the General Services Administration (GSA). An important part of the act concerned the management and accounting of federal property on the basis of its monetary value, a subject hitherto largely neglected. The sections on accounting and auditing of property were apparently drafted by, or in close collaboration with, the GAO for they followed the basic pattern already established by the JAIP and the Accounting Systems Division: the GAO was to prescribe principles and standards to govern property accounting; systems, developed in the agencies, would be reviewed and approved or criticized by the GAO, which would later review and report on them in operation. For many subsequent years, the GAO and the GSA collaborated closely in their endeavors to improve property accounting.

A second major outgrowth of the Hoover Commission recommendations was the National Security Act Amendments of 1949.[34] The amendments were designed principally to integrate the service departments, previously known as the National Military Establishment, into a unified executive Department of Defense and to strengthen the authority of the secretary of defense over its operations. Title IV of the act, which was "tacked on" after the main body of the legislation had been introduced and debated in the armed services committees of the Congress, dealt almost entirely with fiscal management in the Department of Defense and in the three subordinate service departments. It was drafted in the office of the secretary of defense by a consultant, Ferdinand Eberstadt, with the assistance of former task force staff members of the Hoover Commission and persons drawn from the secretary's office, most notably Wilfred J. McNeil, who would become the first defense comptroller.

Title IV established or, in some cases, ratified certain organizational arrangements and practices that would have great influence not only in the Defense Department but in civil agencies as well. This law was the first one to give statutory authorization to the performance budget, which was perhaps the Hoover Commission's most important single proposal. It also set up in the Department of Defense the office of comptroller with the rank of assistant secretary and wide-ranging powers over the budget process, accounting, and program and statistical reporting. Similar structures were required for each of the service departments (the army and the air force already had such offices), and comptroller systems were set up in each of them at every major level of command. All of the services incorporated auditing in their arsenal of activities, and some added other related activities, such as program review and analysis, management studies, and disbursing. The act also authorized the establishment of working capital funds (stock and industrial funds) for the handling of commercial and industrial operations, comparable in many respects to internal "corporations," which bought or produced and sold goods and services to operating units within the military departments.

The JAIP was not involved collectively in the establishment of military comptrollerships in the National Security Amendments of 1949, but the GAO favored the concept of revolving funds in the Department of Defense and Comptroller General Warren endorsed the entire plan because of it. The Bureau of the Budget objected to Title IV on the grounds that the heads of agencies should have authority to prescribe their own suborganizations, and not be subjected to statutory mandates such as the provisions requiring comptrollers. But the title was approved virtually without opposition in both Houses. Thus in some ways the Department of Defense "stole a march" on the civil agencies and on the JAIP. It brought budgeting and accounting together under one "tent," elevated the importance of accounting and of internal auditing, and mandated budgets and accounts related to costs and programs—the central theme of the performance budget.

A third important piece of legislation of that period was the Post Office Department Financial Control Act,[35] which was approved on August 17, 1950. The GAO played a major hand in drafting the measure, and its provisions were in thorough accord with the principles of the JAIP and the efforts of the GAO's Accounting Systems Division. The anomalous situation whereby the GAO was keeping the accounts of the Post Office, which had persisted since 1923, was terminated. The accounting responsibility was returned to the Post Office Department, which was directed to develop and operate an accounting system under principles prescribed by the GAO, with GAO cooperation and subject to its approval. The act also authorized that the GAO conduct comprehensive site audits of postal operations.

Unquestionably the most sweeping financial legislation of the period was the Budget and Accounting Procedures Act of 1950.[36] When President Truman signed it on September 12, 1950, he pronounced it "the most important legislation enacted by the Congress in the budget and accounting field since the Budget and Accounting Act, 1921, was passed almost thirty years ago." Among many other things, it stipulated that the budget set forth "functions and activities of the Government," which was intended to convey the sense of the Hoover Commission's performance budget. It contained other provisions concerning the budget and central financial management in the Treasury Department.

For our purposes, its most significant sections were contained in Title I, Part II, sometimes cited as the Accounting and Auditing Act of 1950. Most of these provisions gave statutory recognition and an encouraging "go ahead" to the principles and programs that were already being pushed. They accorded with the major recommendations of the Hoover Commission's report, *Budgeting and Accounting,* except that proposing an accountant general, as well as those of the Joint Accounting Improvement Program and the GAO's Accounting Systems Division, which played a major part in drafting the bill. A few amended previous legislation to make possible the full implementation of the JAIP's proposed policies. Among its major provisions were that:

- the accounts provide full disclosure of financial operations and adequate information for formulation and execution of the budget;
- maintenance of accounting systems and financial reporting be a responsibility of the executive branch;
- the joint program for accounting improvement (JAIP) continue;
- the Comptroller General, after consulting the secretary of the treasury and the director of the budget, prescribe the accounting principles and standards for the agency systems and for integrating them with the general financial requirements of the Treasury Department;
- the Comptroller General cooperate with the agencies in developing their systems and review and approve them when he deems them adequate;
- as soon as practicable, agency systems be placed on an accrual basis;
- central accounting and reporting by the Treasury Department be consistent with the principles and standards of the Comptroller General;
- when the secretary of the treasury and the Comptroller General agree that existing requirements with respect to requisitioning of funds, advances, and warrants are no longer necessary they may jointly issue regulations to waive them;
- the Comptroller General may discontinue the maintenance of his central accounts when he judges them no longer necessary;
- in determining his auditing procedures and the extent of voucher checking, the Comptroller General "give due regard to generally accepted principles of auditing, including consideration of the effectiveness of accounting organizations and systems, internal audit and control" (the so-called comprehensive audit);
- agencies retain all financial documents whenever the Comptroller General determines they are necessary for site audits.

The 1950 act gave congressional sanction to what was already progressing under the aegis of the Joint Accounting Improvement Program and the

GAO's Accounting Systems Division. None of these changes was accomplished overnight. They were given effect step by step over several years—from about 1948 to 1955. Their net effect in that period was a revolution in federal accounting and in the GAO.

Internal Reshaping of the GAO

As noted earlier, after Comptroller General Warren had decided in late 1949 to change the direction of the GAO, one of his first moves was to institute a managerial and organizational survey by a task force under the direction of Ted B. Westfall. Among the first missions of the group was to assess the usefulness of voucher checking as it was then practiced. The conclusions of that study were that the values were far outweighed by the costs and that in fact a large part of the voucher audit was simply a rote exercise. Sheet after sheet of the vouchers were simply stamped "VA," which meant, not Virginia nor Veterans Administration, but "visually audited," which in turn meant seen or quickly scanned but not examined. Studies of various other checks and of the records kept in the GAO similarly concluded that they were costly and unnecessary or could be better conducted or maintained elsewhere—in the agencies and in the Treasury Department.

The consequences consisted of a series of recommendations, usually followed by administrative action, to alter fundamentally the stance and the functions of the GAO. One by one, agencies were exempted from the requirement of sending their vouchers and accompanying documents to the GAO in Washington (except in the field of transportation, which remained centralized). In turn, the GAO established offices within the various agencies to carry on what were then called comprehensive audits, on a selective basis at the site of operations. GAO field offices were authorized to do the same outside of Washington. The movement of truck and freight cars full of fiscal documents to Washington gradually declined. The audit of individual vouchers, which had been for about thirty years the pièce de résistance of the GAO, was gradually abandoned except where its need was indicated in a comprehensive audit.

For the traditional voucher checking, which was essentially a semi-technical, clerical review of agency bookkeeping, were substituted two quite different kinds of activities. First was the assistance to agencies in the development of accounting systems in accordance with general standards and principles developed by the GAO, followed by GAO review of the systems of individual agencies to be blessed by its approval or criticized by its findings of inadequacies. The GAO had, almost from its start, prescribed forms, classifications, and reports for the agencies, but it had offered little in regard to their overall accounting systems. Pursuant to the provisions of the Budget and Accounting Procedures Act of 1950, the GAO began to issue in 1952 its first *Accounting Principles Memoranda,* which set forth in quite general terms the basic principles of an adequate accounting system in an administrative agency. It was the grandfather of the GAO's current *Policy and Procedures Manual for Guidance of Federal Agencies.* But the basic idea has not changed. Rather than checking on the individual transactions of agencies, the GAO would review the systems whereby the agencies maintained and checked on their own transactions and verify the adequacy of those systems, where necessary, by sample checks of the transactions.

The second substitute for voucher checking was the activity then known, somewhat misleadingly, as comprehensive auditing. Use of the term was apparently derived from the old Corporation Audits Division, which reviewed the totality of the financial condition (income and expenses, assets and liabilities) of the government corporations, more or less modeled on the practices of public accounting firms in the private sector. But from the start, the audits of government corporations went well beyond the accustomed boundaries of public accounting firms. They dealt not only with the financial condition of the government corporations but also with the legality and honesty of their activities and the wisdom and effectiveness of their managerial decisions. As noted earlier, the first of the corporation audits (of the Reconstruction Finance Corporation) entailed ten volumes, and one subsequent audit resulted in several years of negotiations with the corporation's management before a report could be issued.[37]

The extension of corporation-type auditing to the typical appropriation-supported activities of government entailed some modification of terminology. The convenient term was *comprehensive auditing* of the overall adequacy, legality, honesty, and—to a varying extent—efficiency in the application of public funds. Obviously, the GAO could not focus at once on every financial and managerial aspect of an agency's operations; a comprehensive audit would direct its attention to areas of prime importance or where there was reason to expect some deficiency. Therefore, a comprehensive audit was in fact selective, not total as the adjective suggests. The expression was intended to indicate that the audit was not restricted to the review of individual transactions nor to the strictly financial aspects of an agency's operation. The checking of vouchers could be pursued in areas where the general audit suggested that such a review was necessary. But the skills involved in comprehensive auditing differed fundamentally from those of voucher checking: they required investigations of the general system of agency management and of decisions from the top down. Except as a supplement to comprehensive audits where circumstances indicated, voucher checks gradually declined.

A similar fate befell the control over expenditures and receipts and the accompanying record keeping. Most of the GAO records were either abolished or sent to central records storage bases; for them was substituted a

GAO review of Treasury Department accounting and records systems. The GAO had, up to then, been keeping "detailed accounts for appropriations, expenditures, limitations, receipts, public debt as well as personal accounts with accountable officers. In all, maintenance of about 500,000 ledger accounts was discontinued in GAO, and just as important was the elimination of millions of documents that had to be prepared and sent to GAO by Federal agencies."[38]

The Westfall study resulted in fundamental organizational changes. The Postal Accounts Division was eliminated as a consequence of the Post Office Department Financial Control Act of 1950. A postal audits section was retained and later consolidated in 1952 with the old Audit Division, the Corporation Audits Division, and the Reconciliation and Clearance Division into a new Division of Audits.[39] The Accounting and Bookkeeping Division, one of the largest and most influential of all, was simply abolished—along with most of its variegated record-keeping responsibilities.

Concurrent with organizational changes in the headquarters were major adjustments in field operations. It will be recalled that a field organization consisting of six zones and about thirty field stations had been established during the war to audit military contractors. In 1947, the War Contract Project Audit Section, which supervised the operation, was terminated and its responsibilities were transferred to a Field Audit Section of the Audit Division. A number of other duties were assigned to it, including the auditing of practically all civilian payrolls. In 1952, the Comptroller General announced the establishment of twenty-three regional audit offices. The zones were abolished and leadership was vested in an assistant director of audits for field operations. At the same time, the regional offices were given new responsibilities, consistent with the reorientation of the headquarters: comprehensive audit and reporting of the accounts of accountable officers; auditing of the government corporations; review of agency systems of internal control and procedures against GAO standards; and others. This action has resulted in substantial decentralization of GAO operations and personnel to the field (in 1978, about half of the staff were in the field). A few years later, in 1956, the field staff of the Office of Investigations was merged with the field auditing offices, and the Field Operations Division was established. Although there have been a number of consolidations and relocations of the regional offices, the fundamental pattern remains as it was established under Warren's leadership in 1952.

At about the same time, though stemming from a different source, the GAO expanded its audit operations to financial transactions overseas. In 1951 and early 1952 a great deal of concern had been expressed by members of Congress as well as officials of the GAO about the large scale of American expenditures abroad for economic recovery and rehabilitation as well as for the military, principally in Europe and the Far East. At the time, the GAO had no facilities for the audit of offshore overseas expenditures. In the spring of 1952, a GAO team visited Europe for the purpose of surveying the need and feasibility of an auditing program there. As a consequence, the Comptroller General in August 1952 established a European branch with headquarters in Paris. Field stations were set up then and in later months in London, Rome, Frankfurt, Madrid, and French Morocco. A similar survey in the Far East was conducted at about the same time, but for a variety of reasons, one of which was the confusion and congestion occasioned by the Korean War, it was decided to delay establishment of a Far East branch. One was later established in Tokyo (in 1956). Subsequently, the field stations in Europe were abolished, and headquarters of the European branch was transferred to Frankfurt, where it remains today. The Far East branch, which was moved from Tokyo to Honolulu in 1965, and the European branch became the overseas arms of the International Operations Division (now the International Division), which was organized in 1963.

Accompanying the changes in orientation, functions, and organization of the GAO was a radical change in its personnel, in both their numbers and their nature. The total strength of the GAO had reached a peak of almost 15,000 in 1946; it dropped almost by half to a little below 8,000 in 1950, and to just under 6,000 in 1954, the year that Warren resigned. A substantial portion of the reductions resulted from transfers of functions to other agencies, mainly the Post Office and the Treasury departments, although many functions were eliminated totally. The work of Frese and the JAIP in developing a computerized system for the government's check reconciliation process resulted in a reduction of 400 personnel in the GAO and a similar number in the executive branch. Others were simple terminations of "duration" appointments in World War II. But a good many were reductions in force that occasioned no little pain to the incumbents and are said to have severely distressed Comptroller General Warren.

While the total numbers of GAO employees were sharply declining, the numbers of professionals were increasing at an even faster rate. The bulk of the newcomers in the GAO after 1945 were accountants either with degrees in accounting or from business schools with majors in accounting. Although there continued to be "a fringe on (or near the) top" of lawyers, the dominating group of the General *Accounting* Office for the first time became accountants. The number and proportion of CPAs was near zero before World War II.[40] Thereafter, it became the aspired credential for professionals in the GAO. After World War II, and aside from the limited employment of lawyers for the general counsel's office, the only recruitment of professionals in the GAO was for accountants—for the next twenty years. Accountancy thus became the "line" profession of the GAO after 1945. At the time of this writing, the chiefs and deputy chiefs of most of the offices and divisions started with credentials in accountancy. Most of them are CPAs, the majority of whom were initially appointed to the GAO in the years from 1945 to 1955.

One interesting and somewhat paradoxical event during this period was the completion and occupancy, at long last, of the GAO building in 1951. The construction of a single building to house the GAO had been urged by every Comptroller General, beginning in 1922. Plans to enlarge the old Pension Building in the mid 1930s were abandoned because the growth of GAO staff during the New Deal rendered that structure—even after remodeling—inadequate. In 1940 and 1941, Congress authorized funds for a building. The plans were drawn, the site was cleared,[41] and a hole was dug. But all this effort was delayed because of the war. Work was resumed after the war—but on the basis of an anticipated headquarters staff and record-storing requirements comparable to the prewar period. No one had anticipated the comprehensive audits conducted on site, the growth of the regional and overseas offices, and the discontinuance of the bulk of the records, as well as the massive reductions in total personnel. In consequence, the building has never been fully occupied by the GAO, and in 1977 more than two fifths of its office space was being used by other agencies.

Its opening was nonetheless a memorable occasion. At the dedication ceremonies on September 11, 1951, President Truman warmly applauded the work of the GAO and paid special tribute to Comptroller General Warren, under whom, he said:

> the General Accounting Office has handled the biggest auditing job in the history of mankind and has done it well. It has continuously improved its operations so it could serve the people of this country better and more efficiently.

The GAO Transformation in Context

The impact of Lindsay Warren's incumbency as Comptroller General upon the GAO—upon its posture in the government, its relationships with the legislative and executive branches, its functions, and its personnel—was revolutionary. He and his lieutenants switched McCarl's engine, which had been wheeling along for about twenty-five years, to another track. They replaced most of the trainmen and demanded different kinds of qualifications for their jobs. They also changed the nature of the cargo—the kind of work to be done. In the absence of emergency, this was certainly one of the most drastic changes in American administrative history.

The post–World War II turnaround of the GAO was nonetheless consistent with concurrent trends and directions in other areas of federal administration. In budgeting and in management generally, there was the drive to more closely relate programs and activities with their costs and budgets; the general concept encompassed, in ex-President Hoover's term, performance budgeting. The number and the detail of federal appropriations were tremendously reduced, their accent moving from things to be bought to work to be done. The Bureau of the Budget and other federal agencies laid increasing stress on quantified measurement of work and outputs, on production planning and productivity, and on the utilization of financial information for managerial purposes—rather than strictly for checking on legality and accuracy of detail. There was an accompanying push, not everywhere successful, toward greater decentralization of managerial decision making, within the bounds of standards and objectives prescribed centrally.

Parallel developments occurred in personnel management. Following the efforts of the Civil Service Commission to recentralize its operations and controls at the end of the war came rising protests from outside the commission to force greater decentralization. The main theme of the Hoover Commission's report on personnel was parallel to its recommendations on accounting: development of standards centrally by the commission to be enforced by sample inspections and reviews; and conduct of personnel operations within the agencies themselves. A growing share of the traditional citadels of commission activity—recruiting and examining—were delegated to the operating agencies. And the Classification Act of 1949 gave the agencies authority to classify their own jobs, subject to standards established by the commission and subject to its review.

The changes in the auditing and financial control functions of the GAO were compatible with, indeed a part of, larger changes in the conduct of American government generally. But the GAO transformation now seems to have been more striking and more extreme, perhaps because it had the furthest distance to go. In the words of one distinguished accountant, written in 1955: "Thus the agency (GAO) once felt to be the main deterrent to executive self-improvement has become its most ardent sponsor."[42]

Notes

1. Unpublished GAO staff paper, "Accountability, Audit, and Settlement."

2. U.S. Congress, House, Committee on Expenditures in the Executive Departments, *Hearings,* September 5, 1945, p. 10.

3. Ibid., p. 12.

4. U.S. Congress, Senate, Committee on the Judiciary, *Hearings on the Proposed Reorganization Bill,* September 6, 1945, pp. 19-20.

5. Ibid., p. 12.

6. P.L. 263. This change was reflected in the next issue of the

Congressional Directory (79th Cong., 2nd Sess., July 1946), which moved the GAO from "Independent Offices and Establishments" to the legislative branch for the first time.

7. 60 Stat. 837, August 2, 1946.

8. The Government Corporation Control Act, discussed below, listed sixty-three wholly owned and thirty-eight of mixed ownership, a total of 101.

9. They included, for example, the Reconstruction Finance Corporation, the TVA, the Federal Deposit Insurance Corporation, the Commodity Credit Corporation, the Export-Import Bank, the Federal National Mortgage Association, and the Federal Crop Insurance Association.

10. U.S. Congress, Senate, S. Doc. no. 227, 78th Cong., 2nd Sess., August 1, 1944. Much of the work on this study was performed by the GAO under the direction of its then assistant to the Comptroller General, Frank H. Weitzel.

11. P.L. 79-4, February 24, 1945.

12. 59 Stat. 557, 1945.

13. Most of the information in this and succeeding paragraphs is based upon interviews with participants at the time and articles, of which the most detailed is John C. Fenton, "The Corporation Audits Division—Its Legacy to the Seventies," *The GAO Review* (summer 1971), pp. 88-114.

14. He also called upon a number of public accounting firms to conduct the audits of many corporations during the first years after passage of the act while his own staff was being recruited and trained.

15. Morse later became an Assistant Comptroller General, a post in which he served until his death in November 1977. For an example of early audits of government corporations, see the case study on the Commodity Credit Corporation in Erasmus H. Kloman, ed., *Cases in Accountability: The Work of the GAO* (Boulder, Colo.: Westview Press, 1979).

16. U.S. Congress, House, H. Rept. 2713, 79th Cong.

17. As reported by Fenton, "Corporation Audits Division," p. 103.

18. "The Government Corporation Control Act of 1945," *American Political Science Review* 40 (1946):509.

19. The most authoritative work describing these kinds of enterprise is Harold Seidman, *Politics, Position, and Power: The Dynamics of Federal Organization*, 2nd ed. (Oxford: 1975). This usage of the expression "twilight zone" is borrowed from that book, pp. 264 ff.

20. See particularly the works of Don K. Price: *Government and Science: Their Dynamic Relation in American Democracy* (New York: Oxford University Press, 1954); and *The Scientific Estate* (Cambridge, Mass.: Harvard University Press, 1965).

21. Executive Order 8512, August 1940.

22. Frese had been a professor of accounting at the University of Illinois before and again during the New Deal. He later served as Chief of the

Accounting Systems Division of the GAO from 1948 to 1956. Thence, he went to the Harvard Business School as a professor and is now professor emeritus.

23. This story is recounted in the preface to William W. Cooper and Yuji Ijiri, eds., *Eric Louis Kohler—Accounting's Man of Principles* (Reston, Va.: Reston Publishing, 1978), p. 13.

24. U.S. Congress, Senate, Committee on Expenditures in the Executive Departments, "To Improve Budgeting, Accounting, and Auditing Methods in the Federal Government," *Hearings* on S.2054, February-March 1950.

25. In his speech on "Leadership Evaluation in Large-Scale Efforts," in *Improving Management for More Effective Government* (Washington, D.C.: U.S. Government Printing Office, 1971, p. 26).

26. Renamed in 1959 as the Joint Federal Management Improvement Program (JFMIP).

27. The Commission on Organization of the Executive Branch of the Government, established by P.L. 162, July 7, 1947.

28. In its report on *Budgeting and Accounting* (Washington, D.C.: U.S. Government Printing Office, 1949).

29. It may or may not have been coincidental that this meeting occurred just before the 1948 presidential election, which the Republican candidate, Thomas E. Dewey, was widely expected to win.

30. "The Significance of the Hoover Commission Report," *The Yale Review* 39, no. 1 (September 1949):18. Then dean of the Maxwell School at Syracuse University, Appleby had filled a number of high posts in the federal government, including acting director of the budget.

31. Ibid.

32. Ibid.

33. P.L. 81-151, June 30, 1949.

34. P.L. 81-216, August 10, 1949.

35. P.L. 81-712, August 17, 1950.

36. P.L. 81-784, September 12, 1950.

37. See case study on the first audits of the Commodity Credit Corporation in Kloman, ed., *Cases in Accountability*.

38. Ellsworth H. Morse, Jr., "The Accounting and Auditing Act of 1950—Its Current Significance to GAO," *GAO Review* (summer, 1975), p. 28.

39. The first director of the new consolidated Audit Division was in fact the same Ted Westfall who had directed the organization study. Later he resigned to enter the private sector. Still later he became executive vice president of International Telephone and Telegraph, a post from which he retired in 1976.

40. One old-time employee thought there was only one CPA in the GAO during the 1920s.

41. Covering most of the block between G and H and 4th and 5th Streets, N.W.

42. John W. McEachren, "Accounting Reform in Washington," *The Journal of Accounting* (September 1955), p. 31.

5

THE SECOND GAO:
CONSOLIDATION AND
CONTRACT AUDITING, 1954-1966

Some officials handle large sums of public money; it is therefore necessary to have other officials to receive and examine the accounts. These inspectors must administer no funds themselves. Different cities call them examiners, auditors, scrutineers and public advocates.

—Aristotle, *Politics,* ca. 325 B.C.

In the councils of government, we must guard against the acquisition of unwarranted influence, whether sought or unsought, by the military-industrial complex. The potential for the disastrous rise of misplaced power exists and will persist.

—Dwight David Eisenhower, closing address to the American people, 1961

The period treated in this chapter, from the early 1950s to the mid 1960s, was bounded at either end by a "hot" war: Korea at the start and Vietnam at the close. In between, the nation was continuously engaged in a "cold war," which occasioned, or rationalized, the maintenance of a state of semimobilization and enormous federal expenditures for defense and the increasingly sophisticated technologies and tools of warfare. Throughout the period, the auditing of military expenditures, and particularly defense contracts, was a major item on the GAO agenda. On the domestic side, most of these years were relatively quiet. The Eisenhower presidency produced rather few new initiatives, and the mass of legislation associated with President Johnson's Great Society was barely off the drawing boards in 1965.

For much of the GAO and for federal financial management generally, it was a period of consolidation and of continuing movement in directions that had been pretty well set by the close of 1950. There were increasing efforts toward cost-based accounting and budgeting, the performance budget, and computerization of financial processes. "Comprehensive" auditing, as a substitute for voucher checking, became the rule in the GAO, and there was a substantial growth of internal auditing in the administrative agencies. The emphasis in the GAO was more and more on economy and efficiency in the "application" of funds, less on the strict legality of individual payments. In both the GAO and the administrative agencies, there was increasing stress on the full professionalization of accounting and of auditing among their staffs and, from the profession itself, a push to enlarge its influence in the conduct of the public business.

One should not infer that the development of the GAO was smooth or steady. There were problems and setbacks, particularly in the auditing of defense contracts, and there were significant changes in organization and in operating style. Some of the changes are reflective of the changed leadership, and it is to this that we direct our attention in the succeeding section.

Changing of the Guard

The election to the presidency of Dwight Eisenhower in 1952 assured that the next Comptroller General of the United States would be appointed by a Republican president. At that time, Lindsay Warren had just completed the twelfth year of his fifteen-year term. As it happened, Eisenhower was able within a relatively short time to name his own appointees to both of the top jobs in the GAO. On June 29, 1953, only a few months after Eisenhower's inauguration, Assistant Comptroller General Frank L. Yates unexpectedly died. Though little known outside of Washington, Yates was a popular figure on the Hill and in the local press, and his passing provoked a number of warm tributes in the *Congressional Record* and the Washington newspapers.

Pending the presidential decision on a successor to Yates, Warren named his special assistant, Frank H. Weitzel, as Acting Assistant Comptroller General. During the summer of 1953, there was considerable agitation within Congress to appoint one of its own to the job: Robert E. Lee, longtime staffer of the House Appropriations Committee and associate of Senator Joseph McCarthy. But apparently responding to the persuasion of Warren and other supporters, Eisenhower nominated Weitzel to the post in October.[1] In a release to the press about the Weitzel selection, Warren stated that he was "grateful to the President. He will never make a better appointment." Later, when Weitzel was sworn in to the post, Warren announced: "We feel honored and proud that the President came to this Office to fill the vacancy." Actually, the Weitzel appointment was in accord with what appears to have become a standard pattern for those serving as second in command of the GAO. All of them have been lawyers and all except Frank Elliott had previously served many years on the staff of the GAO or the comptroller of the treasury.

Weitzel, who would be the first Assistant Comptroller General to serve out the full fifteen-year term, was respected and well liked on the Hill and in Washington generally, and there was no difficulty about his confirmation. As the press pointed out, his career in the GAO was a prototype of a Horatio Alger hero. Starting as a messenger boy in 1923 at the age of sixteen, he soon earned through his speedy service the nickname of "Zev," the champion racehorse of that time. He worked his way through college and law school in the 1920s and 1930s, and later became a first lieutenant of Warren in bringing about the enormous changes in the postwar period that were described earlier.

Weitzel's confirmation in January 1954 was followed within a few weeks by another unexpected vacancy. On March 29, 1954, Comptroller General Warren notified President Eisenhower of his intention to resign one month later. Warren, who attached a statement from "four eminent physicians," insisted that he was unable for reasons of health to complete the remaining one and one-half years of his fifteen-year term.[2] Two days later, the President accepted Warren's resignation with "a great deal of regret." Warren took that opportunity to send a letter to each senator and representative, notifying them of his actions and summarizing what he considered to be the highlights of his term:

1. elimination of a chaotic situation at the GAO (no Comptroller General for three years, poor relations with the executive branch, low morale);
2. reduction of employees from an April 1946 wartime high of 14,904 to 5,890 (at the time of that letter);
3. collection of illegal payments and debts for the U.S. Treasury in an amount far in excess of the costs of GAO operations;
4. institution of the joint accounting improvement program and the comprehensive audit approach, as well as the accompanying legislation.

Warren concluded this farewell with a reminder of the condition of the GAO when he took office and of his defense against the attack of the Hoover Commission in 1949 and 1950:

> The GAO is *your* agency. To be worth its salt it must continue always to be independent, nonpartisan, and nonpolitical. To be effective, it must always have your wholehearted support and your vigilant safeguarding of its functions and powers. I have no doubt that it will.

The search and designation of a successor to Warren provoked extended conflicts, first between the two houses of Congress and later between some leaders in the Senate and the presidential nominee himself. There seems to have been acceptance on all sides of Warren's position that the Comptroller General is an agent of Congress. Accordingly, Congress undertook to initiate the nomination of someone from its own ranks whom the President would then officially nominate. In 1954, both houses were controlled by the Republicans, and the issue became an intraparty struggle between the two houses. Leaders of the House of Representatives, anxious to preserve their record as the spawning ground for Comptrollers General,[3] selected Congressman W. Sterling Cole (R., N.Y.) and informed the White House of their choice. A lawyer and chairman of the Joint Committee on Atomic Energy, Cole had served nine terms in Congress. In the Senate, where Republicans held a bare majority,[4] the choice for Comptroller General was J. Mark Trice, secretary of the Senate. A lawyer by training, Trice had combined his legal career with service as a Senate page, sergeant-at-arms, secretary for the majority, and secretary for the minority, before assuming his post in January 1953. While Weitzel served as Acting Comptroller General throughout the spring and summer of 1954, neither house would back down or consider any compromise.

In the absence of congressional consensus, Eisenhower informally suggested a compromise candidate, Senator Frederick G. Payne (R., Maine). Although only a first-term Senator, Payne had served as governor of Maine and possessed a background in budgeting and accounting.[5] But Payne's name was not received enthusiastically by congressional party leaders, and the President looked elsewhere.

His choice was Joseph Campbell, whom he had appointed to the Atomic Energy Commission (AEC) a year before. Campbell, a 55-year-old accountant from New York City, had served earlier as treasurer of Columbia University and had worked with Eisenhower when the latter was president of that institution. Although his term on the AEC would not expire until June 30, 1955, Campbell had tired of the work of the commission (and perhaps also of the furor that surrounded the Dixon-Yates contract)[6] and had decided to return to private life. When he accepted Campbell's resignation from the Atomic Energy Commission in September 1954, Eisenhower asked him to consider the vacant position of Comptroller General of the United States. Ten days later, Campbell informed the President that he would accept.[7]

On November 9, 1954, Eisenhower sent his last list of presidential nominees to the Republican-controlled U.S. Senate for its "advice and consent." It included the name of Joseph Campbell to be Comptroller General. The Senate Democrats, led by Minority Leader Lyndon B. Johnson and buoyed by their recent electoral victory through which they would gain majority control of the Senate, postponed any action on "controversial" nominations until the new session in January 1955. Democrats in both houses of Congress criticized the Campbell nomination because of his lack of legislative experience and his association with the Dixon-Yates scandal.[8]

When the Senate adjourned without taking any action on the matter, Eisenhower on December 14, 1954, made a "recess appointment"[9] of Campbell. Later, on January 10, 1955, he sent his official nomination of Joseph Campbell to be Comptroller General of the United States. The

Committee on Government Operations immediately scheduled two days of hearings to receive testimony; although the Democrats had gained a majority and leadership in the Senate, the composition of the committee's senior members remained essentially intact.[10]

Joseph Campbell brought an impressive professional career record in accounting and business management with him to a less-than-enthusiastic Senate Committee on Government Operations. Following his education and military service, Campbell had served in businesses and industrial concerns. He had become a partner in a public accounting firm and had later formed his own firm. Then, in 1941, he had started his service with Columbia University where he became vice president and treasurer and served until 1953. In addition to working with the trustees and University President Dwight D. Eisenhower on a wide range of operational and financial matters (including the management of a sizable endowment and of real estate holdings), Campbell personally supervised the negotiation of up to $85 million in government contracts. During that period, he had occasion to become intimately acquainted with the workings of the federal government. He was heavily involved in the atomic bomb project initially through Columbia University contracts, first with the navy, then with the Office of Scientific Research and Development, then with the Manhattan Engineering District, and finally with the Atomic Energy Commission.[11] Following the war, Campbell had to fit Department of Defense advisory committee meetings (including a chairmanship of the committee that established Brookhaven National Laboratory) into a schedule that already was overcrowded.[12]

As Joseph Campbell testified before the Senate Government Operations Committee on its first day of hearings, he could see a few friendly faces in the room. Senator Bourke B. Hickenlooper (R., Iowa, and vice-chairman of the Joint Committee on Atomic Energy) spoke in Campbell's behalf, saying "there is no man in government for whom I have formed a higher opinion."[13] An equally ringing endorsement of Campbell and of having a CPA as Comptroller General was received from the president of the American Institute of Accountants.[14] But the Republicans could not close their own ranks as Senator Margaret Chase Smith (R., Maine) complained about the President's failure to consult any congressional leaders on the appointment to a legislative agency and about his reluctance to honor the alternation between Senate and House for the appointment.[15]

Chairman McClellan began a Democratic attack by pointing out the nominee's lack of both a legal and legislative background (as opposed to every other Comptroller General to that time, who had possessed both) as well as possible conflicts of interest based on Campbell's service on so many boards of trustees. Although Campbell was able to defend his financial holdings, he had greater difficulty with the barrage of questions concerning his nonlegal background. Senator Henry M. Jackson (D., Wash.) termed the job of Comptroller General as "a quasi-judicial office"[16] and spoke repeatedly of the legal decisions that the Comptroller General must sign. The second day of testimony featured a statement by Senator Albert Gore (D., Tenn.), one of the most persistent critics of Campbell. Gore, who claimed not to be influenced by Dixon-Yates, made the most direct attack on deficiencies in Campbell's background:

> His record is devoid of experiences calculated to steep him in the tradition of the Congress and the urgency for its independence; devoid, too, of experience in interpretation of legislative intent as well as of legal training or judicial review.[17]

Gore then went on to criticize Campbell's appointment directly from the executive branch and his views on making the Atomic Energy Commission (an "independent" agency) more politically responsible to the President.

Campbell, in rebuttal to Gore and with the subsequent endorsement of Senator Karl E. Mundt (R., S.D.), reaffirmed his experience in utilizing the advice of legal counsel as well as in the basic nature of GAO operations, which were more involved with accounting and auditing than legal decisions and claims. Campbell assured the committee of his belief in the independence of auditors and the necessity of serving Congress.

One week later, on March 10, 1955, the Senate Committee on Government Operations approved Campbell's nomination by a vote of eight to four in executive session, and sent the nomination to the full Senate for confirmation. Although the Democrats managed to delay consideration of Campbell's nomination while some reiterated the charges made during the two days of hearings, Senators Gore, Kefauver, Ervin, and others found few joiners in their opposition struggle on the floor of the Senate on May 18, 1955. Predictably, Senator Hickenlooper defended Campbell as a man with "basic honesty and decency," with "impressive experience," and a "leader in his profession."[18] Following a defense of accountants by Senator Payne, the Senate approved President Eisenhower's nomination of Joseph Campbell by voice vote.

Joseph Campbell: The Man and His Administration

Joseph Campbell's tour of duty as Comptroller General began in a congressional storm, and it would end, more than a decade later, in another congressional storm of quite a different kind. His political posture in the government was potentially awkward. He was of course himself a Republican, but through most of his tour the majority of his "bosses" in Congress were Democrats. After 1960, the administration too was Democratic. The effectiveness and the stature of the GAO under these circumstances required more than ever that it maintain its reputation for evenhanded nonpartisanship. The evidence suggests that Campbell was generally successful in this regard. He did not have the advantage of his predecessor, Lindsay Warren, of being a member of the congressional "club." He started with few friends in Congress and rather little experience in working with it. Here too the evidence suggests that Campbell was for the most part successful in overcoming his obstacles. He came to be well respected by many congressmen on both sides of the aisle, and the GAO's reputation for integrity and professional capacity apparently continued to rise during his tenure.

Campbell was the first, and so far the only, accountant to direct the government's General Accounting Office. The fact itself seems somewhat paradoxical, especially in a land that has laid such emphasis on professionalism in public (and private) offices. Even more paradoxical is that his qualifications should be challenged, as they were, on this very ground. But all of his predecessors had been lawyers and came with much experience in, or with, the Congress. He was something of a maverick.

For the most part, he accepted and pushed still further the efforts to reshape the GAO that had begun under Lindsay Warren. The so-called comprehensive audit was extended until it was nearly universal. Centralized voucher checking (except in transportation audits) continued to be eliminated gradually but steadily until it vanished from the GAO scene. There was no effort to reestablish centralized accounts within the GAO. And if anything he pushed harder than Warren had for professionalization in accounting of most of the GAO's upper-level staff. He shared with Warren an almost passionate concern to find, to disclose, and to force the correction of inefficiency and waste of public funds. And he shared with all of his predecessors the insistence upon the independence of the GAO.

But Campbell's operating style was in substantial contrast to that of Lindsay Warren. In the first place, he was much less enthusiastic about working cooperatively with the executive agencies and officials. He personally avoided contacts with other high-level presidential appointees except when they were required by his duties. GAO employees were discouraged from associating with their counterparts in the administration lest they lose their objectivity and independence. He is said to have forbidden the participation of GAO staffers in the federal bowling league for this reason, and to have discouraged their membership in the Federal Government Accountants' Association—even while he was urging those who were qualified to join the American Institute of Certified Public Accountants. The Joint Accounting Improvement Program continued to operate but lost much of its momentum during his tenure. There were few bold cooperative initiatives. The GAO was to assume the stance more of a policeman than collaborator. Although Campbell worked unwaveringly to improve accounting competence in the GAO, there is little evidence that he exerted much effort to do the same in the other agencies of government.

Among those on the present GAO staff who worked under Campbell there is a good deal of difference of opinion about his management. Some liked and admired him, and almost all seem to have respected him. A common, though not universal complaint, is that he insisted upon centralizing control in himself, refused to delegate, and wanted to know everything that went on in the office. Others thought he delegated too much to his line divisions and did not exercise vigorous control over the organization. Some characterize him as a strong and vigorous leader, others as strong but also stubborn and uncommunicative with his staff. He was highly disciplined himself and disciplinary toward others on the staff. Clearly he sought to make the GAO a "tight ship," independent and professional according to the standards of the public accounting fraternity. And he was unafraid to apply those standards and his own standards of integrity when he felt that the course that he and the GAO were pursuing was the right one.

He brought to his office some of the ideology and the ethic of a public accounting firm, examining independently and objectively the honesty, accuracy, and legality of a company's financial condition and statements. In the case of the GAO, the "company" was the executive branch of the government, and the client—the board of directors and shareholders—was Congress and the American people. Campbell described the GAO as "the public accounting agency of the Federal Government."[19] But he accepted the concept of the comprehensive audit, encompassing not only the finances but also the efficiency of management in other aspects of an agency's administration. In this respect, he contrived to push the GAO's scope considerably beyond that of the typical public accountants of his time. Campbell himself described the comprehensive audit as selective; that is, the GAO would pick out the trouble spots—the areas where there were likely to be significant waste or impropriety for intensive review and investigation. GAO reports, especially in the defense area, became increasingly focused upon individual processes, decisions, and particularly contracts that promised to reveal misuse of the taxpayers' dollars. Among other things, as will be shown later, this contributed to a growing emphasis upon defense contracting.

The Second Hoover Commission

Soon after President Eisenhower was inaugurated and more than a year before Joseph Campbell became Comptroller General, a second Hoover Commission was established.[20] Its structure, mode of selection of members, and operating methods (through task forces) were modeled on the first Hoover Commission. There were, however, some important differences. First, the second commission was given jurisdiction to study and make recommendations on public policy as well as on organization and management. Second, it was created and formed by a Republican President and a Republican Congress—although by the time it reported in June 1955 the Democrats had won control of the Senate. Third, its membership and its task forces were generally more conservative and were oriented primarily to the management of private business.[21]

Like the earlier commission, the second one established a task force on budgeting and accounting. Its chairman, J. Harold Stewart, was a CPA and past president of the American Institute of Certified Public Accountants. Its other six members were all CPAs or business executives or both, as were two of its three consultants. Neither the task force nor later the commission itself made any recommendations that would have threatened the status or the powers of the Comptroller General. On the contrary, both expressed their approval of the Joint Accounting Improvement Program and of the work of the GAO. The commission wrote: "The Comptroller General has been, particularly through the General Accounting Office's Accounting Systems Division, an inspiring and constructive influence in developing conscious-ness of the need for accounting reforms in the executive agencies."[22] The bulk of the twenty-five recommendations of the commission were verbatim or slightly modified versions of task force recommendations, and most of them were restatements of objectives previously enunciated by the JAIP and the GAO. It seems safe to surmise that there was considerable consultation with GAO leaders by the task force—and thus indirectly by the commission itself.

The commission's report was short, somewhat technical for the general public, and a good deal less than exciting, even for those who could understand it. Its careful avoidance of the organizational issue surrounding the Comptroller General, which had been a continuing irritant to Mr. Hoover for more than a quarter century, probably dampened widespread interest. Two Democrats on the commission, James A. Farley and Congressman Chet Holifield, made general dissents, primarily on the grounds that the accounting concepts and practices proposed were based on private business experience and were inappropriate to many or most activities of the government. Holifield specifically objected that: "The report tends to exalt the role of accountants." A third member, Congressman Clarence J. Brown, questioned one recommendation, number 7, that proposed appropriations on the basis of accrued expenditures. Otherwise the report was adopted by the commission with little objection or argument.

The commission made two significant recommendations with respect to accounting organization. One was that there be an assistant director of the budget for accounting to develop and promulgate an overall directive for accounting and reporting within the standards prescribed by the GAO and to stimulate the development of competent accounting and auditing staffs throughout the government. The other proposed the establishment in the principal agencies and their subdivisions of comptrollers, apparently modelled on those in the military departments. Both proposals were clearly intended to enhance the quality of accounting in the government, to encourage the professionalization of accounting operations, and to increase the influence of qualified accountants. Neither proposal resulted in legislation, but they apparently did have some, though limited, impact within the administration. President Eisenhower's last two budget directors, Maurice H. Stans and Percival Brundage, were CPAs and they somewhat increased the bureau's emphasis and professional capacities in accounting. A relatively few agencies did in fact establish the office of comptroller, but it did not by any means become a universal or even a general practice.

Most of the other commission recommendations were on themes familiar to the JAIP, the GAO, and indeed the first Hoover Commission: performance classifications and reports; synchronization of organization structures, budget classifications, and accounting systems; cost-based budgets; accrual and cost accounting;[23] better property accounting; better internal auditing in the agencies; and others. Like the earlier Hoover Commission, the second lent outside support and impetus to the movement already being pushed from the inside and particularly within the JAIP, the GAO, and the Bureau of the Budget. In somewhat more specific terms than its predecessor, it urged the linking of management and finance, and of program and performance with budgets, accounts, costs, and reports. A year after the Hoover reports were published, some of the basic elements of such linkage were enacted into law (Public Law 863, August 1, 1956). That law prescribed the accrual basis of accounting within agencies in accordance with principles and standards prescribed by the Comptroller General; cost-based budgets for internal control and as a basis for appropriation requests; and simplified systems for administrative control of funds. It was described by Senator John F. Kennedy, who introduced and cosponsored it, as "the most significant development in the government's financial structure in a decade or more."[24] Kennedy was an optimist, for which he should not be faulted. But passing a law does not make a system, and, for many agencies, it is very likely that the goal implicit in such linkages remains a "will-o'-the-wisp." Nonetheless, that law did stimulate the formation in the framework of the Joint Accounting Improvement Program of a Committee on Defense Participation to develop and install accrual accounting, cost-based budgeting, and related improvements in the military departments and the subsequent adoption of a number of new policies and procedures. Similar work in the civil agencies proceeded apace.

The most significant and later the most controversial of all the commission's recommendations was number 7: "That the executive budget and congressional appropriations be in terms of estimated annual accrued expenditures, namely, charges for the cost of goods and services estimated to be received." A provision embodying this proposal was originally included in the Kennedy Bill of 1956, and it passed the Senate. The House, responding to the leaders of its Appropriations Committee, opposed the provision, and ultimately it was dropped in conference, following a bitter debate between the representatives of the two houses.

That debate continued for the following two years when a number of other bills were introduced—and not passed—providing that budgets be submitted and appropriations passed on the basis of accrued annual expenditures rather than on the basis of the accustomed obligating authority. Comptroller General Campbell strongly recommended it. In his report, dated February 12, 1957, on two Senate bills that would have required it (S.316 and S.434), he wrote:

> The stating of appropriations on an accrued expenditure basis together with the furnishing of cost data to the Congress, as provided by Public Law 863, would provide the best opportunity for improved correlation of programming, budgeting, and accounting. Congressional control of costs and expenditures can only be achieved by the maximum utilization of many tools. The stating of appropriations on an accrued expenditure basis can be made a very important tool for the Congress if effectively installed.[25]

In 1958, a compromise arrangement was worked out whereby appropriations would continue to be made in terms of obligating authority but limitations on accrued expenditures within each fiscal year could be proposed by the President and enacted by Congress for those agencies that the President judged to have their accounts on a satisfactory accrual basis. This compromise was enacted on a temporary and experimental basis, to expire on April 1, 1962, in Public Law 759, August 25, 1958. In his budget proposal for 1960, President Eisenhower proposed accrued expenditure limitations in six appropriations, and, for his 1961 budget, he proposed twelve such limitations. The House Appropriations Committee refused to recommend such ceilings on either occasion, and the legislation died. With it, to all intents and purposes, died the second Hoover Commission's recommendation number 7, which would have put all appropriations on the accrued expenditure basis.

Despite the defeat of its proposals with respect to appropriations on an accrual basis, the second Hoover Commission had a significant impact upon federal financial practices. Professional accounting in subsequent years came more and more to influence federal management generally throughout the government. The Bureau of the Budget increasingly stressed agency budgets based upon costs, which came to be known as "cost-of-performance budgeting." The agencies beefed up their accounting staffs and related their accounts and budgets more closely to general management. The GAO produced an increasing number of manuals and instructions to encourage accrual accounting and, where feasible, accounts and budgets based upon costs. During that period, the profession of accounting reached a new high in its capability and its influence in the federal picture.

Professional Development

The commission's recommendations and the subsequent passage of the Kennedy Bill in 1956 added further outside stimulus to efforts already underway within the GAO. Soon after his appointment as Comptroller General, Campbell embarked upon an ambitious program of professional development in the field of accounting that was, if anything, more aggressive than that of his predecessor, Lindsay Warren. The importance he attached to this program is suggested in his statement before the Independent Offices Subcommittee of the House Appropriations Committee on February 22, 1955:

> From my relatively short experience with the General Accounting Office, I am convinced that our most serious problem is the recruitment of qualified auditors. In the past, the General Accounting Office has made intensive efforts to recruit from the public accounting firms and the colleges and universities, but the results to date have not been sufficient. We need several hundred additional top-flight auditors if we are to adequately carry out our duties and responsibilities. It is my intention to develop every means to obtain the personnel we need.

In 1956, he established an Office of Staff Management to superintend the recruitment, training, and placement of professional personnel in the field of accounting. As director of the new office, he appointed Leo Herbert, a distinguished scholar and practitioner of accounting and auditing from Louisiana, who would serve in that capacity until 1975.[26] Herbert designed and instituted a program of professional development within the GAO that would certainly match or surpass like programs in any other agency, public or private. In the field of recruitment, he obtained authorization from the Civil Service Commission to hire qualified college graduates with majors in accounting without examination and soon was tapping several hundred colleges and universities every year for their top accounting graduates with an intensive outreach program for junior accounting positions in the GAO. In addition, the GAO recruited a few qualified public accountants annually for upper-level hires. During the summer of 1956, he instituted a summer internship program for college-level juniors who might later opt for a career in the GAO. He also began a faculty consultant program to bring in accounting professors so that they might become better acquainted with the

GAO's work and assist in future recruitment. During the Campbell-Herbert years, the number of trained accounting personnel increased steadily and rapidly to the point that they exceeded half of the GAO's staff (see Figures 1 and 2).

The second facet of Herbert's program was in-house training, both for new recruits and for intermediate personnel. The junior appointees were required to take a three-week intensive indoctrination course, followed by several months of on-the-job training. These were followed some months later by a two-week classroom program to equip the juniors to advance to senior levels. A further program of supervisory training was instituted for new supervisors, and specialized courses in particular fields, such as electronic data processing, were also offered. Finally, the GAO offered a CPA review course (after hours in Washington and by correspondence in the field) for those aspiring accountants who sought CPA certificates. The symbol of status and of achievement in the GAO was the CPA, and the professional standing of the organization itself came increasingly to be judged by the proportion of its staff who were CPAs. Campbell waged an unceasing campaign to persuade boards of accountancy in the states to recognize GAO experience as qualifying for the CPA. The number and proportion of the GAO's staff with certificates as CPAs grew impressively during Campbell's term.

The third element of the drive toward professionalism was a placement program, designed to equip all of the GAO's senior professionals to handle almost any type of its work (except legal and clerical). This involved a relatively rapid rotation policy between jobs and between functions, especially at junior levels. New college recruits were rotated among three different jobs with three different supervisors during their first six months. Rotation was less frequent, but still continued after that so that each would have experience in a wide variety of work: systems development, investigations, electronic data processing, and various kinds of audits. The objective was that each person have a complete background before he specialized in any particular field later in his career. As expressed by Herbert: "We need to train each of our accountants and auditors so that he can fulfill the responsibilities of any job at the next level of organization."[27]

The professionalization of the GAO in the field of accounting during the Campbell era was rapid and impressive. Campbell himself later counted it as one of his major achievements as Comptroller General.[28] The small staff of lawyers, who worked principally under the General Counsel, renewed themselves with their own recruitment and training program and were not much affected (although a quite surprising number of present GAO staff have both law degrees and CPAs). In the main, the focus of the staff development program was upon the accounting profession. Campbell endeavored at one point to employ some professional actuaries, principally

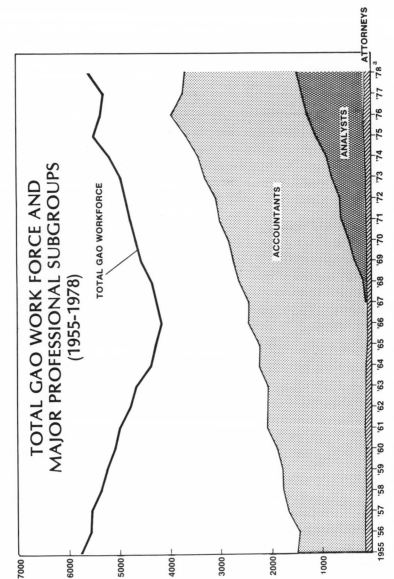

Figure 1

TOTAL GAO WORK FORCE AND
MAJOR PROFESSIONAL SUBGROUPS
(1955-1978)

[a]Based upon their educational and experience backgrounds at time of hiring.

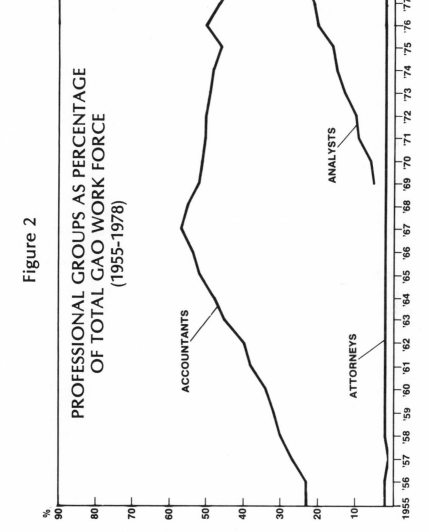

Figure 2

PROFESSIONAL GROUPS AS PERCENTAGE
OF TOTAL GAO WORK FORCE
(1955-1978)

to audit the social security program. But the leaders of the actuarial profession were not in favor, apparently because they did not want certified actuaries reviewing the work of other certified actuaries, and nothing came of it. Otherwise, virtually no professionals from fields other than accounting and law were appointed to the GAO until 1967 after Campbell's resignation.

Implicit in the drive toward accounting professionalism was the conviction that academic training in accounting was the best preparation for all the professional work in the GAO save the legal work. Implicit too was the assumption that an accountant, properly trained and experienced, could perform all the variegated duties of the GAO in all the fields of activity of the national government, even though some of those duties had little to do with financial accounts. During the 1950s and early 1960s, most of its studies had a financial orientation but the emphasis was declining even then. The GAO accounting, or auditing, specialist was being forced by the changing orientation of the agency to become a generalist, well beyond the traditional definition of an accountant.

The GAO Reorganization of 1955-1956

The drive toward an improved caliber of accounting professionalism along generalist lines was but one of several motivating factors that led the Comptroller General to a basic reorganization of the GAO in 1955 and 1956. Others included: increasing concern about losses of public funds through government contracts with private industries; the growth of defense expenditures, especially through contractors; the investigation and recommendations of a congressional subcommittee (the Lipscomb report); and, apparently, declining interest in joint and collaborative programs in accounting systems of executive agencies. The backgrounds of some of these elements are sketched below.

Government Contracts: The "Cheese Squeeze" and the "Zinc Stink"

Comptroller General Warren had laid relatively little emphasis upon government procurement and contracts in his drive to reorient the GAO. On the other hand, in the aftermath of the Korean War, a number of congressional committees had built their public reputations through investigations of alleged extravagance and losses to the government because of loose procedures in negotiating and controlling contracts. These had been conducted usually without benefit of GAO resources. Almost from the beginning of his incumbency, Campbell launched studies of individual contracts, providing fodder for congressional revelations and thus also enhancing the esteem for GAO's independent audits. Early audits of strategic stockpile purchases by the General Services Administration revealed windfall corporate profits and alleged kickback provisions. In the case of copper purchases, Senator John J. Williams (R., Del.) attacked the government's failure to recover $400,000 from three firms, while the House Government Operations Committee publicized a $1 million overpayment for tungsten. Each instance resulted in ample publicity for the GAO's investigation and the oversight capability of Congress.

The legal powers of the GAO were also utilized extensively in Campbell's strategy. An early legal opinion (September 21, 1955) on the improper nature of a $240 million contract between the U.S. Air Force and Western Electric made it possible for House Majority Leader John W. McCormack (D., Mass.) to gain publicity (in the *New York Times* and *Wall Street Journal*) on "how far big business has obtained control of our government." A combination of audit and legal work propelled Emmanuel Cellar (D., N.Y., chairman of the House Committee on the Judiciary) to hold extensive hearings on airline anti-trust activities and the Civil Aeronautics Board, following the GAO's determination that regulated airline fares cost American consumers millions of dollars annually.

One of the best illustrations of GAO activities in this area concerned the purchase of cheese by the Department of Agriculture's Commodity Credit Corporation, which resulted in a $2 million windfall profit for large food processors. Campbell's decision that the manner in which the Department of Agriculture purchased the cheese (42,000 tons) and later resold it to the same companies at a lower price was illegal was prompted by a request from Congressman L. H. Fountain (D., N.C.). While Campbell insisted that the GAO had no legal basis for ordering a "voluntary" refund from the companies, he did encourage Fountain's subcommittee of the House Government Operations Committee to seek an appropriate explanation and some action from Agriculture Secretary Ezra Taft Benson and the Justice Department. Although Benson obtained a contradictory legal opinion on the legality of the contract from Attorney General Herbert Brownell, continued pressure from Fountain and continued publicity in Drew Pearson's "Washington Merry-Go-Round" kept Campbell and the GAO in the forefront of the "cheese squeeze," as it came to be known in the GAO, and solidly against government "irresponsibility."

But not all of the GAO's products had as favorable results. At that time, the GAO still included a sizable Office of Investigations, of about 240 employees, nearly two thirds of whom worked out of some thirty field offices and suboffices. It was entirely divorced from the Division of Audits both at headquarters and in the field and pretty much ran its own program of surveys, inspections, and investigations into almost any facet of any federal agency (or contractor) to examine and report on evidence of mismanagement, inefficiency, fraud, or other irregularity. Staffed largely by investigators (including some alumni from the FBI), rather than trained accountants, it did not pursue the carefully checked and documented procedures of the auditors, and could give rise to embarrassment to the GAO because of charges that it was unable to back up its allegations adequately.

The most celebrated instance was the episode in 1955 that is still referred to by GAO employees as the "zinc stink." Very briefly, it arose from an investigation by the Office of Investigations of the government's purchase by the Defense Materials Procurement Agency (DMPA) of zinc for its strategic stockpile program. Before the GAO report was issued, a copy of its summary was provided, on request, to Senator John J. Williams (R., Del.), who entered the information in the *Congressional Record* and issued a press release that was widely publicized. The report alleged or suggested, among other things: that there was doubt about the need for zinc production at the time; that the types of contracts used were unfavorable to the government; and that there was a possible conflict of interest involved on the part of the deputy administrator of the DMPA who was a "dollar a year" man and whose regular job was president of American Zinc, Lead and Smelting Company, which allegedly profited from the transaction.

In response to vigorous reactions from the press and from the parties concerned, the Joint Congressional Committee on Defense Production held three days of hearings on the subject on July 6, 14, and 27, 1955, in which the top leadership of the GAO and the DMPA as well as representatives of the zinc industries testified. The hearings were acrimonious and inconclusive, but none of the organizations involved came out very well. Comptroller General Campbell was compelled in the last hearing to admit errors in the report and failure to delve deeply enough on certain questions before arriving at conclusions and releasing them for public scrutiny. On many of the major points in the report, he did not back down, but the net effect of the hearings was damaging to the GAO's reputation for thoroughness and factual reliability. In the final minutes of the last hearing, Senator Homer E. Capehart (R., Ind.), the ranking Republican senator on the joint committee, in addressing Assistant Comptroller General Weitzel, said:

> My assumption was you could have found out the truth of this matter, and I think this hearing this morning has perfectly revealed that. . . . Now the thing I object to, and still object to, is that you fellows come in here as prosecuting attorneys—and you have taken that position all the way through—when your job, as I understand it, is to be factual and is to advise us and be just as much interested in defending one side as you are condemning another. Now, maybe I am wrong about it. However, my observation of your attitude all the way through has been one of fighting this thing, of condemning this man and I do not think that is your job. . . . Frankly, I sort of resented it, and I still resent it.[29]

The "zinc stink" raised a number of questions about the GAO's policies and operations: the use of "punitive" investigations by an independent auditing agency; whether reports should not be reviewed by agencies and individuals concerned before release to Congress or to the public; at what stage reports suggesting illegal behavior should go to the Justice

Department; and, perhaps most crucially, whether a separate Office of Investigations should continue to exist.

The Lipscomb Report

Several months before the zinc hearings, in February 1955, a special subcommittee of the House Government Operations Committee had been constituted to study the organization and administration of the GAO. The subcommittee's report, issued in June 1956,[30] represented the first complete review by the GAO's overseeing committee in the House of the ocean of changes that had occurred since 1945. In addition to the "special" designation of the subcommittee and the lack of any systematic oversight of the GAO for six years, the subcommittee was extraordinary in its membership. It was originally composed only of Congressman William L. Dawson (D., Ill., chairman of the full committee) and Glenard P. Lipscomb (R., Calif.), who was also a senior partner in a public accounting firm.[31] Since the bulk of the subcommittee's work and recommendations stemmed from personal interest on the part of the Republican, its product is still referred to as "the Lipscomb report."

The views of Congressman Lipscomb and Comptroller General Campbell, both experienced professionals in accounting, were generally "simpatico" with respect to the objectives and role of the GAO. This seems clear from the decisions on policy and operations taken by Campbell during the period of the committee's existence. Most of Lipscomb's specific recommendations had already been implemented before his report was published. Their differences, as reflected in Campbell's subsequent response to the Lipscomb report in November, 1956,[32] were largely matters of degree, speed, and practicality—not of substance. Both shared the views that the GAO should perform as the government's public accounting firm; that it should concentrate on detailed criticisms of the adequacy and effectiveness of the executive agencies; that it should be independent and free from executive influence; and that it should emphasize its disclosure activities for Congress.[33] Lipscomb urged that the GAO not give "too much consideration to revision of draft reports in response to the views of the agencies before sending the reports to the Congress."[34] But the Comptroller General insisted that it was essential to ascertain all the relevant facts prior to release of its reports and that this required that top agency officials review them and provide such additional information as was relevant. He excepted from this procedure drafts of "investigative reports"—presumably like that produced in the zinc investigation.

The Lipscomb report indicated that the GAO had not carried out the provisions of the Legislative Reorganization Act of 1946 (in its Section 206) directing it to make "an expenditure analysis of each agency in the executive branch" and report its findings to the appropriations, operations, and legislative committees of Congress. It noted that Congress had made no specific appropriations for this purpose and asked the Comptroller General to report on whether implementation was feasible and to recommend "repeal, modification, or implementation of section 206." Campbell responded, in effect, that complete implementation was not possible and that the comprehensive audit program would accomplish most of its purposes. He proposed new legislative language to support this kind of approach.

The main thrust of Lipscomb's other recommendations, however, amounted to a general endorsement of Campbell's policies and efforts, many of which had been given effect by the time the Lipscomb report was issued. They included the extension of comprehensive auditing to more agencies, particularly in the area of defense; abolishment of the Accounting Systems Division as a separate entity; and consideration of whether the Office of Investigations should continue as a separate organization.

Reorganization

In November 1955, Comptroller General Campbell notified the GAO staff of his basic decisions to reshape the organization.[35] Somewhat modified and extended, these were put into effect between then and July 1956. Among their major objectives were to place more emphasis upon auditing in the defense area; to make a clear-cut organizational division between line operations (mainly the audit work plus claims) and staff work (almost everything else); to eliminate the confusion of several GAO divisions intervening in the same executive agencies in an uncoordinated fashion; to extend the comprehensive audit more rapidly; to enlarge and improve GAO professional capabilities in its audit work; to integrate field operations; and to provide a base for systematic relations with Congress.

The organizational pattern that Campbell instituted in 1955-1956 would survive with only slight changes for about fifteen years (until 1971-1972). The only significant structural change during that period was the establishment of the International Division in 1963. The main features of the Campbell reorganization therefore deserve some emphasis.

In the first place, he bifurcated the Division of Audits, then by far the largest of all, into the Defense Accounting and Auditing and the Civil Accounting and Auditing divisions, the latter receiving the larger share of staff. Second, he abolished the Accounting Systems Division, merging its operational work of cooperative development of accounting systems and review of systems in place with auditing responsibilities. The development of general accounting and auditing standards was moved to a new staff Office of Accounting and Auditing Policy. In July of 1956, he abolished the Office of Investigations and joined its work and personnel with the two auditing divisions. Its field offices were also eliminated and their activities and personnel were merged with the existing regional organizations of the old

Division of Audits. The field organizations were headed by a new Division of Field Operations. An Office of Staff Management was set up to recruit and develop professional personnel in accounting and auditing; but the old Personnel Office continued for nonprofessionals. A new Office of Legislative Liaison was established.

Some of the older offices (General Counsel and Administrative Services) and divisions (Claims and Transportation) were not significantly affected. But the impact upon the others, particularly the Office of Investigations and the Accounting Systems Division, was traumatic. A considerable number of their personnel, from the top down, resigned or were encouraged to leave.

The effects of the Campbell reorganization were generally, but not wholly, consonant with the themes of the earlier Warren period. They certainly contributed to the professional competence of GAO personnel and to the dominance of the accounting profession in the GAO. On the other hand, the elimination of the Accounting Systems Division was a setback to the cooperative work with executive agencies toward improving accounting practices, and the joint program thereafter had declining momentum for many years. The audit program, labeled under Campbell as "comprehensive but selective," moved ahead, both in the civil and defense areas. But the organizational division between the two led to a widening distance in objectives and policies, in communications, and indeed in mutual respect.

Both divisons were internally organized on the basis of the government agencies audited. Thus, each major agency or cluster of agencies was audited under the leadership of an assistant director of audits, whose staff, in the case of the Civil Division, was housed on the site—in the agency's headquarters. In the case of civil audits, the basic initiatives and decisions on projects were made by these directors on the sites, subject to periodic job reviews by the division chief and his associates. The Comptroller General apparently played a secondary role in these decisions except where there was vigorous congressional interest. The Civil Audits Division tended to lay heavier emphasis on broad programs and problems of management with less focus on individual and nonrecurring events. On the contrary, the Defense Audits Division increasingly concentrated on individual actions where excessive costs or other faults could be found, most specifically on defense contracts.

Defense Contracting and the Congress

During the term of Comptroller General Campbell, there was increasing emphasis in GAO audits upon expenditures for defense and particularly upon defense contracts with private companies and other organizations in the private sector. This was in part a consequence simply of the enormous amounts of the federal budget for defense purposes and the large portion of those expenditures that went to private contractors. For many of those years, defense expenditures amounted to about half of the federal budget; and nearly half of that defense total was for research, development, and production, conducted for and paid by the government in the private sector. Public concern was enhanced by widespread reports of excessive profits of defense contractors, cost overruns, delays, inadequacies, and sometimes outright failures in the carrying out of contracts. It was further agitated by alleged "buddy" relationships of military and civilian officials in the military establishment and related agencies, such as the Atomic Energy Commission, with private industries, particularly those whose business in large part depended upon defense contracts. A considerable number of public officials, military and civilian, retired from the government to assume top posts with private industries, often the same ones with which they had been negotiating in behalf of the government.

During World War II, the GAO had gained experience in reviewing defense contracts, but it was not until 1951 that Congress granted it permanent authority to examine records of private companies incident to negotiated contracts.[36] There were basically three types of contracts at that time. The first was based upon advertisements and competitive bidding, which was the standard procedure in peacetime until World War II. The second was based upon negotiated agreements as to costs plus a fixed fee, and the third was premised upon the negotiation of the anticipated price at the time of the contracting to or from which the contractor could make a profit or take a loss. The great bulk of defense contracting was on one of the latter, negotiated bases. The GAO had no special investigative powers with respect to the advertised, competitive contracts. But the 1951 act gave it authority, where competitive bidding was not feasible, to investigate and audit company records involved in negotiated contracts of either of the latter two types.

The Defense Department and other agencies favored contracts (known as incentive contracts) based upon estimated costs with provisions for additional profits for "savings" below these estimates to those predicated on costs plus a fixed fee. It argued that this provided contractors with an incentive to save the government's money. A number of congressmen led by Carl Vinson (D., Ga.), Chairman of the House Committee on Armed Services, felt that the contractors were repeatedly stealing from the government by overestimating their prior estimates as a proper reward for their efficiency of performance. The GAO, through its audits in the late 1950s and early 1960s, offered countless examples of this practice and, in a growing number of cases, urged that the agencies ask the contractors to make voluntary repayments of what it considered to be excessive profits.[37] Consequent to these reports and other events, starting about 1959, Vinson began seeking legislation to curb excess profits, particularly in incentive contracts. He received abundant assistance from the GAO, which in fact drafted or participated in drafting various versions of the bill, which eventually in 1962 was enacted as the Truth in Negotiations Act.[38] In 1960,

Comptroller General Campbell testified that the basic essentials in protecting the government's interests in negotiated contracts were maximum competition; complete, accurate, and timely cost information; and selection of the proper type of contract.[39]

Vinson's first efforts passed the House but failed in the Senate. They were generally resisted by the Department of Defense and by representatives of defense contractors. But in 1962, the House passed a bill directed at incentive contracts. The Senate extended it with GAO assistance to cover all large-scale negotiated contracts (over $100,000), and in this form it became law.

The Truth in Negotiations Act was hailed by the chairman of the House Armed Services Subcommittee on Special Investigations, F. Edward Hebert (D., La.), and later in the same words by Comptroller General Campbell in his *Annual Report* for 1962, as doing four important things:

First, it requires more purchasing by formal advertised bidding;
Second, it requires clearer written justification when certain negotiating authority is used;
Third, it will require and produce more competition on negotiated purchasing; and
Fourth, it will safeguard the government against inflated cost estimates on negotiated cost contracts.

Among other things, the bill required advertised, competitive bidding except under certain conditions, specified as exemptions, and required in negotiated contracts that the contractor certify that "the cost or pricing data he submitted was accurate, current, and complete." If it was not, the government could recover the amount by which it had been overcharged. The GAO was made the policeman of the legislation, and it soon became a continuing critic of the implementing regulations in the Defense Department and of the manner in which they were applied. Subsequent events in fact led to a good deal of disillusionment as to the law's effectiveness, both in Congress and in the GAO.[40]

Both before and after the act, the GAO pursued its responsibilities with respect to negotiated contracts with increasing energy. It conducted hundreds of audits in private companies of individual contracts—audits of the fullness and accuracy of their price estimates, of the allowability of their costs and cost increases, of their profits, and so on. Most of its reports were directed to individual contracts and subcontracts of private companies, and almost all dealt primarily or exclusively with deficiencies in the contracts or in their execution that would cost the government money. They named the companies involved and sometimes the names of individual public officials, whom the GAO judged responsible for permitting the alleged deficiencies. A few made front-page stories in the newspapers under headlines with expressions like "excessive prices," "overcharges," "unnecessary costs," "wasteful practices," and so on, some of which were drawn directly from the titles of the GAO reports.

The extent and depth of access to the records of private companies by GAO auditors was repeatedly challenged, and in one outstanding case on the question, *United States* v. *Hewlett-Packard,*[41] the courts affirmed the GAO's power, though the case required five years of litigation. And the powers of GAO to enforce its findings varied from situation to situation. In some cases, it could suspend payments pending further information and negotiation; where there was in its judgment a clear violation of law, it could disallow payments already made; in certain instances, it could refer cases to the Department of Justice; where no recourse to law was available, it could ask the contracting departments to request "voluntary refunds" of what it deemed excessive charges, relying upon the sanctions of corporate "conscience" and public spirit, or of threats to possible future contracts, or of publicity and public opinion. And, of course, it could always report to Congress and the press.

The authors of the original Budget and Accounting Act could hardly have anticipated that their creation, the GAO, would become seriously involved in the internal management and accounting of private businesses, even though their provision of powers to investigate "application" of public funds could be construed to authorize such activity. Subsequent legislation mandated some such auditing, though its extent and its proper boundaries are still not clear. With the development of "government by contract" and the growing suspicion of defense profiteering, one might reasonably argue that the organization created to protect the public purse and to be the watchdog for Congress would have been derelict had it not pursued the activities, the performance, and the costs of business contractors. Further, a number of the committees, subcommittees, and individual members of Congress had requested and even urged GAO inquiries into the practices of defense contractors.

But the GAO was treading on porous ground, nearly quicksand, as it pursued its inquiries into the pricing and charges of defense contracts. Not only was it challenging the largest and most powerful congeries of organizations in the U.S. government—the Defense Department, the Atomic Energy Commission, and others—it was taking on many of the most powerful corporations in the private and "twilight" sectors of the economy—Lockheed, Boeing, General Motors, Westinghouse, Ford, and Hewlett-Packard, to mention a few. The issue was raised by a group of the Congress that one might have expected to support the GAO: the Military Operations Subcommittee of the House Committee on Government Operations, chaired by Congressman Chet Holifield.[42] In response to complaints of some of the defense contractors, the staff of the subcommittee initiated investigations into defense contracting with particular reference to GAO audits in the early 1960s. These studies culminated in extended hearings, beginning in May, 1965, which continued sporadically into July of that year,[43] and which resulted in a report, *Defense Contract Audits,* by the

House Committee on Government Operations on March 23, 1966. The hearings, which with accompanying documents and statements totalled more than 1,000 pages, many in very small print, were probably the most extensive published inquiry into the subject of GAO auditing of contracts to that time. The main topic of the hearings was not the conduct and performance of contracts between the government and private industry, though some of these matters were inevitably discussed, but the nature and propriety of GAO inquiries and audits of such contracts. From the outset, the GAO was the "defendant." Witnesses for the "prosecution" apparently included the majority of the subcommittee and its staff, procurement officials of the federal agencies concerned (mainly in the Defense Department and the Atomic Energy Commission), representatives of private businesses who were heavily involved, and representatives of trade associations.

In his opening statement, Congressman Holifield set the tone and the objective:

> This series of hearings will be directed mainly to contract issues and problems. In view of the great concern that has been shown in industry circles and, recently, in the Department of Defense, over the difficult and sometimes awkward situations created by the GAO audit reports, we believe it is timely to air these problems in public hearings, with all affected parties invited to state their case and to discuss freely their concerns.

More than twenty witnesses testified during the hearings. About half of these represented individual contracting firms or trade associations, and nearly half represented executive agencies, principally from various elements of the Defense Department but also including top officials of the Atomic Energy Commission, the Department of Justice, and the Bureau of the Budget. Almost all of these offered criticisms of the GAO and its practices.[44] The Comptroller General and later the Acting Comptroller General appeared on three different occasions to explain and to defend the GAO record.

The critical tenor of the hearings was established by the first witness, Paul R. Ignatius, assistant secretary of defense (installations and logistics). After noting the sharp increase in the number of GAO reports on defense procurement (from 74 in 1962 to 213 in 1964), Ignatius cited three areas of disagreement between the Department of Defense and the GAO. The first of these concerned the alleged challenge by the GAO of the integrity of government contracts, particularly in its efforts to secure voluntary refunds from contractors when it judged prices or costs to be excessive. Second was the GAO's alleged criticisms or undermining of fixed price contracts in favor of contracts that could be modified on the basis of costs. Third was the GAO's alleged insistence upon government involvement in managerial decisions of private contractors, exemplified particularly by its recommendations that contractors use government-owned computers (and other property) rather than leasing them at government expense. Subsequent witnesses criticized GAO practices and reports on a great variety of grounds: that it was seeking and disclosing business information that should have been private; that it was searching for and publicizing only deficiencies and overlooking favorable aspects of government contracts; that it was identifying companies and individuals as "culprits" and reporting them to the Justice Department before they had an opportunity to defend themselves; that it was seeking favorable publicity for itself; that it was substituting the judgment of its accountants for that of the responsible managers; that it was duplicating the audit activities of the departments; that it was undermining the profit motive and the free enterprise system; and many others.

The responses of the Comptroller General and his various assistants to most of these charges were vigorous and factual. They argued that the GAO had pursued honestly and aggressively the purposes sought in national legislation. Its investigations and actions had been legal, its reports basically correct and defensible. With regard to most of the individual cases raised by the staff of the subcommittee and by the witnesses, its explanations and justifications were persuasive, even though sometimes debatable. The charges themselves were seldom specific with respect to individual contracts and GAO reports. With respect to the GAO's own policies, procedures, and tactics, the GAO responses were sometimes fuzzy and evasive, especially concerning the criteria that guided the choice of contracts to audit, the focusing of reports on particular contracts and contractors, the revelation of names of responsible officials, and other matters. Yet on the whole, the reader of the Holifield hearings, with the advantage of 20-20 vision a dozen years later, comes away with the feeling that the GAO performed reasonably well in its posture as the people's David against the military-industrial Goliath.

In the midst of the Holifield inquiry, Comptroller General Campbell retired for reasons of health (effective July 31, 1965), and the closing testimony for the GAO was rendered by Frank H. Weitzel, then Acting Comptroller General of the United States.[45] Several months later, on March 23, 1966, the House Committee on Government Operations submitted its report, *Defense Contract Audits*, which summarized its findings, raised questions, and in general endorsed decisions already made by the Acting Comptroller General. Weitzel had written a letter to Congressman Holifield on March 4, which was appended to the committee's report. His letter announced that the GAO had reconsidered its policies and practices with regard to government contracting and had determined upon a number of changes. Among the more important themes of the letter were that henceforth:

- the GAO would produce broader studies, focused on causes of deficiencies rather than publicizing individual cases, and therefore the reports would be fewer in number and more comprehensive;
- it would emphasize constructive and corrective changes for the future rather than focusing on errors in the past;
- it would guard more carefully business information of a confidential nature and would report on it only after careful review by top-level GAO officials;
- names and titles of alleged official offenders and recommendations for discipline would not be included in its reports;
- it would not mention in its reports referrals of individual cases to the Department of Justice;
- the titles of its reports would be phrased in constructive and less controversial terms.

The Holifield report was not unanimously supported by the Government Operations Committee. The most vigorous dissent was that of Congressman Jack Brooks (D., Texas), who would a decade later succeed Holifield as Chairman of the House Government Operations Committee. He felt that the report was an effort to muzzle the GAO and to inhibit it from aggressive and fearless inquiry into and disclosure of the facts about defense contracts. He wrote:

> The recommendations and conclusions in this report can only intensify the difficulties confronting the GAO in maintaining an effective contract audit system and in carrying out many other vitally important responsibilities for the Congress of the United States.[46]

The other dissents pursued similar themes. But the Holifield version prevailed.

It would appear from the Weitzel letter and from the subsequent performance of the GAO that the Holifield inquiry gave rise to major changes in the GAO's approach to the whole problem of auditing contracts with private business. The number of reports on defense contracts did decline; their content became more general, their titles less explosive; names were usually omitted. In its report, which was not issued until 1968, the Holifield Committee itself declared that "there has been, in fact, a definite shift of GAO personnel from direct contract auditing to other defense areas."[47]

But the degree to which changes should be attributed to the Holifield inquiry remains debatable. In the spring of 1966, the incoming Comptroller General, Elmer B. Staats, declined to review or criticize the draft of the letter Weitzel was preparing for Holifield. He later stated that "the approach in

Weitzel's letter is one I can support on defense contracts."[48] Staats does not now feel that the Holifield hearings were a particularly significant event in the GAO's history. The basic changes, he thinks, derived from the Truth in Negotiations Act and the development and improved performance of the Defense Contract Audit Agency, which relieved the GAO of many of its onerous tasks in contract auditing. According to one GAO official, the only effect was to change and soften the titles of the GAO's reports, but others felt that the inquiry brought about fairly basic changes in its approach to defense contracts. A most outspoken critic, Richard F. Kaufman, wrote: "The hearings had whacked the GAO in the head, and in some ways it has still not recovered."[49] In a later article he referred to the GAO as a "one-eyed watchdog," largely because he felt it had backed away from defense contract auditing.[50]

Recapitulation

The second decade of the second GAO was in many ways a logical progression of the basic thrusts of the first decade. Less and less effort was directed to the centralized checking of financial transactions until it virtually vanished from the GAO scene. This meant, among other things, that there was greater reliance placed upon the agencies in developing and operating their own accounting systems, including the internal auditing of transactions. The total staff of the GAO continued to decline, reaching a low of 4,148 in 1966, but the professional staff of accountants steadily rose until they comprised a majority of the total staff. The number of attorneys as well as the nature of their work remained about the same, though the number of its decisions grew.

There were, however, significant shifts in emphasis in the accounting and auditing work. In the first place, the abolishment of the Accounting Systems Division in 1956 began a decline in efforts to help the agencies in developing their accounting systems. More attention was given to developing and prescribing standards for agency accounting systems and then reviewing those in place and approving or disapproving them. In 1959, the name of the Joint Accounting Improvement Program was broadened to "Joint Financial Management Improvement Program." It continued to operate and each year issued a report of accomplishments. But the leadership and impetus once provided by the GAO and its accounting systems staff declined, and in fact the principals of the Joint Accounting Improvement Program—the Comptroller General, the secretary of the treasury, and the director of the budget—did not meet at all for several years.

The term *comprehensive auditing* had been introduced after World War II to distinguish the kinds of general, on-site auditing from the older voucher checking conducted in the GAO's central offices. From the layman's point of view, it was probably always something of a misnomer as applied to most government programs other than corporations.[51] In fact few such audits were conducted on a totally inclusive basis. The practice developed, and is now formalized, of first conducting a broad and fairly superficial "survey" of an organization's affairs, selecting the area or areas that appeared most in need of an audit, and then conducting an intensive investigation of those areas. In fact, the term *comprehensive audit* gradually fell into disuse.[52]

It is probable, though not provable, that during the Campbell term GAO audits focused increasingly on efficiency and economy of agency operations with declining emphasis upon reports dealing more strictly with financial accuracy and adequacy of accounts and accounting techniques. They comprehended the need for things and services purchased, the reasonableness of prices, and the effective use of resources—that is, the efficacy of management in general. During the Campbell period, audits in a few cases extended to an assessment of program results—a portent of things to come.[53] Thus, even as the dominance of accountants in the GAO staff grew, the nature of the work extended further and further beyond the accustomed duties of that profession.

Campbell's reorganization of 1956 had important and lasting effects on the internal operations of the GAO. The two new accounting and auditing divisions, civil and defense, became strong, nearly autonomous organizations. Each had vigorous and aggressive leadership and the social as well as the organizational distance between the two grew to something resembling a chasm. Though each was internally organized primarily on the basis of the individual government agencies dealt with, their perceptions of purpose and their modus operandi differed sharply, and there was little communication between them. After the establishment of the International Division in 1963, likewise quite independent of the others, there were, as one observer put it, three GAOs, each a power center unto itself. He might have said that there were four GAOs, because the attorneys who inhabited the Office of the General Counsel were also different, separate, and powerful.

Addendum 1: The Dixon-Yates Controversy

The Dixon-Yates affair, which arose during the first years of the Eisenhower administration, became one of the most heated political issues at the time and a focal issue between liberals (mostly Democrats) and conservatives (mostly Republicans). It also became an issue of official morality. It was one of the most complicated situations in recent times, and it is impossible to summarize here except in the most generalized terms. It was the subject of many articles and a few books.[54] Underlying it was a basic theme of the Eisenhower campaign in 1952 and of his administration: to reduce, or at least to restrain, the incursion of government into the private sector, particularly in the field of electric power.

It began, long before the Eisenhower presidency, with a formal agreement between the city of Memphis, Tennessee, and the Tennessee Valley Authority that the latter should provide power to Memphis until 1958. Some months before the Eisenhower election in 1952, the TVA sought appropriations to build a steam power plant at Fulton, Tennessee, to supply the growing needs of Memphis. Later, to counteract this proposal, which would have carried the TVA's power production business well beyond the borders of the Tennessee Valley, the Eisenhower administration sought other alternatives that would restrain TVA growth and assure the development of the private power industry. The administration, working principally through top officials of the White House, the Bureau of the Budget, and the Atomic Energy Commission, developed a proposal with representatives of private electric utilities in the south to produce the electricity for Memphis from privately owned power sources built on contract with the AEC. The arrangement would be negotiated between the AEC (specifically its chairman, Lewis L. Strauss) and the private utility representatives, bypassing the TVA. The power would be bought by the TVA and sold to Memphis. The utility representatives were Edgar H. Dixon, president of the Middle South Utility System, and Eugene A. Yates, chairman of the board of the Southern Company, a utility holding company. The TVA and its Democratic supporters in Congress and elsewhere viewed the Dixon-Yates contract as a first step in destroying the TVA, an improper if not illegal action of the AEC, and an excessive if not fraudulent gift of public funds to private utilities. The fight raged for two years, 1953 to 1955, when the City of Memphis decided to build its own steam plant. President Eisenhower, who had ordered the AEC to negotiate the contract, was compelled on July 11, 1955, to direct that it be cancelled. Subsequently, Dixon-Yates sued the government for the costs it had incurred and ultimately lost in a decision of the Supreme Court.

Although the GAO was not a directly involved party in Dixon-Yates, the long-range impact on it may well have been more important than on any other organization. It was called upon a number of different times for reports or testimony on various questions. Its representative on all of these occasions was Frank Weitzel, first in his capacity as Acting Comptroller General and later, after Campbell's nomination, as Assistant Comptroller General because Campbell had disqualified himself, having previously served on the commission. Aaron Wildavsky described Weitzel's performance on one of these occasions as "brilliant."[55]

The first involvement of the GAO was in May 1954 when representative Chet Holifield, then a leading minority member of the Joint Committee on Atomic Energy, became interested in the Dixon-Yates proposal and wrote the GAO requesting information about it. Weitzel responded in a letter recommending that consideration be given to granting the contract to the lowest bidder after advertising. Later, in September, when the Joint

Committee on Atomic Energy asked the GAO for comments on the terms of the contract, Weitzel sent, and subsequently testified about, a detailed critique and suggested that the contractor might "make a killing at the expense of the Government." Apparently in response to Weitzel's objections, the administration forced changes in the contract, and in November Weitzel testified that the changes had met his principal objections.

In July 1955, the chairman of the Atomic Energy Commission requested a ruling from the GAO as to whether the commission could spend its appropriation to terminate the Dixon-Yates contract. Weitzel later informed the commission that the conflict-of-interest statutes might have been violated and that no settlement should be made that did not reserve to the government the power to have the issue judicially determined. This was a major reason why the Dixon-Yates combine went to court to sue the government for its costs. Eventually the Supreme Court ruled that there had been indeed a conflict of interest.[56]

More important, however, for the future of the GAO was the fact that, when the Dixon-Yates contract was being considered, Joseph Campbell was a member of the Atomic Energy Commission. He apparently did not play an active role, but he was the only member of the commission who supported the chairman, Lewis L. Strauss, and voted for the contract. This created difficulties for Campbell with the Democratic Congress and particularly with representative Chet Holifield, who would later become chairman of the House Government Operations Committee. It also created difficulties within the GAO in the relationship between the Comptroller General and the Assistant Comptroller General. The continuing inquiries to Weitzel and his responses, which by inference were critical of his boss, were a source of embarrassment and estrangement between the two men. It is interesting that Campbell directed so much of the GAO's attention to government contracts with private industry after having been "burned" by the Dixon-Yates contract.

Addendum 2: Accrual Accounting and the Federal Financial System

Historically and to this day, federal accounting has been based upon two elements: obligations and the movement of cash—that is, cash expenditures and receipts. What Congress appropriates is new obligating authority (now called budget authority and including the authority to lend money). This is authority to enter into obligations that generally result in immediate or future expenditures of government funds (now called outlays and including loans). Cash expenditures and receipts are recorded as of the time the money actually moves. The overall size of the budget for any given year is normally stated in terms of cash expenditures and receipts, and the relation between the two determines the condition of balance, surplus, or deficit.

For many elements in the budget, as in the payment for personal services, obligations and cash expenditures usually occur at about the same time. But when the government commits itself to a future payment through a contract or a grant, for example, the obligation and the actual payment may be temporally separated by months and years. This is particularly true in the cases of construction, large-scale (not off-the-shelf) procurement, research and development contracts, project grants to state and local governments, and so on. When these kinds of outlays are substantial, neither obligations nor cash expenditures provide an appropriate base for relating the costs of a program or activity to the actual work performed or results achieved.

The accrual basis of accounting, which is in addition to and not a substitute for obligation and cash accounting, is essential for developing information on program costs.

> Accrued expenditures are the charges incurred during a given period requiring the provision of funds for:
> (1) Goods and other tangible property received;
> (2) Services performed by employees, contractors, grantees, lessors, and other payees; and
> (3) Amounts becoming owed under programs for which no performance or current services are required (such as annuities, insurance claims, other benefit payments, and some cash grants).
> Expenditures accrue regardless of when cash payments are made.[57]

In most normal cases, when a contractor provides goods or services, they are recorded as accrued expenditures when they are received by the government. "However, when a contractor manufactures or fabricates goods or equipment to the Government's specifications, *constructive receipt* occurs in each accounting period when the contractor earns a portion of the contract price, and the accrual takes place as the work is performed"[58] (emphasis added).

Similarly, income accrues when it becomes due or legally owed, regardless of when the cash is received. It is perfectly possible for agencies to keep their accounts on an accrual (as well as obligation and cash) basis, and still seek and receive their appropriations on the basis of obligating authority. It would likewise be possible, and many authorities have recommended, that appropriations be made for accrued expenditures, or on the basis of obligating authority but with limitations on accrued expenditures in any given year. But this so far has not been done in spite of the recommendations of the second Hoover Commission and other groups before and after it.

Notes

1. At the same time, he nominated Lee as a member of the Federal Communications Commission.

2. Warren was able to take advantage of the recently enacted Public Law 83-161 (enacted on July 28, 1953), which amended the Budget and Accounting Act of 1921 to provide for a pension at full pay for life to any Comptroller General (but not Assistant Comptroller General) who retires with a disability after ten years of service. This provision is similar to that for federal judges.

3. Both Fred Brown and Lindsay Warren were veterans of the lower chamber, although Brown also served one term as U.S. Senator from New Hampshire.

4. Of the ninety-six Senators, there were forty-eight Democrats and forty-seven Republicans. The addition of one Independent (Wayne Morse) and the Vice President (Richard M. Nixon) gave the GOP a one-vote margin as majority party.

5. Payne, a graduate of Bentley College of Accounting and Finance in Boston, was *not* a lawyer. Before his two gubernatorial terms in Maine, Payne served as that state's commissioner of finance and director of budget.

6. The Dixon-Yates controversy is briefly described in Addendum 1 to this chapter.

7. Campbell reportedly joked that he was trading salary for security; the new position represented a $500 pay cut from his $18,000 per year remuneration with the commission, but it provided him with a fifteen-year term instead of the year and a half that remained on his appointment.

8. Congressman Chet Holifield (D., Calif.), who was holding a hearing of the Joint Committee on Atomic Energy investigating the Dixon-Yates contract on the day that Campbell's nomination was announced, called it "a travesty on justice" (*Washington Post* and *Times-Herald,* November 10, 1954).

9. Under law, the nomination must be submitted to the next session of Congress within forty days for confirmation.

10. The 1955 committee included eight holdovers from the previous Congress: Democrats McClellan (chairman), Jackson, Kennedy, Symington, and Humphrey; and Republicans McCarthy (former chairman), Mundt, and Smith. The new members were Democrats Ervin and Thurmond and Republicans Cotton, Bender, and Martin.

11. U.S. Congress, Senate, Committee on Government Operations, *Hearings on the Nomination of Joseph Campbell to become Comptroller General of the United States,* February 2 and March 3, 1955, p. 4.

12. Campbell served on the Boards of Trustees of Teachers Insurance and Annuity Association, Central Savings Bank, Trinity College, New York

State Chamber of Commerce, Manhattanville Neighborhood Center, and American Reserve Insurance Co.

13. *Hearings,* p. 21.

14. The same individual, Maurice H. Stans, who would become Eisenhower's director of the Bureau of the Budget.

15. *Hearings,* p. 14. Senator Smith believed that the Comptroller Generalship was to be rotated between Senate (Brown) and House (Warren), and back to the Senate. Her objections may have stemmed from the President's backing down on the nomination of her colleague from Maine, Senator Payne.

16. *Hearings,* p. 15.

17. *Hearings,* p. 28.

18. *Congressional Record,* May 18, 1955, p. 2676.

19. Joseph Campbell, "Recruiting, Training, and Professional Development of Accountants in the General Accounting Office," *U.S. General Accounting Office Staff Bulletin* 2, no. 2 (August 1957):33.

20. The Commission on the Organization of the Executive Branch of the Government, P.L. 108, July 10, 1953.

21. It was a conservative period in American history. Five of the twelve members of the second Hoover Commission were in fact alumni of the first. The majority of these were conservative in their orientation, as were the majority of their new colleagues. In fact, the only member of the second Hoover Commission who could be considered to represent the liberal wing was Chet Holifield (D., Cal.).

22. Second Hoover Commission, *Budget and Accounting,* p. 59.

23. See Addendum 2 to this chapter for a descr̃iption of accrual accounting.

24. *Congressional Record,* 84th Cong., 2nd Sess., June 19, 1956, p. 10557.

25. U.S. Congress, Senate, *Financial Management in the Federal Government,* 92nd Cong., 1st Sess., Vol. 2 (Washington, D.C.: U.S. Government Printing Office, 1957).

26. After his resignation from the GAO in 1975, Herbert accepted an appointment as professor of accounting at the Virginia Polytechnic Institute, where at the time of this writing he is still teaching.

27. Leo Herbert, "Professional Development in the United States General Accounting Office," *U.S. General Accounting Office Staff Bulletin* 2, no. 8 (February 1958):26.

28. In an interview with the author, June 23, 1977.

29. U.S. Congress, Joint Committee on Defense Production, *Hearings,* 1955, p. 172.

30. U.S. Congress, House, H. Report 2264, 84th Cong., 2nd Sess., June 6, 1956.

31. If Lipscomb had belonged to the majority party, he undoubtedly

would have been subcommittee chairman; therefore, the necessity for including Dawson's name. Rep. Clare R. Hoffman (R., Mich., ranking minority member on the full committee) was also listed as ex officio.

32. Comments of the Comptroller General of the United States on Report of the Committee on Government Operations, House of Representatives, entitled "The General Accounting Office—A Study of its Organization and Administration with Recommendations for Increasing Its Effectiveness." H. Report 2264, 84th Cong., 2nd Sess., November 1, 1956.

33. H. Report 2264, pp. 18-19.

34. Ibid., p. 4.

35. Unlike the reorganizations of Warren before him and Staats later (see chapter 6), Campbell apparently reached these decisions unilaterally—without benefit of a survey or recommendations by a reorganization planning committee. He did rely on two of his immediate assistants, Robert F. Keller and Karney A. Brasfield, in developing his plan.

36. By P.L. 82-245, October 31, 1951.

37. Between 1957 and 1962, the GAO reported overcharges of more than $61 million, of which about $48 million was recovered by the government. U.S. Congress, House, Subcommittee *Hearings on Relation of Cost Data to Military Procurement*, 88th Cong., 1st Sess., 1963.

38. P.L. 87-653, September 10, 1962.

39. U.S. Congress, House, Special Subcommittee on Procurement Practices of the Department of Defense of Committee on Armed Services, *Hearings*, 86th Cong., 2nd Sess., pp. 406-7.

40. For example, Herbert Roback, a principal staff assistant to Congressman Chet Holifield, later wrote: "Today, almost five years after the Truth in Negotiations Act was passed, there is strong impression in some Congressional quarters, reinforced by the GAO, that the statutory requirements are being ignored by Government and Contractors alike." "Truth in Negotiating: The Legislative Background," a paper (processed) presented to the American Bar Association, Section of Public Contract Law, Honolulu, August 8, 1967.

41. Hewlett-Packard Co. v. United States, 385 F 2d. 1013 (9th Cir. 1967).

42. Holifield represented a district that contained no significant defense industries. On the other hand, he was the second ranking Democratic representative in the entire delegation of California, a state that contained a large number of defense plants. He was later to become for many years the chairman of the House Government Operations Committee.

43. U.S. Congress, House, Subcommittee of the Committee on Government Operations, *Hearings on Comptroller General Reports to Congress on Audits of Defense Contracts*, 89th Cong., 1st Sess., May 10–July 8, 1965.

44. One of the few witnesses who did not specifically criticize the GAO was Elmer B. Staats, then deputy director of the Bureau of the Budget, who

would within a year be appointed Comptroller General of the United States.

45. A number of persons have suggested that Campbell retired because of the heat generated by the Holifield hearings. On the basis of our own inquiries, we are convinced that he was seriously ill and withdrew under doctors' orders. Campbell was a man of conviction and courage and would not willingly quit under fire.

46. U.S. Congress, House, H. Rept. 1132, *Defense Contract Audits*, 90th Cong., 2nd Sess., p. 28.

47. Ibid., p. 9.

48. *Armed Forces Management*, November 1966.

49. Richard F. Kaufman, *The War Profiteers* (New York: Bobbs-Merrill, 1970).

50. "The One-Eyed Watchdog of Congress," *The Washington Monthly* (February 1971).

51. *Webster's New Collegiate Dictionary* defines *comprehensive* as "covering completely or broadly; inclusive."

52. The bible for the guidance of GAO audits is still entitled the *Comprehensive Audit Manual*, a vastly enlarged and amended version of the manual originally issued in 1952 (see chapter 4). It would probably be more accurately described today as a comprehensive manual of auditing than a manual of comprehensive audits. Its content nowhere refers to "comprehensive audits."

53. Examples of such end result assessments include:

1. *Selected Permissive Activities of the Alcohol and Tobacco Tax Division* (1961), a report to the Congress on the overall policies and procedures of the Alcohol and Tobacco Tax Division of the IRS and a report to the commissioner on those findings that were within the authority and responsibility of the field offices to address;

2. *Problems Associated with the Statutory Requirement for Design of the Interstate System to Accommodate Traffic Foreseen for the Year 1975* (1963), which stated that certain highways constructed during the later years of the program may not adequately serve traffic shortly after their completion;

3. *Weaknesses and Problem Areas in the Administration of the Imported Fire Ant Eradication Program* (1965), which noted that there had been a net increase in the number of acres infested with fire ants since the program was started in 1957 and expressed the opinion that the success of the program was doubtful for several reasons.

54. Most of this summary is based upon Aaron Wildavsky, *Dixon-Yates Controversy: A Study in Power Politics* (New Haven, Conn.: Yale University Press, 1962).

55. Wildavsky, *Dixon-Yates Controversy,* p. 137.

56. U.S. Petitioner v. Mississippi Valley Generating etc., 364 U.S. 520, January 9, 1961.

57. U.S. General Accounting Office, *Manual for Guidance of Federal Agencies,* Title 2, Accounting, pp. 2-18.

58. Ibid.

6

THE THIRD GAO:
PROGRAM EVALUATION AND
SERVICE FOR CONGRESS, 1966-1978

New occasions teach new duties;
Time makes ancient good uncouth.

—James Russell Lowell, *The Present Crisis*, 1844

It is better to advise than upbraid, for the one corrects the erring; the other only convicts them.
—Epictetus, *Encheiridion*, ca. 110

Backdrop

The years between the 1960s and the late 1970s will certainly be recorded by future historians as a period of great turbulence. At its beginning were the development under an aggressive Democratic president and the passage by a willing though divided Congress of a flood of domestic legislation in the fields of education, health, welfare, the environment, civil rights, housing, transportation, urban development, and others. The implementation of these measures, however, was accompanied by growing national involvement in an increasingly unpopular war that came to overshadow and retard the momentum for domestic change. Vietnam, protests about civil rights and other domestic problems, and a series of assassinations roused the youth of the nation—particularly at the colleges—the blacks, and many of both the poor and the intellectuals. They took part in protests, civic disturbances, and riots that were unprecedented in the memory of most Americans. Vietnam ended the presidential career of Lyndon B. Johnson and was probably the major factor in the return of the Republicans to the White House in 1969.

Until he became engulfed in the Watergate crisis, President Richard M. Nixon was increasingly aggressive, positively in international affairs except for the gradual pullout and the final collapse of South Vietnam, and negatively on the domestic front. His conflicts with Congress, which was controlled by the Democrats throughout those years, grew more and more bitter, both with regard to Vietnam and his efforts to reduce or abandon domestic programs and their attendant expenditures. Even before the culminating confrontations about Watergate and impoundment, Congress was taking steps to gain—or regain—authority and initiative over the government's activities. It developed and passed a number of bills aimed at starting or changing federal programs, a good many of which were vetoed; it passed legislation to limit the President's authority to involve American troops overseas; it established for itself the means to provide a congressional budget; it joined the latter bill with another to limit the President's assumed powers to impound funds; it passed legislation to assure the openness of documents in the executive branch, the disclosure of the financing of presidential campaigns, and the protection of the privacy of citizens; it refused to act on presidential reorganization proposals that would have concentrated more power in the White House.

The various inquiries that preceded and followed Nixon's resignation made it embarrassingly clear that Congress had not been very effective in its oversight role. So it took steps to strengthen its capacity in this regard too: it enlarged its committee staffs, gave new responsibilities to its two existing staff agencies—the GAO and the Congressional Research Service (previously the Legislative Reference Service)—and established two new ones—the Congressional Budget Office and the Office of Technology Assessment.

The ascendancy to the presidency of Gerald Ford and then of Jimmy Carter seems not to have dampened the ardor of Congress to build its capacity to direct and oversee the executive branch. Between 1965 and 1977, the total outlays for the legislative branch grew from $0.2 to $1.1 billion.[1] During the same period, the GAO's expenditures grew from $45 to $162 million, but its proportion of the congressional total declined from 21 to 15 percent.

In one further respect did Congress manifest its efforts to better control executive agencies: its growing concern about the effectiveness of the various programs it had established and funded in terms not only of managerial efficiency, but also in terms of results measured against congressional intent. This was a response to widespread criticism that many if not most of the new undertakings of President Johnson were not achieving their goals. In part, Congress was simply following Johnson's lead in this respect, for in 1965 he had initiated a broad executive program, the Planning-Programming-Budgeting System (PPBS), involving among other things the analysis and evaluation of program effectiveness. Congressional leaders and many of the legislative committees picked up the idea in the late 1960s, and soon Congress was requiring program evaluation as a part of some of its substantive legislation. Further, it was directing its own agencies—specifically the GAO and the Congressional Research Service— to get into the act on behalf of Congress.

These governmental developments provided a changing backdrop for the "third GAO"; they also helped propel the GAO in directions considerably different from those pursued by Comptroller General Warren two decades earlier.

New Leadership

Another significant force toward new roles for the GAO was its new leadership, beginning in 1966 with the naming of a new Comptroller General. It will be recalled that Joseph Campbell resigned the post for reasons of health on July 31, 1965, before the close of the Holifield hearings. For the second time, Frank Weitzel became Acting Comptroller General pending the appointment and confirmation of a successor to Campbell, which did not come until seven months later. Weitzel was widely respected on the Hill, and some congressional leaders are reported to have recommended his appointment as Comptroller General to President Johnson. A rumor to that effect was reported in the press, and it may have hurt his chances. Another man who is said to have been suggested was Bernard L. Boutin, then administrator of the General Services Administration.

But there is little evidence that Johnson seriously considered anyone other than the appointee he ultimately named, Elmer B. Staats, then deputy director of the Bureau of the Budget. The President thought highly of many career public executives, and among them Staats was one of the most eminent. When his name was suggested, Johnson made his decision almost immediately[2] and nominated him on February 11, 1966. Staats had earlier been offered and had declined several high posts in the administration and was still considering Johnson's tentative offer of Comptroller General when the President made his announcement. Staats' qualifications and background for the post were if anything more unusual than had been those of Joseph Campbell. He was neither a lawyer nor accountant but a Ph.D. in economics and political science from the University of Minnesota. His public service career included work in the Bureau of the Budget under five different presidents, beginning with Franklin D. Roosevelt, and he had been its deputy director under four of them (Truman, Eisenhower, Kennedy, and Johnson); since then, he has been Comptroller General during four presidencies: Johnson, Nixon, Ford, and Carter. During the Eisenhower administration, Staats served five years as executive director of the Operations Coordinating Board (now defunct) of the National Security Council. But his main experience was with the Bureau of the Budget, and it had involved much work with and testimony before congressmen and congressional committees.

Although he was by no means partisan,[3] a member of the congressional "club," or a lawyer, the Staats nomination was greeted enthusiastically in Congress and in the press. When the Senate Committee on Government Operations held hearings on his confirmation on March 2, 1966, Chairman McClellan (D., Ark.) introduced him as "eminently qualified" with "a long and distinguished career." Senator Henry M. Jackson (D., Wash.), who had questioned Joseph Campbell's qualifications for the job because of his lack of legislative or legal experience, stated that no one came to the job of Comptroller General "better equipped than Elmer Staats." Most of the senators' statements were testimonials in the appointee's behalf. The committee voted unanimously for his confirmation, and two days later he was confirmed in the Senate. At the swearing-in ceremony in the East Room of the White House on March 8, President Johnson paid tribute to his loyalty and dedication, cited him as a "builder, not a doubter," and prepared him for possible future unpleasantness with the remark that: "When Mr. Staats hears some of the things that will be said about him in the next fifteen years, he may want to remember the nice things that were said today." In private, Staats asked the President what he thought the job of Comptroller General was. Johnson replied, "to make sure that the laws and programs are carried out as both the President and Congress intended them."[4]

Two years later, another change in leadership was forced when the term of Assistant Comptroller General Frank H. Weitzel expired on January 17, 1969, three days before President Nixon's first inauguration. Weitzel had served almost from the beginning of the GAO in 1923 and had risen successively from messenger boy to second in command. He had great impact on the many changes in development of the organization. Staats believed that Weitzel's successor should likewise be a GAO career man and a lawyer (in view of the fact that he himself was not). His own choice, which he communicated to the White House, was Robert F. Keller, then the GAO's general counsel.

Keller's nomination by President Nixon was not, however, a foregone conclusion. Although well liked and respected in the Congress, he had little political support. Further, he had played a leading role in the controversy between the Comptroller General and the administration's Departments of Labor and Justice over the legality of the Philadelphia Plan (described in chapter 7). The Comptroller General's negative decision on the plan was announced just three weeks before Nixon made his choice. Finally, the Republican side of Congress, specifically Representative Frank T. Bow (R., Ohio), the ranking minority member of the House Appropriations Committee, was pushing for another candidate: Robert C. Gresham, minority staff director of that committee. Staats was therefore delighted when President Nixon announced from San Clemente Keller's nomination. The following day, Staats said that Keller "has demonstrated that he can serve as Assistant Comptroller General in a most admirable way."[5] His confirmation presented no serious problems. The Senate Committee on Government Operations voted unanimously to confirm, and he became the fifth Assistant Comptroller General on October 3, 1969.

Elmer Staats was widely acquainted with people in the executive branch and in Congress, but when he arrived at the GAO he knew almost no one there—possibly a reflection of the insularity of the organization. Like most of his predecessors, he brought no one with him, not even a secretary, feeling that bringing in a "retinue" would be the likeliest way to alienate the organization, particularly if many came from his old agency, the Bureau of the Budget.

After he became Comptroller General, Staats was the only "stranger"[6] in the GAO's upper hierarchy. But there were many components of compatibility. Staats was an orderly and seasoned government official; the GAO was an orderly and seasoned government agency. And though Staats was neither an accountant nor a lawyer, as all of his new professional associates were, they had similar backgrounds of working with, or on, executive agencies and with Congress, its committees, and its members. Further, Staats recognized the importance to him of the organization's support.

Among his first tasks was to acquaint himself with the people and to identify those who seemed most promising for future leadership posts. He visited almost all of the GAO's field offices. And he made a round of calls on committee and subcommittee chairmen in Congress, partly to obtain their counsel. Most of them, while not critical of the GAO, had made little use of it. In fact, the GAO's primary congressional clients were the House Committees on Government Operations, Appropriations, and Armed Services. At an early date he determined to make the GAO's work for all of Congress more timely, more relevant, and closer to the cycle of appropriations and legislation. This effort to make the GAO more useful to Congress became an underlying impetus for the GAO's directional changes in the years ahead.

The transition to Elmer Staats in no way resembled the turmoil that often accompanies political transition in the executive branch. He learned about his organization, its activities, and its principal personnel. He made few immediate changes, partly in recognition that a number of the division and office chiefs would retire within a few years. Major reorganization would come later, but in his first year he did make several significant changes. He changed the Defense Division from its departmental structure (army, navy, air force) to a functional base, crossing departmental lines (research and development, procurement, manpower, and so on). He set up the GAO's first Program Planning Staff and its first Information Office. And he expanded the older Accounting and Auditing Policy Staff into an Office of Policy and Special Studies. The following year, in December 1968, he combined the two personnel offices, the Office of Staff Management (for professional personnel) and the Office of Personnel (for nonprofessionals), into a single Office of Personnel.

Soon after his confirmation, Staats took steps to revivify the Joint Financial Management Program. He called a meeting of its leaders, the secretary of the treasury, the director of the Bureau of the Budget, and himself, and with their agreement invited John W. Macy, chairman of the Civil Service Commission, to participate as a full-scale member. This move was designed to stimulate the commission's participation in the recruiting and development of personnel in the fields of financial management throughout the government. In May of 1966, President Johnson, on the stimulus of members of the Joint Financial Management Improvement Program (JFMIP), issued a memorandum to each department and agency head requesting immediate action to improve financial management practices to accord with the standards and principles required by the Comptroller General, to work with the Civil Service Commission for the improvement of professional personnel in that field, and to make sure that each agency's financial information and reports were adequate to support the planning and management of its programs.

Program Evaluation

Probably the most significant development in the nature of the GAO in the first dozen years of Staats' term was the changing emphasis in its auditing activities toward program evaluations. This thrust began quietly and grew gradually, with no such overturn of practices and personnel as accompanied Warren's "revolution" before and after 1950. It stemmed from a number of sources: congressional needs and concerns; preceding and accompanying developments in the executive branch; and the interests and objectives of Staats himself and of some of his new colleagues in the GAO.

The idea of program evaluation was by no means a new one in business or in government. In conjunction with systems for planning and allocation of materials, it had been used during World War II, and in the fifteen years following that war there was increased interest in the subject, particularly in the planning and development of weapons systems. Leaders in the field were principally microeconomists, who developed sophisticated techniques for the analysis of proposed new military hardware and the evaluation of its effectiveness. When Robert S. McNamara became Secretary of Defense in 1961, he engaged in high-level positions a number of such economists, and they began immediately to develop for the Defense Department what they labeled a Planning-Programming-Budgeting System. It involved a number of elements: precise definitions of objectives; consolidating of related activities in program "packages"; comparative analyses of alternative means of attaining the objectives, including projections of their costs and effectiveness; and translating these into budgetary plans, followed by evaluation of costs and results to lead to a new round of analysis and budget making. A central feature was to consider not only the input side of the budget, the costs, but also the program results, the outputs in terms of objectives.

If the 1950s had been the era of accountant ascendancy in federal management, the 1960s was the era of economists—at least until 1969. All three of the budget directors and several assistant directors who served under Presidents Kennedy and Johnson were economists. They had encouraged experimentation with PPBS techniques in some of the civil departments in the early 1960s. In August 1965, President Johnson, impressed by McNamara's apparent success with PPBS in the Defense Department and mindful of criticisms of the costs and alleged ineffectiveness of some of his new programs, ordered the installation of PPBS systems in most of the rest of the government, under the direction of the Bureau of the Budget. At that time, of course, Elmer B. Staats was deputy director of the budget.

The Johnson directive resulted in frantic work, reams of paper, and probably, over the long pull, more sophisticated decision processes. Nixon formally abandoned it in 1971, and substituted for it a system known as Management by Objectives, which was later followed by Carter's Zero Base Budgeting. But the PPBS emphasis upon analysis of program results against their costs and upon the consideration of alternative means of achieving objectives was in the Washington air in the 1960s and it remains there today. It is interesting that one of the early GAO studies under Staats was a *Survey of Use by Federal Agencies of the Discounting Techniques in Evaluating Future Programs,*[7] and the following year it published a *Survey of Progress in Implementing the Planning-Programming-Budgeting System in Executive Agencies.*[8]

Congress too was growing concerned about the evaluation of the results of the programs it was legislating and funding. In the same year as Johnson's PPBS directive, it wrote into the Elementary and Secondary Education Act of 1965 a provision requiring the administering agency to report to it on the implementation and effects of its Title I. This provision was added to the bill at the insistence of Senator Robert F. Kennedy (D., N.Y.). In 1967, Congress turned to the GAO for a major program evaluation. In the Economic Opportunity Act Amendments of that year, it included in an amendment, known for the senator who introduced it, Winston L. Prouty (R., Vt.), a requirement that the GAO review and report on the effectiveness of the principal programs authorized by the act—that is, the poverty programs. This was by far the most ambitious study of its kind the GAO had made to that time. Many GAO auditors had their initiation in program evaluation; in addition, a number of consultants were hired from outside to assist in the process. Among their activities were interviewing program participants, analyzing selected manpower programs, and assessing the program evaluation techniques of the administering agencies. The study resulted in a major report with recommendations, transmitted to Congress on March 18, 1969, and some fifty supplementary reports on individual program sites.

Another major evaluation study, completed in 1970, concerned the effectiveness of the water pollution construction grant programs set up by the federal and state governments to aid municipalities. In the same year, the GAO initiated a review of the effectiveness and validity of the Office of Economic Opportunity experiment on the negative income tax in New Jersey.

The GAO no doubt already had legal authority under the Budget and Accounting Act of 1921 to make program evaluations through its power to investigate all matters relating to the "application" of public funds. But in 1970, Congress made it specific in the Legislative Reorganization Act:

> The Comptroller General shall review and analyze the results of Government programs and activities carried on under existing law, including the making of cost benefit studies, when ordered by either House of Congress, or upon his own initiative, or when requested by any committee of the House of Representatives or the Senate, or any joint committee of the two Houses, having jurisdiction over such programs and activities.[9]

The GAO's responsibilities in connection with program evaluation were considerably expanded in 1974 by certain provisions of the Congressional Budget and Impoundment Control Act.[10] These are discussed in a subsequent section. That act prompted the development of a new staff within the GAO to provide a focal point for its program evaluation work, which in 1976 would become the Program Analysis Division.

The expanded scope of auditing was reflected in revisions of its *Comprehensive Audit Manual,* the original version of which had been issued in 1952. The primary purposes of GAO audits are there stated to be:

1. To evaluate the efficiency, economy, legality, and *effectiveness* with which Federal agencies carry out their financial, management, and *program responsibilities.*
2. To assist the Congress and Federal agency officials in carrying out their responsibilities by providing them with objective and timely information on the conduct of Government operations together with our *conclusions and recommendations.*[11]

The *Manual* goes on to say: "Our audits should extend into all important aspects of an agency's operations. They are not restricted to accounting matters or to books, records, and documents."[12]

Audits were until fiscal year 1978 classified in three categories, as audits of (1) financial operations and legal compliance; (2) efficiency and economy of operations; and (3) program results. The first of these roughly reflects the concept of the GAO's audit role (though not its techniques) during the McCarl era; the second, the additions of Warren and Campbell (which had been contemplated by the authors of the Budget and Accounting Act of 1921); and the third, the developments that, though begun earlier, are principally associated with the Staats regime. In practice, the second and third often overlap since both may include evaluations of management effectiveness.

The first category, audits of financial operations and legal compliance, are defined to include four types: (1) reviews of accounting systems in operation; (2) examination of financial statements; (3) audits and settlement of accounts/pay audits; and (4) financial management improvement. These have declined in relative emphasis and are now estimated to consume no more than one tenth of the GAO's auditing resources.

Audits of program results are intended to "evaluate whether desired results or benefits of agency programs and activities are being achieved and whether the objectives established by the Congress are being met."[13] The *Manual* contemplates that audits of program results may sometimes justify recommendations to Congress to reconsider its objectives as well as alternative approaches to achieve them at lower cost. But this broad charter is somewhat qualified: "Our objective is *not* to become the 'think tank' for the Congress on the best solutions to pressing national problems. Nor is it our job to assess overall national program priorities or budget funding requirements."[14] In the light of ambiguities in the interpretation of "program results" and the evident fact that many GAO studies did not really fit in that, or any other, category, the Comptroller General in the fall of 1977 ordered that it be divided into three separate categories:

- *audits and evaluations of results of ongoing programs,* which would be oriented primarily to effectiveness in terms of outcomes of what is now happening;
- *analyses of costs and benefits of alternative approaches,* oriented to problems of the future and the probable implications of differing options for meeting them; and
- *special studies,* a potpourri of work that fits nowhere else, including studies of methodology, new techniques, broad surveys for internal planning purposes, and others.[15]

Of these, the second would appear pretty close to providing a "think tank" for Congress.

The potential scope of GAO audits comprehends almost all executive branch activities (though there are a few specific exemptions and limitations on its inquiries). It is obvious, however, that a complete audit of the management and the end results of many departments or agencies or even of larger programs would be virtually impossible. Actually the GAO makes proportionately few large-scale audits of major programs, though those that have been made consume a considerable amount of staff time. In numbers of audit reports, the great majority are on relatively limited, finite, and sometimes geographically localized questions of performance and results in sectors of federal agencies. The variety of their subject matter is tremendous, as is the variety in terms of manpower costs, length, and time. The GAO now has more than 1,500 projects underway and is issuing reports at the rate of about ninety per month, or four per working day.[16]

Some GAO studies, such as the financial audits of government corporations, are mandated by law. Some are responses to requests by chairmen of committees and subcommittees of Congress, and some are requested by individual members of Congress. But the majority—nearly two thirds—are initiated within the GAO on the independent authority of the Comptroller General.

The GAO's Program Planning Staff has maintained statistics since 1972 classifying the GAO's audit work in terms of staff-years for the three categories of audit described above. The record of the six fiscal years 1972-1977 (see Table 2) shows a persistent increase in the proportion of work directed to "program results" to the point at which it absorbs nearly half of the GAO's audit resources. Very probably, if the data were available back to the beginning of Staats' term, "program results" would then have accounted for less than 10 percent.

Examples of audits in the "program results" category in recent years include:

Federal-state income tax administration (November 1975). Based on an investigation of the ability of state governments to collect taxes from military personnel, the GAO found that the lack of a regular weekly withholding of state taxes from military personnel caused problems for both individuals and state tax units. Despite Defense Department opposition to ending the prohibition on payroll tax withholding, the GAO was able to mobilize enough support from other government agencies and armed services newspapers to convince Congress to have "pay-as-you-go" privileges extended to the military in the Tax Reform Act of 1976.

Water pollution control facilities (December 1975). The GAO examined the data used by one state to obtain funding for the construction of several pollution control facilities and found that the data did not clearly demonstrate the need for water treatment, nor did the state adequately analyze the cause or alternative solutions for the water quality problem. At the conclusion of the GAO's field audit, state officials indicated that they would reevaluate their decisions; the state later announced a total capital cost savings of $13.5 million by amending its original plans.

Planning for government hospitals (April 1976). The GAO found, in the case of a planned military hospital, that the criteria for expected use were inaccurate, and developed a new computer model for estimating need (which can be applied to other government agencies' hospital construction programs). Congress delayed appropriations for the new hospital until the

TABLE 2

Percentages of GAO Work by Program Category[a]

	1972	1973	1974	1975	1976[b]	1977
Financial	14	13	14	12	11	10
Economy & Efficiency	56	53	54	52	49	41
Program Results	30	34	32	36	40	49

Source: The GAO's monthly "Overview Report."

[a]
The data are indicative of trends and are probably less than precise. Some GAO studies fall in none of the three categories; some are "crossovers" that might be classified in two or three of them; and there is probably a tendency of the auditors to give the benefit of any doubt to "program results" in view of the interests of Congress and the GAO's management.

[b]
Not including the transition quarter to the new fiscal year, July 1 to September 20, 1976.

GAO's report was ready, and the Defense Department agreed with the GAO's revised estimate of needed capacity.

Automobile safety (July 1976). In response to a request from Congress, the GAO obtained data from the major American automobile manufacturers on the costs of incorporating federal safety features in passenger cars and compared these costs to various estimates of the "benefits" that accrue from the installation of the features. Although the GAO reported to the congressional committee that the value of the lives and injuries prevented exceeded the cost of installing safety features, no immediate congressional action was taken.

Welfare payments (November 1976). The GAO found that one government agency did not have adequate information on the benefits provided to welfare recipients from other federal grants programs and that the information was not used in computing the eligibility or the amount of welfare benefits. When the department accepted the GAO's recommendations and modified its eligibility system, it reported a reduction of 35,000 ineligible recipients and a savings of $60 million in overpayments.

Military medical school (May 1976). The GAO conducted a cost-effectiveness analysis of two alternative programs for the recruitment of military physicians through (1) armed forces health professions scholarships to students at existing medical school facilities, and (2) construction of a proposed Uniformed Services University of the Health Sciences. Although the GAO concluded that the first alternative was more cost effective and presented three options for reinforcing its utility, Congress decided to continue plans for construction of the new medical school, citing various non-cost-related factors.

Department of Energy and Natural Resources (July 1977). As part of its overall evaluation of energy policy decision making and organization, the GAO recommended that Congress create a Department of Energy and Natural Resources, expanding the President's concept of an energy department to include some Interior Department functions, various economic and noneconomic energy regulatory activities, and others. The politically and bureaucratically favorable climate for the creation of an Energy Department and the President's desire to equip the new agency with some—but not all—regulatory functions reduced the likelihood of this proposals's passage amidst many recommendations that were enacted.

Problems Attending the GAO's Movement Toward Program Evaluation

Despite the impressiveness of the statistics and the examples cited above, the development of the program evaluation emphasis in the GAO has been gradual, usually cautious, and less than uniform. Some of the line divisions have moved into it aggressively, some hesitantly or reluctantly. The shift away from traditional auditing concerns has depended in part on the interests of divisional leadership and the interests and capabilities of staff, both in the headquarters and in the field.

There are reasons for caution. One is that the evaluation of programs depends upon "soft" data, especially in social fields. Another is that initial responsibility for evaluation of the effectiveness of executive programs lies in the executive branch. The proper role of the GAO as a legislative agency is not altogether clear-cut. A third reason for caution—and probably the most important—relates to the larger role of the GAO in the governmental system. Studies of the effectiveness of governmental programs lead to findings that in turn lead to recommendations to abolish, change, or renew programs or to establish new ones: that is, GAO reports, based on program evaluations, often contain proposals to change public policy. The GAO is one of very few federal agencies that make *public* recommendations for policy changes across the whole executive branch of the government. To the extent that its studies are in controversial political areas, its recommendations almost inevitably force it into fields that are politically sensitive in Congress. Oversight and accountability, focused on past performance and results, can transform themselves noiselessly to advice on policy and action in the future, even when they were not labelled "analyses of costs and benefits of alternative approaches." A good many of the GAO's reports in recent years have pointed to, or explicitly recommended, changes in legislation and federal policy. This could conceivably portend a major change in the stance of the GAO from auditor in the direction of being a policy staff, a change that could become at least as profound as that initiated during the term of Lindsay Warren from voucher checker to financial and management auditor.

Developments in Defense and Procurement

During the late 1960s the GAO's audit work in the military field followed a course somewhat parallel to that in domestic affairs. Its primary focus shifted from individual defense contracts to broader studies of the effectiveness and costs of major weapons systems, procurement practices and procedures, financial management and controls, supply systems and like matters. The work of auditing individual contracts was left increasingly to the Defense Contract Audit Agency, set up in 1965. But the Holifield hearings of 1965 did not signal the termination of congressional interest in cost overruns and other alleged abuses in defense contracting. The prominence given to the TFX (F-111) and C-5A scandals sparked a renewed concern by several congressional committees, resulting in frequent requests for GAO studies on specific cases of defense contractor spending.

The GAO was in effect whiplashed between two contending sets of committees, subcommittees, and leaders in Congress. One of these sought to constrain and contain the GAO's investigations in military procurement; it was led by a majority of the House Committee on Government Operations (including Congressman Holifield), the majorities of the two Armed Services Committees and of the military subcommittees of the Appropriations Committees. The other was critical of the GAO's alleged failures to penetrate with sufficient vigor the inefficiencies and extravagance of the Defense Department and the "military-industrial complex." It was represented principally by Senator William B. Proxmire (D., Wisc.) in his capacity as chairman of the Joint Economic Committee, leaders in the Senate Committee on Government Operations like Senators John McClellan (D., Ark.) and Abraham Ribicoff (D., Conn.), and a considerable number of others. Proxmire became increasingly critical of what he regarded as inadequate GAO monitoring and reporting on defense contracts, particularly with regard to the C-5A—the Lockheed affair. He

and others sought in a variety of ways to enlarge the GAO's responsibilities
and powers in this area. Most of these arguments came to a head in 1969, the
year the House Appropriations Committee dubbed "the year of the cost
overrun."[17]

That year, Proxmire's Joint Economic Committee published a report on
The Economics of Military Procurement,[18] which outlined a number of proposed
new responsibilities for the GAO. It should:

1. conduct a comprehensive study of profitability in defense contracting;
2. develop a weapons acquisition status report for Congress on a
   periodic basis;
3. develop a military procurement cost index;
4. determine the feasibility of incorporating the "should-cost" method
   of estimating contractor costs ("should-cost" meant the cost based
   upon the best available current indicator, rather than the historical
   record); and
5. compile a defense-industrial personnel exchange directory.[19]

Comptroller General Staats later testified on these proposals before the
committee and indicated his reluctance to undertake most of them. He
stated that the main responsibility for developing the information relating to
proposals 2, 3, and 5 should be vested in the Department of Defense. He felt
that proposal 1 would require broad legislative authority as well as
additional staff resources. Proposal 4 would be considered, but only along
with historical costs. Proxmire responded with some acerbity: "We would
like to call you our watchdog, but in view of your response to this
committee's recommendation I just wonder if we should."[20]

The pressures on Congress to limit military spending and its growing
exasperation with what some of its members regarded as concealment or
failure to report accurate data on its costs by the Defense Department led to a
spirited debate on the floor of the Senate in the spring of 1969 when it was
considering the Military Procurement Authorization Bill for 1970. A host of
amendments were introduced to direct the GAO to make more intensified
studies and reports on weapons systems, contracts, and related matters. Most
of these were defeated, but two of considerable significance passed. One,
introduced by Proxmire, directed the GAO to make a study of the profits
made by defense contractors and subcontractors. Staats had earlier agreed
with Proxmire to conduct such a study on a one-time basis rather than
periodically as the senator had proposed earlier. The study resulted in the
GAO report issued in 1971, *Defense Industry Profit Study.*[21]

The second amendment, introduced by Senator Richard Schweiker (R.,
Pa.), called for an elaborate system of quarterly reporting on all major

contracts by the Defense Department and required the GAO to audit the reporting system and report on it annually to Congress. The GAO would also conduct its own audits of individual contracts and for this purpose was given the right to subpoena the books and records of the procuring agency and the contractor. The amendment passed the Senate by a single vote, 47 to 46. Later, on the request of Congressman Mendel Rivers, chairman of the House Armed Services Committee, Comptroller General Staats wrote a letter to Rivers stating what steps the GAO planned to take to improve its reporting on weapons systems, contractors, and costs, and indicating that passage of the amendment prescribing a particular form of reporting and review would be unwise. He further stated that the GAO's authority in this field was already adequate and that it would obtain the necessary information "with the aid of the appropriate Congressional committees."[22] The amendment was unsuccessful in the House and the subsequent conference committee and did not become law.

But the Senate debate on the Schweiker and other amendments provoked Senator Abraham Ribicoff (D., Conn.) to hold hearings before the Senate Subcommittee on Executive Reorganization, of which he was chairman, on the *Capability of GAO to Analyze and Audit Defense Expenditures.*[23] The first witness, Comproller General Staats, testified on September 16, just four days after his letter to Rivers. He told again of the GAO's plans to report to Congress annually on defense contracts, emphasized the GAO's work in the area of program results, including those in the Defense Department, and announced the creation within the GAO of a new group to analyze and report on weapons systems acquisitions. As part of his testimony, Staats released to the committee a letter that he had written to Senate Armed Services Committee Chairman John Stennis a month earlier, indicating the GAO's attempt to have future defense-oriented reports concentrate on certain areas.

1. Currently estimated costs compared with the prior estimates separately for (a) research, development, and engineering, and (b) production.
2. The reasons for any significant increase or decrease from cost estimates at the time of the original authorization and the original contract.
3. Options available under the contract for additional procurement and whether the agency intends to exercise any options, and the projected cost of exercising options.
4. Changes in the performance specifications or estimates made by the contractor or by the agency and the reasons for any major change in actual or estimated differences from that called for under the original contract specifications.

5. Significant slippages in time schedules and the reasons therefor.[24]

Also on that occasion, Staats specifically requested that Congress grant him subpoena power to compel the "production of those books, accounts, and other contractor records."[25] He has repeatedly requested subpoena power since 1969, but it has not been granted except for certain specific and limited purposes.

The questioning during the Ribicoff hearings was generally friendlier to the GAO than had been that of Proxmire. For example, Senator Charles Percy (R., Ill.), ranking minority member, said:

> I would hope that the GAO could say to itself that it has a creative role that the Congress cannot do without. . . . I think we really need an expanding, continuing creative role for the GAO. You are one of the few agencies that can do that—and not just respond to specific requests—unless they are broad enough.[26]

The Monitoring of Major Acquisitions

A further response to congressional concern about military procurement was the GAO's creation in 1969 of a Major Acquisitions Group to carry on continuing reviews of major weapons systems at various stages of the acquisition cycle—from formulation of the system's concept through the phases of contract definition, development, production, and deployment. The purpose of this undertaking was to determine the basic sources of cost growth, schedule slippage, and deterioration of performance characteristics in order to make recommendations for improvement of the acquisitions process. Beginning in 1970, the GAO made annual (later, semiannual) reports to Congress on the financial status of major acquisitions of weapons systems. In 1975, the report was extended to include major acquisitions of the civil agencies.[27] In recent years, although the acquisitions reports continue to be issued, this work has been overshadowed by intensive studies of the missions, suitability, need, effectiveness, and costs of individual systems. Examples of these include studies of the B-1 bomber, GAMA Goat, AWACS, Trident submarine, M-1 tank, and a variety of missile systems. Examples of recent GAO studies of weapon systems include the following.

Termination of Condor missile program (February 1976). Using the military departments' own testing and evaluation results, the GAO advised the Congress that the proposed Condor missile system was unlikely to perform its function under hostile conditions, and that existing weapon systems could perform the same function more effectively and at a lesser cost. Congress halted naval acquisition of the missile system in the next appropriations bill, saving approximately $458 million.

Cancellation and reinstatement of navy hydrofoil (March 1976). The GAO determined that the navy's procurement of patrol hydrofoil missile ships was not cost effective or operationally effective. The secretary of defense concurred with the GAO's recommendations and the President included the missile on a budgetary rescission list submitted to Congress. Congress, however, refused to allow cancellation of the hydrofoil and the Defense Department ordered five additional ships from the contractor.

Cost Accounting Standards Board

In 1968, the agenda for Congress included a two-year extension of the Defense Production Act of 1950,[28] the omnibus legislation for defense contracting procedures. In a bill sent to the Senate in the spring of 1968, the House of Representatives, on the initiative of its Committee on Banking and Currency, added a provision calling for an eighteen-month study by the GAO on the feasibility and applicability of uniform cost accounting standards for defense contractors. Although the provision was resisted by the Republican members of the Senate Banking and Currency Committee, the Senate as a whole—prodded by Senator Proxmire (D., Wisc.)[29]— incorporated it into the 1968 amendments to the Defense Production Act.[30]

The GAO, in preparing its report on cost accounting standards for negotiated defense contracts in excess of $100,000, was specifically directed to work in cooperation with the Bureau of the Budget, Department of Defense, and representatives from the accounting profession as well as large defense contractors. Its report, which was delivered to the chairmen of the House and Senate Committees on Armed Services and on Banking and Currency, concluded that it would be feasible to establish and apply cost accounting standards to provide a greater degree of uniformity and consistency in cost accounting as a basis for negotiating and administering procurement contracts.[31] Additional conclusions focused on the level of detail in the standards, applicability to nondefense work, cost of implementing the standards, need for standards of disclosure and consistency, and access to records. Following extensive hearings on the GAO report, Congress added a new section to the Defense Production Act,[32] calling for the establishment of a Cost Accounting Standards Board (CASB).[33] It would be an agent of Congress, independent of the executive departments, and would consist of the Comptroller General as its chairman and four other members of his choosing. Its basic function is to promulgate cost accounting standards designed to achieve uniformity and consistency and to make regulations for the implementation of the standards.

Although the Cost Accounting Standards Board is not a part of the GAO, its work requires a considerable amount of time by the Comptroller General and represents another link between the legislative branch and the accounting profession. The other four board members—who also serve on a part-time basis—represent specific constituencies: two are required to be from the accounting profession, one from industry, and one from a federal department or agency.

Since 1972, the Cost Accounting Standards Board has issued annual progress reports to Congress as well as periodic restatements of its objectives, policies, and concepts. Elmer Staats, as chairman of the board, has "changed his hat" before Congress and the accounting profession on occasion to carry out his statutory responsibilities with the CASB, quite distinct from his responsibilities in the GAO. In an audit report to Congress on the CASB,[34] the GAO noted that "promulgations issued by the Cost Accounting Standards Board have profoundly affected defense contractors and procurement offices. The board and the Department of Defense should be commended for their efforts to implement this highly complex program."[35] There is no doubt that the CASB has had a significant effect on government procurement, the role of the Comptroller General, and the relationship of the accounting profession to the legislative branch.

Commission on Government Procurement

Between 1966 and 1969, a plethora of proposed legislation was filled with the intent of instituting a special study of government procurement. Finally, with the enactment of Public Law 91-129 on November 26, 1969, a twelve-member blue-ribbon bipartisan Commission on Government Procurement was officially established. Based on a bill introduced by Representative Holifield (with a companion Senate bill by Senator Henry M. Jackson), the legislation that led to the commission rejected proposals for a separate study by either Congress or the executive branch, opting in favor of a commission with representatives from the legislative and executive branches and from the public. The Comptroller General was the only statutory member of the commission.[36]

The commission was organized to provide in-depth coverage of the procurement process in three ways: (1) the environment in which procurement occurs; (2) the sequence of procurement events; and (3) types of procurement. Although the commission was limited to a staff of 50 professional members, the services of almost 500 persons were loaned to the commission on a full-time or part-time basis. Of the thirteen study groups established by the commission to examine specific areas of procurement, GAO representatives served on ten groups.

As the study groups completed their work, the twelve commissioners (guided by a five-person Executive Committee, including the Comptroller General) produced a report of four volumes and 149 recommendations, and delivered the material to Congress on December 31, 1972. In early 1973, Congressman Holifield, who had served as vice-chairman of the commission, in his capacity as chairman of the House Government Operations Committee requested that his fellow commissioner, Comptroller General

Staats, monitor for Congress the effectiveness of the executive branch in implementing the commission's recommendations.

From 1973 to 1975, the GAO issued five progress reports on the status of the recommendations by the Commission on Government Procurement and on the status of legislation the commission believed was needed to implement sixty-four of its recommendations. At the end of that two-year period, the GAO was able to report that the executive branch had established policy on 77 of the 149 commission recommendations, with 64 of those recommendations adopted and 13 rejected.[37] Congress passed a number of bills on procurement, including one to give effect to the commission's first recommendation: establishment within the Office of Management and Budget of the Office of Federal Procurement Policy.[38]

The GAO as Agent of Congress

The shifts in the GAO's work were responsive to changes that were proceeding in the Congress (see chapter 9). From the start in 1966, Comptroller General Staats endeavored to impress upon congressional leaders the resources and the potential of the GAO and its loyalty and dedication to the legislative branch. During this period, there was increasing effort to make GAO work more useful and relevant for congressional needs, actual and predicted. The effort took various forms: increasing numbers of reports addressed to Congress as a whole and to a broader variety of its committees and subcommittees; more frequent testimony by GAO officials on legislation currently under consideration; more assignments of GAO staff on detail to congressional committees; more advisory services and briefing meetings for congressmen and their staffs. An Office of Congressional Relations was established to monitor and coordinate the GAO's congressional activities, and GAO officials in all its divisions were encouraged to work more closely with congressional counterparts on common problems. Between 1966 and 1977, the percentage of the GAO's professional staff time allocated to direct assistance to Congress grew from about 10 percent to about 35 percent.

In an effort to make GAO reports more useful, each was introduced with a brief nontechnical digest, and the GAO started issuing a monthly newsletter listing all of its reports published during the previous month. It augmented its immediate services in the internal management of Congress, such as accounting systems and audits of the Senate and House restaurants, the House Stationery Revolving Fund, the Capitol Guide Service, and others.

General Legislation Affecting the GAO

During the same period, Congress enacted a number of laws which would modify and generally enhance the GAO's responsibilities. One of the most important of these was the *Legislative Reorganization Act of 1970*,[39] the first major congressional realignment since 1946. The act called upon the GAO to participate in the development of a standardized budgetary and fiscal information system, to conduct cost-benefit studies of federal programs when requested by congressional committees or on a self-initiated basis, and to "review and analyze the results of Government programs and activities."[40] It further provided for direct congressional use of GAO employees and reports. For the first time, Congress required federal agencies to submit written statements of action taken in response to GAO recommendations within sixty days of the release of a GAO report or decision. Most of these provisions did not add new powers to the GAO, because they were already authorized, at least by implication, in the Budget and Accounting Act of 1921. But they did reemphasize the congressional intent to make further use of the GAO, particularly in the area of program analysis and evaluation.

The same act renamed the Legislative Reference Service as the Congressional Research Service (CRS) and gave it responsibilities some of which are only narrowly distinguishable from those of the GAO. The CRS was called upon to advise any requesting committee of Congress on the advisability of proposed legislation, on its probable results, and on possible alternatives.[41]

Beleaguered by four years of vetoes of appropriation bills and outright impoundments at the hands of the President, and facing the prospect of a landslide election mandate one week hence, Congress in 1972 chose to seek an effective means of establishing responsible legislative control of budget totals by creating a Joint Study Committee on Budget Control.[42] The same act designated the GAO as the representative of Congress for impoundment control, and tied together the problems of budget reform and impoundment control for the first time. In 1973, Comptroller General Staats testified before the committee on his proposal to improve congressional control over the budget. He also detailed the possible utilization of the GAO by Congress as part of a new legislative system to consider and monitor the budget: (1) analyses of budget justifications; (2) assignment of staff; (3) obtaining information and analyzing data; and (4) improving budgetary, fiscal, and program information for Congress.[43] This expanded role for the GAO in congressional budget deliberations was embraced in the Study Committee's final report (April 18, 1973) and became the basis for consideration of new budget legislation.

In 1974, Congress passed a bill that many regard as the most important in the field of budgeting since the Budget and Accounting Act of 1921: the Congressional Budget and Impoundment Control Act of 1974.[44] That act, the product of years of congressional frustration, deliberation, and discussion, was aimed to provide Congress a more effective voice in the making of budgetary decisions and in determining budgetary priorities, and to give it teeth in protecting its appropriations against presidential impoundments. Its first six titles provided a very complex procedure for acting on the budget within Congress and a schedule to cover the process; they changed the beginning of the fiscal year from July 1 to October 1, established budget committees in each house, and created a new Congressional Budget Office (CBO) as a staff source of information, developer and analyst of budgetary options, and scorekeeper. The tenth title, which had been developed originally as a separate bill, provided machinery for congressional control over the impoundment of funds (discussed in chapter 7).

Title VII of the 1974 act amended the Legislative Reorganization Act of 1970 to give additional and more specific responsibilities to the GAO in connection with the review and evaluation of federal programs, including the development and recommendation to Congress of methods to make such evaluations, authorization for the GAO to hire outside experts to assist in evaluations, a requirement that the Comptroller General include in his annual report a statement of his activities in this area, and an authorization for him to establish an Office of Program Review and Evaluation—the beginnings of what would later become the Program Analysis Division. Title VIII of the act, likewise an amendment of the Legislative Reorganization Act of 1970, similarly enlarged upon and specified in greater detail the GAO's responsibilities for the building of informational systems in connection with budgetary questions, including the development—in cooperation with the secretary of the treasury, the director of the Office of Management and Budget, and the director of the Congressional Budget Office—of standard terminology, classifications, and definitions of program and budget data. It provided further that information of this type be made available to state and local governments, as appropriate. Titles VII and VIII provide a considerable part of the current workload of the GAO's Program Analysis Division.

Of somewhat lesser significance was another bill, passed during the same year, the General Accounting Office Act of 1974.[45] It consisted of a miscellaneous collection of provisions, designed "to streamline and modernize the role and responsibility of the GAO, so that it may more fully utilize its resources as an arm of Congress."[46] It relieved the GAO of making an audit annually of all government corporations and provided instead that each wholly owned corporation or corporation of mixed ownership be audited "at least once every three years." It transferred the responsibility—along with the personnel and funds—for auditing transportation vouchers and claims to the General Services Administration. It gave the GAO the authority to audit certain nonappropriated fund activities, such as the military exchanges, commissaries, clubs, and theaters. Finally, it offered a miscellany of benefits to the GAO, including employment of additional consultants, control of GAO space requirements in the GAO building, and others.

Perhaps more important than these provisions were two that the GAO sought—and is still seeking—but that were not enacted. The first was authority to issue subpoenas for information required by law to be furnished the Comptroller General when the agencies and contractors failed to produce it. The second was to empower him to bring court action on his own authority for information or action, independent of the Department of Justice.[47]

Legislation Affecting GAO Jurisdiction and Access

During the first twelve years of the Staats term, Congress passed a number of laws affecting the GAO's powers of access to records, documents, and books and its jurisdiction for conducting and reporting on audits. In general, these have had the effect of broadening the scope of the GAO's responsibilities. They fall in several categories. First, when Congress sets up new organizations and programs it has become fairly common, though not universal, practice to include "boiler plate" language giving the GAO audit authority and rights of access. Examples include the Corporation for Public Broadcasting, the Postal Service, the National Railroad Passenger Corporation, the U.S. Railway Association, the Federal Energy Administration, the Trans-Alaska Pipeline Liability Fund, the Susquehanna River Basin Commission, and many others.

A second category is the empowering of the GAO to audit parts or all of activities that were previously exempted. Such extensions of audit authority have in recent years been enacted in connection with public housing programs, the Inter-American Development Bank, the District of Columbia, the Internal Revenue Service, and most recently the bank regulatory agencies, including the Federal Reserve Board. In some cases, Congress has directed the GAO to conduct an audit of specified organizations and programs as it did with respect to the Office of Economic Opportunity and the Small Business Administration. Some agencies are still totally or substantially exempt from GAO investigations,[48] and proposals to extend its jurisdiction over some of these are now under consideration. They include the Federal Bureau of Investigation, the Central Intelligence Agency, and the discretionary accounts of the executive branch.

A third category of broadening the GAO's scope and access concerns federal grants or other financial assistance to state and local governments. In general, the GAO's audit authority has not been construed to extend to funds transferred to other governmental jurisdictions since they lose their federal identity once the transfer has been made. But during the 1960s and 1970s, Congress has with increasing frequency added provisions to its specific legislation to authorize GAO access to the records of grant recipients for purposes of examination, audit, and report. Such a provision has been included, for example, in connection with grants for law enforcement, education, airports, clean air, alcohol and drug abuse, mental health, intergovernmental personnel, occupational safety and health, water pollution, general revenue sharing, and many others. In addition, the Intergovernmental Cooperation Act of 1968[49] required that the Comptroller General, on request of any congressional authorizing committee, make a study of any federal grant-in-aid program to determine its effectiveness, efficiency, procedures, and possible conflicts or duplication with other programs.[50] Collectively, these many acts have opened up a tremendous new territory of potential GAO concern.

The fourth category concerns GAO access to and audit of the records and books of recipients of federal funds in the private sector through contracts or subsidies. In the field of defense contracts particularly, GAO auditing authority extends back to the period before World War II; however, the general effect of recent legislation has been to extend and strengthen it, especially in domestic areas such as health and other areas of research, education, and energy. A particularly important example was the Energy Policy and Conservation Act of 1975,[51] which gave the GAO the responsibility to verify energy data submitted to the government from corporations in the energy field. For this purpose the GAO was empowered to have access to the records of companies and persons who furnish energy information to any federal agency (other than the IRS), to issue subpoenas, and to assess and collect civil penalties up to $10,000 for violations.

New Kinds of Professionals

With the growing emphasis on new kinds of audits and studies directed to management generally, program results, and special problems—in addition to the traditional financial accounting and auditing work—it became increasingly evident that the GAO needed to develop new kinds of skills and orientations among its professional personnel. When Staats became Comptroller General in 1966, the GAO professional staff included about 100 attorneys, and 2,250 accountants or persons whose educational and experience backgrounds were primarily in financial accounting and auditing. In 1967, the GAO began a program to expand and enlarge upon that professional base, a program that is still growing as this is written. Staats did not initiate any large-scale changes through separations and replacements as had Comptroller General Warren at the close of World War II. Rather, he worked gradually through the modification of processes already underway. The program had four major facets: recruitment, training and development, placement and assignment policies, and use of outside consultants.

Recruitment

In fiscal year 1968, the GAO, through its college recruitment, hired its first professionals in fields other than accounting and law. They included eleven management analysts, nine mathematicians, six economists, two statisticians, and one engineer—all hired directly out of college. In 1969, the number increased to 190, and it increased almost every year after that to 1976. In addition, the GAO annually has hired at upper levels persons who had previous work experience in other agencies, often in work other than accounting. The majority of new recruits continued to be accounting majors, but their numbers did not far exceed the accountants who left the agency, so that the total number of accountants remained substantially the same. Their proportion of the total professional staff (see Figure 3) steadily but very gradually declined. On September 30, 1977, of the 4,085 professional staff, 2,496 had entered as accountants and auditors—about 60 percent. The remainder were distributed as follows:[52]

Business and public administration/management	630
Attorneys	126
Actuaries and other mathematical scientists	111
Claims adjudicators/examiners	73
Engineers	27
Computer and information specialists	57
Economists and other social scientists	232
Personnel management specialists	43
Transportation specialists	12
Other	278
Total	1,589

About 1,100 of the professional staff now have advanced degrees; more than half have master's degrees in business administration (391) or accounting (183). But that the accounting credential is still valued within the organization is evident in the steady increase of CPAs in the GAO, whose number reached 646 in 1977.

Indicative of Staats' interest in strengthening the GAO in fields other than accounting were his appointments to the very highest posts, as the opportunities presented themselves, of nonaccountants with considerable experience from other federal agencies, principally the Bureau of the Budget. His first opportunity came in 1969 when Robert F. Keller, the GAO's general counsel, was appointed Assistant (later Deputy) Comptroller General. He named, as the new general counsel, Paul G. Dembling, a lawyer with long administrative as well as legal experience in various federal agencies, most recently as general counsel for the National Aeronautics and

Figure 3

TOTAL GAO WORK FORCE (1922-1978)

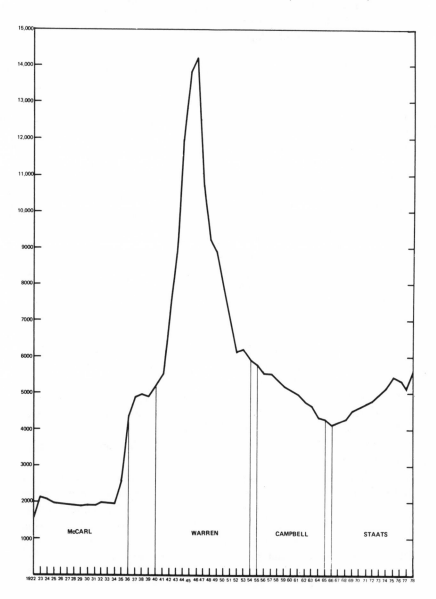

Space Administration (NASA). Between 1969 and 1974, Staats named four others who would soon become Assistant Comptrollers General or GAO division chiefs from outside the career ranks. None had training or experience in accounting, and all were alumni of the Bureau of the Budget. Two of these had long experience in public management; one was trained in political science but had concentrated his career in the area of natural resources and energy. The fourth was an economist with experience focused on welfare and human development.

Training Programs

Although the new "management team" encouraged the attainment of advanced degrees and certificates by staff members, the GAO continued to rely primarily on internal courses with supplemental on-the-job training. The personnel director, though he had an academic background, was an advocate of the in-house approach to training and development. He said:

> The college classroom seldom is the place where one finds the knowledge of how to audit the highly complex programs the General Accounting Office staff member encounters. Generally, through our office-sponsored training programs and on-the-job experience he can develop this ability.[53]

The internal training courses were expanded to encompass some of the new and technical areas for which auditors needed expertise: systems analysis, automated data processing, management theory, quantitative techniques, and so forth.

Placement and Assignments

It may be recalled that under Comptroller General Campbell, the GAO instituted a vigorous rotation program for its younger and middle-grade professional personnel, particularly in its Civil Division. It aimed to make all of the auditors generalists, capable of handling any kind of auditing work at the next higher level. Rotation to different supervisors, different functional areas, and differing kinds of responsibilities was mandatory from the entering grade to the journeyman grades. The generalist concept continued to prevail. During the 1970s, however, it became increasingly evident—at least among some of those in top positions—that there was need for a higher level of functional specialism and expertise. The requirement of rotation after the first year was eliminated in December 1975, and, although some of the divisions still carry on rotation programs of their own, there is growing recognition of the value of specialized knowledge and skills in different areas of activity. A fuller discussion of current assignment practices is contained in chapter 11.

Consultants

But as the GAO's concerns increasingly focused on federal programs and their effectiveness, it has utilized a growing number of outside consultants, expert in the particular fields under study. Some of its divisions maintain extensive lists of consultants who may be called upon to advise, assist, or participate in the framing and conduct of particular studies. They include a wide variety of experts in business and various professions and in the academic fraternity. Most of them are not accountants. The GAO seldom contracts its projects out to private consulting firms or individuals, although it is not unusual for it to propose to other agencies that they contract for external studies and advice. Some of these proposals concern studies on accounting and auditing systems, fields in which the GAO has long had its greatest expertise.

The reliance upon outside consultants varies greatly among the divisions and offices of the GAO. In general, they are used most intensively by the newer divisions that deal with energy and with economic problems. Some of the older ones use them hardly at all. The Comptroller General himself has a consultant panel of about twenty-five prominent leaders from business and the professions, many of whom have had prior experience in Congress or in high executive posts. He is also advised by a group of about twenty-five educator-consultants. This group was initially established by Comptroller General Campbell and consisted principally of deans of business and accounting schools. It has recently been expanded to include administrators and professors from a wide variety of disciplines, including physics, engineering, and various social sciences. Both of these groups meet twice a year.

The changes in personnel policies during the first dozen years of the Staats term were consonant with and supportive of the shifts in the emphases of its work. They encouraged a greater degree of specialization along lines of federal programs, a declining stress on accounting and financial auditing, a growing search for persons competent in program management, and increasing outreach to specialists outside the government. The process has been gradual and the results to this time rather uneven. But the directions are quite clear and consonant with the directions of the GAO as a whole.

Reorganization

Like most of his predecessors, Comptroller General Staats moved slowly and carefully in reorganizing the GAO. And, like them, his organizational changes were consistent with the changing philosophy of the GAO's mission at the time. As indicated earlier, he made a few minor changes soon after his appointment. But his basic reorganization came five and six years later.

By 1971, the needs for reorganization were accompanied by opportunities. During that year, Congress, in response to Staats' request, changed the title of the Assistant Comptroller General to Deputy Comptroller General.[54] By a later law the same year, it authorized the establishment of four new positions of executive level (generally equivalent in rank to the assistant secretaries of departments).

In February 1971, Staats appointed an Organization Planning Committee to develop proposals for reorganization. That group was composed entirely of GAO officials and was chaired by Deputy Comptroller General Keller. The first among the committee recommendations, slightly modified by Staats, went into effect on July 1, 1971. An Office of Policy and Program Planning was established to group the existing functions of the Program Planning Staff and the policy work of the Office of Policy and Special Studies. This office would serve as the Comptroller General's principal adviser in the areas of policy formulation, long-range planning, internal review, and publications. At the same time, the nonstaff work of the Office of Policy and Special Studies became the basis for a new divison, the Financial and General Management Studies Division. It was given primary responsibility for financial management, systems analysis, actuarial work, statistical sampling, automatic data processing, intergovernmental audit standards, and somewhat later the review and approval or disapproval of agency accounting systems.

Later in the year, Staats accepted the Keller Committee's recommendation that a new division be established for procurement, based upon four perceived needs for: (1) a uniform approach to the audit and review of procurement; (2) centralization of GAO expertise in the procurement field; (3) increased attention to procurement policy and procurement actions in areas that may not now be receiving sufficient attention; (4) a vehicle for follow-through on recommendations that would be made by the Commission on Government Procurement the following year. Although he agreed with the committee's recommendation, Staats decided not to implement the idea until early 1972, when it could be announced with the rest of the audit division changes and its staffing could be accomplished on an orderly basis.

On January 25, 1972, a little less than six years after he had taken office, Staats announced his decisions on reorganization in an eight-page memorandum to all employees of the GAO. He reviewed the background and work of the Keller Committee, as well as the various changes in the role and workload of the GAO, and cited the four benefits that he hoped would result from the reorganization: (1) acceleration of the growth of program and functional expertise among senior staff; (2) provision of more opportunities for staff growth and advancement; (3) facilitation of the timely completion of the GAO's work; and (4) assistance to the Comptroller General in dealing with his expanded responsibilities.

Figure 4

ORGANIZATIONAL CHANGES OF THE
GENERAL ACCOUNTING OFFICE, 1971-1972[a]

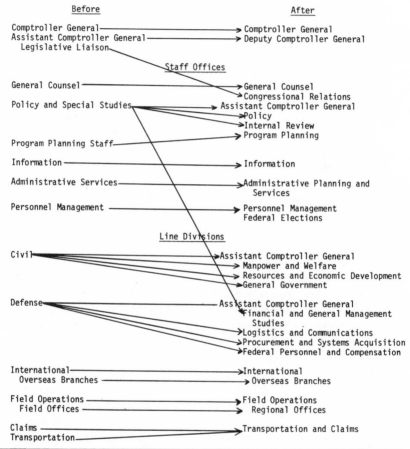

a/The lines are intended to indicate only the sources and destinations of the
major functions and personnel. There are a number of movements of activities
at lower organizational levels that are not shown.

The major changes in the reorganization proposal (see Figure 4) were the elimination of the two accounting and auditing divisions (civil and defense) and the creation of six new operating divisions, each with responsibilities for government-wide programs and functions. They would be called: Logistics and Communications Division, Procurement and Systems Acquisition Division (as recommended in 1971), Federal Personnel and Compensation Division, Manpower and Welfare Division, Resources and Economic

Development Division, and General Government Division.

In the same memorandum, Staats announced that, taking advantage of his new authority to fill four new positions at an executive level, he was creating three posts with the title of Assistant Comptroller General. The first of these went to Ellsworth Morse, who would direct three staff offices: internal review, policy, and program planning. The other two Assistant Comptrollers General would have direct line authority over a group of audit divisions. A. T. Samuelson, formerly director of the Civil Division, was a natural choice to fill the position of Assistant Comptroller General (for domestic programs), with responsibility for the three divisions that were essentially carved out of his former bailiwick: general government, resources and economic development, and manpower and welfare. The three choices to head these divisions were not surprises; all had been deputy or associate directors under Samuelson in the old Civil Division.[55]

The International Division remained intact, but the four other new divisions—financial and general management, logistics and communications, procurement and systems acquisition, and federal personnel and compensation—were grouped under another new Assistant Comptroller General (management reviews), Thomas D. Morris. Morris was the second top-level Staats appointee from outside the GAO. He came with long and varied management experience in both the private and public sectors. He had served in the TVA, the Bureau of the Budget, as assistant secretary of defense (both for installation and logistics and for manpower) and in a number of other capacities. Staats had appointed him as special assistant to the Comptroller General in October 1970, and with the reorganization he became Assistant Comptroller General in charge of four of the new divisions in April 1971.[56] To head the four new divisons, Staats again relied on GAO insiders. Three of them had been deputy or associate directors of the old Defense Division, and the fourth had been a regional office manager.

The interpositions of two Assistant Comptrollers General between the various line divisions and the Comptroller General proved to be an interim arrangement. In 1974, the two Assistant Comptrollers General were transferred to staff positions and the division directors reported directly to the Office of the Comptroller General. Morris was placed in charge of the GAO's management services in 1974, a capacity in which he served until he resigned in 1975.[57] Samuelson also retired in 1975.

A number of other shifts and additions in the GAO's organization were made during the years following 1972, but they have not fundamentally altered the basic thrust of the overhaul of that year. In 1972, Staats hired Phillip S. Hughes to head up the election campaign financing effort that was thrust upon the GAO in that year. Hughes, like Staats, had had long experience in the Bureau of the Budget, and in fact succeeded Staats as its deputy director when Staats became Comptroller General. Hughes later became the fourth Assistant Comptroller General. With the creation in 1974 of the Federal Election Commission, most of the GAO's responsibilities in campaign financing were terminated, and Hughes was assigned to the development of certain special programs, notably in the fields of energy and program analysis. He brought in from the outside two social scientists to head up these two programs, both of whom had had prior experience in the Bureau of the Budget. The two, with their staffs, in 1976 "spun off" from Hughes' office to become directors of two new divisions: the Energy and Minerals Division and the Program Analysis Division. The latter division was given the main GAO responsibilities under the Congressional Budget and Impoundment Control Act of 1974, as described in a later section.[58] It was already directed to undertake the new responsibilities of the Comptroller General for reviewing and approving or disapproving questionnaires, forms, and surveys proposed by the independent regulatory agencies.[59]

A few months later, in February 1977, Hughes resigned,[60] and Morse passed away in November 1977. Thus, of the four authorized Assistant Comptroller General appointments, none remained at the time of this writing.

Three other organizational changes are worthy of note. In 1972, the GAO set up its first technical library, reflecting to some extent its gradual shift from straight financial auditing to managerial and programmatic concerns. In 1973, a separate Office of Congressional Relations was established.[61] And in 1974, following passage of the General Accounting Office Act of that year,[62] the functions and personnel of auditing transportation vouchers were moved to the General Services Administration. The GAO had employed some 400 technical and clerical personnel in that work, and one of the consequences of the transfer was that the overall work force of the GAO in fiscal year 1976 showed a decline—for the first time since the first year under Elmer Staats.

The Claims Division and the Office of General Counsel, plus of course the Comptroller General and the Deputy Comptroller General themselves, remained as the only organizational vestiges of the first GAO. But the GAO's original powers remained intact and indeed somewhat enlarged; and they could be called upon when the need arose.

Among the line divisions, there have been some changes in jurisdiction and in personnel assignments in top positions. But in the main, the thrusts of the 1971-1973 reorganization remain. The structural orientation to broad categories of executive branch organization are reflected in the various auditing divisions; a greater degree of program specialization has thus been made possible. The number of top-level positions was tremendously increased with the addition of four executive level slots, and a great increase of super-grade positions with the more than doubling of the number of auditing divisions, each with its director, deputy director, and associate directors. The average age of top-level incumbents was considerably reduced, and it remains relatively lower than in most federal career systems. The opportunities for leadership and intervention from the top grew through the flattening of the structure and the development of staff services. Congressional relations, up and down the line, were enormously expanded and became more systematized.

The reorganization was accomplished without substantial changes in the nature—the educational background, the training and indoctrination, and the experience—of leadership personnel. Except for the two new divisions that were established in 1976 (the Energy and Minerals and the Program Analysis divisions), almost all of the division directors, deputies, and associates were individuals recruited and experienced before the arrival of Elmer B. Staats. Almost all were initially educated as accountants and experienced as auditors in the old civil and defense audit divisions. The majority of them are CPAs. Any changes in their orientations, in their views of the world and of the GAO's role in it, came from their own adaptability, flexibility, and responsiveness to changing work demands and to the new leadership, not from any shifts of boxes in an organization chart. It should further be noted that the reorganization did not directly affect the GAO's regional offices where nearly half of its staff works.

* * *

The changes of the Staats regime were less rapid and less dramatic than were those of Comptroller General Warren after World War II. This was probably due in part to the fact that he inherited a staff that was much more in keeping with the times, and the needs of the times, and more professional and tractable, than did Warren. Staats inaugurated no massive infusion of new people or separations of the older ones. Rather, he worked with what was there, gradually brought in different kinds of recruits, promoted to upper positions those in whom he had confidence, and restructured the organization in ways that would facilitate the effectuation of the GAO's mission as he viewed it.

Notes

1. As estimated in the 1978 budget. It should be noted, however, that as the GAO pointed out at the time of its budget hearings, a substantial part of outlays for the legislative branch are for noncongressional purposes.

2. According to John W. Macy, then chairman of the Civil Service Commission and principal presidential advisor on appointments. Interview, November 16, 1977.

3. In recognition of his facility in serving both parties as deputy director of the budget, a political position, his colleagues there, after his designation as Comptroller General, presented him a seat cushion for his desk chair with an elephant on one side and a donkey on the other. Interview with Comptroller General Staats, June 29, 1977.

4. Interview with Comptroller General Staats, June 29, 1977.

5. Memorandum to the GAO staff from Comptroller General Staats, August 27, 1969.

6. The term is borrowed from Hugh Heclo, who used it to characterize political executives in his recent book, *A Government of Strangers: Executive Politics in Washington* (Washington, D.C.: Brookings Institution, 1977). Heclo had in turn borrowed it from James Madison in the *Constitutional Debates, June 2, 3, 1787*. (Quoted in Heclo, p. 84).

7. Comptroller General's report to Joint Economic Committee of Congress (B-162719), January 29, 1968.

8. Comptroller General's report to Congress (B-115398), July 29, 1969.

9. P.L. 91-510, October 26, 1976, Sec. 204.

10. P.L. 93-344, July 12, 1974.

11. *General Accounting Office Comprehensive Audit Manual*, part I, chapter 2, p. 1. Emphasis added.

12. Ibid., p. 3.

13. Ibid., p. 5.

14. Ibid.

15. Memorandum from the Comptroller General to the heads of divisions and offices, October 20, 1977.

16. Examples of the GAO's studies—how they were initiated, how they were done, and what their impact was—are contained in the companion volume: Erasmus H. Kloman, ed., *Cases in Accountability: The Work of GAO* (Boulder, Colo.: Westview Press, 1979).

17. U.S. Congress, House, Committee on Appropriations, *Report on Department of Defense Appropriations Bill, 1970*, H. Rept. 91-698, 91st Cong., 1st Sess., 1969, p. 47.

18. U.S. Congress, Subcommittee on Economy in Government of the Joint Economic Committee, *The Economics of Military Procurement*, 91st Cong., 1st Sess., 1969.

19. U.S. Congress, Joint Economic Committee, *Hearings on The Military Budget and National Economic Priorities*, 91st Cong., 1st Sess., 1969, part 2, p. 714.

20. Ibid., p. 721.

21. B-159896, March 17, 1971.

22. Letter to L. Mendel Rivers from Elmer B. Staats, September 12, 1969.

23. U.S. Congress, Senate, Subcommittee on Government Operations,

Hearings on *Capability of GAO to Analyze and Audit Defense Expenditures,* September 16 and 17, 1969.

24. Ibid., pp. 102-4.

25. Ibid., p. 9.

26. Ibid., p. 11.

27. For further information about these reports, see Kloman, *Cases,* "Financial Status of Major Systems Acquisitions."

28. P.L. 81-774, September 8, 1950.

29. In addition to his number two position on the Senate Banking and Currency Committee, Proxmire also served as chairman of the Joint Economic Committee and member of the Joint Committee on Defense Production.

30. P.L. 90-370, July 1, 1968.

31. B-39995(1), January 19, 1970.

32. Proxmire had not waited until the GAO report was received officially; he filed his legislation (S. 3302) on December 23, 1969.

33. P.L. 91-379, August 5, 1970.

34. *Status Report on the Cost Accounting Standards Program—Accomplishments and Problems,* PSAD-76-154, August 20, 1976.

35. Ibid., p. 25.

36. The others were two members of the House of Representatives and a public member appointed by the speaker of the House; two members of the Senate and a public member appointed by the president of the Senate; two members of the executive branch and three public members appointed by the President of the United States.

37. *Executive Branch Action on Recommendations of the Commission on Government Procurement,* PSAD-75-61, March 17, 1975, p. 20.

38. P.L. 93-400, August 30, 1974.

39. P.L. 91-510, October 26, 1970.

40. Ibid., Sec. 204.

41. Ibid., Sec. 203.

42. P.L. 92-599, October 27, 1972.

43. Testimony of Comptroller General Staats before the Joint Study Committee on Budget Control, March 7, 1973.

44. P.L. 93-344.

45. P.L. 93-604, January 2, 1975.

46. U.S. Congress, Senate, S. Rept. 93-1514.

47. As will be discussed in a later chapter, the second of these powers was provided in the case of impoundments by the Congressional Budget and Impoundment Control Act of 1974. The Comptroller General has been granted the subpoena power in certain specific cases, but not in general.

48. Among them are a few private-public corporations, such as COMSAT.

49. P.L. 90-577, October 16, 1968.
50. Ibid., Sec. 602.
51. P.L. 93-153, November 16, 1973.
52. *GAO Annual Report*, 1976, p. 221.
53. "What the Professional Staff Member in the U.S. General Accounting Office Must Know in the Future," speech by Leo Herbert, Jackson, Mississippi, October 19, 1967.
54. P.L. 92-51, July 9, 1971.
55. As of this writing, all three men continue to hold the same division director positions, although the names of the Resources and Economic Development and the Manpower and Welfare divisions have been changed to Community and Economic Development and Human Resources divisions, respectively.
56. See Figure 4.
57. Morris later became the first inspector general of the Department of Health, Education and Welfare (see chapter 10).
58. P.L. 93-344, July 12, 1974. However, the task of policing presidential impoundments was subsequently transferred to the Office of General Counsel.
59. This responsibility had previously been vested in the Office of Management and Budget. It was transferred to the GAO by P.L. 93-153, November 16, 1973.
60. After several temporary and intermediate assignments, Hughes became an assistant secretary of the new Department of Energy.
61. Congressional relations had previously been handled by a small staff under the general counsel and later the Deputy Comptroller General.
62. P.L. 93-604, January 25, 1975.

7

THE THIRD GAO:
THE COMPTROLLER GENERAL AS AN
INDEPENDENT OFFICIAL, 1966-1978

If a man will begin with certainties, he shall end in doubts; but if he will be content to begin with doubts he shall end in certainties.
　　　　　　　　　—Francis Bacon, *The Advancement of Learning,* 1605

No man is allowed to be a judge in his own cause, because his interest would certainly bias his judgment, and, not improbably, corrupt his integrity. With equal, nay with greater reason, a body of men are unfit to be both judges and parties at the same time.
　　　　　　　　　—James Madison, *The Federalist Papers, No. 10,* 1787-1789

Although the GAO, like other federal agencies, is a creature of Congress and although much of its work is directed to the service of Congress, the Comptroller General possesses certain continuing powers of a nonlegislative nature that he may exercise with substantial independence. Some of his decisions may be appealed to the courts; some may result in special legislation; some have been contested and have led to open confrontation. Most of these "independent" powers were inherited by the Comptroller General from his predecessor, the comptroller of the treasury, in 1921: the settling of accounts, the disallowance of payments judged by the GAO to be illegal or improper, the issuing of advance decisions on the legality of proposed expenditures, the countersigning of warrants, and the settling of claims for and against the government. Some of these powers are invoked only occasionally,[1] but their existence is considered a potent persuader for other GAO activities. Two of those inherited powers continue as major activities of the GAO: the rendering of legal advice, opinions, and decisions, mainly on matters involving financial questions, and the settlement of claims.

A few other "independent powers" have developed, or were legislated, since 1921. One is the review and decision on disputes raised by disappointed bidders for federal contracts, generally known as "bid protests." Although there is precedent for this activity from the early years of the GAO, it did not become a very significant element in the GAO's work until the 1960s. In quite a different arena, the GAO was required by the Budget and Accounting

Procedures Act of 1950 to prescribe accounting principles and standards for federal agencies and to review and approve or disapprove the accounting standards they proposed. Later, in 1972, the Comptroller General was required by law to investigate and police the financing of presidential election campaigns, a responsibility that proved to be temporary. Still later, in 1974, he was called upon to monitor presidential impoundments of appropriated funds and authorized to take legal action against the executive branch when the provisions of the law were violated.

Legal and Related Powers

Since the beginning of the GAO, an important responsibility of the Comptroller General has been the rendering of decisions and the provision of advice on the interpretation of legislation and the legality of individual financial transactions. He and his predecessor, the comptroller in the treasury, have been required by law since 1894 to respond to inquiries from the various executive agencies, their heads and their accountable officers, on the legality of proposed payments in advance. He resolves disputes between agencies and businesses concerning government contracts. Many of these inquiries result in rulings by the Comptroller General that are final and binding on the executive branch, though some may be appealed to the courts.[2] In addition, he is frequently called upon by members and committees of the Congress for opinions on legal interpretations of existing law, and for comments on drafts of proposed legislation.

Most of this work is carried out within the GAO by the Office of the General Counsel, staffed principally by about 140 attorneys. That office also assists the other GAO divisions by advising them and sometimes participating with them on individual projects in which legal questions arise; and it reviews all of their reports to assure that the findings and recommendations are consistent with statutory requirements.

Over the years, the decisions of the Comptroller General (and his predecessor, the comptroller of the treasury) have cumulated to enormous numbers. They are very nearly the bible, verse, and multiple footnotes on law in the national government, a basic reference guide for officials of federal agencies. They are available to Congress, the courts, and the public. The more important ones are brought together annually and published as *Decisions of the Comptroller General*. The current workload is also enormous. During fiscal year 1977, the Office of the General Counsel reported that it had disposed of more than five and a half thousand legal matters. A substantial proportion of these concern rather small, one-time questions, and some are very technical. On the other hand, the Comptroller General produces a number of interpretations every year with broad and enduring implications on public policy.

The largest single area of GAO legal activity is that of procurement law, which accounts for nearly two fifths of its cases. The majority of these arise from protests of disappointed bidders against agency procurement decisions. Some come from questions of the heads and accountable officers in the various executive agencies, and from congressional inquiries. An increasing number arise from complaints against state and local governments on bids for federally financed contracts. And some in fact come from the courts, both federal and state, seeking GAO advice on procurement actions under litigation.

The second largest area of GAO legal work is the interpretation of statutes regarding the rights of agencies to expend funds on programs and projects. Third are rulings on the pay, rights, and benefits of federal personnel, both civilian and military. The remainder of the legal work is scattered among a wide variety of legal-financial questions covering nearly the gamut of federal activities. The range of the GAO's legal work is suggested by the following examples of recent decisions and opinions:

- it advised the leaders of both houses of Congress on the meaning and interpretation of the Impoundment Control Act soon after the act was passed;
- it ruled that foreign funds acquired by the Treasury Department could not be used to support congressional travel abroad (corrective legislation with stronger reporting requirements was soon passed);
- it ruled that the Department of Labor had no authority to allow payments in violation of its regulations under a grant program to the state of Rhode Island;
- in a bid protest involving a contract for certain fighter airplanes, it ruled that the Department of the Navy was not required by law to expend funds provided in a lump-sum appropriation when the statute does not specify its specific purpose, notwithstanding the intent as indicated in committee reports and floor statements.[3]

Bid Protests[4]

The rendering of opinions on appeals of disappointed bidders who failed to win government contracts is a relatively recent GAO activity and was modest in its beginnings. It is now one of the most time-demanding and occasionally contentious of GAO activities. In 1977, the GAO rendered formal decisions on 820 protests from disgruntled bidders for government contracts. The procedure is simple, inexpensive, and quick for the aggrieved parties, and these are its main attractions. It requires only a letter from the protesting bidder to the GAO, which then requests a statement of the facts from the agency involved, offers an opportunity for rebuttal by the disappointed bidder, holds a conference of the interested parties, and then renders an opinion as to whether the contract action taken or proposed is supported by law and regulation. The GAO opinion is not necessarily final. If it is against the protester, he may still try to carry his case into court; agencies almost invariably comply with decisions against their contract actions. On a contract award already made, the agency must report to a number of congressional committees on corrective action it will take in response to the Comptroller General's recommendation for corrective action.[5] Decisions against an agency's proposed action to award a contract are binding on the basis that any payment made pursuant to a contract awarded after notice that such award would be improper can be disallowed by the GAO.

During his first few years in office, the first Comptroller General, McCarl, rendered advance opinions on about a dozen requests from executive agencies with regard to procurement. Then in 1925, he responded to a protest of a disappointed bidder against the Panama Canal authorities—the first published GAO decision on a bid protest from a private contractor. Its opinion was against the canal but did not result in any relief to the protester. Fifteen years later, however, the Supreme Court, in a celebrated decision on a case questioning a determination of the secretary of labor, not alone ruled in favor of the secretary's decision but also indicated that the litigator had no standing in court to sue the government on such a matter involving the administration's interpretation of a procurement law.[6] The Court held that "judicial restraint of those who administer the Government's purchasing would constitute a break with settled judicial practice and a departure into fields hitherto wisely and happily apportioned by the genius of our polity to the administration of another branch of Government."[7] That decision could be construed to mean that aggrieved bidders had in effect only one place outside the executive branch in which to seek relief—the GAO. In some subsequent cases, however, the courts have qualified that ruling as to standing in court and have overruled or modified some of the GAO's bid protest opinions.

Meanwhile, the volume of bid protests handled by the GAO grew phenomenally after the 1960s—from about 200 per year to more than five per working day in 1977. The reasons are essentially related to convenience and practicality rather than law. The procedure provides the protesters an unbiased listener for their grievances inexpensively and relatively quickly. Some persons outside the GAO have complained that the bid protest procedure is too slow. On the other hand, the informality of the procedure permits relatively rapid handling, certainly in comparison with normal judicial actions. On the average, a bid protest from the date of receipt in the GAO to the reaching of a decision takes eighty to ninety working days. Even if the protestors lose, as they do in the majority of cases, they have the satisfaction of knowing that their views were considered, and sometimes agencies take corrective action. It is a convenience to the agencies to have an impartial arbiter to which their aggrieved clients may turn—short of the courts—especially since relatively few GAO decisions result in reversals or additional costs. A good many are withdrawn or amicably settled and adjusted without a formal decision. It is useful to Congress and also to individual congressmen beleaguered by aggrieved constituents to have their own agency overseeing executive branch procurement. The GAO itself considers it desirable to assure the integrity of the procurement system, to correct deficiencies in the system, and to contribute to improvements in the regulations governing federal procurement.[8]

In the last dozen years there have been a bewildering variety of court opinions on procurement bidding actions and the weight, if any, that should be given to GAO decisions. But the Department of Justice has never recognized the GAO's power to render decisions on bid protests that are binding on the executive agencies. This has led to more or less open conflict between the attorney general and the Comptroller General on at least two recent occasions. In 1971, the latter officer sent to the former for comment a proposed revision of the GAO's bid protest procedures. Attorney General John Mitchell responded in a letter on June 14, 1971, in which he vigorously stated the Justice Department position that the awarding of contracts was "purely an Executive function"; that the GAO, "as an arm of the legislative branch, should be limited in these matters to the advising of the procurement agencies on a purely voluntary basis"; that it "has no authority to regulate the withholding of awards"; and that the GAO's powers were to postaudit, not to render advance decisions on the protest of private bidders.

The issue was drawn again in late 1976 when the administrator for federal procurement policy (in the Office of Management and Budget) proposed changes in the federal procurement regulations that included the statements that the final decisions on bid protests are the responsibility of the heads of the executive agencies involved and that the views of the Comptroller General are advisory and not binding. Comptroller General Staats wrote a letter to the administrator objecting that the regulations should make clear that his opinions are not merely advisory but are authorized in law, in court decisions, and that his ruling on bid protests is consistent with the recommendations of the Commission on Government Procurement. The administrator then asked the attorney general his opinion. Attorney General Griffin B. Bell responded on March 17, 1977, endorsing the proposed regulations as written, contradicting Staats, and relying on essentially the same arguments that Mitchell had used six years earlier.

About a year later, the Congress resumed consideration of the proposed Federal Acquisition Act of 1977, bringing together and modernizing a great variety of procurement legislation on the books from preceding decades. Such a law was one of the principal recommendations of the Commission on

Government Procurement. Title VII of that bill specifically authorized the Comptroller General "to decide any protest submitted by an interested party in accordance with rules and regulations he shall issue," and provided that those "proceedings shall be informal to the fullest extent possible." A proposed provision that his decisions be binding upon the executive branch was deleted specifically to avoid the constitutional question. And a provision was added to assure aggrieved bidders standing in court should they wish to appeal actions of executive agencies or the Comptroller General for judicial review. It is possible that this bill, if passed, will resolve the long-standing dispute between the Comptroller General and the attorney general on bid protests.

The Philadelphia Story[9]

One of the most interesting and celebrated recent confrontations between the Comptroller General and the executive branch arose in connection with the application of civil rights conditions to government contracts. In 1966, the Department of Labor proposed that bidders for such contracts be required to submit affirmative action programs for approval by its Office of Federal Contract Compliance prior to the award of the contract. During the following two years the idea was tested in several cities, and President Johnson in February 1968 proposed regulations to make the requirement nationwide.

The involvement of the Comptroller General in this instance was initiated by the objections of a single congressman, William C. Cramer (D., Fla.), who wrote the Comptroller General to question the requirement that contractors produce an "acceptable" affirmative action program without advising them in advance as to what the minimum standards for approval were. In response, the GAO wrote the secretary of labor a conciliatory letter but stated that the failure to specify minimum standards of affirmative action was a violation of competitive bidding regulations.[10] The Labor Department replied that its aim was to encourage "the utmost in creativity, ingenuity and imagination" on the part of contractors in developing affirmative action proposals, and that it feared that any minimum standards it might set forth would in effect become maximum.

Representative Cramer, unsatisfied by this response, wrote again to complain that the so-called Philadelphia Plan, requiring such affirmative action programs, which had been adopted for that city the previous year, had not been changed in response to the Comptroller General's ruling. The latter then issued a stronger statement, to the effect that:

> In our view where federally assisted contracts are required to be awarded on the basis of publicly advertised competitive bidding, award may not properly be withheld pursuant to the Plan from the lowest responsible and otherwise

responsive bidder on the basis of an unacceptable affirmative action program, until provision is made for informing prospective bidders of definite minimum requirements to be met by the bidder's program and any other standards or criteria by which the acceptability of such program would be judged. . . . The present lack of specific detail and rigid guideline requirements for an acceptable affirmative action program . . . permits denial of a contract to the low bidder to be based on purely arbitrary or capricious decisions, and award to be made on the basis of similar decisions.[11]

In the spring of 1969, the Department of Labor, now under the Republican leadership of President Nixon, gave in. It issued instructions that the area coordinators of the Office of Federal Contract Compliance provide a "range of minority manpower utilization of each of the designated trades" with each invitation for bids, and contractors were required to include in their proposals their own ranges, equal to or better than those of the office.[12]

Comptroller General Staats was satisfied on his initial objection, but soon would raise quite a different one on the legality of the requirements as set forth by the Department of Labor under the Civil Rights Act of 1964. After an exchange of correspondence with the solicitor of labor, he issued a new ruling to the general effect that the requirement of contractors' meeting goals in minority employment made race a factor in hiring and that in fact such goals amounted to racial quotas, which were expressly prohibited by the Civil Rights Act.[13]

The matter was then referred in the administration to the attorney general, who issued a formal opinion flatly contradicting the Comptroller General: "The United States as a contracting party may not require an employer to engage in practices which Congress has prohibited. It does not follow, however, that the United States may not require of those who contract with it certain employment practices which Congress has not seen fit to require of employers generally. . . . The employer may have a right to refuse to abandon his customary hiring practices, but he has no right to contract with the Government on his own terms."[14]

This overt confrontation on a politically explosive issue led to vigorous controversy on the Hill. In general, the southern and conservative congressmen supported the Comptroller General, and the liberal group (on the racial issue) supported the administration's Philadelphia Plan—in a curious reversal of political roles. Senator Sam Ervin (D., N.C.), leader of the former contingent, implored that the Senate not "shirk the Constitutional responsibility of Congress to maintain control over appropriations,"[15] and he introduced an amendment to the Supplemental Appropriation Bill of 1970 that would explicitly prohibit federal expenditures on any "contract or agreement which the Comptroller General of the United States holds to be in contravention of any Federal statute."[16] Unfortunately for Ervin the bill came up a few days before Christmas, 1969, and Congress was anxious to adjourn for the holidays. President Nixon threatened to veto any bill containing such a provision;[17] the House gave in and the Ervin amendment was defeated. But Nixon preceded his veto warning with a statement never before enunciated by a President: "that the amendment need not be stricken but that it should be modified to permit prompt court review of any difference between legal opinions of the Comptroller General and those of the Executive, and to permit the Comptroller General to have his own counsel (rather than the Attorney General) to represent him in such cases."[18]

Before the Philadelphia Plan could be implemented in Philadelphia, an association of contractors sued to enjoin the inclusion of its provisions in invitations for bids for a certain construction contract. They lost the case in the federal district court, which upheld the plan;[19] on appeal, they lost again;[20] and the Supreme Court denied certiorari. At least for the time being, the Labor Department had won the battle, and the Comptroller General had lost. He took no further action in the matter.

The Philadelphia story was not unique in some respects but it was certainly not a typical episode in the GAO's history. The way it arose—on a complaint of a single representative in Congress—was unusual for a major issue. The complaint ultimately rested on an alleged violation, in a projected program for federal procurement, of a law—the Civil Rights Act—adopted for a quite different purpose than federal contracting. It was a case in which the Comptroller General in effect took a side on a high political (as well as legal) issue about which Congress, his bosses, was sharply divided. Ultimately, his office became a focus of confrontation between Congress and the President. The final arbiter on the instant case was the judiciary, but it ruled on the merits, not on the question of whether the attorney general or the Comptroller General should prevail. The latter issue is still moot.

Impoundment Control and the Case of Staats *v.* Lynn et al.

In 1974, following a period of growing frustration in Congress over the multiplying impoundments of appropriated funds by President Nixon, Congress passed the Impoundment Control Act.[21] The act was in part an effort to give Congress ultimate control over impoundments and to sidestep the constitutional issue that was being raised in a number of court cases over the constitutionality of presidential reservations of appropriated funds in the absence of specific congressional authority to do so.

The act that President Nixon signed in June 1974, two months before he resigned, provided highly complicated procedures for the reporting and considering of proposed presidential impoundments and made the Comptroller General the monitoring and enforcing authority. The President was required to report to Congress and to the Comptroller General any impoundment he wished to invoke with a justification for it. The latter was required to analyze each such proposal and himself report on it to Congress. Further, he was required to report to the Congress any de facto impoundment of funds that the President did not report. Either house could negate temporary impoundments (called deferrals) by a simple majority vote; and permanent impoundments (called rescissions) could not go into effect unless both houses voted positively for them within forty-five legislative days. If Congress disapproved an impoundment in either of these ways, the President was required to release the funds. And if he failed to do so, the Comptroller General was empowered to bring suit in federal court to compel release of the funds after twenty-five days notice to the Congress of his intention to initiate such action.

The act added important new responsibilities to the GAO and particularly its General Counsel who subsequently was given the responsibility to investigate, keep track of, and prepare reports for the Comptroller General on all impoundments. For the most part, the White House (through the Office of Management and Budget) has reported most proposed impoundments; the Comptroller General discovered only ten unreported impoundments in the first two years following the act and these were all subsequently resolved. During that period, almost $41 billion of impoundments was reported, and the Congress disapproved 39 percent of them. Most were temporary impoundments—deferrals—and the bulk of these were approved. But of the $8 billion proposed for rescission, Congress failed to approve four fifths.[22] The great bulk of the President's proposed rescissions were in domestic fields—nearly 95 percent. Deferrals, or temporary impoundments, were also predominantly in domestic programs. Defense programs accounted for about 20 percent. But perhaps most significant is that the total impoundments declined sharply from the first year, 1975, to the second, 1976. In 1975 the dollar amount of funds proposed for impoundment was two and a half times that in 1976.

In only one instance in the first three years of experience with the Impoundment Control Act did the Comptroller General take legal action against the administration to enforce it, and that occasion almost brought about a constitutional confrontation. In very summary form, the case was begun on September 20, 1974, when President Ford sent to Congress a bundle of impoundment proposals, including one to defer $264 million in contract authority for a housing program. Virtually all of the Democratic leaders of the Senate—the majority leader and the chairmen of most of the standing committees—signed a letter to Comptroller General Staats insisting that he carry out the law as they had intended it.[23] The Ford proposal for a deferral, which the GAO said was really a rescission, was turned down by Congress, and the President refused to release the funds.[24] On April 15, 1975, the Comptroller General brought suit to compel the

President to release the funds in an action altogether unique in American history.[25] Two months later, the attorney general, acting for the defendants, filed a motion to dismiss on the grounds that the provisions of the act empowering the Comptroller General to bring suit were unconstitutional and that therefore he had no standing in court. The claim of unconstitutionality rested on two arguments: (1) that the action was brought to "enforce the law," which is a power assigned to the executive branch; and (2) that the action did not constitute a "case or controversy" between the contending parties—the suit could be called "*The Congress* v. *The President,*" which would be unconstitutional since the Constitution provided means other than the courts to resolve controversies between the branches of government. Both arguments rested partly on the premise that the Comptroller General is part of the legislative branch, an agent of Congress.

The Comptroller General responded to this motion on July 28 with an extensive brief built around three main points: (1) that the Comptroller General was not executing the law but rather was suing to compel executive branch officials to execute it; (2) that he was not acting as an agent of Congress in this suit but as an independent officer who has duties of both a legislative and executive character and his decision to sue was a discretionary act; and (3) that even if in this action he were to be construed as an agent of Congress, he could, like members of Congress, bring lawsuits to protect legislative interests. The Comptroller General's brief strongly asserted his executive as well as legislative responsibilities in that he is both an agent of Congress and an independent officer.

Neither the motion nor the suit reached the point of trial and judicial decision. On October 17, 1975, Secretary of Housing and Urban Development Carla Hills announced that the housing program in question would be reactivated and that funds would be released. The two contending parties agreed that there was no need for further continuation of the suit, and it was dismissed. Thus was resolution of the constitutional question on the status and role of the Comptroller General again deferred; but the arguments on both sides drew the issues involved more sharply than before. And it is of course perfectly possible that another impoundment case will arise and go all the way through judicial process in the future.[26]

The Campaign Financing Experience

Early in 1971, the Democratic leadership of the Senate introduced a bill to regulate, restrict, and disclose the financing of federal election campaigns and where necessary to initiate prosecution of violators. After nearly a year of consideration, hearings, and debate, the bill, considerably amended, was approved by Congress on January 19, 1972. It was signed into law by President Nixon on February 7, 1972, and became effective sixty days later, April 7, 1972, as the Federal Election Campaign Act of 1971 (P.L. 92-225).

During the course of the congressional deliberations, the Comptroller General on a number of occasions voiced his vigorous opposition to placing administrative, audit, investigative, or enforcement responsibilities in connection with elections upon the GAO in order that it might maintain its reputation for independence and objectivity, free from political considerations. He even suggested at that time the establishment of a nonpartisan election commission to carry out these tasks.

In spite of his objections, the act as passed gave major responsibilities to the GAO with respect to presidential and vice-presidential campaigns. The secretary of the Senate and the clerk of the House were given somewhat comparable responsibilities with respect to House and Senate candidacies. But the big and immediate job for that year was the presidential election. Even before the bill had become law, Comptroller General Staats formed a task force to plan for this new undertaking, and before the act became effective he had formed an Office of Federal Elections to administer the duties of the Comptroller General. A little later, he appointed Phillip S. Hughes to direct the office and its operations. Hughes assembled a staff of about twenty-five professionals, mostly drawn from the GAO itself, and relied heavily upon the existing resources of the regional offices of the GAO. In accord with the act the Comptroller General formed a Clearinghouse of Election Administration to gather and disseminate information on election administration throughout the United States, and for this purpose appointed an ad hoc advisory committee including political practitioners and experts.[27] The Office of Federal Elections conducted or contracted for a variety of studies relevant to elections, including intensive studies of election administration in seven states, a survey of state election laws, a survey of state and local election boards, and studies of voter registration systems, of voter counting methods, of the use of computers in elections, of absentee registration and voting, of the training of election officials, and of the costs of administering elections.

But the more immediate and urgent tasks of the GAO's Office of Federal Elections concerned the famous, and infamous, political campaigns of 1972. In the course of a few weeks, it had to develop and issue regulations and guidelines for the candidates and the thousands of committees spending money for them; receive, analyze, and audit their reports; summarize and publicize their findings; investigate questionable financing practices; and decide upon whether to report infractions of the law to the Department of Justice. Utilizing its discretion, the GAO referred only what it considered to be major infractions for prosecution.

During and following the presidential campaign of 1972, the GAO's Office of Federal Elections issued a great many reports concerning questionable practices of campaign financing, many of which became central issues in the Watergate investigations. Perhaps most significant of all was the report on its initial audit of the Finance Committee to Reelect the President, released on August 26, 1972, widely publicized, and referred to the Department of Justice. It included a number of apparent and possible violations of the act, among them that campaign contributions had been used to finance the Watergate break-in. Later reports disclosed the cash contributions of Robert L. Vesco to Maurice H. Stans, the financing of a college student to play "dirty tricks" on Democratic primary candidates, cash payments to Watergate defendants and their attorneys, and, on the other side, illegal contributions to the Humphrey campaign. The workload of the Office of Federal Elections was extraordinary. Between March of 1972 and the end of September 1974, it responded to about 10,500 requests for forms and instructions and more than 12,000 telephone inquiries; it received nearly 20,000 reports and statements from about 2,800 committees, totalling 140,000 pages of information, and it furnished for inspection nearly 28,000 copies of reports.[28]

However effective the GAO's efforts in connection with campaign financing were, they proved to be transitory. In 1974, Congress voted to establish a Federal Election Commission,[29] which took over all of the Comptroller General's responsibilities in this area. The Comptroller General had indicated that he might be willing to continue the election work and take on the policing of congressional campaigns; but he did not resist the idea of an independent commission, which he had in fact proposed two years earlier. It may be that the GAO's work in connection with the 1972 presidential election was simply too effective for some congressional stomachs.

The experience of the Office of Federal Elections was thus short lived, but it had a lasting impact upon the GAO. It had never had authority to audit and report on political campaigns; indeed no one else had either. It was in virgin territory in carrying out the provisions of a federal act that was itself "virgin." It was called upon to receive reports on, to ferret out, to investigate, and to report on contributions to presidential campaigns with the utmost expedition, and speed had not been a watchword of most GAO operations. Its work was carried out under the continuous surveillance of the press and other media during a political campaign that proved to be the most explosive and scandalous in modern American history. Despite criticisms, the GAO accomplished its mission with no lasting allegation that it was unfair, partial, inaccurate, or foot dragging. The venture, which had at first been shunned and feared by a good many leaders of the GAO and for which it demonstrated little enthusiasm at the start, probably in the long run enhanced its reputation. The Office of Federal Elections demonstrated that the GAO could utilize its resources quickly and produce prompt, impartial, and honest reports in a situation that seemed treacherous and threatening to many of the values that the GAO had long sought to protect: integrity, accuracy, impartiality, and objectivity. Its reports did not go through the protracted and detailed review process of other GAO reports; indeed, some of the reports were released within three days after they were written.

The demonstration of the Office of Federal Elections was not lost upon others in the GAO itself. That office became a launching pad for new or growing activities in problem areas involving innovation and some risk taking. With the departure of the campaign financing activities, Staats instructed Hughes, then an Assistant Comptroller General, to develop different kinds of staffs and programs under his wing in an Office of Special Projects. One major area for the new office was energy, then emerging as a number one public issue. Another was to provide a focal point within the GAO for its program evaluation activities and to carry out the GAO's responsibilities growing out of the congressional budget legislation. Both later spun off as full-fledged operating divisions, but their seeds had been planted during the federal election experience.

The Handling of Claims

A GAO responsibility of ancient vintage is the adjudication and settlement of claims for and against the United States. The Budget and Accounting Act of 1921 provided (in Section 305) that: "All claims whatever by the Government of the United States or against it . . . shall be settled and adjusted in the General Accounting Office." In point of fact, the majority of claims are settled between the parties and the government agencies concerned without reference to the GAO. But a good many are referred or appealed to that organization for settlement; some go to the court of claims, and a few find their way to the federal district courts.

The claims are of two types. *Debt claims* are made by government agencies when the agencies are unable to collect from individuals debts to the government or where there is doubt as to the amount due or the legal liability of the parties involved. The GAO investigates the cases and, if it is unable to collect the amount due or reach an appropriate compromise, refers them to the Department of Justice and helps that department to prosecute them. These number nearly 50,000 per year, usually in fairly small amounts; in recent years, the majority have arisen from overpayments of educational benefits by the Veterans Administration.

Payment claims are those made by individuals against government agencies for amounts alleged to be due for services rendered the government or losses to the government by its employees, contractors, private citizens, state and local governments, and others. These are considerably fewer in number than debt claims (about 7,000 in fiscal year 1977), but greater in total dollars involved (about $165 million in fiscal year 1977). Most arise from recent actions, such as those growing out of the Vietnam evacuation, but a few are more than a century old. These include, for example, claims filed for horses shot during the Civil War and the loss of a merchant vessel during the War of 1812.

Much of the claims work is routine in character, but a few involve extensive investigation and legal analysis. As in the cases of bid protests, the GAO's claims activities are essentially a service to the agencies and individuals involved. It provides a convenient, relatively inexpensive means of resolving disputes between public agencies and individuals by an agency generally regarded as impartial and authoritative.[30]

Financial Management

Changes in the stance and activities of the GAO in the area of financial practices in the decade following the Staats appointment were less spectacular and less widely understood than in other areas. Except for noisome scandals, financial management is seldom the object of newspaper headlines or even of much congressional interest beyond a very few congressmen in a very few subcommittees. In proportion to the GAO's total workload, that directed strictly to financial management continued to decline—to about ten percent at the time of this writing. Yet, during this period there were major shifts in federal financial practices to which the GAO made substantial contributions, and there were significant changes in the GAO's own posture and responsibilities in the financial area. The GAO retains and, in some quarters at least, treasures its authority to disallow payments that it considers illegal or unethical, though it seldom uses it. In the main, it relies upon the internal auditors in the various federal agencies to check on the propriety of payments; it then audits the operations of the internal auditors. Its main concern is the adequacy and reliability of *systems* in the operating agencies, not individual payments and receipts.

Viewed in retrospect, the changes made during the first decade of the Staats term were gradual and incremental, but they were also fundamental. He did not view the GAO as a public accounting firm for the government as had his predecessor, Joseph Campbell. In the financial area at least, he envisioned the GAO as one of several instruments, executive and legislative, to improve the financial management of the government. And he thought the two branches could and should work together. This underlying theme was demonstrated in a variety of activities which are summarized in the paragraphs that follow.

The President's Commission on Budget Concepts

In 1967, President Lyndon Johnson established and appointed a sixteen-member Commission on Budget Concepts to make recommendations on the content, organization, and presentation of the federal budget. The commission was a mixed body of private citizens and prominent federal officials, chaired by a prominent banker who became secretary of the treasury. Comptroller General Staats was a member, and the GAO contributed a great deal of staff time to its various task forces. The commission's report[31] recommended perhaps the most far-reaching changes in the format, inclusiveness, and definitions in the budget since 1921. Its basic thrust was that the budget be unified and comprehend virtually all federal financial transactions, whether or not they are appropriated, such as operations of trust funds, loans, and other matters previously excluded.[32]

All of the commission's major recommendations were approved by the President, and all but one were put into effect almost immediately. But the one exception was, for the GAO, one of the most important of all. The commission recommended that all revenues and expenditures be shown in the budget in terms of accruals rather than cash, and that budgetary surpluses and deficits be stated in terms of accruals rather than cash receipts and outlays. The commission's proposal did not go as far as that of the second Hoover Commission, which had recommended that appropriations be made in terms of accrued expenditures rather than obligating authority. The President's 1967 commission did not propose to change the base of appropriations. But its recommendations would have significantly changed the amounts of surpluses and deficits.[33]

However, the accounts of some of the largest agencies and programs in the government, including most of the Department of Defense, were maintained on a cash rather than an accrual basis. The Bureau of the Budget (later the Office of Management and Budget) deferred action on this recommendation year by year until, in 1972, it deferred it indefinitely, and shifted the responsibility of pushing for the implementation of the proposal to the Joint Financial Management Improvement Program. The GAO was, and is, the lead agency of the JFMIP, and accrual accounting had been a major GAO objective for many years.

The Review and Approval of Accounting Systems

It may be recalled that the Budget and Accounting Procedures Act of 1950 provided that the Comptroller General prescribe accounting principles and standards for agency systems; cooperate with the agencies in developing their systems; and review and approve them when he deems them adequate. It also prescribed that all agency accounting systems be placed on an accrual basis "as soon as practicable." The GAO has always included accrual accounting among its principles and standards and made it requisite for approval of an agency accounting system—though exceptions have been allowed when accruals were deemed infeasible. But the Accounting Systems Division, which had been the prime mover in cooperating with the agencies in the development of systems, was abolished in 1956, its functions and personnel being combined with the audit divisions. Thereafter, there was declining emphasis upon cooperative work with the agencies and little organizational focus for review and approval of agency accounting systems. The number of accounting systems that were actually approved by the GAO grew at a snail's pace.

In 1964, 1966, and again in 1967, the House Committee on Government Operations held hearings on the GAO's authority and progress in approving agency accounting systems and considered, but did not pass, statutory changes to strengthen its enforcing powers. Comptroller General Staats, however, undertook to centralize within a single staff the advice, review, and approval functions. A new division, the Financial and General Management Studies Division (better known within the GAO by the acronym FGMSD, pronounced "figmas"), was established in 1971, and these activities became a responsibility of that division. This was in some respects a revival of the old Accounting Systems Division of the late 1940s and early 1950s, although the size of its systems approval staff is only about two thirds that of its predecessor.

During the same period, the procedures for handling accounting systems were changed and formalized. First, the GAO separated the approval of agency principles and standards (within the more general GAO prescription of principles and standards) from the approval of accounting systems in operation. Then, in 1967, the procedure was extended to three steps: approval of principles and standards; later, approval of system design; and still later, approval of systems in operation. A further modification occurred in 1969. The basic approvals became the first two steps. Audits of systems in operation would be conducted by a separate group (within FGMSD) later, as time and priorities permitted. This is the present practice.[34] Under it, the proportion of agency accounting systems approved by the GAO in their statements of principles and standards grew to about 98 percent in 1977; and the proportion of those whose designs have been approved grew to about 60 percent in 1977. Only 32 of the 198 systems that had been approved by 1977 were approved prior to 1966. Unfortunately, some of the largest federal systems in terms of the dollars involved are not approved, particularly those in the Departments of Defense and Health, Education and Welfare. Probably a bit more than one third of federal expenditures are accounted for under systems whose designs have been approved by the GAO.

While agency accounting practices have considerably improved in terms of the GAO's standards, particularly in the last decade, it is equally clear that they still have a very long way to go. There are three principal kinds of obstacles. The first is political: the appropriations committees and subcommittees of Congress, particularly those involved in defense, have not been enthusiastic about accrual accounting, preferring to consider the simpler and traditional cash and obligation accounts. A second obstacle is administrative: accrual accounting is more difficult and more costly than accounting on the basis of cash, which would have to be continued anyway. The third obstacle has to do with the tools of enforcement: the GAO has no feasible "club in the closet" for those who do not live up to its rules. It could conceivably be empowered to stop payments of delinquent agencies, but the punishment would grossly exceed the crime, and it would penalize many who had no part in the crime.

The problems of enforcement of federal acts directed to internal administrative practices are demonstrated in other measures. The act sponsored by Senator John F. Kennedy in 1956[35] directed that, in addition to accrual accounting, all agency budgets should be cost based. This requirement has not been modified, yet it is probable that, at the time of this writing, the number of agencies whose budgets are truly cost based could be counted on the fingers of two hands. There is no machinery for enforcement beyond persuasion, and persuasion is not very effective if the appropriations subcommittees in Congress are not themselves persuaded.

Interagency Cooperation: The Joint Financial
Management Improvement Program

The development of accounting systems on a cooperative basis between the GAO and individual agencies was paralleled by the renewal of the cooperative efforts of the JFMIP during the late 1960s and the 1970s. It will be recalled that one of Staats' early actions as Comptroller General was to arrange for the participation of the chairman of the Civil Service Commission in the joint organization. Later, when responsibilities of the Office of Management and Budget for financial management policies were transferred to the General Services Administration in 1973, the administrator of that agency became a full-fledged member. But in 1975, these functions were moved back and the General Services Administration dropped out of the JFMIP. It operates today with four agency members. The principal officers seldom convene, but each has designated a representative for his agency (the GAO's representative is the director of the FGMS Division), and these four meet about once a month as a steering group to provide general direction. In addition, each operating agency has named a liaison officer for his agency to work with the JFMIP.

During its first twenty-five years, the JFMIP (originally the Joint Accounting Improvement Program) operated without any permanent staff of its own. Most of its work was conducted or led by staff from the GAO. In 1969, it established an office of executive secretary, drawn from one of its sponsoring organizations. Then, in 1973, it created the office of executive director with a small permanent staff to provide continuing leadership of its work.

The principal functions of the JFMIP are to serve as coordinator, stimulator, and catalyst toward the improvement of financial management practices throughout the government. It has sponsored and assisted a number of individual agencies in the development and conduct of innovative and experimental projects in the area of financial management; sponsored seminars and training programs in the field; and helped in the establishment of programs in financial management at universities—most notably, the Institute for Applied Public Financial Management at American University. It has also participated in government-wide studies directed to specific financial problems, such as the use of letters of credit in connection with federal grants to state and local governments; a system for electronic fund transfers of recurring federal payments from the Treasury; studies of statistical sampling procedures in the audit of financial transactions; the management of money within federal agencies; and the use of operating budgets within agencies. Beginning in 1973, it assumed leadership in efforts to improve productivity in federal agencies and served as information gatherer, clearinghouse, and reporter on such efforts. In 1975, Congress established a National Center for Productivity and Quality of Working Life,[36] and the following year the work of the JFMIP in this area was transferred to the center. In 1977, it undertook a major inquiry, led by staff assigned from the GAO, directed to the improvement of auditing practices in state and local governments.

But perhaps the most significant role of the JFMIP over the years has been symbolic. It has been an institutional expression of efforts in the federal government to cooperate in the improvement of financial management practices. And the principal leader of these efforts has in fact been a legislative agency, the GAO. In this regard, the JFMIP has reassumed essentially the same stance as when it was founded in the late 1940s, though its posture today in terms of what went before is less radical and its activities probably less prominent.

Intergovernmental Cooperation: The Intergovernmental Audit Forums

The deluge of new federal programs involving grants to state and local units of government during the 1960s gave rise to growing concern about the propriety, the efficiency, and the effectiveness with which those funds were spent by the recipient units. The jurisdiction and scope of federal agencies, including the GAO, to audit the application of funds after they had been transmitted to state and local governments was sometimes doubtful, and thorough, comprehensive federal audits, even where legally possible, were practically infeasible. The machinery for auditing at state and local levels varied tremendously, as did their approaches, techniques, and capabilities. Further, in those grant programs in which two, three, or more levels of government contributed funds, there was the possibility of duplication in auditing and sometimes of working at cross purposes.

By 1970, it had become evident to Congress, to the executive branch, and to the GAO that the national government should do what it could to improve auditing standards and practices in state and local jurisdictions and to foster cooperation and coordination among all the levels of government in their conduct of audits. In that year, under the additional stimulus of the Legislative Reorganization Act of 1970, the GAO undertook preparation of standards for governmental auditing for state and local as well as federal governments. It was published by the GAO during 1972 under the title of *Standards for Audit of Governmental Organizations, Programs, Activities, and Functions.* This has been followed in succeeding years by a series of supplements and other publications providing more detailed guidelines, case examples, and directories (of state and federal audit organizations).

In a meeting in September 1972 of the Comptroller General, the assistant director of the Office of Management and Budget, and six state auditors, it was proposed that there be established on the national and regional levels audit councils for the purpose of improving the planning and coordination of auditing efforts at all levels of government. The proposal received widespread endorsement, and there was subsequently established a National Intergovernmental Audit Forum in Washington and a pilot regional forum in the Southeast Region under the auspices of the GAO's regional office in Atlanta. By the fall of 1974, intergovernmental audit forums had been established in all ten of the federal regions.

The national and the ten regional forums have become significant continuing mechanisms for exchanging information and views, solving problems, implementing audit standards, coordinating auditing efforts, and doing cooperative audit work. They meet two to four times a year and periodically there is a conference of representatives from all of them. Most of their membership consist of federal, state, and local auditors, though a few program officials are also members. Although each was chartered individually and they are organizationally independent of one another, their leadership and most of their financial support (about half a million dollars) comes from the GAO. The chairmanship of the national forum alternates between officials of the GAO and the Office of Management and Budget while six of the ten regional chairmen have been GAO regional managers. All of their executive secretaries are GAO officials.

Although the audit forums can point to some achievements already in their young lives, their greatest promise lies in the future. Simply getting acquainted, carrying on dialogues about common concerns, and identifying mutual problems are a contribution to the workings of the federal system. From the standpoint of the GAO, they offer channels through which to educate and give operational meaning to its audit standards and to extend the sights of state and local auditors beyond the traditional limits of financial reviews to its own, broader objectives of auditing managerial effectiveness and program results. Auditors at all levels may more effectively tackle problems of standardizing and simplifying federal grants and the auditing of them, test and conduct audits on a joint basis, enlarge the confidence and trust in the work of the auditors of other jurisdictions, and approach problems of mutual concern on a more understanding basis.

The Impact of the Computer on Financial Management and Auditing

State and local governments, like federal agencies, have had increasingly to deal with automatic data processing in managing and auditing their finances. Beginning in World War II and accelerating rapidly thereafter, computers have tremendously increased the speed and the capacity to handle information, including of course accounting information. By 1976, there were more than 9,000 computers in the federal government, costing over $10 billion per year. Only a fraction of computer use is directed to financial management and auditing, but the bulk of federal payrolls and other payments are now handled by computers.

The computerization of financial practice has greatly complicated the management and auditing of federal expenditures. In the United States system of financial control, from the time of Alexander Hamilton, individual officers, designated as disbursing or certifying officers, were held personally accountable before making or authorizing payments. Auditors in the agencies and in the central auditing agencies—under the comptroller of the treasury or later in the GAO—would check the propriety and accuracy of each transaction on the basis of checking the paper evidences. Any discrepancies or mistakes that could not be corrected or otherwise adequately explained, would be the basis for disallowing payments, and the officers who authorized them would be personally accountable to make them up to the government.

The principle of personal accountability of certifying officers has not changed. But the documents themselves on which their payments are based may not exist or, where they do, are often in widely scattered geographic locations. In computerized systems, their amounts and supporting information are entered on tapes, and the computers make the calculations and reconciliations and even write the checks. This means that the certifying officers, as well as the auditors who check up on them, are basically dependent not only on the pieces of paper that support their transactions, as in the past, but also upon the adequacy of the computer systems and the safeguards that can be built into those systems.

Much of the GAO's work in the areas of financial accounting and auditing has therefore come to concern the ever more complex and sophisticated computer systems. It includes advice and the issuance of reports on accounting and financial information systems, automated payroll and property accounting systems, and systems for the internal audit—as well as GAO audit—of accounting systems in operation. Most of this work is centralized in the GAO's Financial and General Management Studies Division, which now accounts for more than two thirds of all of the GAO's work specifically in the financial field. In addition, that division provides technical assistance to all the operating divisions of the GAO when their studies require specialized expertise in automatic data processing, systems analysis, statistical science, and actuarial science.

In Retrospect: The Third GAO and Its Predecessors

The years of 1966 to 1978 witnessed a gradual but persistent change in the GAO's perception of its purpose and an enlargement of its scope. In governmental circles, particularly in the legislative branch, the change and enlargement have contributed to an image of considerably greater stature and confidence. The Comptroller General himself has become more visible and more influential, a situation reflected in the substantial number of important assignments, official and unofficial, he has been given beyond the running of the GAO.[37]

The Comptroller General has retained most of the specific powers bestowed upon him by the Budget and Accounting Act of 1921 and has acquired some new ones along the way. A few, like the rendering of decisions and advice on legal questions, have grown in importance and influence. Some, particularly in the areas of financial accounting and controls, were changed both in law and practice. The original provisions became simply obsolete and irrelevant because of the exploding growth and scope of federal activities, as well as technological and professional advances. In these fields, the GAO has moved from a plodding and laggard second cousin to a posture of leadership, not alone in federal management but increasingly in society at large.

Since World War II, the change in the GAO's attitudes and approaches have generally, though not always, been in certain common directions:

- from frugality in expenditures toward effectiveness;
- from audits for legal compliance toward reviews of management;
- from suspicion of and hostility to the executive branch toward cooperation and collaboration;
- from individual transactions toward systems and problems;
- from a punitive approach toward a corrective approach;
- from nearly total independence toward interdependence with Congress;
- from concerns about the past toward concerns about the future;
- from concentration of auditing in itself toward devolution to executive agencies;
- from strictly financial matters toward costs and results of programs.

The processes of change are far from complete and probably never will—or should—be. It is at least doubtful that, in the summarization above, the first items of the pairs mentioned should ever be totally neglected in behalf of the second items.

The changing activities of the GAO have to a considerable extent mirrored the differing perspectives on the GAO's objectives of the four men who have governed it through most of its history. Comptroller General Staats has made it clear that in his view the purpose of the GAO is to improve the performance of government—wherever and however it can be improved. Probably all of his predecessors would agree. But each would have taken a somewhat different position on the question of what the GAO should do to improve it. McCarl would no doubt have held that the GAO should make sure that public financial transactions are honest, legal, and frugal. Warren would have argued that governmental improvement depended partly on collaborative efforts with the executive branch in improving financial management and on the audit of financial systems. Campbell would likewise have relied on the audit of financial systems plus the review of problem areas to spot, penalize, and correct faulty transactions—especially in the area of contracts. Staats would maintain these functions but lessen their importance in comparison with the assessment of the effectiveness of government programs and advice to Congress and the executive branch on how to improve it.

The disparate views of these four Comptrollers General were not as inconsistent as may at first glance appear. Each of them was at least roughly consonant with the values, mores, concerns, methods, and technologies of the government and the society during the period in which they served or began their service. It should therefore be useful to examine the GAO from the standpoint of its role in the federal government and American society today.

Notes

1. For example, warrants are now used almost solely to authorize expenditures when appropriations have not passed the Congress and continuing expenditures are authorized by congressional resolutions. A most interesting recent example of the disallowance of expenditures was the GAO's threat to disallow payments for Secret Service protection of Spiro Agnew after he had resigned from the vice presidency—a threat addressed to the secretary of the treasury. And a little known vestige of the settlement power is that the Comptroller General every month issues a certificate of settlement to cover the salary and expense allowance of the President of the United States.

2. The "finality" of GAO decisions has been challenged from time to time by executive agencies, especially the attorney general.

3. A number of other illustrations of GAO legal work are discussed in the succeeding sections of this chapter on bid protests, the Philadelphia plan, and impoundment control. In addition, the companion volume, Erasmus H. Kloman, ed., *Cases in Accountability: The Work of the GAO* (Boulder, Colo.: Westview Press, 1979), includes two cases focused on Comptroller General decisions, dealing with intervenor expenses and a bid protest. Four other cases illustrate legal contributions to GAO audits and evaluations: those dealing with the FBI, the liquid metal fast breeder reactor, *Mayaguez*, and crime in federal recreation areas.

4. Much of the historical material in this section is based upon an article by Thomas D. Morgan, "The General Accounting Office: One Hope for Congress to Regain Parity of Power With the President," *North Carolina Law Review* 51 (October 1973).

5. Section 236 of the Legislative Reorganization Act of 1970, P.L. 91-510, 31 U.S.C. 1176.

6. Perkins v. Lukens Steel Co., 310 U.S. 113 (1940).

7. Ibid.

8. For an illustration of bid protest activities see "Bid Protest: Lockheed and the Space Shuttle Solid Rocket Motors," in Kloman, ed., *Cases in Accountability*.

9. Some of the historical material in this section is based upon the article, cited earlier, by Thomas D. Morgan, "The General Accounting Office."

10. 47 Comp. Gen. 666, 669 (1968).

11. 48 Comp. Gen. 326, 328 (1968).

12. "Order to the Heads of All Agencies from Assistant Secretary of Labor Arthur A. Fletcher Announcing the Revised Philadelphia Plan 6, 9 (June 27, 1969)," reprinted, 115 *Congressional Record* 39 (1969):951-53.

13. 49 Comp. Gen. 59 (August 5, 1969).

14. 42 Op. Att'y Gen. 37, pp. 5, 9.

15. U.S. Congress, Senate, 115 *Congressional Record* 39 (1969):126.

16. Section 904, H. Rept. 15209, 91st Cong., 1st Sess. (1969).

17. In a statement on December 22, 1969, the President wrote that he shared "the Attorney General's serious doubts as to the constitutionality of this amendment and may have to withhold my signature from any legislation containing it." *Presidential Documents 1778* (1969), week ending Saturday, December 27, 1969.

18. Ibid. If the omnibus GAO Bill (H.R. 12171, 95th Cong., 2nd Sess.) now before Congress passes, such authority would be provided the Comptroller General.

19. Contractors Association of East Pennsylvania v. Secretary of Labor, 311 F. Supp. 1002 (E.D. Pa. 1970).

20. 442 F. 2nd 159 (3rd Cir. 1971).

21. P.L. 93-344. The act was joined with the Congressional Budget Act and passed as Title X of the Congressional Budget and Impoundment Control Act.

22. These data are drawn from the *Review of the Impoundment Control Act of 1974 After Two Years*, Comptroller General's Report to Congress, OGC-77-20, June 3, 1977.

23. In an extraordinary message, dated October 10, 1974, signed by Senators Robert Byrd, Cannon, Eagleton, Ervin, Fulbright, Hartke, Jackson, Magnusson, Mansfield, McGhee, McClellan, Moss, Muskie, Randolph, and Stennis.

24. The funds for the program had initially been impounded before the passage of the Impoundment Control Act, apparently at the instance of Secretary of Housing and Urban Development James T. Lynn. After Lynn was transferred to become director of the Office of Management and Budget, he acted to renew, or continue, the impoundment. The GAO's argument that it was truly a rescission rather than a deferral was based on the allegation that, after the deferral, there would be insufficient time to obligate the funds before the authorization expired.

25. Initially the defendant named in the suit was President Ford. This was later changed to James T. Lynn, director of the Office of Management and Budget, et al. The suit was filed in the U.S. District of Columbia, Civil Action no. 75-0051.

26. The issues are discussed in greater depth in chapter 8.

27. Among its members were Bryce Harlow, former counsel to both Presidents Eisenhower and Nixon, Herbert Alexander, executive director of the Citizens' Research Foundation, and Richard Scammon, former director of the Bureau of the Census.

28. These data and much of the other factual information in this account are drawn from the Comptroller General's Report to the Congress, *Report of the Office of Federal Elections of the General Accounting Office in Administering the Federal Election Act of 1971*, ACG (OFE) 74-5, February 6, 1975.

29. The Federal Election Campaign Act Amendments of 1974, P.L. 93-443, October 15, 1974.

30. For brief examples of this work, see the claims cases in Kloman, ed., *Cases in Accountability.*

31. *Report of the President's Commission on Budget Concepts* (Washington, D.C.: Government Printing Office, October 1967).

32. The "unified budget" would replace the three different budgets previously in use: the so-called administrative budget, the consolidated cash budget, and the national income accounts budget.

33. In 1975, the accounting firm of Arthur Andersen and Co. issued a report, *Sound Financial Reporting in the Public Sector*, that contained

consolidated statements of assets, liabilities, revenues, and expenses of the federal government on an accrual basis for 1973 and 1974. For each of the following two years the Treasury Department published comparable prototype Consolidated Financial Statements. All of these showed enormous accrual benefits (up to $152 billion in 1975), primarily because of the annual increase in liabilities for future payments in social security and various pension plans. For a variety of reasons, the usefulness of these early reports, beyond experimental development, is questionable.

34. For an illustration of the GAO's work in reviewing agency accounting systems, see the case on "Bureau of Land Management Accounting System" in Kloman, ed., *Cases in Accountability.*

35. P.L. 863, August 1, 1956.

36. P.L. 94-136, November 28, 1975.

37. Among his many extracurricular activities are included a variety of statutory assignments, permanent and temporary. As noted earlier, he is a member and leader of the permanent Joint Financial Management Improvement Program (since 1948), and the Cost Accounting Standards Board (since 1970). He is also a statutory member of the Technology Assessment Advisory Council, which is intended to guide the work of the Congressional Office of Technology Assessment (since 1974). He served as a prominent member of the (nonstatutory) President's Commission on Budget Concepts (1967), the Commission on Government Procurement (1969-1972), the National Commission on Electronic Fund Transfers (1974-1977), and the Federal Paper Work Commission (1974-1978). Through a variety of other activities, he has been recognized nationally and internationally as a professional leader in governmental auditing, public and business management, political science, and other fields.

PART TWO

EMERGING ROLES OF THE GAO

Accountability and Independence in American Governance

The General Accounting Office was founded principally to provide a means whereby the executive branch of the federal government and its responsible officers could be held accountable for their actions, particularly in the realm of finances. The word *accountability* was not then widely used, but the argument for creation of a GAO was compatible with the assurance of accountability in the sense we use the word today. Such assurance remains the central but not exclusive mission of the GAO. The current Comptroller General has himself suggested that the middle word of its title should be construed as "accountability" rather than "accounting" in its usual sense.[1] At the same time, the GAO is substantially independent in respect to many of its own decisions and activities. These two concepts—accountability and independence—are central to this study. But their meanings and relationships are elusive and have themselves changed over the years.

Accountability and independence seem at first to be reciprocal: the more of one, the less of the other; in the lingo of economists, the two appear to constitute a "zero-sum game."[2] And the dictionary lends credence to this view. One is accountable if he or she has to "report, explain, or justify"; one is "answerable," presumably to someone else. Independence, on the other hand, is defined as "freedom from subjection, or from the influence of others" and as "exemption from external control or support."[3] In practice, of course, the distinction is a good deal less than clear-cut, particularly when applied to organizations. An agency may enjoy substantial independence so that it may more effectively hold others accountable. The measure and the means of both accountability and independence may be formal or informal, official or psychological.

Difficulties in the zero-sum approach to accountability and independence arise partly because we apply the two to different kinds of action or evidences of action by a given individual or agency; we utilize different kinds of measures and criteria in assessing those actions; and we assess them at different stages in the action process: in the planning stage, or during the operating stage, or in the postmortem stage. Thus an agency of government may be given substantial independence in determining what it does and at the same time be held rigidly accountable for every item it buys, an approach reflected in much of the work of the "first GAO." Or it may have substantial independence in its individual financial transactions but be held rigorously accountable for the results and overall costs of its actions, a practice more typical of the "third GAO." A good many agencies, of which the GAO is only one, may on paper have a great deal of freedom of action, but they will have to justify what they are doing and have done in some detail when they come back for next year's appropriations. The appropriation process itself is a tool of accountability. On the other hand, some agencies that on paper appear to be severely restricted in their freedom of action may in fact perform with almost complete independence because they are confident that no one in a position to hold them accountable will pay any attention. Anticipation of the actions of others is a major element of the "game" of independence-accountability.

Yet the idea of accountability is probably as ancient as organized government itself—or at least any government in which there is or was some form of delegation of authority. In democratic or republican systems, it is an important though often neglected principle that officials be held accountable for their public actions directly or indirectly to the people, the "citizen sovereigns." In the past, it applied principally to actions reviewed after the fact, and it carried the likelihood or certainty of redress or penalty for those who failed to act legally, properly, and in the public interest. It was and remains the disciplining extension of the essentially moral concept of responsibility. Indeed, until our governors are saints, it is difficult to imagine how a responsible democratic polity could survive without the principle and some tools of accountability.

Even in simple times, accountability was hard to define and harder to assure. But there seem always to have been three essential elements. The first of these is *information*: information about the decisions and actions of those individuals and organizations who are held accountable to those others who are holding them to account. So the nature and usefulness of the information provided—its honesty and accuracy, completeness, specificity, relevance, adequacy, and timeliness—have always been critical attributes of accountability. The nature of the information provided to the GAO is central to the understanding of its roles.

A second requisite of accountability is that there be some individuals or organizations, outside *receivers and/or discoverers* of the information, who are able and willing to examine it, investigate it if necessary, digest it, and report it or initiate appropriate action based upon it. And the third has to do with *recourse* on the basis of such information (1) to correct deficiencies and improve performance and/or (2) to reward honorable and effective performance or penalize dishonesty, concealment, fraud, inefficiency, or ineffectiveness. Historically, the greater emphasis was placed on the second kind of recourse, particularly the imposition of penalties. Among the cruder tools of enforcing accountability in the negative sense have been death, replacement, removal, demotion, elimination or reduction of authorities or resources, and legal action, either civil or criminal or both, to redress grievances. Less extreme but still significant instruments to penalize failures in performance include reprimands, loss of repute among superiors, peers, and subordinates, social penalties on self and family, and countless others. Instrumental to all of these, and increasingly potent unto itself, is simply disclosure and publication. The key to accountability is thus, quite simply, information—the openness with which an individual or agency operates and the access to information by persons outside who are in a position to do something about it, if necessary, and the ways in which relevant information is selected, processed, and utilized. There are, however, legitimate constraints on the disclosure and exposure of information in pursuit of accountability (discussed in chapter 10).

The idea of the independence of different agencies of government has at least two connotations, related but quite different from each other and both in potential contest with the principle of accountability. The first concerns the degree of freedom, without public scrutiny, with which an individual or agency makes decisions and carries them out. This involves the constraints on disclosure suggested in the preceding paragraph. It includes also the large number of public corporations and other public enterprises that operate according to standards and objectives not historically associated with government and for which the normal instruments of accountability in government would be ineffective or actually damaging. Possibly the most important areas where independence is espoused are those of new or changed policies and programs for which there are few guidelines, little experience, and no routines. In such situations, a strict enforcement of accountability might severely inhibit creativity, imagination, experimentation, and risk taking.

A second construction of independence concerns the freedom of an individual or agency from outside pressures or influence in the reaching of its decisions and the carrying out of its activities. In this sense, independence is nearly synonymous with objectivity: freedom from hierarchical, political, special interest, personal, or other partial bias. This interpretation of independence has been best exemplified in America by the judiciary and indeed the entire judicial system. Judges are protected by long or indefinite terms in office and by immunity from removal except for the grossest behavior, and, through a great variety of procedural requirements, from pressures from specially interested groups. The Comptroller General has received somewhat, though not quite, comparable protections in his term of office, partly on the grounds that some of his duties are quasi judicial. And despite vast differences in their views of the job, all of the Comptrollers General have vigorously defended their independence, often while challenging the independence of other agencies in the first sense described above. In other words, independence from outside influence seems to be a requisite for assuring against excessive independence on the part of accountable agencies in their decisions and actions.

Accountability and Social Dynamics

The problems associated with accountability in government have been difficult from the beginning of Western civilization—since the Babylonians and ancient Greeks. The questions have ranged widely, and many of them are still relevant. In what ways and to what extent is one accountable for the actions of his subordinates? To whom is an individual accountable? For what, and according to what criteria is he accountable? At what stage in the action process? What is the recourse if he has misused his authority and trust or failed in his endeavors? And by whose authority or through what means is such recourse to be effected? The institutionalized mechanisms that we inherited from the Middle Ages today seem quite direct and elementary. They were based primarily upon one-to-one relationships, usually between superior and subordinate; upon the cumulation of individual transactions; upon quantitative measures, normally in terms of money; and on direct recourses in terms of rewards and penalties, some of which were brutal. They were grounded in the concept that each individual should be held responsible for his use of public resources, that is, money that was not his own. To a considerable extent, these ideas and practices were carried over to organizations, even three and four centuries ago when organizations themselves were simple; and some of them survive in the financial systems of today.

It has been the experience in the Western and the Westernizing worlds that as the complexity of society grows, the size and complexity of government grows even more. By the same token, the demand for effective accountability in government is accompanied by an increase in the difficulty of assuring such accountability. The old, direct meaning and means of accountability are much less than adequate in a vastly changed and changing society with a government that is endeavoring to be responsive to its dynamic demands.

The point may be illustrated by the continuing erosion of the boundaries between zones of society and government, which once were reasonably clear and useful distinctions for viewing and handling social problems. For example, the line between what is governmental and what is nongovernmental, between the public and private sectors, is now little more than a blur in many areas. To what extent and in what ways should government hold private citizens and private or semipublic institutions—businesses, nonprofit organizations, associations—accountable when they are carrying out public purposes with public money?

A second kind of blurring has occurred between the boundaries that once fairly clearly divided responsibilities of different levels of government: federal, state, and local, and, more recently, international. In consequence primarily of the explosive growth of grants-in-aid, every level of American government is involved, financially or operationally or both, in almost every major governmental activity. To what extent and in what ways should the federal government hold state and local governments accountable in their performance of programs in which it has declared an interest and for which it has contributed funds? The same question applies to international organizations, most of which receive the largest contributions from the United States.

A third kind of obfuscation of traditional boundaries has occurred with respect to the different functions and responsibilities of the executive agencies of the federal government itself. Who is to be held accountable for the effectiveness of programs in which several different agencies take part, short of the President himself?

A final example of the clouding of boundaries has occurred in connection with the time-honored division of powers among the legislative, executive, and judicial branches and the association of each of these with a particular institution of government. These separations, though pervasive in national and state constitutions and to a lesser degree at the local level, were never clear-cut and perfect. The President—and most of the state governors— were always constitutionally involved in legislative matters, and the judiciary established its involvement through its self-asserted powers of interpretation of constitution and laws. In recent decades, most policy legislation has originated in the executive, and legislatures have in effect delegated legislative responsibilities outright to executive agencies. Further, a number of agencies, of which the GAO is but one, have been established with frankly acknowledged executive, legislative, and judicial powers, constituting what some have labelled a fourth branch of government, not contemplated in the American Constitution. Congress, through its powers associated with oversight, investigation, legislation, and appropriation, has long been intimately involved in the execution as well as the passage of the laws.

The mixing or sharing of powers has further confused the problem of governmental accountability. Under the original concept, the courts could assure that the laws were justly carried out, the President could be held periodically accountable through the fixed term and the election process, and Congress could be similarly held accountable through the election process. From the beginning, it seems to have been accepted that Congress had a special responsibility to assure the accountability of the executive in the performance of governmental programs and the expenditure of public funds. But the extent and the means of doing this were not spelled out in the Constitution, and they have been objects of search and argument for 200 years. They are central to this study.

The process of blurring the boundaries separating the public and private sectors and the levels, branches, and functions of government has been going on since the forming of the republic. But it was greatly accelerated during the current century and particularly after the onset of the Great Depression about 1930. In other words, a great part of it has happened since the GAO was established in 1921. The history of the organization may be interpreted partly as a response to the accelerating complications of maintaining accountability. These complications provide underlying themes in the discussion of the GAO's posture and problems at the time of this writing, discussed in the chapters that follow.

Notes

1. As in his speeches before the Australian Society of Accountants, February and March 1977, on "The United States General Accounting Office: Its Role As An Independent Audit and Evaluation Agency" (processed).

2. I am indebted for this thought and some of the other ideas in this section to Harvey C. Mansfield, Sr., "Independence and Accountability for Federal Contractors and Grantees," and Bruce L. R. Smith, "The Public Use of the Private Sector," Bruce L. R. Smith, ed., *The New Political Economy: The Public Use of the Private Sector* (Carnegie Corporation of New York, 1975).

3. Both definitions are drawn from the *Random House Dictionary of the English Language* (New York: Random House, 1967).

8

THE GAO IN THE
GOVERNMENTAL SYSTEM

Our Constitution is so simple and practical that it is possible always to meet extraordinary needs by changes in emphasis and arrangement without loss of essential form.
　　　　　　　　　　　—Franklin D. Roosevelt, *Inaugural Address*, 1933

Without criticism and reliable and intelligent reporting, the government cannot govern.
—Walter Lippman, address, International Press Institute Assembly, London, 1965

The first thirty years of the GAO's history were punctuated by frontal assaults on its locus in the government, its powers, the tenure of its chief, and its very existence as an agency. Many of these attacks stemmed from reorganization study groups and from Presidents—Wilson through Roosevelt (with the single exception of Coolidge). After Roosevelt, no President has launched an attack on the organization as such, and it has consistently been exempted from the executive reorganization machinery ever since 1939. Indeed, it does not appear that the Presidents from Truman on paid it much attention; neither the Comptroller General nor the GAO is discussed in the memoirs of most of those who have so far published memoirs—Truman, Eisenhower, Johnson, and Nixon.[1] This apparent reversal in presidential attitudes may be attributed to the cooperative approach instituted by Comptroller General Warren, the massive changes in the nature of GAO operations associated with Warren and later Staats, and the assumption that a majority in Congress would not let any substantial portion of the GAO's powers return to the executive branch.

But there are still problems associated with the status, powers, and independence of the Comptroller General in his relation to the executive branch that arise in connection with specific issues—like the Philadelphia Plan, the impoundment controversy, and the bid protest procedure (described in chapter 7). One's general impression is that the GAO does its best to finesse these problems and avoid open confrontations. But this is not always possible. The problems are not unlike those that were argued in the 1920s, 1930s, and 1940s and stem from the same unique posture of the GAO in the governmental system. One aspect of them is legal and constitutional;

another has to do with management, its effectiveness and responsibility.

Independence: The Constitutional Question

The legal problem arises from the separation of powers—legislative, executive, and judicial—on which the drafters of the Constitution relied heavily. It is true that at several major and crucial points they introduced one branch of government into the operations of another, as in the presidential veto of legislation and the senatorial power to review and approve presidential appointments and treaties. Later the Supreme Court interpreted its powers to extend to the review of the constitutionality of legislation and the review of executive action. Clearly the separation of powers was never intended to be ironclad. Furthermore, the founders left certain matters particularly ambiguous. One of these was the area of financial control. As noted in chapter 1, the First Congress, following its first major debate, came down primarily though not unequivocally on the side of the executive branch when it established the comptroller in the Department of the Treasury, appointed by the President with senatorial consent, and removable by him.

The Budget and Accounting Act of 1921 substantially reversed the original position with regard to financial control; all of the powers of the comptroller of the treasury and the auditors were transferred to the GAO, explicitly "independent of the executive departments," and a few new ones were added. The GAO was made responsible to the Comptroller General, but to whom he was responsible was not specified.

A strict construction of the separation of powers might lead to the conclusion that the Treasury Act of 1789 was in error or the act of 1921 was in error, or parts of both were wrong; but such a literal construction would be questioned today. For ninety years, Congress has set up "independent" bodies, notably the regulatory commissions, in which are joined legislative, executive, and judicial powers, and the courts have upheld their legitimacy. There appears to be no argument that the Comptroller General is and should be independent of the executive branch in those activities that are primarily legislative in character. Congress can quite properly utilize its own agent to make sure its laws and appropriations have been carried out and to investigate and report findings and recommendations on problems that are or may become of legislative concern. All sides agree that in these matters the GAO is accountable to Congress, although the Comptroller General insists on his independence even of Congress in selecting the majority of his projects and in the objectivity of his investigations and of the recommendations that grow out of them.

Historically, the stickier question has concerned the GAO's exercise of powers of an executive or quasi-judicial character and the degree to which the Comptroller General's opinions are binding on the executive branch.[2] Some of these powers, like the disallowance of payments and the countersigning of warrants, are rarely used, but their existence lends authority to other GAO activities. The argument today is not whether these powers are legislative or executive or judicial; all appear to agree that they are not legislative. The main question is whether or not the Comptroller General may make decisions or take actions on his own in areas that are not legislative in nature.

The attorney general has repeatedly, though rather infrequently, contended that the decisions of the Comptroller General are only advisory on the executive branch, with final decision short of appeal to the courts resting in the executive branch. His position includes several arguments: that the Constitution provides that "the executive Power shall be vested in a President" (Article II, Section 1); that "he [the President] shall take care that the laws be faithfully executed" (Article II, Section 3); and that the Comptroller General is an officer of Congress since, though he is appointed by the President with the consent of the Senate, he cannot be removed by the President. In short, the Comptroller General is specifically and only an agent of Congress, a position that Congress itself declared in the Reorganization Act of 1945 when it described the Comptroller General and the GAO as "a part of the legislative branch of the Government." In fact, the former attorney general, John Mitchell, in his letter to Comptroller General Staats of 1971 concerning bid protests, quite clearly implied that in his opinion the provision of the Budget and Accounting Act of 1921 that all the powers of the comptroller of the treasury and of the auditors be transferred to the Comptroller General was unconstitutional. He wrote:

> However, we continue to feel that those sections should be construed as investing with G.A.O. only post-audit duties. The broader reading of those sections, as formerly applied to the Comptroller of the Treasury, an Executive Branch officer, should not be carried over to the activities of the Comptroller General, a Legislative Branch officer. To do so raises serious constitutional objections about G.A.O.'s binding the Executive Branch or its officers in advance through its authority to settle and adjust accounts.[3]

The Comptroller General's response to these arguments includes a number of different points. He agrees that he is ultimately accountable to Congress. This accountability is exercised in a variety of ways: through the annual appropriations process; through the requirement that he submit to Congress a complete annual report of his activities; through reviews of his work by oversight and special committees of Congress; through other reports and testimony before congressional committees; through the fact that his actions and recommendations are subject to legislative action or judicial review; and through the fact that Congress can remove him for specified cause or by impeachment. On the other hand, Congress has deliberately delegated to him a number of powers of nonlegislative character primarily to assist it in assuring the financial accountability of the executive agencies. In respect to these actions, the Comptroller General is an independent officer of the United States, substantially independent of either branch.

The argument is strengthened by a reading of the "necessary and proper" clause of the Constitution, which indicates that the founders intended that Congress exercise the ultimate power of the government, including both the executive and legislative branches:

> To make all Laws which shall be necessary and proper for carrying into Execution the foregoing Powers, *and all other Powers vested by this Constitution in the Government of the United States, or in any Department or Officer thereof.* (Emphasis added.)[4]

According to this view, Congress can set up agencies, vest them with powers, and attach conditions to their performance as it wishes.[5] Among those conditions may be included surveillance by the GAO.

The dual capacity of the Comptroller General—as an officer of Congress and as an independent officer—has been recognized and affirmed in one federal court case (though the question has not reached the Supreme Court). In the most explicit judicial statement on the subject, Judge Alexander Holtzoff of the District Court of the District of Columbia, after describing the Comptroller General's legislative responsibilities, stated that:

> The Comptroller General has also a second status as the chief accounting officer of the Government. . . . This is an executive function and in performing it the Comptroller General acts as a member of the Executive Branch of the Government. The dual status of the General Accounting Office is not anomalous, for many regulatory commissions fulfill in part a legislative function and in part carry out executive duties. . . . Thus we have developed in comparatively recent years a fourth type of Government agency—one that combines two kinds of basic powers.[6]

Relevant to the constitutional issue are the unique provisions concerning the appointment, term, and removal of the Comptroller General. Like other officials in the executive branch, members of the regulatory commissions, and federal judges, he is appointed by the President with confirmation of the Senate. His legally fixed term of fifteen years is longer than that of any other officer of the United States.[7] He cannot be reappointed. Barring resignation, death, physical or mental incapacity, or extremely bad behavior, the Comptroller General is assured his tenure if he wants it, and not a day more. His term is equivalent to almost four presidential terms and is about six times the actual tenure, in recent years, of the average presidential appointee to high political offices in the executive branch. Since the founding of the office, Presidents Coolidge, Hoover, Truman, Kennedy, Nixon, Ford, and Carter have had no opportunity to appoint a Comptroller General.

The fact of presidential appointment lends some support to the Comptroller General's argument that he may perform nonlegislative functions. The absence of presidential removal power is key to the attorney general's argument that he is an officer only of the legislative branch. In fact, the question over removal power seems to him to be crucial—as it seemed to the members of the First Congress in 1789. But the appointment provision is also crucial. Different proposals to change the appointment, removal, and term of the Comptroller General and his deputy are currently under consideration in the Congress (see chapter 9).[8]

After fifty-seven years, the legal status and powers of the Comptroller General and the GAO remain in some respects disputed. But the GAO continues to operate and to change. The ambiguity and the allowance for dynamics that it permits may be an asset for the responsiveness and accountability of American government.

Independence: The Operational Questions

Some students and practitioners of public administration were for several decades sorely exercised about the powers of the Comptroller General because, they alleged, those powers infringed upon the administrative responsibilities of the managers in the executive branch. If a manager is to be held responsible for carrying out legislation, he must have the tools to direct and control his organization. Insofar as the Comptroller General is involved in or interferes with or impedes such activities, he is charged with violating a first principle of administration. As a legislative officer, he should confine his work to a prompt postaudit of executive branch activities. And he cannot do that objectively and disinterestedly if he has had a major part in the current controls and decisions; otherwise, he is in effect auditing his own work.

The main theme of the argument was consistently held by almost every major study group up to, but not including, the second Hoover Commission and by almost every scholar who wrote on the subject. The most conspicuous exception was the Institute for Government Research (later the Brookings Institution) and its director, W. F. Willoughby, who had a major hand in drafting the Budget and Accounting Act. He later wrote a book in 1927 describing, defending, and extolling the GAO and containing a series of recommendations to strengthen the GAO's powers, particularly in the field of accounting.[9] Even Willoughby changed his mind. In a still later book in 1936, he wrote critically of the "failure to distinguish between these essentially different functions (audit and control). . . . The most striking example of where this faulty procedure has been followed is presented by the national government, which, in creating its General Accounting Office . . . has vested the performance of these two functions in the hands of the same officer—a procedure which has given rise to much trouble in operating a system which otherwise has great merits."[10]

The massive changes within the GAO after World War II, the joint accounting program, and the Budgeting and Accounting Procedures Act of 1950 defused most of the criticisms that had been directed at the "first GAO." The GAO got out of the business of trying to keep books for the whole government, recognized the primary responsibilities of the operating agencies for developing and operating their own accounting systems, and encouraged the development of internal auditing within agencies; it concentrated increasingly on "comprehensive" postaudits conducted on the sites of operations, as its critics had said it should. Indeed, most of the scholarly commentators seem to have lost interest in the subject even though the Comptroller General has lost very few of his old powers. Further, he issues principles and standards on agency accounting systems and reviews and approves the principles and designs of those systems and their effectiveness in accounting—functions that some consider properly executive. The old issue is still there, but most of the time it is "simmering on a back burner."

The GAO's Posture in the Government

In relation to most of its day-to-day decisions and work, the question of the GAO's independence has taken on a quite different cast. The more pressing problem today is: To what extent is or should the GAO be independent in the choice of its projects, in the conduct of its studies, and in deciding what should go into its reports? Congress or various elements of it have frequently acknowledged, sometimes tacitly, that the Comptroller General has and should have a range of discretion on these matters. On the other hand, a not infrequent congressional criticism is that the GAO is insufficiently responsive to its needs and requests and to those of its committees and members. The GAO perceives its roles and its purposes in somewhat different terms than do the committees, subcommittees, and individual members and staffs of Congress, and it has far greater knowledge of its own staff resources and how they may most effectively be utilized—at least in its own perception of its purposes. Further, it would probably be next to impossible to develop any sort of consensus within Congress as to what the GAO should or should not do.[11]

There is another consideration. Although it is generally agreed that the GAO's primary boss is Congress and although the majority of its products are made for and go to Congress, whether or not on congressional request, it has a number of other audiences who receive and may be importantly affected by its reports. Among them are the executive branch and the various agencies of which it is composed (that may or may not welcome the GAO's observations and recommendations);[12] the media (the press, television, and radio), and through them the general public;[13] and a great variety of groups and interests affected by GAO studies, like state and local governments, international organizations, businesses contracting with the federal government, universities and other nonprofit enterprises, public interest groups, and others.[14]

The GAO insists that it must be largely independent in the selection, conduct, and products of its work in order that it may effectively assure the accountability of agencies in the executive branch. Without such independence, its efforts might lack objectivity and freedom from bias, and be subject to partisanship and political and special interest pressures. The independence of one agency thus appears to be essential to the accountability of others.

The main stock of the GAO's trade with its multifarious clienteles is information, mainly though not exclusively information about the conduct and the results of the work of the executive branch of the federal government. It searches for such information, organizes and synthesizes it, reports it, and makes recommendations, or in some instances decisions, growing out of it. In the larger part of its work, the GAO seeks and reports factual information that is countable, quantifiable, and provable. Much of this "hard" information has to do with finances—expenditures and costs in relation to results and the manner in which finances are managed. This emphasis is an outgrowth of the organization's historical development, of the inclinations and capabilities of many of its personnel, and of the interests of Congress. In recent years, there have been an increasing number of GAO studies on matters that are only remotely or indirectly related to finances, but the financial orientation remains strong.

Under the general umbrella of information, the GAO performs in a variety of roles. Since its inception, it has been referred to as the *watchdog* of the Treasury for Congress. Clearly the first GAO, under the direction of Comptroller General McCarl, perceived itself in such a role, but there is at least some question that its methods—mainly the review of individual vouchers—were very effective. Since that time, the GAO has relinquished the responsibility of overseeing or reviewing all or even a major part of individual federal expenditures and revenues. The dimensions of such an undertaking today in relation to the GAO's resources are far beyond the realm of possibility: it would mean that each of its professional employees, if all spent full time on this aspect of the work, would have responsibility annually, on the average, for overseeing the expenditure and receipt of about $100 million. Yet there may be some preventive, psychological value in the watchdog metaphor; the very fact that the GAO is "out there" and might make a check on transactions probably encourages greater care and inhibits peccadilloes.

If one likes the canine analogy, the term *bird dog* would be a more apt label for much of the GAO's work today. It selects and points to its prey, searches it out, retrieves it, and delivers it to the "hunter" (Congress and others). Unable to cover the entire universe, the GAO must be highly selective in choosing its targets and must have both patience and skill in searching them out. This kind of activity overlaps with the GAO's role as *investigator* of suspected wrongdoing and, more emphatically in recent years, of problems where improvements might be made, whether or not wrongdoing is involved.

The GAO is an *evaluator* and *critic* of proposed agency accounting systems and systems "in place," of agency program evaluation systems, and to an increasing extent of executive programs themselves, mostly of programs already underway but sometimes of program proposals that are still under consideration. The evaluation of federal programs is one of the most significant functions of the GAO, the one to which nearly half of its resources are directed; and it is a function for which the posture and the reputation of independence are crucial. Most federal agencies conduct internal evaluation and auditing systems, and very probably most of these studies are useful and valuable to those agencies. But they are almost necessarily parochial, bounded by the objectives and the limits of the individual agencies concerned. Further, in areas of actual or potential political controversy, they are inhibited against criticisms of programs that their administration endorses—or their reports are suppressed. There is no government-wide evaluation program in the executive branch at this time, and it is doubtful that, were there one, its findings would be made public if they were adverse to the objectives or the reputation of the executive branch. In general, one must conclude that the GAO's programs so far have been selective (with some emphasis on financial matters) and focused on problems, not comprehensive. But the potential is there, and it is almost nowhere else.

Among its many roles, the GAO acts as *technical assistant* and *management consultant* with regard not alone to accounting and other financial management systems but also to managerial problems of almost every stripe. Its posture as consultant differs from that of most private consulting firms in that (1) it usually enters upon its studies without invitation of the agency studied and (2) its findings and recommendations frequently go beyond the agency concerned. Its reports normally go not only to that agency, but to the Office of Management and Budget, to the appropriate elements of Congress, and to the public; and the agency must later report to Congress what actions it has taken to implement the recommendations.

Its evaluative functions often lead, implicitly or explicitly, to a role as *policy adviser*, both for the agencies and for Congress. There are dangers for the GAO in this role, especially in controversial areas. Its reputation for neutral, nonpartisan objectivity, above the political fray, could be threatened were it often to take sides and appear as a lobbyist on disputed issues. Most of its legislative recommendations to Congress, of which there are several dozen every year, concern the manner in which legislative intent is carried out. But some in certain fields (for example, energy) can hardly avoid political implications.

The GAO performs in the roles of *judge* and *rule maker* in the thousands of decisions the Comptroller General issues annually that, as in common law, become governing on federal agencies for like situations in the future. Its decisions on claims likewise are of a judicial character. It continues to be a *financial auditor* of government corporations and of certain other organizations, although this activity has declined proportionately in the last two decades.[15] In a number of ways the GAO serves as a *teacher*. For years, it has produced manuals on accounting, auditing, data processing, and related subjects for the benefit of other federal agencies, and most recently for state and local governments. Its Office of General Counsel has during the last few years been issuing manuals on contracts and procurement, personnel law, and other matters. Its Program Analysis Division has issued a number of reports on the techniques and problems of program evaluation. And GAO personnel frequently participate in professional conferences and training seminars dealing with such subjects as these.

The bulk of the GAO's work can be described as problem-oriented, applied research, an expression that many would find more accurate than "auditing." In the last few years, it has undertaken some studies that would qualify as *developmental research*, directed at enhancing knowledge in broad problem areas that might contribute to better policies and practices in the future. One of these was a review and analysis of the *Mayaguez* incident.[16] The incident itself was closed when the study was begun, and it was intended not to provide better solutions for the *Mayaguez* incident, but to contribute to the understanding of the processes and problems of crisis management and thus, it was hoped, to enhance the government's ability to handle crises in the future. Another study, still underway, is that of the problems of the aged in Cleveland, Ohio, and of the effectiveness of various public and private agencies in dealing with these problems. The study, which is utilizing a variety of sophisticated social science survey techniques, is intended to enhance understanding of the problems of the aged and to contribute to wiser policy and programs in the future.

Finally, the GAO is to a limited extent and usually in an indirect way an *ombudsman*. It responds very selectively to citizen complaints about governmental performance, alleged injustices, and alleged extravagance or waste. Some of these complaints are received directly or through its field staffs; some are forwarded by congressmen and their staffs; and some are from federal employees, often through the channels of their agencies. Indeed, its consideration of protests of contract bidders is, in a sense, an ombudsman function.

This enumeration of the roles of the GAO may not be complete and exhaustive. It should be sufficient, however, to indicate that the GAO has a great number of different roles that together constitute a complex package. Some of these roles—such as technical assistant, policy adviser, and judge—may not seem totally consistent; yet role conflict does not appear to be a major concern within the GAO. However, there is a good deal of differing opinion, both inside and outside the organization, on the emphasis and the resources that should be applied to each of the GAO's different roles.[17]

The GAO, the Media, and the Public

The GAO's independent status is illustrated and also enhanced by its open and cooperative relations with the press and other media. The bulk of its reports, whose primary destinations are Congress, congressional committees, and members, and which are not enshrouded under security classifications, are also delivered to news representatives and organizations. A growing and already substantial number of these reports become the basis of newspaper stories, sometimes on front pages, and of television and radio coverage. Between 1972 and 1976, the number of GAO reports that were given nationwide, in-depth media coverage grew from 31 to 180, or about one every other day. Testimony of the Comptroller General and other GAO officials before congressional committees is likewise frequently reported in the papers and sometimes broadcast on television programs.

Until the arrival of Comptroller General Staats in 1966, the GAO did not maintain a public information office (and in fact issued a number of reports criticizing executive departments and agencies for maintaining large publicity staffs). Relations with the media—and relations with Congress—were handled by an assistant to the Comptroller General, who was generally an attorney with previous experience in the Office of the General Counsel. Although critics accused the GAO—particularly under Campbell—of being a publicity mill, the organization maintained a policy of releasing audit reports through congressional offices and of minimizing direct media-auditor contacts. Particularly sensitive or controversial reports either were released as congressional committee prints or were announced to the press by individual congressmen.

Under Staats, the GAO has developed a distribution system that channels audit reports to news organizations based on subject-matter interest. For the most "newsworthy" blue-book reports, the GAO provides copies to the press as soon as distribution on Capitol Hill is completed. Furthermore, it sometimes schedules press conferences to explain significant or technical audit findings to media representatives. One observer of the GAO attributed these changes in the GAO's relations with the press to changes occurring in Congress: no longer monopolizing the information flow to Congress on the status of federal programs, the GAO can best call congressional attention to its work through well-placed media coverage of audit reports.

The rise of two closely related phenomena in recent years—the accent on investigative journalism and the renewed interest in government accountability—has provided both the GAO and the media with a new set of common interests in their evolving relationship. Even the traditional audits performed by the GAO—financial reviews—became the basis for national media attention, although the GAO had not suddenly changed its modus operandi. In 1977, for example, GAO audits of congressional printing clerks and of the Smithsonian Institution became the subjects of nationwide headlines and editorials. The emphasis on investigative reporting, however, has created one headache for the GAO: competitive news organizations and overly zealous agency officials have sometimes released ("leaked" in current parlance) draft audit reports before they were officially issued to Congress, embarrassing the Comptroller General and/or the congressional requester.[18]

The influence of the GAO upon the media has not been a one-way street. As noted earlier, about 35 percent of the GAO's work stems from direct congressional requests, and members have a natural interest in exploring any government subject, particularly any deficiency, that might receive newspaper space. Indeed, both Congress and the GAO have long realized that praiseworthy reports do not make "news." In addition to viewing the GAO in the capacity of "an in-house Ralph Nader," as in the previous examples of press use of GAO reports, Congress also tends to use GAO audits to corroborate the charges made by public interest groups such as Nader's, or to investigate causes championed by the media. The 1975 GAO report on the use of Red Dye No. 2 in foods received immediate press attention because Congress claimed that it was the first independent examination of the issue, and because the GAO agreed with consumer advocates that the additive should be banned by the Food and Drug Administration.

Not insignificant in determining the relationship between the GAO and the media have been the demands that Congress—as a body, through its committees, and by individual members—has placed on it. Dependent upon electoral support from the home district constituency and aware of the power of the media in attracting votes, congressmen have used the GAO extensively as a basis for press releases and news accounts for their local audiences. In fact, it may be surprising that this practice is not considerably more widespread. Simultaneously, the GAO is forging its own relationship with the media by lessening the controls formerly exercised on that relationship by Congress. If an audit is performed at the request of a specific member and that member does not care to publicly release the findings of the report, the GAO will no longer "bury" the audit or refuse to divulge the contents. New regulations promulgated by Staats in 1977[19] provide for GAO release of all audit reports, without the specific authorization of the requesting members, as long as the members have had the opportunity to release it themselves.

The GAO's Role in Government Contrasted with That of Auditing Firms in the Private Sector

For a period of about twenty years, 1945-1965, the overriding thrust of the GAO's development was to make it an effective financial auditor of governmental operations. The basic model was the auditing firm in the private sector, generally known as the public accounting firm, and the recruitment of professional personnel was directed almost exclusively to auditors trained for and sometimes experienced in the audit of private enterprise. Comptroller General Joseph Campbell made this concept explicit when he said in 1957 that the GAO is the "public accounting agency of the U.S. Government."[20] Structurally and superficially—and excepting the unique position of the popularly elected President of the United States— the business and governmental models appear quite comparable (see Figure 5).

There are similarities between the two in certain fields, such as the GAO's audits of government corporations, but overall, the differences considerably exceed the likenesses. Even in purely structural terms, the stance, activities, and internal organization of the shareholders of most businesses differ in kind from those of citizens in relation to the government of the United States. Few if any boards of directors resemble in any significant respect the U.S. Congress, any more than do their presidents resemble the President of the United States. Both the public accounting firms and the GAO treasure their independence and their adherence to professional standards, but the nature of their independence and standards differs.

The differences in their respective arenas of operation are also significant. In overall financial terms, at least, the condition of business firms can be measured against fairly well understood criteria: balance sheets, profit and loss statements, liquidity, earnings per share, and so forth. Except for business-type enterprises in the federal government, most of these are not usable by the GAO, the objectives of whose studies hinge upon substantive laws and appropriations. There are seldom profits or losses, earnings, or shares in specific dollar terms. Objectives of government programs are often

Figure 5

AUDIT RESPONSIBILITY AND LINES OF AUTHORITY IN PRIVATE SECTOR AND PUBLIC SECTOR ENTERPRISES

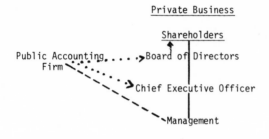

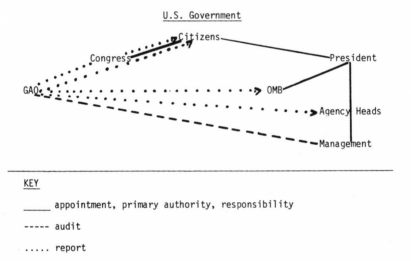

KEY

_____ appointment, primary authority, responsibility

- - - - - audit

· · · · · report

if not usually imprecise, so that the GAO must rely heavily upon nonquantifiable, nonfinancial measures of outputs and outcomes of social programs whose economic benefits at best can be roughly estimated. In other words, the GAO, like other governmental evaluators, must in much of its work depend upon judgment, supported as far as possible by accounting or statistical data.

Perhaps the most significant ·distinction between the GAO and public accounting firms lies in the historic, traditional, and still dominant responsibility of the auditing profession in the business world: attestation.

"First, the usual commercial attest audit is built around the concept of verifying the representations of management. In fact, by and large, it is confined mainly to the financial statement representations of management —as when an auditor issues (or fails to issue) an unqualified certificate attesting to the validity of the financial statements prepared by the management of the company under examination."[21] Most GAO "audits" are very different in both the initiating and reporting phases. The GAO selects the area, method, and scope of its studies, and decides on the nature, destination, and recommendations of its reports.

In fact, most GAO reports bear very little resemblance to the audits of public accounting firms in the private sector. Except in the audits of government corporations, they do not attest to the accuracy and fairness of agency reports. Instead, the GAO produces its own reports, most of which are submitted to the agencies for review and criticism. Agency comments are considered and may occasion modifications in the GAO report, and, where the GAO does not agree, are included in or appended to it. The product, however modified following agency review, goes to Congress and the public. Most GAO reports are basically its own, not attestations of or comments on the honesty and accuracy of the reports of others.

The absence of the "attest" function in most of the GAO's work is only one of a great many differences between it and public accounting firms. In the private sector, the employing firm may define the limits and scope of independent audits within the framework of professional standards;[22] it selects and may dismiss its outside auditors. On the contrary, the GAO, sometimes under mandate or request from Congress, defines its own limits and scope. Public accounting firms are paid for their work by the companies engaging their services; the GAO pays its own way from its appropriations. The former operate in a market that is highly competitive; the GAO is a monopoly, although it may enlist an outside group to assist or replace it on specific projects. Further, the GAO is not legally accountable for the accuracy of its products (though it may be held politically accountable). If, for example, it fails to discover and report fraud, the primary responsibility rests with the agency involved, not the GAO. In contrast, the courts, certain regulatory commissions and committees of Congress, and the financially concerned public have increasingly held that public accounting firms should be held accountable when they attested to inaccurate information about the financial condition of their clients.

Another conspicuous difference between the GAO and public accounting firms is reflected in the scope, coverage, and nature of both their reports. The GAO's reports are essentially oriented to problems of management, programs, and effectiveness, problems that are largely selected by the GAO itself. They normally conclude with statements of findings and recommendations. In their attest function, public accounting firms issue reports that are essentially certifications that verify whether or not the financial statements of management are in accordance with generally accepted accounting principles. It would be beyond the scope of a CPA firm, in its attest capacity, to report publicly on the defects, dangers, or environmental hazards of a product line, or on poor planning or quality control in the firm's general management.

Many public accounting firms, of course, have instituted management advisory services to make studies and recommendations on problems perceived by the management of a business that have to do with managerial efficiency and effectiveness. In this capacity, they are in no significant way different from other private consulting firms. The problems to be studied are defined by management, and the consulting services are contracted and paid for by management, which may or may not implement the recommendations and may or may not issue the reports publicly or even to their own superiors in the corporate structure. Agencies of the federal government as well as state and local units have been increasingly contracting for such advisory services from accounting and other consulting firms—and these include the GAO itself. Within the public accounting firms, their attest activities are organizationally divided from their consulting work.[23] For the former they employ almost exclusively CPAs and other accountants; for the latter, specialists from a wide variety of professions.

As noted earlier, both the GAO and the public accounting fraternity lay emphasis upon their professional standards. The attest reports of CPA firms normally include assurance that the audit was conducted in accord with "generally accepted auditing standards"; and GAO attest reports on public corporations usually include the same assurance. Like other well-established professions, accountants and auditors, through their professional organizations, have long enunciated standards and principles to guide and discipline practitioners of the profession. Soon after the GAO extended its commercial-type audit work to noncorporate government agencies in the late 1940s it recognized the need for its own manual for such auditing, which was first published in 1952.[24] That early effort leaned heavily on the standards of the public accounting profession, but even then, because of the nature of the organizations being audited, went considerably further.[25] The Accounting and Auditing Act of 1950 vested in the GAO the responsibility for prescribing accounting principles for all federal executive agencies, and in 1952 the GAO issued its first *Statement of Accounting Principles and Standards for Guidance of Executive Agencies in the Federal Government*. In 1957 it produced a statement on internal audit principles and concepts. Thus, a federal agency was enunciating principles and standards for most federal accounting and auditing activities in the national government, whereas in the private sector the issuance of auditing standards was, and remains, a private initiative of a professional association, the American Institute of

Certified Public Accountants (AICPA).[26]

As the GAO's studies extended further and further from the traditional financial audits, its standards increasingly differed in content from the accustomed auditing standards. In 1972 when it published its general standards for governmental audits as guidelines for audits of state and local as well as the federal governments,[27] it defined "audits" in entirely different terms from those traditionally used in the private sector: "not only work done by accountants in examining financial reports but also work done in reviewing (a) compliance with applicable laws and regulations, (b) efficiency and economy of operations, and (c) effectiveness in achieving program results."[28] Later in the same year, the AICPA issued a *Codification of Auditing Standards and Procedures* that declared in its foreword: "This statement (on auditing standards) is not intended to apply to the function of independent auditors insofar as they relate to tax practice and management services." However, the AICPA includes a Management Advisory Services Executive Committee, which periodically publishes pamphlets in a "Guideline Series," and in 1977 issued a pamphlet primarily to explain and illustrate the GAO's own standards for government audits.[29] In the introduction of that document it is stated that: "Ultimately, a publication similar to those in the AICPA's audit guide series should be issued covering government economy, efficiency, and program results evaluations as well as financial audits."[30] It thus appears that the GAO has assumed leadership of the accounting fraternity generally through its enunciation of auditing standards that are far broader than is common in the private sector.

Both the GAO and auditors in the private sector lay emphasis on their independence and objectivity. Objectivity depends in theory on independence, but, as must be abundantly clear, independence is never complete in an interdependent society—it has limits and operates within constraints. Both the GAO and auditors in the private sector depend ultimately for their credibility, their viability, and even their survival upon their reputation as objective, impartial agencies; yet neither is completely independent. The GAO is ultimately dependent upon support in Congress, which is itself to some extent responsive to support or criticism from the executive branch, the media, special publics, and the general public. Public accounting firms are immediately dependent upon the businesses that do and will (or will not) engage their services; they are secondarily dependent upon their credibility and reputation for objectivity—particularly in the business community and in government agencies, such as the Securities and Exchange Commission, that exercise surveillance over business activities of various kinds. The accounting profession has recently been the object of criticism and attacks— in Congress and in the courts—on the grounds that it is not independent, that it has "gone to bed with" the businesses whose financial integrity it is engaged to attest. Some have gone so far as to propose that the profession's self-governing, self-disciplining powers be removed and replaced by governmental regulation.[31]

The GAO has likewise occasionally been criticized for "going to bed with" the agencies it examines. But the potentially more critical threat to the GAO's independence is that some of its reports, which cannot be proven by quantifiable, indisputable "facts," are perceived and attacked as being partial to one or another side of a policy or program issue or in behalf of some congressmen against one or more executive programs. The further it moves into controversial and judgmental matters of public concern, the greater the risks of charges of lack of objectivity and independence.

For the GAO and for CPA auditors in the private sector, the reputation for independence is lifeblood. But the threats to that reputation, the criteria for measuring it, and the possible recourses are very different. A central element in the difference is simply politics. The GAO lives in a political world continuously; public accounting firms are drawn into that world from time to time and sometimes draw vitriolic political attack. But their ethos is basically one of business. The GAO's is one of government; and government is, among other things, politics.

Notes

1. The recently published *RN: The Memoirs of Richard Nixon* (New York: Grosset and Dunlap, 1978) is an exception; in it there are several references to audits of Nixon's campaign organization by the GAO's office of Federal Elections (see chapter 7). But there is nothing about the GAO as an organization.

2. As indicated in chapter 7, these powers include the settling of accounts and the disallowance of payments judged by the GAO to be illegal or improper, the issuing of advance opinions on the legality of proposed expenditures, the rendering of decisions on protests of bidders for federal contracts, the prescribing of accounting principles and standards, the countersigning of warrants, the settling of claims for and against the government, the bringing of suits to compel the release of impounded funds, and a number of others.

3. Cited in chapter 7.

4. U.S. Constitution, Article I, Section 8, cl. 18.

5. For a comprehensive and scholarly presentation of this argument, see William W. Van Alstyne, "The Role of Congress in Determining Incidental Powers of the President and of the Federal Courts: A Comment on the Horizontal Effect of the Sweeping Clause," *Law and Contemporary Problems* 40, no. 2 (spring 1976):101-34.

6. United States ex rel. Brookfield Const. Co., Inc. v. Stewart, 234 F.

Supp. 94 (D.D.C.), affirmed in 119 U.S. App. D.C. 254 (1964).

7. Some officers are of course appointed for indefinite or lifetime terms; they include judges and "inferior" officers appointed within the classified civil service or other protected services.

8. The Supreme Court recently made the point clear and unequivocal that appointive officers of the United States must be appointed by the President and confirmed by the Senate; in Buckley v. Valeo, 424 U.S. 1 (1976).

9. W. F. Willoughby, *The Legal Status and Functions of the General Accounting Office of the National Government* (Baltimore: Johns Hopkins Press, 1927).

10. W. F. Willoughby, *The Government of Modern States*, rev. ed. (New York: Appleton-Century, 1936), p. 487.

11. Further discussion on these topics is contained in chapter 9.

12. See chapter 10.

13. Discussed in a later section in this chapter.

14. See chapter 10.

15. Its role of auditor is further discussed in the closing section of this chapter.

16. Described in Kloman, ed., *Cases in Accountability: The Work of the GAO* (Boulder, Colo.: Westview Press, 1979).

17. See chapters 9, 10, 11.

18. A recent example was the premature release of a GAO study on the potential dangers in liquid natural gas logistics, which was in draft form for comment by the Department of Energy when "leaked" to the press.

19. Mainly in consequence of the GAO's embarrassment resulting from congressional release of the *Mayaguez* reports in the heat of the 1976 election campaign. See the case study on the *Mayaguez* incident in Kloman, ed., *Cases in Accountability*.

20. Joseph Campbell, "Recruiting, Training, and Professional Development of Accountants in the General Accounting Office," *U.S. General Accounting Office Staff Bulletin* 2, no. 2 (August 1957):33.

21. William W. Cooper and Walter F. Frese, "Turnaround at the GAO," in W. W. Cooper and Yuji Ijiri, eds., *Eric Louis Kohler—Accounting's Man of Principles* (Reston, Va.: Reston Publishing, 1978), p. 143.

22. "Independent audits" in this section are used to describe audits conducted by public accounting firms or the GAO and are to be distinguished from "internal audits" conducted on a continuing basis and paid for by the managements of private businesses or government agencies.

23. One of the principal sources of recent congressional criticism has been that the separation is insufficient: that the desire to expand consulting services has contributed to loss of independence and objectivity in the attest work. See U.S. Congress, Senate Committee on Government Operations,

Improving the Accountability of Publicly Owned Corporations and Their Auditors (Washington, D.C.: U.S. Government Printing Office, November 1977), pp. 16-17.

24. The GAO *Comprehensive Audit Manual,* September 1, 1952.

25. Karney A. Brasfield, "Development of GAO Auditing Standards and Their Relevance to Practice of Public Accounting," in Cooper and Ijiri, eds., *Eric Louis Kohler,* p. 161.

26. AICPA is also interested in government auditing. Two of its recent publications include: Cornelius E. Tierney, *Federal Financial Management: Accounting and Auditing Practices* (New York: AICPA, 1976); and Cornelius E. Tierney, *Federal Grants-In-Aid* (New York: AICPA, 1977).

27. *Standards for Audit of Governmental Organizations, Programs, Activities And Functions,* June 1972.

28. Ibid., p. 3.

29. *Guidelines for CPA Participation in Government Audit Engagements to Evaluate Economy, Efficiency, and Program Results.*

30. Ibid., p. 2.

31. U.S. Congress, Senate, Committee on Government Operations, *The Accounting Establishment: A Staff Study* (Washington, D.C.: U.S. Government Printing Office, 1976).

9

THE CONGRESSIONAL
ENVIRONMENT OF THE GAO

It is the proper duty of a representative body to look diligently into every affair of government and to talk much about what it sees. It is meant to be the eyes and the voice, and to embody the wisdom and will of its constituents. Unless Congress have and use every means of acquainting itself with the acts and the disposition of the administrative agents of the government, the country must be helpless to learn how it is being served. . . . The informing function of Congress should be preferred even to its legislative function.

—Woodrow Wilson, *Congressional Government,* 1885

The most important part of the political world in which the GAO operates is the Congress of the United States. Probably more than ever before, the GAO is an "agent" of Congress. It may be a "part" of the legislative branch, but it is not realistically a "part" of Congress. Like most other agencies in the government, it is dependent upon Congress for its powers, its resources, and ultimately its existence. The bulk of its work, however it is initiated, is directed to perceived or predicted needs of Congress, and its effectiveness depends heavily on whether Congress utilizes its products. But it has a distinct identity and a considerable degree of independence in terms not only of law but also of discretion in its program and internal administration. It may be of some psychological and symbolic significance that its headquarters are not on Capitol Hill in Washington, D.C., where or near which the other congressional support agencies are located, but about as far from the Capitol as it is from the White House (a mile or so). The bulk of GAO personnel are scattered around Washington and environs, around the country in regional offices, and around the world in overseas branches.

The GAO's dependence on Congress is not a one-way street. In its legislative, oversight, and informational activities Congress is increasingly dependent upon the GAO, for the GAO is very probably its best source of information about what is actually going on in the executive branch—outside of that branch itself. The relationships between Congress and the GAO can hardly be described as a "street." They are a network of multifarious pathways connecting segments of both organizations—or, in some cases, failing to connect them. The GAO and Congress are interdependent, their relationships multiple and complex.

It has been noted earlier that many of the rather dramatic changes that have occurred within the GAO were largely generated by its own leaders, particularly the Comptrollers General; but this is not the full picture. In the last dozen years, more or less, there have been multiple changes in Congress—in membership, leadership, attitudes, and internal organization. These changes, beginning approximately with the term of Comptroller General Staats, have had great impact on the GAO, so much so that one's understanding of that organization would be seriously deficient if it were not considered in relation to the changing posture and nature of Congress itself.

The Emergent Congress

Many of the specific congressional reforms in this recent period may quite properly be credited to certain individual leaders and groups within it. But the real generator of change in Congress was very probably the American society outside it. As described in the opening pages of chapter 6, this recent period was one of almost continuous turbulence. Popular disaffection with government in general, including Congress, became widespread. Congressional disaffection with the presidency, ignited by Vietnam, likewise grew to the point of the forced resignation of President Nixon. Increasing numbers of congressmen were frustrated by the apparent inability of Congress to make decisions on public policy issues and to control the executive branch.

Many of the recent developments in Congress have a fairly extended history; for convenience, they may be traced at least to World War II and the Legislative Reorganization Act of 1946, which immediately followed it. They include the efforts of that act to reduce the number of committees, to rationalize and more clearly define their respective turfs, to regularize procedures, and to gain more effective control over the budget. Many of those postwar efforts at reform were not conspicuously successful. The broader but also larger committees created many subcommittees, which heightened rather than lessened the narrowly focused specialisms that the committee reforms had intended to correct; the universally recognized rule of seniority governed the oligarchic leadership of the majority and minority heads of committees and subcommittees; the dominant authority of the Rules Committee in the House and the continuing power of filibuster in the Senate operated to frustrate majority coalitions in both houses; the effort at systematic congressional control of the budget was a total failure. During most of the Eisenhower years, under the skillful though cautious leadership of Democratic Speaker Rayburn and Majority Leader Johnson, Congress managed to cooperate with the President on some issues. Later, following the Kennedy assassination, President Johnson at the peak of his popularity was able to push through Congress an avalanche of social legislation under his slogan of the "Great Society." In the main, these new programs were products of presidential, not congressional, initiative and leadership.

The new beginning of congressional change, which is still underway, may be dated from the last years of the Johnson administration. Some members and some committees were roused to question the effectiveness and the political consequences of the domestic programs that they themselves had enacted; others vociferously objected to the growing dimensions of defense expenditures and to enormous cost overruns on military contracts. As early as 1965, Congress was considering new measures to enlarge its participation in the framing of policy and in the control of its execution.

Near the close of the Johnson administration, one of the President's staff aides described the executive and legislative branches as "separate but unequal";[1] Congress was clearly the "less than equal" party. Much of the legislation and other actions during the succeeding years were efforts to redress the balance, to enhance the effective influence of Congress. Some of the more important laws enacted to this end have been described earlier (in chapter 6).[2] In many other ways Congress undertook to curb or check executive initiative. It increasingly attached to its substantive legislation provisions that the agencies evaluate the effectiveness of legislated programs and report their evaluations back to Congress. It made more and more legislation temporary, subject to annual or periodic review and reenactment; and committees in both houses subsequently gave serious consideration to "sunset" bills, which would require that most substantive legislation be in effect temporary, expiring every several years (five to ten in different bills), a procedure designed to require thorough reexamination and reevaluation in light of experience, and enactment of new legislation. When Congress delegated legislative authority to administrative agencies through the power to issue regulations or make decisions, it increasingly attached requirements that such regulations or decisions could become effective only after one or both houses, or sometimes designated congressional committees, had an opportunity to review and approve or disapprove them—the so-called legislative veto.[3]

Further, Congress has recently assumed far greater initiative with regard to basic substantive legislation than in the past—at least as far back as the revolution of 1910, which dissolved the power of the dictatorial speaker, Joseph G. Cannon (R., Ill.). The old maxim that "The President proposes; Congress disposes" is a bit too simple to describe current congressional behavior. Congress considers, questions, revises, substitutes, and passes or refuses to pass executive proposals. Perhaps the most striking illustration of the changed posture is in connection with the new congressional budget organization and procedures. The President still proposes his budget, but Congress proceeds to set up its own, with its own targets in terms of total figures and priorities. It has instituted rather elaborate procedures in order to discipline itself and its various committees to stay within those budgetary boundaries or, at least when they are changed, to be consciously aware of the overall impact of the changes. Congress has in fact taken the initiative in a number of substantive areas, even in cases in which the President has submitted his own proposals: energy, social security, the environment, the space program, public housing, taxation, and other areas.

Congress is playing an increasing role in what some have called second-stage initiatives—changes in existing programs and operations growing out of legislative oversight, evaluations and audits.[4] Oversight by Congress of the executive branch has been practiced in a piecemeal way almost since the founding of the republic, but it was most clearly enunciated in the Legislative Reorganization Act of 1946, which provided that:

> To assist the Congress in appraising the administration of the laws and in developing such amendments or related legislation as it may deem necessary, each standing committee of the Senate and the House of Representatives shall exercise continuous watchfulness of the execution by the administrative agencies concerned of any laws, the subject matter of which is within the jurisdiction of such committee; and, for that purpose, shall study all pertinent reports and data submitted to the Congress by the agencies in the executive branch of the Government.[5]

The provision was modified and somewhat strengthened by the Legislative Reorganization Act of 1970. Three years later, the House established a bipartisan Select Committee on Committees under the chairmanship of Richard Bolling (D., Mo.) to restructure its committee system. That group proposed that all House legislative oversight activities be concentrated in the Government Operations Committee. This recommendation was defeated, but a milder substitute, emanating from a special committee of the Democratic Caucus, was adopted. It prescribed that all the standing committees in the House incorporate the oversight function within their regular activities and recommended that each establish an oversight subcommittee. According to many of the observers who have addressed the topic, oversight is still less than adequate with respect to most administrative activities. A reason sometimes attributed is that congressmen have little incentive to engage themselves actively except in areas of high public interest and potential drama—as in the recent investigations of intelligence activities. Among the many demands upon congressmen, oversight is said to enjoy a relatively low priority.[6] Another student attributes the relative slowness in the development of oversight activities not to congressional incentives but to fear that centering of the oversight function in a single committee (as was proposed by the Bolling Committee) or in one subcommittee of each standing committee would deprive the other committees and subcommittees of power.[7] Nonetheless, few would question that the effort and attention given to oversight of the administration have greatly increased in recent years.

In several other ways Congress has demonstrated that it would not simply acquiesce to pressure from the executive branch. Its law to curb presidential impoundments of appropriated funds[8] resulted in a dramatic decrease in the number of impoundments, and a very substantial proportion of proposed permanent impoundments (rescissions) were in fact nullified by Congress. The Senate approved the President's proposed Panama Canal treaties only after protracted debate and modification, and only by two votes. The Senate's power to approve or disapprove presidential appointments was exercised in connection with two Nixon nominees to the Supreme Court. Both houses undertook in effect to remove his incumbent director of the Office of Management and Budget, Roy Ash, but failed because of a presidential veto. They later succeeded in making the director and deputy director of the Office of Management and Budget—theretofore exclusively the President's choice—subject to confirmation by the Senate. In 1977, the Senate was embarrassed when President Carter's appointee as director of the office, Bert Lance, whose appointment it approved without serious investigation, came under criticism for his financial dealings and subsequently resigned. The activities of his successor, James T. McIntyre, especially in financial matters, were subjected to the closest scrutiny before he was confirmed, the Senate inquiry being based on a thorough audit by the GAO.

The cumulative evidence of congressional assertiveness and aggressiveness is indeed impressive: the requirements for evaluation of executive programs; increased oversight activities; the legislative veto; initiative in substantive legislation; the congressional budget; the control of impoundments; the more extensive senatorial review of treaties and presidential appointments. How lastingly effective the effort to redress the balance between the "separate but unequal" branches is a question for future historians. But the vigor of the effort and its impact upon congressional behavior can hardly be doubted.

One other factor has had great significance in the emergent Congress: the increasing complexity of the issues with which it must deal.[9] This is a reflection in part of the growing interrelatedness and interdependence of various elements of the national and world societies. It is in part a result of the demand that the federal government do something about a growing variety of problems. And it is in part a consequence of the recognition of the interrelatedness of problems: that decisions in foreign affairs affect domestic matters, that decisions about energy have "spillover" effects upon the environment, the economy, and quality of life as do those about education affect unemployment, housing, crime, and so on. As Congress has sought a more assertive role in policymaking, the need for more understanding—in breadth as well as depth—of problems has magnified.

For purposes of this study, it is significant that the GAO was, in one or another way, involved in and affected by virtually all of the changes and developments cited above. In fact, the growth in function, influence, and difficulties of Congress was approximately contemporaneous with the development of the "third GAO" in the first dozen years of Comptroller General Staats.

Devolution, Democratization, and Centralization

The growing assertiveness of Congress was accompanied and to a considerable extent occasioned by changes in the nature of its members, in organization and procedures, and in power structures of the two houses, particularly the House of Representatives.[10] During the 1950s and the early 1960s the liberal-moderate Democrats and some like-minded Republicans were repeatedly frustrated by what they considered a "coalition" of Republicans and conservative southern Democrats. They were frustrated further by the systems whereby committees largely dominated congressional processes and outcomes; the committees themselves were dominated by their chairmen, who sometimes exercised nearly dictatorial powers in their respective jurisdictions; and the leadership of the committees on both sides of the aisle were protected by the traditional but unlegislated rule of seniority.

In 1959, the disaffected Democrats formed an unofficial organization, known as the Democratic Study Group, in the House to lend some cohesion, leadership, and information on issues. In the late 1960s it gave greater attention to the structure and organization of the House and provided a principal impulse to the basic changes that occurred in the 1970s. Its influence was enhanced by changes in the composition of the congressional membership, particularly on the Democratic side, in the direction of higher proportions of liberals and moderates to the point that a clear majority of the Democrats would be classified as liberals and only a minority of the whole House, including Republicans, were conservatives.[11]

Many of the newcomers, in both House and Senate, were independent minded, reform-oriented persons, eager to set their stamp on legislative actions. Perhaps most important, they were relatively independent of party ties and commitments. Many were in effect independent political entrepreneurs who owed little to their party organizations. They were quickly disaffected by the committee system, the powers of committee chairmen, and the norm of seniority particularly in the selection of committee chairmen. They were considerably younger than the incumbents and younger than most of their predecessor freshmen. In the House, they included a rising number of women and blacks—though these groups were still disproportionately low in relation to their share of the national population. The new senators and representatives defied the age-old norm that the freshman term was one of apprenticeship during which they should watch, listen, and be quiet. Most of them became active and articulate spokesmen on issues soon after they entered Congress.[12]

These developments contributed to major shifts in power and in style during the early and mid 1970s, particularly in the House and particularly in the majority Democratic Party. The changes were mainly in the directions of devolution and dispersion of powers from the "old guard" to the Democratic membership, democratization of procedures, and greater openness of congressional operations, including public access to bill mark-up sessions and conference committees. Part of these developments was made possible by the growth in numbers of subcommittees, a trend that had begun two decades earlier. Between 1955 and 1975, the number of standing subcommittees in the House grew from 83 to 139. Through a series of reforms in the early 1970s, the Democratic caucus of the House vastly increased the powers, resources, and importance of the subcommittees. In 1973, in what was dubbed the "Subcommittee Bill of Rights," it required that subcommittees have fixed jurisdictions, authorization to meet and hold hearings, and adequate budgets and staffs. It further removed the power to appoint subcommittee chairmen from the committee chairmen, providing instead that they be chosen by a vote of the Democratic caucus within the standing committee. An earlier reform (in 1971) had limited subcommittee chairs that could be held by individual members to one. The powers and status of committee chairmen were further reduced—or at least threatened —by other changes instituted in the period of 1970 to 1975. The methods and mechanics of their selection at the beginning of every Congress were changed so that the Democratic caucus could have a real choice by majority vote. The seniority rule was no longer sacrosanct, and in fact three of the old-time chairmen were replaced by the Democratic caucus. The chairmen lost the powers to determine the number, size, and majority party membership of subcommittees, to control referral of legislation to subcommittees, or to prevent their committees from meeting. Somewhat comparable changes had occurred or were occurring in the Senate and among congressional Republicans.

One effect of these developments was a widespread dispersal of powers and influence among congressmen, including the newer and younger members. In 1978, half of the Democratic members of the House (144 of 288) chaired at least one standing committee or subcommittee. Among the Republicans, far fewer in total numbers, the proportion of ranking minority members was considerably higher. In the Senate, most first-term Democrats received at least one chairmanship of a subcommittee on the day they entered on duty, and, on average, each chaired almost two subcommittees. In 1978, nearly nine of every ten Democrats in the Senate were chairmen of at least one committee or subcommittee.

Another manifestation of the dispersal of traditional committee authority in the two houses was the growth of a variety of informal organizations, crosscutting the official committee structure and representing common policy concerns of their members. Many of these have their own small staffs, financed by allocations from their members. The first and probably still the most influential is the House Democratic Study Group, which grew in size to over 150 members in 1978. It has been emulated to some extent from the Republican side of the aisle by the House Republican Conference and the so-called Wednesday Group. A variety of other crosscutting groups with more specialized concerns in both houses have been formed for blacks, for Hispanics, for women, for New Englanders, for rural representatives, for Vietnam-era veterans, and other groups.

It is somewhat paradoxical that the dispersal of power has been accompanied and to a considerable extent made possible by a centralization of power, particularly in the House. The far-reaching changes in rules and procedures of the 1970s were foreshadowed by the activation in 1969 of the House Democratic caucus under pressure from the Democratic Study Group. Theretofore, for many decades the caucus had been a dormant organization, meeting only at the opening of each new Congress to ratify committee assignments determined in advance by the Committee on Committees, which was composed of the Democratic members of the Ways and Means Committee. Thereafter, the caucus could be called once a month if fifty of its members signed a petition, with an accompanying agenda, for the meeting. In 1975 the caucus adopted a change requiring the chairman to call a meeting of the caucus on the third Wednesday of each month. The chairman can cancel any monthly caucus but not two consecutive monthly caucuses. Most of the changes in House rules and procedures in the succeeding years, some of which are summarized above, emanated from the House Democratic caucus. A number of the changes instituted by the caucus tended, and were intended, to strengthen party leadership: in the caucus itself, in the Steering and Policy Committee that it created with significant powers on a continuing basis to develop and guide legislative strategies, and in the role of the speaker of the House. The powers of the speaker were significantly enhanced in a number of ways. He was empowered to chair a revised Committee on Committees; to nominate the Democratic members of the Rules Committee; to chair the Steering and Policy Committee; and to substantially control the referral of bills. He was further given a much strengthened party whip organization.

The recent changes in House organization and procedures have thus been in two directions: to devolve powers and influence to subcommittees and individual members; and to strengthen overall party leadership through the Democratic caucus, the Steering and Policy Committee, and the speaker. The former movement has unquestionably been more pronounced and effectual than the latter. Both meant a lessening of influence by the chairmen of the standing committees. Somewhat comparable though less dramatic changes have been occurring in the Senate and within the Republican organizations in both houses.

These various developments have already had significant consequences for congressional operations, for those organizations and persons that are called upon to assist its diverse elements, and for the executive agencies that must deal with them. The number of different subcommittees and individual members who exert power and influence has multiplied in most policy areas. The range of subjects in which the various elements of Congress are interested beyond a superficial level has greatly broadened, and the degree of specialization of subcommittees in different problem areas has greatly increased.[13] Despite efforts to strengthen party leadership and discipline, strong subcommittees and members have grown stronger and more independent in their activities—though not always in their legislative achievements. All of these factors, coupled with the distrust of the information and proposals from executive agencies, have contributed to a tremendous growth in congressional demands for information, evaluation, analyses, forecasts, and advice on difficult and often highly technical policy issues. And these demands have been a principal reason and justification for the increasing reliance upon congressional staffs and support agencies.

Congressional Staffing

One of the most significant developments in American national government in recent years and particularly during the 1970s has been the growth in size and influence of congressional staffs.[14] Again the Legislative Reorganization Act of 1946 may be considered the benchmark. Prior to that legislation, congressional staffs had been rather small, their growth rate low, their professionalism slight. The act provided the first official recognition of professionalization of committee staffs.[15] It marked the beginning of rapid and steady growth that has continued to the time of this writing—in the staffing of individual members, of committees, and later of subcommittees. The extent of this growth is reflected in Table 3. In the spring of 1978, there were on the payroll of Congress a total of 18,056 employees: 11,544 in the House and 6,512 in the Senate. Three quarters of these were on the staffs of committees, subcommittees, and members. The grand total was more than ten times the number on the payroll of the Executive Office of the President and nearly three times the total personnel of all the congressional support agencies combined. It should be borne in mind that the number of representatives has not materially changed in many decades and the number of Senators has increased by only four (for Hawaii and Alaska). On average, the Senate employs sixty-five persons for every senator; the House, twenty-seven for every representative.

TABLE 3

Personal and Committee Staffs of Congress in Selected Years, 1947-1978

	House		Senate		
Year	Committee	Personal	Committee	Personal	TOTAL
1947	193	1,440	290	590	2,513
1967	589	4,005	621	1,749	6,964
1972	783	5,280	918	2,426	9,407
1976	1,548	6,939	1,534	3,251	13,272
1978	2,274	7,226	1,268	3,575	14,343

Source: Data based upon Fox and Hammond, Congressional Staffs, p. 171,
except for the 1978 figures, which are based on data compiled by
the Office of the Doorkeeper of the House, May 1978, and by the
Office of the Secretary of the Senate, March 1978.

Although the rate of growth since 1947 has been consistently high, by far the greatest part of it in terms of numbers has been during the most recent decade. Further, a significant proportion of that growth has consisted of professional personnel, most of whom are well-educated people in the fields of law, journalism, political science, and other social and physical sciences and many of whom have had substantial experience in executive branch agencies. This is true of committee and subcommittee staffs particularly, but also of the personal staffs of individual congressmen. With the growth in specialization has come a great increase in specialization in the subject matter of government operations and legislation, reflecting the variegated interests of the committees and subcommittees and of the individual congressmen who lead or participate in those groups. Overall, the result has been a large-scale increase in the capabilities of Congress, as a whole, to deal with a broad range of subjects; and a large-scale increase in the capabilities of committees, subcommittees, and individual members to work in depth on individual and specialized problems, legislation, and oversight.

The influence of congressional staffs on the nature of congressional operations and legislative products varies widely in different fields, but few observers would question that in general it is substantial, if not overwhelming. Senator Robert Morgan (D., N.C.) may have exaggerated when he said in 1976 that "this country is basically run by the legislative staffs of the Members of the Senate and the House of Representatives,"[16] but the dependence of senators and representatives upon their staffs is unquestioned. The impact of congressional staffs on congressional actions is difficult, probably impossible, to measure with any exactitude. But, in addition to their traditional roles of dealing with and responding to constituents and assisting in political campaigns, the staffs now serve their congressional superiors in overseeing executive agencies and operations, in dealing with public agencies and private interests, in investigating current and future public problems, in planning and conducting hearings, and in planning and drafting legislation. They are principal recipients and filters of information for their chiefs and principal links in the chains of communications within Congress, and between Congress and the outside world. An outstanding, though not altogether unusual, example of staff influence on legislation was the drafting of the Congressional Budget and Impoundment Control Act of 1974, certainly one of the most significant pieces of legislation in this century, which was hammered out by a conference of staff representatives of a number of House and Senate committees.

It would be inaccurate to characterize congressional staffs and their members in terms of an average or a type. They are a variety of informal organizations and individuals; most of them would hardly fit the normal model of a bureaucracy. Compared with most other legislative or executive agencies, the professional staffs of Congress are young (median age in the mid 30s), well educated, with limited experience and rather short tenure in Congress (median of four to five years). Particularly among the personal staffs, primary loyalty is to their congressional boss or sponsor; they tend to be partisan and ideologically sympathetic with his or her party and views. Among the principal drives of many—but certainly not all—congressional staff members is to further the interests and reputations of the congressmen whom they principally serve. This contributes to conflicts over "turf" and prestige within Congress and with others outside it; and close linkage with a member of Congress, particularly if he or she is a prominent political figure, does not encourage self-imposed anonymity or humility.

On the other hand, there are a number on congressional staffs who have made, and are making a career of congressional service. They provide a degree of continuity, experience, and wisdom about the workings of American government that is very nearly essential to the effective operation of a fluctuating Congress. Furthermore, there is a small but significant and growing movement of professionals between the staffs of the Congress and executive agencies that probably enhances the understandings and compatabilities on both sides.

The growth of congressional staffs may be another illustration of Parkinson's law about the inevitability of organizational growth—though here in a nonbureaucratic setting. Staffs discover or learn of new problems, and pursue them—and therefore beget new staff. As principal controllers of the variety of information systems within Congress, the powers of different staffs grow—but they are to some extent counteracted by one another. For those outside who must deal with Congress, the growth and proliferation of of congressional staffs are a source of increasing complexity in relationships and priorities.

The Congressional Support Agencies

Augmenting its many staffs, for its legislative and oversight work the Congress also utilizes the informational and analytical resources of four principal agencies: the Congressional Research Service (CRS), which is organizationally a part of the Library of Congress; the General Accounting Office; the Office of Technology Assessment (OTA); and the Congressional Budget Office (CBO).[17] These four have certain characteristics in common: they are responsible primarily or exclusively to Congress; they all conduct research; most of their products go to Congress or some element thereof; each has congressional committees (and in the case of the OTA also a congressional board) that exercise oversight responsibilities (though the oversight committees are in every case different); they all have a single chief (a director or the Comptroller General); they are all intended to be, and for the most part are, nonpolitical and nonpartisan; their staffs are highly professionalized, though in different fields of specialization; more than most of the congressional staffs, they are organized on a hierarchical basis, though the degree of bureaucratization differs widely among them. During the decade ending in 1978, all four of the agencies assumed roles, objectives, and ways of operating that were compatible with and reflective of the transformation of Congress itself that was summarized earlier. The two older support agencies, the CRS and the GAO, changed and grew markedly during that period. The other two, the OTA and the CBO, were created during the 1970s as direct responses to congressional concerns in their particular fields (see Table 4).

The oldest of the four is the Congressional Research Service, originally established in 1914 as the Legislative Reference Service, which is a semi-autonomous department of the Library of Congress. Begun as a source of legal advice and service for Congress, it developed as a resource for general assistance and information, derived primarily from documents available in the Library of Congress. It provided, on request of any committee or member of Congress, factual historical data, digests, bibliographies, material for speeches, and other information. It was accurately named a

TABLE 4

Total Employment by Congressional Support Agencies, 1968-1978

	1966	1968	1970	1972	1974	1976	1978 (Jan.)
General Accounting Office	4136	4221	4516	4713	4954	4870	5382
Congressional Research Service	208	264	298	399	565	721	791
Congressional Budget Office	-	-	-	-	-	193	202
Office of Technology Assessment	-	-	-	-	42	103	136
Total Congressional Support Agency Personnel	4344	4485	4814	5112	5561	5887	6511
GAO Percentage of Total Employed	95%	94%	94%	92%	89%	83%	83%

Source: Budget documents.

reference service, and its work was generally regarded as responsive, neutral, quick, and reliable. The change in name to Congressional Research Service, which came in the Legislative Reorganization Act of 1970, sparked a substantial enlargement in the size of the organization, in its responsibilities, and in the professional capabilities of its staff. That act directed that it provide objective analyses on policy issues for Congress, and following its passage, the CRS employed increasing numbers of professional researchers in a variety of fields, mainly the social sciences. While continuing its earlier reference services for Congress, its emphases shifted toward longer-range and deeper studies of policy issues. Unlike the GAO, its reports refrain from making specific recommendations, though some balance the pros and cons in a manner that makes recommendations implicit. Most of its products are not made public unless the congressional committees or members for whom they are made choose to release them. Consequently, CRS studies have only infrequently been publicized. Within Congress, its work on specific and immediate requests is widely appreciated because it responds to most requests expeditiously and factually. Some members of Congress and some of their staffs are critical of CRS reports as too scholarly, too academic, and insufficiently relevant to the legislative bills with which they are immediately concerned. But similar criticisms have been voiced about the work of the other support agencies.

Beginning in the late 1960s, the House Subcommittee on Science, Research and Technology[18] conducted hearings concerning the impact of scientific and technological change upon society and the need of Congress for information about the subject. It developed a bill that, following some rather severe amendments on the floor of the House, became the Technology Assessment Act of 1972.[19] The act provided for an Office of Technology Assessment to be headed by a director appointed by and responsible to a Technology Assessment Board, which is a bipartisan mix of senators and representatives. In addition, it established a Technology Assessment Advisory Council, consisting of distinguished scientists in a variety of fields plus two ex officio members: the Comptroller General and the director of the Congressional Research Service. Under direction of the board, the Office of Technology Assessment was designed to make in-depth studies of the long- and short-range impact of current and probable future technological developments and to provide "early warnings" of possible deleterious consequences of such developments. Although all of the support agencies rely upon outside consultants to some degree, the OTA from the outset has utilized consultants, specialized panels, and contracts with outside groups to a greater extent. Its "in-house" staff (about 130 in 1978) is the smallest of the support agencies; it develops and monitors outside work and produces some studies of its own.

In its first years the OTA had a number of problems, some of which were still being thrashed out in 1978. Some have to do with internal government and direction among its board, its Advisory Council, and its director. The roles of the three are not clearly spelled out. The influences of the board, almost by definition a political if bipartisan body, upon the choice of projects, the choice of personnel, and internal administration have contributed to confusion in its programming and management. The appropriate responsibilities of the Advisory Council have not been agreed upon and defined. Some observers feel that the board's choice of projects has carried it considerably away from the original congressional intent of forecasting and analyzing the long-range impact of technological developments and of analyzing different strategies for dealing with them. Partly as a result of this, its relationships with the other support agencies have been uncertain. This is true with all three of the others but particularly with the CRS and the GAO, both of which have responsibilities and personnel concerned with technological developments.[20]

The Congressional Budget Office was created by the Congressional Budget and Impoundment Control Act of 1974. It is a servant primarily of the budget committees of the two houses, which were established by the same act to guide, monitor, and police the congressional budget procedures provided in that act. The CBO is charged with a number of specific responsibilities by the act, including "scorekeeping" on actual and proposed authorizations, appropriations, expenditures, and revenues. It analyzes the short- and long-range financial and economic impacts of proposals from the executive branch and from the various legislative committees and conducts economic studies for its two supervising budget committees and for other elements in Congress. About one third of the CBO's work is routine "scorekeeping" on the status and progress of the budget; about one fifth concerns overall fiscal policy; and most of the remainder is the economic analysis of policy. The CBO is directed by a professional economist, and the bulk of its professional staff are economists; it built up its staff very rapidly in its first two years and since then has leveled off at about 200 persons.

The four congressional support agencies differ substantially from the congressional staffs, and the support agencies and the staffs in some ways complement one another. The former are more institutionalized, and less immediately responsive to swings in the makeup and membership of Congress. Their ties with committees, subcommittees, and individual members are less political, less partisan, and less personal, and their goals and norms are tied more to their respective professions and the institutions employing them than is true of most of the staff professionals in Congress. In these respects, they can be more professionally independent and objective. There are conspicuous exceptions on both sides, but it is generally true that the support agencies and their personnel are able to take a longer view on governmental problems than are the members and staffs of Congress, tied as they are to the shifting currents of legislative priorities, to the interests and demands of interest groups and constituencies, to hearings and roll calls, and to calendars of forthcoming elections.

In comparison with each other, the differences among the support agencies are more striking than the similarities (see Figure 6); and among the four, the GAO is the most different. Its size in 1978 was more than four times that of the other three combined. Between 1970 and 1978, the CRS grew by 165 percent, while the GAO grew by only 19 percent; but in numbers, the GAO's growth was substantially greater, 862 employees added compared to 493 for the CRS. The GAO is the only support agency that maintains part of its staff "on site" in the various executive departments and agencies in Washington, D.C., and that operates field establishments in the United States and overseas. All of the others operate only through headquarters offices in Washington. The GAO is the only support agency whose head is constitutionally an officer of the United States, nominated by the President

Figure 6

CONGRESSIONAL SUPPORT AGENCIES

	Congressional Budget Office	Congressional Research Service	General Accounting Office	Office of Technology Assessment
Founding Date	1974	1914	1921	1972
Oversight Committee	House Budget Committee and Senate Budget Committee	Joint Committee on the Library and the Rules Committees	House Gov. Oper. Committee and Senate Gov. Affairs Committee	House Science and Technology Committee, Senate Commerce, Science & Technology Committee a/
Appointment of Director	by Speaker of House and President Pro Tempore of Senate	by Librarian of Congress	by President with confirmation of Senate	by Congressional Technology Assessment Board
Term of Director	Four years	No fixed term	Fifteen years	Six years
Expenditures (in millions) (fiscal 1977)	9.6	20.5	157.1	7.3
Total Number of Employees (Jan. 1978)	202	791	5,382	136
Predominant Professional Background of Staff	Economics	Social Sciences; Law	Accounting; Management; Social Sciences; Law	Physical Sciences
Field Staff	NO	NO	YES	NO
Overseas Staff	NO	NO	YES	NO
Highest Priority of Requests	from Budget Committees	from Members or Committees on legislative business	from Committee Chairmen	from Technology Assessment Board
Public Release of Reports	some mandated; others requester's permission	at discretion of requester	YES	YES

a/ OTA is immediately under the Technology Assessment Board, a joint congressional group.

and confirmed by the Senate. And, though all of the four operate through personnel systems largely protected from patronage, the GAO is the only one completely governed by the civil service system under the direction of the U.S. Civil Service Commission (now the Office of Personnel Management).[21] Partly in consequence of its greater size as well as the disciplined procedures it inherited from the accounting profession, the GAO's work and products are more formal, routinized, and institutionalized than those of the others. The bulk of its reports, including all of those that include recommendations for Congress, are signed by the Comptroller General, whereas in the CRS individual staff members are credited with authorship of their reports, and in the OTA the director normally identifies the names of project directors. Those reports of the CBO that are required by statute are issued over the name of its director, but all its reports list their authors.

The GAO has more independence than the other support agencies in the determination of its work and its priorities. Its reports include specific recommendations for action; those of the others in the main do not. All of the agencies give the recipients of requested reports in Congress the opportunity to make public the report findings before "going public" themselves. All self-initiated GAO reports except those that are classified for security reasons are public. The major reports of the OTA are published, as are those of the CBO; in contrast, the CRS generally produces multiple copies of studies for wider distribution only with the permission of the congressional requester. The GAO is the only one of the four that formally obtains comments from the executive agencies concerned and includes statements of disagreement when they occur. This practice, however, seems gradually to be declining even in the GAO, which is relying more and more on informal consultation with the agencies.

The organizational culture of each of the four agencies is distinctive, though there are some common features. The CBO is the domain of analytical economists whose education and experience—and many of whose future careers—are not in Congress but in professional groups in executive agencies of the government or in research institutions, policy analysis staffs, or universities. Their norms, standards, and aspirations are those of their professional peers, which are often in conflict with the pressing demands of Congress for quick analyses of proposed bills and their economic consequences. Turnover of CBO professional personnel is relatively high.

The OTA is among other things a kind of bridge between the scientific and technological communities in the nation and Congress. Its staff suffers strains somewhat similar to those of the CBO, between professional excellence and the demands from its board and elsewhere in Congress for studies on immediate problems rather than long-range technological assessments. Not all of those demands in the OTA's first years were on subjects with high technological content. Both the CBO and the OTA are closely tied to, and constrained by, their oversight groups in Congress: the House and Senate budget committees for the CBO, and the Technology Assessment Board for the OTA.

The CRS has concentrated its traditional reference services—responding to immediate requests for information, data, legislative digests, and so on—in a single division, freeing most of its more specialized research staff for longer-range studies. It relies heavily upon the unmatched printed resources of the Library of Congress, and upon its highly developed computer systems for storing and retrieving information. The CRS rarely conducts field studies. It responds to requests from committees, subcommittees, and members all over Congress, as well as its sister support agencies, and the range of subjects with which it deals is almost unlimited. Its senior staff include persons with national reputations in their fields. It is constrained by law and tradition from unwittingly taking sides on issues and from losing its reputation for evenhanded, nonpartisan reports that present pros and cons of various alternative courses of legislative action (though the constraints are sometimes evaded). Specially tailored research and directed writing can be requested from the CRS by a congressional client, but such predetermined products are identified as such and are not offered as a "normal" objective creation of the service.

The organizational culture of the GAO is treated in chapter 11 of this book. Here we would point out only a few of the features that most contrast with the other support agencies. First is that, since the bulk of the working staff pursues its studies at or near the sites of executive branch agencies in Washington, D.C., and in the field, its working staff is more attuned to the climate of the executive branch than to that of Congress. The background of many of its staff and of their own experience in the GAO contributes to greater emphases upon financial aspects of government operations, financial management, and management generally. With respect to the executive agencies, it operates from a base of independent authority as well as of potential influence upon congressional decisions. By and large, it is probably less oriented toward scholarly norms than the other three, and more toward governmental action.

Although the main thrust of the work and the services of each of the four support agencies is different, the boundaries are in some areas indistinct and there are possibilities of overlap, competition, and unnecessary duplication of effort. All, for example, prepare policy analyses, and all are involved in "futures"—forecasts of consequences of different courses of governmental action. The CBO and the GAO have closely linked responsibilities in connection with the budgetary process. Any or all of them may be called upon by different congressional committees or members to analyze the same problem or the same piece of legislation—as happened in 1977 when all four produced different and uncoordinated reports on the President's energy program.[22] Not all such work is undesirable. Even when working on the same subject, the different agencies may bring to bear different perspectives, different knowledge, and different emphases; the totality of such overlapping products may be useful, an example of what has been called "constructive duplication."

Nonetheless, much concern within Congress has developed about unnecessary duplication and about rivalry, competition, and jealousy among the four agencies. The inclusion of the Comptroller General and the director of the CRS on the Technology Assessment Advisory Council was one reflection of that concern. Later, the Commission on the Operation of the Senate commissioned five studies and reports by outside experts, one on each of the support agencies and a synthesizing study on all four,[23] that addressed the problem. There have been a number of other congressional studies and reports of the four agencies, and all of them raised the questions of duplication and coordination.[24] In general, these various investigations reported little evidence of needless duplication, but urged greater collaboration and coordination in planning and carrying out projects, and the institution of more joint projects.

It may be noted that the only places in Congress where the four agencies are dealt with together are in the subcommittees on the congressional budget of the two appropriations committees. Both have expressed concern about the matter, and at the insistence of the Senate Appropriations Committee the four agencies in 1976 established a Research Notification System managed by the CRS, which provides a computer printout every month on nearly all projects of all the agencies that were recently completed or are currently underway. New and completed projects are reported every two weeks. In addition, senior officials representing each agency meet regularly to encourage better coordination. The Comptroller General issued a directive to all of the GAO's professional personnel announcing and urging systematic coordination with the other support agencies, both formally and informally. There are still disputes over "turf" between support agencies, some of which arise from the preferences and the knowledge of the congressional committees that use their services. Based on previous experiences and committee jurisdiction, the staff of committees continue to utilize the support agency with which they are most familiar, regardless of existing competence in other support agencies.

The developments described—the tremendous growth in numbers and influence of subcommittees, congressional staffs, and the four support agencies—may have reached their apex in 1978. Complaints about the numbers of staff are frequently voiced by congressmen, as are complaints from the staffs themselves about the overcrowding of their offices. All four of the support agencies are apparently in a no-growth or slight-growth situation, reflecting restrictions on their budgets.

GAO Services to Congress

On Friday mornings of almost every week, the top officials of the GAO— the Comptroller General, the Deputy Comptroller General, the general counsel, the chiefs of the staff offices and the operating divisions, and certain others—convene primarily to discuss recent and prospective contacts with and presentations to the various elements of Congress. Chaired by the Comptroller General, or in his absence the Deputy Comptroller General,

Figure 7

TOPICS DISCUSSED AT
OFFICE OF CONGRESSIONAL RELATIONS MEETING,
FEBRUARY 28, 1978

I. Topics Relating to Congressional Hearings and Briefings Involving
    the GAO
    National Visitor Center
    Mexico-U.S. drug traffic
    Pipeline safety (primarily for liquid natural gas)
    Research and development on materials
    Coast Guard efforts in cleaning up oil spills
    Litton Industries
    GAO appropriations
    New York City finances
    Paperwork legislation
    President's Reorganization Plan on Equal Employment Opportunity
      Commission
    Centrifuge plant siting
    Humphrey bill on foreign aid
    Costs of swine flu program
    Sunset legislation

II. Other Topics that May or May Not Involve Hearings
    Taxation of Americans abroad
    GAO access to records on alcohol, tobacco, and firearms
    Bottle returns--request of Massachussetts legislator for GAO
      testimony on its report
    Cost of All Volunteer Force
    Renegotiation Board and foreign military sales
    Senator Glenn to be responsible for GAO oversight in Senate
    Audit of current funding for Clinch River Breeder Reactor
    Study of Mitre Corporation contract with Office of Telecommunications
      Policy
    Report and bills on administrative law judges

these meetings are organized and generally superintended by the GAO's Office of Congressional Relations (OCR), and they are referred to as OCR meetings. In their content and focus they illustrate the greatly increased emphasis within the GAO on its services to Congress. As Figure 7 illustrates, the variety of subjects with which GAO and Congress are concerned is tremendous. The development of the OCR meetings itself was an expression of the growing concern about congressional relations within the GAO. They were begun early in the Staats term for discussions among the Comptroller General, the Deputy Comptroller General, and the congressional liaison officers. After the GAO reorganizations of 1971 and 1972, participation was extended to the division chiefs and the other staff leaders. They became, in fact, general staff meetings of the top GAO officers directed primarily to current issues before or soon to be before Congress.

A very great part of the GAO's relations with Congress are informal, unofficial, and therefore hardly measurable. They involve consultations, conferences, dialogues, oral reports, and correspondence between GAO staff members and congressional staffs. They encompass the projection and planning of reports, briefings during and following the conduct of GAO studies, preparation for hearings, including the questions to be asked of various witnesses, advice and interchange on legislative provisions, and sometimes the drafting of legislation. Most of these interchanges are between the staffs of the OCR and the operating divisions of the GAO on one hand and the congressional staffs of committees, subcommittees, and members on the other. The Comptroller General's main contacts are with members of Congress, particularly the leaders and leading members of the committees and subcommittees. The Deputy Comptroller General estimates that his contacts are divided about equally between congressional members and ranking officials of congressional staffs.

The recent growth and the dimensions of interactions between the GAO and Congress are suggested by the GAO's statistics descriptive of their more formal relationships[25] (see Table 5). During 1977, the GAO received (and counted) a few more than 1,500 requests for information and studies from Congress, divided about evenly between requests from individual members and requests from committees and subcommittees. In that year, it produced 1,082 reports of which 71 percent were addressed to the houses of Congress as a whole, its committees, subcommittees, or individual members. The balance went to officials of executive agencies. Of the grand total, 16 percent were addressed to individual members of Congress. The proliferation and dispersion of congressional subcommittees, staffs, and interests, discussed earlier in this chapter, were reflected in the origins and nature of requests and reports. Most of the committees and subcommittees in Congress made at least one request of the GAO; and its reports back to committees (or their subcommittees) were addressed to twenty-one different committees in the House and seventeen in the Senate. Whereas a dozen years earlier the bulk of GAO reports were addressed to just three committees in each house— appropriations, armed services, and government operations—these committees combined accounted for only 41 percent of the requested reports in 1977.

In the three-month period of February through April 1978, the GAO received requests for thirty-one studies from committees and for eighty-two from subcommittees of the House. In the same period, Senate committees requested sixteen studies, and subcommittees, thirty-eight. The largest numbers of House requests came from the committees and subcommittees on interstate and foreign commerce, government operations, appropriations, and judiciary—more than ten in each case. In the Senate, only the committees and subcommittees on governmental affairs and appropriations submitted more than ten requests.

An increasingly significant vehicle of GAO communications to Congress is through the testimony of its officials in formal hearings before committees

TABLE 5

Direct Assistance of the GAO to the Congress, 1965-1977

	1965	1967	1969	1971	1973	1975	1977
Proportion of GAO Staff Time Devoted to Direct Assistance to Congress	a/	a/	10 (est.)	20	25	34	35
Audit Reports Addressed to: b/ Congress as a Whole,	411	161	177	173	152	199	330
Committees & Sub-					180	178	265
committees,	167	177	204	287			
Members					172	255	174
Appearances for Testimony	22	18	24	30	38	69	111
Reports on Pending Legislation	476	530	496	632	575	266	302
Number of Staff Assigned to Committees	72	106	73	91	68	95	102
Number of Committees Served With GAO Staff	19	23	14	21	19	35	25

a/ Not available.

b/ Most of the reports addressed to Congress as a whole are self-initiated; most of those addressed to committees, subcommittees, and members are in response to congressional requests. The reports to committees and members are not separately available for the years prior to 1973.

and subcommittees. Congress requests such testimony frequently about recent studies the GAO has made relevant to current legislative proposals; about ongoing, still unfinished studies; or to seek information and advice on current legislative problems about which, through prior studies and contacts, the GAO has acquired expertise. At some hearings, the Comptroller General or his deputy testify, supported by senior staff who have specialized on the subject under consideration. On other matters, appropriate division chiefs, their deputies, associates, and project directors appear. The frequency of GAO testimony has risen sharply in recent years. During 1978, the GAO testified on 164 different occasions—on the average, about once every legislative day. For example, during the first three months of 1978, the Comptroller General or the Deputy Comptroller General testified on the following subjects:

- the Panama Canal
- additional cost of the all-volunteer armed forces
- crime in federal recreation areas
- status of productivity data in the budget process
- Commodity Futures Trading Commission
- managing material research and development
- the President's Reorganization Plan No. 1 of 1978
- budget estimates for fiscal year 1979

In a variety of other ways the GAO provides assistance to Congress. On the request of congressional committees, it analyzes and advises on pending legislation. In recent years, it has endeavored to reduce the number of such requests to bills that were likely to receive serious consideration and about which it could offer knowledgeable assistance. In 1977 it reported on 302 bills that were under consideration. It lends staff to congressional committees and subcommittees to assist in their studies and investigations: in 1977, a total of 102 GAO staff members assisted twenty-five different committees on the Hill. Its Office of General Counsel provides legal advice on request from Congress and, often in tandem with other GAO units, develops legislative proposals and language.

In short, the GAO's orientation is increasingly toward Congress and the services it can render Congress. Its image and self-image as an "agent" or "part" of Congress was pronounced in the rhetoric long ago. As of 1978, the image more clearly resembles the actuality than ever before. In the breadth of subject matter with which it deals, it has endeavored to match, and in many ways has encouraged, the broadening of congressional concerns. Congress has in recent years become increasingly diverse and complicated; in consequence, the GAO's relationships with it have likewise been increasingly complex. Given the multifarious forces that operate on Congress, it would be speculative to assess the impact of GAO inputs on congressional outputs. Yet the GAO has clearly played a role sometimes as initiator, sometimes as critic, sometimes as reinforcer of congressional predispositions, and often as armament to strengthen congressional efforts to assert itself in the governmental system.

Congressional Perceptions of the GAO

Congressional acquaintance with the GAO and its evaluation of the GAO's work and usefulness are matters of paramount importance for two principal reasons. The first arises from the fact that Congress is the GAO's principal client and constituent. The extent to which the GAO is a contributing institution in American government depends heavily upon the degree to which Congress trusts, pays attention to, and in fact uses its products in its lawmaking and oversight functions. The second is the fact that the GAO is totally dependent upon Congress for its powers and its funds. Normally, the GAO must go it alone when it seeks, or resists, new powers and when it justifies its annual appropriations; it commands little support from outside constituencies.

It is impossible to make a blanket appraisal of congressional perceptions of the GAO. This is partly because it is a many-sided creature, and few if any are in a position to view the GAO as a whole. For example, the present Comptroller General and Deputy Comptroller General appear to be widely esteemed within Congress—and this was true of most of their predecessors. Yet some of those most effusive in their praise of the top leadership are mildly or severely critical of individual divisions and of people in the organization down the line with whom they deal.

The other side of the problem is the wide variety of perspectives represented by the committees and subcommittees, by individual members of the two houses, and by the congressional staffs. All these views defy generalization. Some members and staff have little or no acquaintance with the GAO, and are barely aware of its existence. Some perceive it exclusively as a financial accounting and auditing organization, a view that is reinforced by the continuing use of the old titles and of the term "audits" to describe its studies.[26] On the other hand, many of the members of the committees and subcommittees having to do with its powers and resources—and the staffs of those members and committees—are fairly knowledgeable about the GAO's activities. They include the GAO oversight groups—the Senate Governmental Affairs Committee and the House Committee on Government Operations—and the legislative branch subcommittees of the two appropriations committees that deal with its funds. Other committees and subcommittees rely upon it to varying degrees, as stated earlier, and usually on the one or few specialized elements of the GAO whose work falls within their respective jurisdictions.

Few senators or representatives have time to read more than a handful, if any, of GAO reports, even in fields of primary interest to them. The pressures of time and scheduling have become a major problem for most congressmen. A recent study of the allocation of time of representatives showed that, on the average, they spent only eleven minutes of their working day reading in their offices.[27] An earlier study in 1975 of a sample of representatives revealed that the majority spent an average of less than thirty minutes in legislative study outside their areas of special interest and activity.[28] Some may scan the digests of a few GAO reports, but most rely on staff to call attention to and brief them on the pertinent ones. Their personal contacts with GAO personnel are most frequently with those at the top level—the Comptroller General, the Deputy Comptroller General, the general counsel, the directors and deputies of divisions with whose work they are most concerned, and sometimes with project directors and staffs down the line who are working on problems that are of particular interest to them. Most of the day-to-day contacts between Congress and the GAO are carried on by committee and personal staffs who serve as a filter of communications in both directions and also not infrequently as initiators, negotiators, planners of hearings and briefings, and users of GAO reports.

In the course of this study, we have met with some members of Congress and staff members who were relatively familiar with the GAO or some parts of it. Their responses were widely disparate, but they suggest—but certainly do not prove—certain observations. One is that the members are generally less knowledgeable about and more favorable toward the GAO than their staffs. Most described the GAO as very useful, a few, as essential to the effective operations of Congress. There appeared to be no distinction in the views of Democrats and Republicans, and several commented on the GAO's nonpartisanship.

The staff members with whom we talked were generally favorable toward the GAO, but some were critical of some aspects of its work and a very few were caustic. The criticisms did not run to the accuracy and reliability of its findings but to the choice of projects, the toning down of reports, and the timeliness of its submittals. Some thought it insufficiently responsive to Congress and thought that the Comptroller General should be less independent, particularly in the choice and definition of projects. Several considered the GAO too gentle in its treatment of executive agencies and criticized its practice of "clearing" reports through those agencies before submitting them to Congress. A few felt that it avoided controversial, political topics, while others criticized it as too political. Some thought that it was too submissive to the executive agencies and others that it was too deferential toward the prominent members of Congress as against lesser members. Some felt that it leaned too heavily on provable, quantifiable facts to protect itself, while a few felt that it should revert to being a pure audit agency and leave recommendations on legislation to congressmen (and their staffs).

Clearly the objectives of the GAO as perceived by its own leadership differ from those perceived by some congressional staff people. Some of the latter view it either as a pliant tool for their congressional mentors (and sometimes themselves) or as a competitor in digging out and publicizing information that may be politically significant. Some congressional staff members request or utilize GAO studies that they think lend support to the positions of their congressional bosses, and avoid those that might weaken those positions.

In 1976 and 1977 two congressional studies, cited earlier, relevant to the usefulness of the GAO to Congress were conducted. Both relied to some extent on questionnaire surveys addressed to members and to committee and subcommittee chairmen. The first of these was a study of the four support agencies done by a group of scholars for the Commission on the Operation of the Senate, the final paper of which was a comparative analysis of all four prepared by Ernest S. Griffith, formerly the director of the Legislative Reference Service.[29] The second was by the House Select Committee on Congressional Operations and dealt solely with the GAO.[30] In general, the findings of the two surveys and the conclusions drawn from them, insofar as they covered the same ground, were consistent. In regard to the quality of its reports and other services, the GAO received high marks. The reports were widely, though not unanimously, regarded as thorough, accurate, and nonpolitical. The respondents of the House survey gave GAO studies the highest ratings for their reliability and accuracy. Somewhat lower but still favorable grades were attributed to their usefulness, responsiveness, comprehensiveness, and clarity. Some of the Senate respondents were critical of what they regarded as "overcautiousness" in declining to report information that might offend or in watering down language.

Both House and Senate groups were critical of the timeliness of GAO products: they took too long; they were not timed to meet legislative deadlines; and they were sometimes so late that they were useless. Both attributed these problems in part to the processes of review within the GAO and outside in the executive agencies. In the trade-off between speed and accuracy they considered that the GAO leaned too far toward the latter. The House report went a step further in alleging that GAO reports cost too much in time and resources in relation to their value.

Directly or by implication, both the Senate and House groups deplored what they regarded as still a too heavy emphasis on financial accounting and auditing among GAO personnel. The Senate report pointed to the absence of sociologists, psychologists, and social workers on the GAO's staff and its alleged inability to evaluate social programs in human terms. The House report urged that efforts to broaden the perspective of the auditors, trained in accounting, be increased and that the number of professionals educated in fields other than accounting be increased to at least 50 percent of the GAO's professional staff.

The covering reports of the two congressional groups, as distinguished from the studies of their staffs and consultants, emphasized deficiencies and recommendations for improvement rather than general appraisals of their contributions. The Senate Commission on the Operation of the Senate, in a brief page-long section of its final report, described the GAO as the "primary field investigation agency available to Congress," which is "generally regarded as a reliable source of audit, review, and related services." But it went on to criticize "what some members of Congress perceive as an inability to evaluate programs in terms of their social effects," an alleged slowness in responding to requests, and a difficulty in recruiting and training nonaccounting professionals. It recommended closer relations and better communications with Congress, strengthening of its program evaluation capability, enlarging the multidisciplinary makeup of its staff, and related actions.[31]

The summary of the House Select Committee on Congressional Operations, which dealt exclusively with the GAO, was more extensive and more explicit. It described the GAO as a "valuable asset to the Congress" and stated that a "substantial majority of the agency's Congressional clients . . . have a generally high regard for the quality, professionalism, and integrity of its services and products and for the competence of its personnel." The summary report then proceeded to a series of criticisms: "frequent lack of timeliness in the delivery of services requested by the Congress"; "certain bureaucratic rigidities"; "some lack of responsiveness to requests for (a) more comprehensive overviews of areas and issues . . . and (b) shorter term, quick response analyses of specific problems"; the failure to achieve an "effective integration of accounting skills and techniques, associated with its older functions, with the evaluative and analytical tools of the policy sciences required by its post-1970 responsibilities."[32]

It should be understood that both the Senate and House reports were directed primarily to identifying deficiencies in the GAO and recommending directions for improvement. In this respect they were similar to most GAO reports about the executive agencies. Very probably, the reports as well as the responses to the questionnaires on which they were partially based were products principally of congressional staffs, subject to a varying carefulness of review by the congressmen who attached their names to the reports.

However favorably or critically individual congressional committees, members, or staff view the GAO, there appears to be little disposition to diminish or limit its powers and scope. In fact, the reverse tendency is more prevalent. During the 1970s, Congress has quite consistently added to the GAO's responsibilities, augmented its powers of access to information, and extended the scope of its audit authority to agencies and programs previously exempted from its jurisdiction (see chapter 6).

Recent and Proposed Legislation Affecting the GAO

Sunset Bills

In recent years, interest has risen among certain segments of the Congress, particularly the Senate, in legislation that would force Congress to reevaluate acts declaring public policy and authorizing public programs, and to reenact them with such modifications as seem appropriate or let them expire. In order to discipline Congress in its oversight responsibilities, authorizing legislation (with certain specified exceptions) would be limited to a period of years after which it would go out of existence unless the Congress took affirmative action to renew it. Such requirements, generally known as "sunset laws," have already been adopted in some twenty states, particularly with regard to their regulatory activities.

In 1978, there were under consideration in the Congress several "sunset" bills, different in their particulars but built upon the same theme: to require on a systematic, scheduled basis the reconsideration of existing legislation with the threat that it would die unless affirmatively acted upon.[33] All would require the executive agencies to submit information, analyses, evaluations, and reports to the appropriate congressional standing committees on their various programs. The extent to which those committees would call upon the congressional support agencies, including particularly the GAO, to appraise the agency evaluations, to submit independent evaluations, or to otherwise facilitate or police the process is not clear. But if any such legislation is passed, it will very probably increase the GAO's responsibilities in program evaluation—possibly by a quantum leap.

The Policing of Congress Itself

For many years, the GAO has provided auditing services to Congress in connection with its business-type operations such as its barber shops, restaurants, and other activities. These have not been a source of concern, and in fact the GAO maintains an "on-site" office in the U.S. Capitol. In the wake of the Watergate affair, the behavior of congressmen and indeed the legislative process itself have been objects of increasing criticism from the media, public interest groups, and even members of Congress. The criticisms have been periodically restimulated by scandals: misuse of staff and of public funds, improper behavior of individual members, acceptance of bribes, failure to reveal financial transactions, improper financing of political campaigns, failure to regulate lobbying activities effectively, and others. Both houses set up committees on ethics, and a number of bills and resolutions were introduced. These measures have included requirements for full disclosure of members' finances, periodic auditing of the finances of each senator and representative and some of their staffs, and tighter regulation of lobbying activities.

A central problem with regard to all of these undertakings is that of enforcement. Who, or what agency, should be empowered to police Congress and the behavior of its members? This responsibility involves, generally, the collection of information, the verification of its completeness and accuracy, the making public of its findings, and when appropriate the referral of potentially criminal infractions to the Department of Justice for prosecution. Congress would be reluctant to authorize such a responsibility to an executive agency responsible to a President. Congress is ill equipped to do it itself, and an internal self-review would have doubtful credibility. A private firm would likewise enjoy little credibility, especially since any adverse findings might be subject to congressional reprisals. The sponsors of these measures have been inclined to place the responsibility in an independent agency, outside Congress but within the legislative branch: the GAO. The policing agent for most of the measures that have been proposed, including those already enacted, is in fact the Comptroller General.

The posture of the GAO as the policeman of and for Congress is potentially uncomfortable: it will be policing and indirectly disciplining its own bosses. On the other hand, the choice of the GAO for this responsibility is an affirmation of its reputation as a credible, evenhanded, and reliable instrument of government.

The GAO and the Civil Service System

It may be recalled that the GAO's charter in 1921 provided that: "All laws relating generally to the administration of the departments and establishments, shall, so far as applicable, govern the General Accounting Office."[34] Most important of the potential administrative constraints were undoubtedly the executive budget process and the civil service system under the direction of the Civil Service Commission. The GAO was effectively removed from the executive budget process after the Reorganization Act of 1945, which declared it to be a "part of the Congress." But it has remained within the civil service system, subject to the rules, regulations, investigations, and directives of the Civil Service Commission (now the Office of Personnel Management). For many years, the relations of the two agencies were friendly and mutually accommodating.

In the 1970s, the GAO undertook studies of personnel problems in the executive branch including some on the civil service system that were directly or indirectly critical of the work of the commission itself.[35] Then in 1976-1977, the commission conducted a thorough study of personnel operations within the GAO. The report of that study had not been released at the time of this writing.

Meanwhile, GAO officials became increasingly critical of the constraints of civil service, especially as they applied to an agency of Congress—not in the executive branch. Furthermore, they cited the inconsistency of two agencies, one in the legislative branch, the other in the executive branch, studying and writing reports about each other. The conflict of roles seemed obvious.

During 1978, GAO officials drafted legislation for submission to Congress that would exempt the agency from most of the civil service standards, regulations, and controls applicable to such central personnel functions as recruiting, selecting, promoting, and classifying. Most GAO employees would continue to be paid under the civil service pay structure and would continue to enjoy the same benefits as other civil service personnel: job protection, equal employment opportunity, and transferability to other agencies.

During the same period, the Carter administration proposed to Congress its federal personnel reform legislation and reorganization plan. It is interesting and probably significant that the Carter proposal specifically exempted from several of its provisions personnel of congressional agencies, including the GAO. Further, the proposed legislation gave the GAO monitoring responsibilities with regard to some personnel operations.

The Appointment and Term of the Comptroller General and His Deputy

It has been recently proposed that the Comptroller General and his deputy be appointed by the leadership in Congress and that the length of term be reduced to seven years. There have also been suggestions that either officer be removable by a simple vote of one or both houses of Congress. The intent, and the effect, of such proposals would be to make both offices more immediately responsive to and dependent upon approval by Congress and specifically its majority party. Collectively, they would make both officers of Congress rather than officers of the United States. The areas in which the Comptroller General is legally or operationally independent would be drastically reduced.

During 1978, the Comptroller General offered a counter proposal for consideration in both houses of Congress.[36] It provided that on or near the occurrence of a vacancy in the office of Comptroller General there be established a congressional commission, composed of the leadership in each house and of the chairmen and ranking minority members of the House and Senate government operations committees, that would submit to the President a list of at least three names as potential nominees for the office of Comptroller General. The President could nominate one of these names or could request additional names if none were satisfactory to him. The person ultimately selected by the President would be subject to senatorial confirmation. Another part of this proposal provided that the Deputy Comptroller General be appointed, and removable, by the Comptroller General himself.

*   *   *

The heaviest emphasis of this chapter has been upon the changing nature of the Congress. The GAO contributed to congressional changes in a variety of ways. But in the main, its own changes have been in response to what it perceived to be concerns of Congress—past, present, and future. It is still true that a substantial part of the GAO's efforts is directed to projects of very slight or partial concern to Congress and the nation. But its increasing emphasis has, for the decade to 1978, been upon what Congress wants or upon what the GAO thinks Congress should or will want. The most dominant influence on the GAO's work is therefore the Congress, more now than ever before. The usefulness of the GAO can hardly be judged apart from the aggressiveness, strength, and needs of Congress.

Notes

1. Joseph A. Califano, as quoted in Harlan Cleveland, *The Future Executive* (New York: Harper and Row, 1972), p. 42.

2. For example, the Legislative Reorganization Act of 1970, the Technology Assessment Act of 1972, the War Powers Resolution of 1973, and the Congressional Budget and Impoundment Control Act of 1974—signed under severe pressure as one of the last official actions of President Nixon.

3. Several bills, now under consideration in the House, would make all regulations applicable to the private sector subject to a legislative veto.

4. Richard M. Pious, "Sources of Domestic Policy Initiatives," in Harvey C. Mansfield, Sr., ed., *Congress Against the President* (New York: Praeger, 1975), pp. 98 ff.

5. Section 136.

6. For example, Morris S. Ogul, "Congressional Oversight: Structures and Incentives," in Lawrence C. Dodd and Bruce I. Oppenheimer, eds., *Congress Reconsidered* (New York: Praeger, 1977), pp. 216-20.

7. Lawrence C. Dodd, "Congress and the Quest for Power," in Dodd and Oppenheimer, *Congress Reconsidered*, pp. 295-96.

8. Impoundment Control Act of 1974, P.L. 93-344, Title X of the Congressional Budget and Impoundment Control Act.

9. On this subject, see particularly Allen Schick, "Complex Policy-making in the United States Senate," Congressional Research Service, a processed paper prepared for the Commission on the Operation of the Senate, June 10, 1976.

10. Much of what follows applies most specifically to the House, though comparable developments, more gradual and less striking, were proceeding in the Senate. Most of the changes to be described were initiated by the Democratic Party, which held the majority of both houses, sometimes by a two-to-one margin, throughout the period, and indeed for more than two decades. This has been the longest period of one-party control of both houses of Congress in this century.

11. These data and much of the other information about recent congressional developments are based primarily upon two books: Harvey C. Mansfield, Sr., ed., *Congress Against the President;* and Lawrence C. Dodd and Bruce I. Oppenheimer, eds., *Congress Reconsidered.* Particular reference should be made to the Mansfield article in the first of these on "The

Dispersion of Authority in Congress," and to that by Dodd and Oppenheimer on "The House in Transition." Reference should be made also to the fifteen articles on "Changing Congress: The Committee System" in *The Annals of the American Academy of Political and Social Science* (January 1974). For an analysis of the growth and development of the Democratic Study Group, see Arthur G. Stevens, Jr., et al., "Mobilization of Liberal Strength in the House, 1955-1970: The Democratic Study Group," *American Political Science Review* 68 (June 1974):667-81.

12. It is interesting that in the debates of 1978 over the Panama Canal treaties, the principal stumbling block became a resolution introduced by freshman Senator Dennis DeConcini (D., Arizona), theretofore almost unknown outside of his state and not hitherto involved in international relations. The second treaty was passed in a form acceptable to Panama only after negotiations by the Senate leaders and the President with DeConcini on new, modifying language.

13. With regard to individual members, specialization seems to have worked in opposite directions in the two houses. The representatives, normally confined to one or two committee and subcommittee assignments, have become more specialized within the jurisdictions of those assignments. Senators, on the other hand, are normally spread over a variety of committees and subcommittees and are freer to express their views outside the jurisdictions of their committees. In 1976, on the average each senator served on nearly four different committees and more than fourteen subcommittees. See Schick, "Policymaking in the Senate," p. 24.

14. Much of the information in this section is drawn from or based upon the thorough study by Harrison W. Fox, Jr., and Susan Webb Hammond, *Congressional Staffs: The Invisible Force in American Lawmaking* (New York: The Free Press, 1977).

15. Section 202.

16. Quoted from the *Congressional Record* by Fox and Hammond, *Congressional Staffs*, p. 1.

17. Not included in this group of congressional support agencies, as they are commonly labelled, are the Cost Accounting Standards Board and a number of other agencies that are responsible to Congress and part of its overall budget, including the Library of Congress, the Government Printing Office, the Architect of the Capitol, and others.

18. Of the Committee on Science and Technology.

19. P.L. 92-484, October 13, 1972.

20. For a comprehensive exploration of these and other problems of the OTA, see U.S. Congress, House Subcommittee on Science, Research and Technology, *Review of the Technology Assessment Act* (U.S. Government Printing Office, 1978).

21. The CRS is within the purview of the central personnel agency with

respect to classification and certain other matters but it is exempt from the competitive service for purposes of hiring. The central personnel activities of the Civil Service Commission were assigned to the new Office of Personnel Management on January 1, 1979, pursuant to Reorganization Plan No. 2 of 1978.

22. See the case study on this subject in the companion volume, Kloman, *Cases in Accountability: The Work of the GAO* (Boulder, Colo.: Westview Press, 1979).

23. *Congressional Support Agencies* (Washington, D.C.: U.S. Government Printing Office, 1976).

24. The most intensive of these were studies of each agency initiated by the Joint Committee on Congressional Operations and conducted by staff. The latest of these, *General Accounting Office Services to Congress*, was completed and published by the House Select Committee on Congressional Operations in 1978.

25. The data presented here and in Table 5 are based primarily upon the Comptroller General's annual reports to Congress, secondarily upon data provided within the GAO.

26. For example, in a report on Congress and foreign policy, a House subcommittee contemplated the creation "of an 'assessment office' which would 'audit' and analyze policy options and decisions the way GAO audits governmental financial activities." Special Subcommittee on Investigations, House Committee on International Relations, *Congress and Foreign Policy* (Washington, D.C.: U.S. Government Printing Office, January 2, 1977), pp. 12-13.

27. U.S. Congress, House, Commission on Administrative Review, "Work Management," vol. 2, *Administrative Reorganization and Legislative Management* (Washington, D.C.: U.S. Government Printing Office, 1977), p. 18.

28. Donald R. Matthews and James A. Stimson, *Yeas and Nays: Normal Decision-Making in the U.S. House of Representatives* (New York: John Wiley and Sons, 1975), p. 20.

29. *Congressional Support Agencies: A Compilation of Papers* (Washington, D.C.: U.S. Government Printing Office, 1976).

30. *General Accounting Office Services to Congress: An Assessment* (Washington, D.C.: U.S. Government Printing Office, 1978).

31. *Toward a Modern Senate* (Washington, D.C.: U.S. Government Printing Office, December 1976), pp. 61-62.

32. The above summary and quotations are all drawn from the summary statement in *General Accounting Office Services to Congress: An Assessment*, pp. vii-viii.

33. During the Ninety-fifth Congress, the Senate considered both S. 2 (Muskie) and S. 1244 (Biden); House attention focused mainly on

H.R. 10421 (Derrick).

34. Budget and Accounting Act, P.L. 67-13, Section 306.

35. Until the establishment of the Federal Personnel and Compensation Division in 1972, the GAO had made rather few strides on personnel management. Since then, its work in this area, which extends not only to civil service but also to military and other personnel systems, has become increasingly extensive. Among those in which the Civil Service Commission was involved have been reports on federal white-collar pay systems (FPCD-76-9, 1975), classification of white-collar jobs (FPCD-75-175, 1975), and administrative law judges (FPCD-78-25, 1978), to mention a few.

36. Incorporated in H.R. 12171, 95th Congress.

10
THE GAO, THE EXECUTIVE BRANCH, AND OUTSIDE INSTITUTIONS

In the past two decades the Federal budget has increased from $70 to nearly $370 billion. Popular wisdom to the contrary, the number of full-time Federal civil servants has remained relatively constant. How does the Government manage?
—Daniel Guttman and Barry Willner, *The Shadow Government*, 1976

The auditor is like the inspector, the regulator, the policeman or social scientist: he cannot get very far without the cooperation of his subjects. If he is too critical, he will lose the cooperation of his subjects and if he is not critical enough, he will lose his value to the public.
Harold Orlans, "The Contract State—or is it the Welfare State of the Professional Classes?" (unpublished, undated)

As changes in the legislative branch have contributed to basic modifications in the role and operations of the GAO, so have changes in the responsibilities and activities of the federal government, operating through its executive branch. The latter category of changes have been as profound as the former. Directly or indirectly, federal concern begins with the first evidence of human conception and extends to death; it includes the food we eat, the air we breathe, the water we drink, the houses we live in, our education, our cultural and recreational activities, our employment and conditions at work, our safety from all sorts of hazards, our income, almost ad infinitum. Though it seems anomalous, the recent surge of sentiment against government and its growth has been accompanied by demands that it do more, that it extend its responsibilities into more and more fields of hitherto private, nonfederal, or nonexistent activity.

The extension of federal responsibilities in the past quarter century has obviously been tremendous. But the more astonishing fact is that these new or greatly enlarged responsibilities have not been accompanied by any significant growth in the size of the federal establishment itself—in the amount of services and goods it produces or in the number of people it employs. Among the more important devices for effectuating these greater responsibilities has been a vastly increased system of regulation of institutions and individuals outside of the government, with accompanying penalties for violations. Another has been the provision of inducements in the form of subsidies, loans, guarantees, and particularly tax privileges, many of which are now better known as tax expenditures. But most important have been direct cash (or sometimes in-kind) payments to individuals and the utilization of nonfederal institutions, public and private, for the carrying out of nationally legislated programs.

Most of the more traditional responsibilities of the federal government continue as before. But the newer ones, especially since World War II, have entailed fundamental changes in the nature, costs, and methods of federal administration.

The Changing Nature of Federal Spending and Operations

The increases in federal outlays since the early post-World War II years have, on the surface, been enormous. Between 1947 and 1977, they grew by well over 1,000 percent, from $35 billion to over $400 billion. A large part of that growth was occasioned by inflation; the value of the dollar declined by about three quarters. In dollars of constant (1972) value, the outlays increased by almost three times from $98 billion to $280 billion. When related to the increase in population, the growth remained substantial on a per capita basis —about 92 percent (in constant dollars) in thirty years. When related to the growth in the national economy, the growth in total budget outlays was considerably lower: from about 15 percent of gross national product (GNP) to about 22 percent, or a total percentage increase of about 40 percent. However, since the close of the Korean War, the ratio of total federal outlays to the gross national product has been quite stable, hovering a little below or above 20 percent.

The growth of budgetary expenditures is, however, somewhat misleading. A substantial and increasing portion of them is not included in computing the GNP, even though the parts that are excluded have a substantial indirect effect on the total economy. The only parts of federal budgetary expenditures that are counted in the national income accounts are its direct payments for goods and services—that is, for the personal services of federal employees and for goods and other services purchased for federal use. Since the close of the Korean War, federal expenditures for goods and services have steadily and greatly declined in relation to the GNP except for a "bump" upward during the Vietnam period. In the final year of the Korean War, 1952, federal payments for goods and services amounted to over 13 percent of GNP. By 1977, they had dropped to a little less than 7.5 percent. Nearly two thirds of these federal payments are for purchases of national defense, not domestic activities. The proportion of the GNP directed to federal purchases of goods and services for purposes other than defense in 1977 was 2.7 percent.[1]

One further clue to what has been happening in the federal government lies in its employment statistics. Except for rather sharp increases followed by more moderate declines in connection with both the Korean and Vietnam wars, total civilian employment by the federal government has been remarkably stable for nearly three decades. Overall, it has grown slightly but its growth has been at a lower rate than that of the American labor force and slightly lower than the growth of the total population that federal workers serve. Measured in terms of numbers of federal civilian employees (including the Postal Service) per 1,000 in the population, the figure for the end of 1977, 12.83 employees, was the lowest since 1950, and the ratio is still very slightly declining.[2] The number of military personnel has of course declined sharply since Vietnam and the institution of the all-volunteer armed forces. In relation to the total population, civilian and military employment combined had dropped to 23 per 1,000 population in 1977, compared with 32 in 1967, 31 in 1957, and 25 in 1947.[3]

These seemingly contradictory data—the greatly increasing federal expenditures, the astonishing drop in the proportion of federal purchases to gross national product, and the declining ratio of federal employment to population—are a consequence of fundamental shifts in the purposes, emphases, and methods of federal operations. In addition to its older, traditional functions, the federal government has become an enormous exchanger of money, which it receives mainly in the form of taxes (including insurance contributions) and pays out to individuals and institutions, mostly in cash or credits, according to criteria quite different from those on which taxes are based. The fastest growing and currently the largest single portion of federal expenditures is labeled by economists as "transfer payments," not generally for services rendered the government but for the sustenance and benefit of the recipients. In the quarter century of 1952 to 1977 these rose from 17 to 41 percent of federal expenditures, more than two fifths of the federal budget (see Table 6). The bulk of these are payments to individuals for social security, medicare, unemployment benefits, veterans' benefits, retirement, and a variety of other income support programs. A second kind of transfer payments are those made for interest on the debt. Interest payments have not changed significantly in relation to the total of federal spending, running about 7 percent. But, when these two kinds of transfers are combined, they amount to nearly half of federal expenditures.

Another variety of federal payments consists of grants-in-aid to state and local governments. During the quarter century of 1952 to 1977, these grew in geometric proportions. In terms of current dollars, they approximately doubled every five years, rising from $2.5 billion in 1952 to $66 billion in 1977. In relation to total federal expenditures, they grew from 4 percent in 1952 to 16 percent in 1977.

The only segment of federal expenditures that has significantly declined is

TABLE 6

Expenditures of the Federal Government Sector of
the National Income and Product Accounts
Selected Fiscal Years, 1952-1977[a]

	A. B I L L I O N S O F D O L L A R S						
	Purchases of Goods & Services	Transfer Payments	Grants-in-Aid	Net Interest	Net Subsidies to Government Enterprise	Total Federal Expenditure	Gross National Product
1952	47.2	11.1	2.5	4.5	.8	66.0	347.2
1957	48.1	16.3	3.7	5.3	2.6	76.0	442.8
1962	61.0	27.2	7.6	6.4	4.1	106.2	563.8
1967	86.0	39.4	14.8	9.6	5.2	154.9	796.3
1972	100.9	78.9	32.6	14.1	6.4	232.9	1,171.1
1977	140.7	169.7	66.0	29.3	6.1	411.8	1,890.4

	B. AS PERCENTAGES OF TOTAL FEDERAL EXPENDITURES						
1952	71	17	4	7	1	100	-
1957	63	21	5	7	4	100	-
1962	57	26	7	6	4	100	-
1967	56	25	10	6	3	100	-
1972	43	34	14	6	3	100	-
1977	34	41	16	7	2	100	-

	C. AS PERCENTAGES OF GROSS NATIONAL PRODUCT						
1952	13.6	3.2	0.7	1.3	0.2	19.0	100
1957	10.9	3.7	0.8	1.2	0.6	17.2	100
1962	10.4	4.8	1.3	1.1	0.7	18.8	100
1967	10.8	4.9	1.9	1.2	0.6	19.4	100
1972	8.6	6.7	2.8	1.2	0.5	19.9	100
1977	7.4	9.0	3.5	1.5	0.3	21.8	100

Source: The Economic Report of the President (Washington, D.C.: U.S.
Government Printing Office, 1978), Appendix B, Table B-74,
p. 343.

a/
These figures do not include the total expenditures of certain
federal enterprises, particularly the Postal Service. Its expenditures in 1977 were about $16 billion, most of which were pur-
chases of goods and services.

purchases of goods and services, and here the shift has been dramatic. As a
proportion of total expenditures, such payments dropped by more than half
—from 71 percent in 1952 to 34 percent in 1977. But this is only part of the
story. A very substantial portion of these expenditures consists of contracts
and grants to institutions and individuals outside of the federal government:
to private businesses, universities, other nonprofit organizations, consultants, international organizations, foreign governments, and others. They go

for research and development, procurement of major equipment, construction of various kinds of public works, assistance to developing nations, payments to international organizations, and a multitude of other purposes.

We have been unable to locate reliable statistics that would show the total amounts of spending for federal programs that are carried out by the government itself in comparison with those that are farmed out to other institutions and individuals. There are a number of clues that the latter category is very substantial and probably greater than the former. Some agencies, like the National Aeronautics and Space Administration and the Department of Energy (and its predecessors), have habitually relied upon private contractors for a large share of their activities. Most major equipment of the armed forces, including weapons systems, is produced by private contractors. Most major federal construction, such as buildings and dams, is produced on contract. In 1977, military procurement awards amounted to more than $55 billion. In the same year, civilian procurement awards amounted to more than $25 billion. Almost three quarters of federal obligations for research and development for 1977, which totaled $23.5 billion, were allocated to industrial firms, universities, and other nonprofit institutions. Only 26 percent were conducted by the federal government intramurally.[4]

Thus about half of all federal spending consists of direct payments for income security, interest on the debt, and similar direct payments. About one third of the remainder goes to state and local governments in the form of grants-in-aid to carry out federally sponsored and supported programs or for unspecified purposes (revenue sharing). One third or more of that remainder goes to other institutions outside of the federal government, also to carry out federally sponsored and supported programs and procurement. On the other side, this means that only about 15 percent of federal spending is directed to activities that the federal government performs itself; and more than half of this amount is applied to the operations, maintenance, and personnel compensation of the armed forces.

The basic shifts outlined above have profoundly influenced the content and nature of federal administration. The direction and control of operations that are within the orbit of particular organizations are different and far less difficult than carrying on programs through institutions that have other or additional objectives and perceptions than those of the federal government. A great part of federal administration today consists of planning, coordinating, preparing and issuing regulations and contracts for, negotiating, paying for, overseeing, inspecting, auditing, and evaluating the work of others. It requires some degree of federal involvement in the affairs of sovereign American states and their subdivisions, of sovereign foreign nations, of international organizations, of business enterprises endeavoring to compete (or monopolize) in a market system, of both public and private universities and colleges, and of a wide variety of other profit and nonprofit organizations, some of which are in the twilight zone of semipublic, semiprivate. Some of these, like community action and a variety of health and neighborhood agencies, owe their existence wholly or partially to federal fiat or encouragement. The problems of this kind of administration are complex, subtle, and often politically sensitive.

The extent to which federal direction and controls should accompany its dollars into the rest of the public sector and much of the private sector is a multidimensional problem of law, propriety, administrative efficiency and effectiveness, and politics. To what degree and through what mechanisms should federal agencies be held accountable for the costs and the results of programs carried out by others? How can and should those agencies assure the accountability of organizations outside the federal government, presumably sovereign unto themselves or otherwise independent in a free market system, for their use of federal money to carry out federal objectives? How can accountability be assured without infringing upon the independence and the integrity of those thousands of organizations and individuals that receive and spend the largest part of federal outlays?[5]

The GAO continues to direct much attention to the efficiency and effectiveness of programs conducted by federal agencies. But the larger and growing problems concern federal spending to individuals and to organizations wholly or partly outside of the federal government. In short, how does one agency—the GAO—hold other federal agencies accountable for programs that they do not themselves conduct?

The GAO and the Executive Branch

Since 1950, the GAO's response to this question has been straightforward and deceptively simple: the primary responsibility for seeing to it that federal dollars, to whomever they may go, are spent honestly, wisely, and in accord with congressional intent rests on the agencies that spend or transfer them. This principle applies equally to federally operated programs, to grants and contracts for goods and services carried on by others outside the government, and to direct transfer payments to individuals. For this purpose, the GAO has quite consistently encouraged the agencies to build their own staffs for internal accounting and auditing; it has published standards and guidelines for internal (and external) auditing and, more recently, for program evaluation; it has urged that these audits and reviews be as independent as possible within each agency and that the internal audit units report directly to the heads of their agencies. On an infrequent spot-check basis, the GAO audits and evaluates the work of the agency and its evaluators and auditors,[6] who greatly outnumber GAO professionals. It checks the adequacy of auditing, accounting, and evaluation systems and makes recommendations for improvements.[7]

But the bulk of GAO studies are not checks on the audits and evaluations of others. Most are conducted by the GAO itself on its own or on congressional initiative and without collaboration on the part of auditors or evaluators in the agencies involved. Most are directed to problems and deficiencies, small or large, perceived, surmised, or anticipated. Before it initiates a new study of its own, it normally checks it out with the internal auditors in the agencies to avoid duplication and repetition and to make use of relevant material already available. A large part of the fact gathering is conducted on the site of agency (not GAO) operations in headquarters and field, or at the site of private recipients of federal funds or of governmental recipients at state and local levels. An increasing proportion of GAO effort in these studies is directed to the effectiveness of systems, whereby federal programs are planned, implemented, and controlled, in terms of results accomplished, rather than to individual transactions. For nationwide programs, evaluations are normally made on the basis of samples, often utilizing the field resources of a small number of regional offices in different parts of the country. The studies are usually begun only after a series of informal and formal communications between appropriate program officials of the agencies involved and GAO officers, both in Washington and the field, and conferences where the purposes, methods, and constraints are thrashed out. Findings of the studies are often conveyed to, and discussed with, the appropriate program officials before the draft reports are prepared. Customarily, these drafts are transmitted for agency comment, and criticisms or agreements of the agencies are subsequently incorporated in the final report.

A number of top GAO officials have assured this writer that the purposes of the GAO and of the managers of the agencies whose programs it evaluates are fundamentally compatible; both seek to improve the efficiency and effectiveness of federal programs. But this generality glosses over some equally fundamental differences in the stances of the two: the mission of the agencies is to plan, sell, and do, or sponsor and finance other institutions in doing; while the mission of the GAO is to examine, review, criticize, and propose better ways of doing. One is the playwright and producer, the other the drama critic, but with the added responsibility of proposing how the production can be improved. Though ultimately their aims may coincide, the nature and channels of their responsibility are different, their perspectives are different, the criteria for their rewards and penalties are different. A federal program manager is no more likely than a drama producer to welcome adverse criticisms from the outside, especially when they are expected to be publicized.

But anxiety about outside criticism is far from universal. GAO reports sometimes strengthen the hands of agencies, and particularly those of upper-level managers, in doing things or gaining congressional support for changes they wanted anyway. Through their reports and other communications, the GAO frequently provides managers with useful information and suggestions difficult to obtain through internal channels. For example, it was a significant source of information for some of President Carter's reorganization teams. Expressions of appreciation and commendation to the GAO from executive agencies are not infrequent. Furthermore, in those agencies for which much of the work is carried on by outside contractors and grantees, agency and GAO objectives in auditing and evaluating are essentially parallel, not adversary. Both are external auditors and evaluators of programs conducted by organizations outside the federal government. The internal auditing and evaluating units within executive agencies are to some extent competitors of the GAO and to some extent mutual supporters. The GAO, through its own studies, has often been critical of those units, directly or by implication. On the other hand, it has consistently supported their development and strengthening. On a few occasions, it has brought to light situations that the internal reviewers had discovered but which were suppressed.

The posture of GAO evaluators differs too from that of internal auditors and other evaluators within the executive agencies. They are less constrained by the policy and programmatic objectives and the positions of political and career executives in the executive branch. Critical findings and reports are less likely to be risky for their own careers, and are less likely to be suppressed or compromised by superiors in the executive organization. Most of all, the GAO has a broader potential scope. It can, and increasingly does, conduct studies across the board encompassing many or all federal agencies on topics like the alleviation of poverty, procurement, energy, the effects on the economy of federal regulation, benefits for the aged, and federal compensation. On questions of this kind, the GAO's potential strength is unique. The Office of Management and Budget has comparable jurisdiction but lacks the professional resources, especially in the field, and is to a considerable extent constrained by its necessary allegiance to the immediate interests and programs of the President. The GAO can sometimes take a longer range view.

Against these actual or potential strengths, the GAO suffers disadvantages. Most of these derive from the simple fact that it is outside the organizations that it is studying and outside the day-to-day decision processes. Its personnel, even when they are located on agency sites, are not normally privy to the information and processes that lead to decisions. Their access to such information, post facto, is often restricted and inadequate. They are neither participants in nor observers of most agency decision making. Very few of them have had much experience in program management beyond their own unique agency. And only a small proportion have had significant education or experience in the specialized and professionalized fields to which they are assigned.

Perceptions and Relationships

A popular story one hears in the corridors of the GAO building concerns the introductory meeting of a GAO official with the manager of a p. ogram he is about to audit. The manager greets the auditor, saying: "I am glad to see you." The auditor responds: "I am here to help you." These statements are described by the raconteur as two of the biggest lies told in Washington today. The story exaggerates the typical situation. But it is no doubt frequent that a manager feels that this visitor has come to find things to criticize, to report them to his bosses, to his supervising subcommittees in the Congress, and, if they can be made to appear newsworthy, to have them published in the media. And the auditor is likely to feel that if he finds and reports nothing wrong, he will have failed in his mission and squandered GAO time and money—and possibly damaged his own reputation among his superiors and peers.

An arm's length relationship is not unique to GAO personnel. It applies to other outside investigators, auditors, researchers, reviewers, and even budget and personnel officers who are beyond the control of the head of the operation that is being examined. Indeed, if such a relationship did not exist, there might well be suspicion of collusion and conflict of interests. The social distance, the reserve, and the formality that characterize some of the interchanges between the GAO and agency personnel may be more pronounced than for some other kinds of outsiders, probably because of the GAO's potential access to superiors in the executive agencies, the Executive Office of the President, committees and staff in Congress, and even the press. The interpersonal relationships of the two are more relaxed than in the past for a number of reasons. There is no conscious policy within the GAO to stand apart, as there certainly was during the terms of McCarl and Campbell. GAO personnel participate with executive officials in many professional gatherings and associations. A good many of them are encouraged to enroll in training programs with other officials. Many of them occupy offices on the sites of the agencies that they are studying, and talk and lunch with members of these agencies. In fact, among the small number of GAOers with whom this writer talked, there seemed to be rather little concern about their relationships with executive branch officials, apart from questions about access to information. Their principal interpersonal concern was about their relationships with each other in the GAO's own organization and with congressional staff.

To our knowledge, there has been no systematic attempt to assess the attitudes and thinking of executive officials about the GAO; the remarks that follow are based upon a small and random sample of conversations, letters, memoranda, testimony, and other documents. As in the Congress and the public at large, there are a good many in the executive branch who know little about the GAO, or if they are aware of it, share the common misconception that it is only an external financial auditing agency like public accounting firms in the private sector. Among those who have direct relationships with the GAO, and have been subjects of some of its reports, there is a wide disparity of opinion. Some with whom we talked made statements to the effect that if there were not a GAO, one would have to be invented. Some were very complimentary of Comptroller General Staats but thought he was not moving fast enough or that he had insufficient influence on the operating staff. Others expressed the view that he was moving too fast and overreaching the capabilities and proper scope of his organization, especially in the area of program evaluation. There were expressions of enthusiasm about the GAO's work, especially among groups who were benefited or strengthened by GAO recommendations—like those in accounting and internal auditing or those concerned with simplifying and rationalizing intergovernmental relations.

The criticisms that we heard about the GAO from executive branch officials were in many cases the opposite of those we heard from congressional staff. Some of the former charged the GAO with being overly critical and selectively negative about small or unrepresentative practices when most of the activities on which it was reporting were being performed well. Some averred that it sought out things that would provide political fodder for individual congressmen and for the press. Some were particularly sensitive that the GAO allegedly failed to issue positive reports, even when all or most of what it found about an agency's performance was favorable. A few charged that the GAO's negative posture contributes to popular disaffection toward government generally and to the damaged morale of managers and employees specifically. Some expressed their belief that the GAO is too responsive to Congress and fails to recognize that many administrative problems originate, not in the executive branch, but in Congress itself.

One of the more frequent criticisms made by executive agency officials is that many GAO professionals approach their tasks with the backgrounds and perspectives of auditors. These criticisms were partly directed against what some referred to as the "accounting mentality," the predisposition to seek and rely upon hard numbers and dollars on the "bottom line" with insufficient consideration of qualitative factors. They were partly directed against what was construed to be insufficient understanding of and sympathy with the problems of management and policymaking. Some went so far as to suggest that all or many GAO personnel should gain experience in management in the executive branch before assuming supervisory responsibilities in the GAO. This has in fact happened but not very frequently.

Another complaint comes from professionals in specialized agencies—such as educators, military officers, doctors, or scientists—who contend that GAO reviewers lack the professional know-how to analyze or audit professional activities. Much the same complaint has applied, over the years, to economic analysts or budget officers making judgments in professionalized fields in which they are not specialized. The GAO has sought to counter this charge through its hiring policies, its use of consultants, and its increasing use of interdisciplinary teams. But some of its old-timers retort with an ancient GAO aphorism that "you don't have to be a chicken to smell a bad egg." Indeed, some managers in the executive branch carry the metaphor further by alleging that the chicken who hatched the egg might be the last to complain about its smell, i.e., that the professionals who run the programs might be the least qualified to appraise their own decisions and performance.

One further complaint of some executive branch officials has to do with the timing of GAO studies. Its auditors and evaluators usually come in after the fact—after decisions have been made and programs implemented. They enjoy the advantage of "Monday morning quarterbacks": hindsight. They do not have to make the decisions when the consequences are uncertain, the information partial, and the pressures in various directions great. They come in later when the results can be measured and the information is more complete, making it much easier to identify mistakes or ways in which the job could have been done more efficiently.

The degree of prevalence and the validity of these various reactions and their effects are impossible to assess, for no systematic study has been made. Most career federal officials are conditioned to investigations and reviews by outsiders. A number of GAO officials stated that the only serious problems they had in dealing with the executive branch were in new programs or programs in which the GAO had not previously been involved: that in areas in which it had already been engaged, there were usually not many difficulties. But in some degree, an adversary relationship is inevitable: it is written into the Constitution, into the nature of human beings, and into the pride and self-definition of different professions.

Yet in no aspect of the GAO's work is cooperation more necessary than in the gaining of access to information. Over the last several years, the GAO has sought and obtained from Congress legislative authority to provide it with access to records and documents relevant to audits and evaluations of a number of agencies where such information had previously been denied or severely restricted.[8] Even where the GAO has legal access, there are laws, executive directives, and recognized proprieties that must be observed in the way information is gathered and used. These include restrictions for reasons of national security, personal privacy, executive privilege, and others. Such limitations often require careful advance planning and negotiation if the investigations are to be useful and at the same time protective of such laws and proprieties.[9] The working out of these arrangements entails a considerable degree of cooperation between the outside reviewers and the subjects of their reviews. But quite apart from legal authorities and restrictions, cooperation between the two sides is almost essential in the ordinary course of auditing and evaluating. Outside reviewers do not always know what documents and other information they should seek and are available. The "auditees" may decline to tell them. Or they may delay in providing them, or conveniently forget or hide documentary materials that they fear might be used against them. Such behavior bears a certain amount of risk because of the GAO's known access to administrative superiors, to Congress, and to the press.[10]

On the basis of interviews with a number of GAO officials, it is the impression of this writer that this kind of behavior is the exception rather than the rule, except in segments of a few executive branch organizations. For the most part, the "rules of the game" are observed on both sides, even when the two consider themselves adversaries. A system of checks and balances such as ours could grind to a stalemate of hostile camps were there not a substantial foundation of respect and trust, one for the other.

The Evaluation of Executive Branch Programs

For reasons discussed in the previous chapter, various elements of Congress have indicated their growing concern about their oversight responsibilities with particular reference to the results of programs enacted by Congress and carried out in the executive branch. Yet most observers to the time of this writing apparently agree that systematic congressional oversight is still only modest in scope and effectiveness; the activity remains relatively neglected as it has been through most of United States history.[11] Much of it is ad hoc and temporary, reactive to immediate issues and scandals.

Nonetheless, Congress has increasingly called upon the executive agencies to conduct and report on evaluations of the effectiveness of the programs they administer. The GAO has consistently expressed its view that the initial responsibility for program evaluation should rest with the various executive agencies. Comptroller General Staats wrote in 1974 in a letter to the chairman of the Joint Committee on Congressional Operations, that:

> It is our view that program evaluation is a fundamental part of effective program administration. The responsibility, therefore, rests initially upon the responsible agencies. However, in our opinion, the executive agencies too frequently issue reports without adequate consideration of congressional needs ... and GAO can help to identify these needs for consideration by the agen-

cies. . . . GAO can assess the objectivity and validity of agency studies. . . . We believe the Congress and GAO, as an arm of Congress, should also have capability to make evaluations of programs. The GAO reviews and evaluations of programs should not, however, supplant the agencies' responsibilities in this area.[12]

The GAO's work in connection with program evaluations falls into four different categories.[13] The first and by far the largest is the studies it conducts itself of the effectiveness of government programs, either on congressional request or on its own initiative. For such studies, it has two potential advantages over evaluations conducted by the agencies themselves: objectivity in reviewing work in which it has no self-interest, and the ability to review the cumulative effects of programs that cross agency and budgetary lines.[14]

The second category is the review, for the benefit of congressional committees, of the validity and veracity of agency evaluation studies. This work can be accomplished either as the synthesis and analysis of several agency studies[15] or as the appraisal of a larger evaluation of a single agency.[16] This function has recently been broadened to include "quality control" of agency evaluation systems[17] as well as appraisals of entire products that emanate from those systems.[18]

Congressional committees increasingly mandate evaluation studies and reports when they draft legislation for new programs or reauthorization of old ones. Sometimes they seek GAO assistance in specifying program objectives and devising meaningful criteria whereby their effects may be measured. This work, which constitutes the third category of GAO work in program evaluation, is sometimes referred to as an "evaluability assessment."[19] A few pieces of legislation, such as the Forest and Rangeland Renewable Resources Planning Act,[20] have incorporated such provisions, and at least one Senate resolution has been offered to require that the Comptroller General review and approve the program objectives of all new programs prior to passage.

The fourth category of GAO work in this area is the preparation and publication of documents to guide and explain evaluation techniques to interested participants in the policy process: legislators, administrators, analysts, and auditors. These range from the theoretical *Evaluation and Analysis to Support Decisionmaking*[21] to the practical *An Audit Use of the Chi Square Test for Independence.*[22] A forthcoming study, which was commissioned by the GAO from the Social Science Research Council and which should attract considerable attention from the professional research community, deals with the "reanalysis" of the results of social experiments for use in policy development.[23]

Program evaluation is barely distinguishable from cost-effectiveness analysis, from program analysis, and from policy recommendations. It is basically an effort to introduce scientific methodology or simply factual data into the consideration of decisions, whether the decisions are made on the administrative or the legislative sides, or both. In the complex society of America in the 1970s, it may be the most promising, but also the most difficult and the most fallible, of aspirations. Except in certain areas in which objectives may be defined in limited terms of time and without too much concern about external effects, program evaluation falls considerably short of being a science; it is more nearly an art, educated by technique and methodology but fueled by judgment and hope. This is particularly true with respect to social programs, the programs directed to the quality of human life. The Congress of the United States reflects, somewhat imperfectly, the pluralistic society that it represents. The more important laws that it passes are compromises and accommodations of varied interests. In consequence, a large number of its acts can state their objectives only in general and hortatory terms. Some of them are competitive with or even contradictory to other acts it has previously passed.

The GAO and the Office of Management and Budget

The Office of Management and Budget (OMB) and the GAO share a number of organizational similarities. It will be recalled that the GAO was created partly as a counterpart to the Bureau of the Budget, forerunner to the OMB, in the Budget and Accounting Act of 1921, an enactment that many legislators interpreted to be a quid-pro-quo exchange between the President and the legislative branch (see chapter 2). Both were perceived as instruments of economy and efficiency; both were, and remain, unique in that they enjoy virtually complete jurisdiction in the executive branch; and the subject matter with which they deal—the finances, management, and programs of the government—are broadly speaking the same. In addition, the GAO and the OMB entered into the area of overall government management from a base of financial management (financial auditing and budget examining, respectively), activities that tend to place both organizations in an adversative position towards the executive departments and agencies.

These likenesses are offset by more deep-seated dissimilarities that characterize their work and responsibilities. The OMB is a staff agency of the President and must be geared to providing him advice and counsel as well as to carrying out his legislative and budgetary programs. It would be impossible for the GAO—or any other legislative branch agency—to function as a true staff agency, since the Congress, as a collective, 535-person body, cannot take action like a single, hierarchical boss such as the President. Likewise, the work required of the OMB by the President differs markedly from the demands placed on the GAO by Congress. The bulk of the OMB's operations are tied to the annual budget cycle and the President's legislative program and must take into account the political exigencies that accompany budgetary and legislative decisions. While the GAO is of course involved in the congressional consideration of the budget and its attendant time cycle, and in legislation, it retains considerable leeway in choosing the areas of its study as well as considerable freedom in programming and scheduling its reviews.

Additional differences between the GAO and the OMB stem mainly from the organizational and operating styles that have developed in the two agencies during the fifty-seven years since their creation. The most obvious differences are their size and spread. The OMB is about one ninth the size of the GAO and has no permanent staff outside of Washington, D.C. Both have highly professionalized career staffs, though the nature of their professional backgrounds differ to some extent. But in recent years, the OMB has imposed a buffer of several layers of non-career appointees between its career staff and its director and the President. The OMB's smaller size makes possible a higher degree of flexibility than characterizes the GAO, and its employees have generally been more mobile in moving to and from other executive branch agencies.

The nature and distribution of the OMB's products are entirely different from those of the GAO. The OMB of course produces the President's budget and a variety of documents relating to it, in the name of the President. For the President, it drafts executive orders, reorganization plans, and other official documents. It issues to executive agencies circulars, guidances, memoranda, and other messages. Most of these do not go to Congress, and few find their way to the general public. The bulk of the GAO's reports go to the Congress or some sector of it; most of them go to the media and are available for purchase by the general public.

The OMB has not reviewed the GAO's budget for many years. And the GAO does not audit or evaluate the OMB's internal operations (although in various GAO studies OMB directives and policies are sometimes scrutinized). It made an unsuccessful try to do so many years ago—when Elmer B. Staats was still deputy director of the budget. In these regards, the GAO-OMB relationship is quite the opposite from that between the GAO and the central personnel agency (see chapter 9).[24]

The GAO's relations with the OMB have probably been most continuous and effective in financial management and subjects closely related to it. These began in the late 1940s with the collaborative arrangement now known as the Joint Financial Management Improvement Program. Both the GAO and the OMB seek to improve agency accounting and fund control systems. The GAO has responsibility for approving the former, and the OMB has authority over the latter. Similarly, the regulation of internal audit systems is officially in the hands of the OMB, but the professional leadership in this area and the testing of agency systems rest upon the GAO. Since the establishment in the OMB of the Office of Federal Procurement Policy, the relationships between that office and the GAO's general counsel have been fairly close.[25] Both the GAO and the OMB have work underway in intergovernmental fiscal administration although here the OMB's interests and resources seem to have been declining while the GAO's have been growing. In these areas there has been a good deal of cooperation and coordination.

This has been less true in matters of program and general, as distinguished from financial, management. The OMB requires agencies on which the GAO has made recommendations to report to it within sixty days what they are doing or planning to do about them or to explain why they should not be carried out. This responsibility apparently ranks fairly low in the OMB's system of priorities and has been largely routinized. Some GAOers complain that the OMB does not follow through; others, that communication between the two, formal and informal, is a one-way street, in which the GAO does the talking while the OMB simply listens. At least some of the OMB's personnel refer to their counterparts in the GAO as "dabblers" who can explore problems and make recommendations but do not have the crucial responsibility for decision.

Yet, in some substantive areas the degree of mutual respect, the sharing of information and ideas, and the extent of coordination have grown considerably in recent years. The relations between the two are not exactly intimate; probably in the nature of our system of government they will not and cannot be. But they certainly are not as remote as they once were.

The recent directions of the two organizations offer something of a paradox. According to many observers and employees, the OMB's attention to management problems began to decline with the accession to leadership by economists in the early 1960s. Since the word management was put into the OMB's title in 1970, its concern with broad managerial problems has declined more rapidly. Increasing emphasis has been placed on finances, costs, and budgets. During the same period the GAO has been increasing its work in program management. One commentator went so far as to suggest that, in their interests and application of resources, the present-day GAO resembles the Bureau of the Budget of the early 1960s more than does the OMB; and that the OMB bears a stronger resemblance to the second GAO of Warren and Campbell than does the third GAO of Staats.

The Inspectors General

In 1976, Congress enacted a law establishing in the Department of Health, Education and Welfare (HEW) a new Office of Inspector General to superintend a department-wide program of auditing and investigations.[26] HEW spends more than one third of the total federal budget, and most of its outlays are to individuals and institutions outside the government in the forms of grants, subsidies, income support payments, and contracts. The Office of Inspector General was created in response to widespread charges and suspicions that a substantial portion of this spending was being wasted or misused because of inadequate controls, inefficiency, and outright fraud.[27] The new office was given substantial independence within the department. The inspector general and his deputy were both to be appointed by the President with consent of the Senate but on the basis of professional, nonpolitical criteria. They were directed to report regularly to the secretary and, through him, to the appropriate committees of the Congress. The new office had two basic functions: to conduct or supervise audits, both external and internal, of federal funds flowing through the department; and to conduct investigations of suspected fraud or abuse. In carrying out these tasks, the inspector general was specifically directed to cooperate and coordinate with the GAO.[28]

The idea of such centralized offices for auditing and investigations in civilian agencies "caught on." A few other agencies established comparable offices on their own authority. Then, during 1978, the Congress passed a bill[29] requiring a number of other departments and agencies to institute inspectors general with basically similar powers and duties.[30]

The GAO consistently supported the purposes of this bill though it recommended a number of changes in its specific provisions. In its testimony, it urged that more emphasis be given to systematic auditing, less to investigations of individual instances of possible fraud. It also recommended that the scope and purposes of audit, as defined in the act, be extended to cover not only legality, economy, and efficiency but also effectiveness in terms of program results. It proposed that the title of the officer, inspector general, be broadened to inspector and auditor general.[31] The GAO apparently perceives these new offices within the larger departments and agencies not as competitors but as collaborators in the review of the operations of the executive branch.

The GAO and the Outsiders

The opening section of this chapter emphasized the growing reliance of the federal government upon outside organizations and individuals to carry out its programs. With regard to accountability for these programs, the GAO's posture and mission are, or should be, essentially the same as the administering agencies: to assure that federal moneys are delivered to and expended by their recipients in the most efficient ways possible and in accord with congressional intent. But the problems attending federal accountability for programs once—or several times—removed from direct federal control are different and more subtle than those for programs directly operated by federal agencies. Some of these problems and the GAO's part in dealing with them are summarized in the paragraphs that follow. They are treated in five main categories: grants to state and local governments; contributions and other assistance to international agencies; contracts and other relationships with private industry; grants and contracts to not-for-profit institutions; and transfer payments, mainly for income support.

The GAO and the Federal System

The differentiation of responsibilities among the different levels of American government was never altogether clear-cut. In the apt expression of Morton Grodzins, federalism has long been a "marble cake" in which there was blending among the different levels, rather than a "layer cake," in which each level was separated and largely independent of the others.[32] But for the first century and a quarter of American history, the main foci of responsibilities were pretty well understood by citizens as residing in one or another level of government. The federal government had foreign relations, defense (though with considerable input from the states through the militia, later the National Guard), the post office, and interstate commerce and communications. Local governments provided most direct services to citizens, including police, fire, water, waste disposal, streets and roads, elementary and secondary education, and many others. In terms of operations and expenditures, the states were least of the three, though their responsibilities grew in fields of higher education, highways, prisons, and mental and other health institutions. Yet, for the most part and despite some exceptions, each unit of each level of government operated fairly independently of the others. And each depended upon its own revenues to meet its expenditures, primarily if not exclusively. Each could devise and effect its own system of accountability, however imperfectly.

There had been grants from the federal to state and local governments, originally in the form of land, since preconstitutional days. They were substantially expanded before World War I (a few years before the founding of the General Accounting Office), principally for vocational education and highways. They virtually exploded during the 1930s and again in the 1960s. In consequence, today every level of American government is involved, operationally and financially, in almost every governmental activity. Federal grants to state and local government amount to about 16 percent of the federal budget, and they continue to rise. Federal aid provides more than one quarter of all the funds state and local governments spend, and it extends into most of the functions of government—education at all levels, welfare, health, transportation, housing, and crime control, to mention but a few. Through general revenue sharing for which the purposes of spending are not specified, it potentially influences almost every facet of state and local activity.

Obviously, the federal government is heavily dependent upon state and local governments for the delivery of services in which it has a large program and political interest. And state and local governments are heavily dependent upon the federal government for funds. This situation gives rise to knotty questions of accountability. Are federal grants—some or all of them—properly to be considered as financial aids to local and state governments in carrying out the "sovereign" powers and responsibilities of the latter? Or are they a device to effectuate national policy in which the states and local units are used essentially as instruments of national programs? Responses to these questions are relevant to the extent of outreach of federal accountability for state and local operations and finances.

There can be no single answer. Some have argued that when the federal government contributes to activities that were historically and traditionally state/local in nature, like education or crime control, its demands for accountability should be relaxed, whereas in those areas where there is an emphatic national interest, such as in the construction of airports and interstate highways, it should be more demanding. When general revenue sharing was under consideration, Comptroller General Staats spoke out against it, basically on the grounds that the recipient governments could not be held accountable for the ways in which they spent federal funds.[33] The problem has been exacerbated in recent years by the growing demands of Congress, the executive branch, and the GAO for evaluations on the results of federally supported programs of state and local governments, for these involve federal judgments—and presumably corrective actions—on the effectiveness of officials who are politically or administratively responsible to another unit of government. If such actions were carried out fully with respect to all programs that receive federal support, they might have the practical effect of transforming our system of governance from a federal to a unitary state.

The GAO has been involved in the intergovernmental accountability problem in a number of ways. Over the years, it has conducted many investigations and studies of the operations of federal grant programs in various fields. Its findings and recommendations are usually addressed to the responsible federal agencies and Congress, not to the nonfederal jurisdictions that are carrying out the programs, and their emphasis is on improving federal laws, regulations, and surveillance and thus indirectly state or local administration. As discussed earlier, the GAO has endeavored to improve evaluation techniques by the responsible federal agencies, including their evaluations of programs carried out through state and local governments. It has undertaken to broaden the scope of state and local audits and to improve the capabilities of state and local auditors through its manuals, technical assistance, meetings and forums, and cooperation, including the promotion of the use of state and local audits to satisfy federal audit requirements. On a few occasions GAO and state auditors have cooperated in the audit of state and local activities that are supported with federal funds.

The original revenue sharing act of 1972[34] provided that the GAO review compliance with its provisions. When the act came up for renewal, the GAO made a number of recommendations to strengthen its antidiscrimination provisions and enforcement, to require public reporting of budgets (including shared revenues), and to strengthen state and local auditing. Provisions along these lines were incorporated in the 1976 act that extended the program.[35]

By congressional mandate, the GAO has become intimately involved in the internal management and fiscal affairs of two major cities, Washington, D.C., and New York City. In the case of Washington, it was called upon to carry out studies on various aspects of its administrative processes, the adequacy of its records, and its accounting and auditing practices. In New York, the GAO reported on the probable long-range fiscal viability of the city, the adequacy of its accounting systems, and the ability of the city to meet its budgetary goals.[36] As this is written, GAO work is continuing in both cities.

Over the long pull, its most important contributions may be in its efforts to simplify, rationalize, and encourage reforms in the grant system and intergovernmental relations generally. It has developed close cooperative relationships with other groups that share these concerns: the appropriate subcommittees of the Congress; the Office of Management and Budget; the Advisory Commission on Intergovernmental Relations (ACIR); and the various public interest groups of state and local public officials. Examples of recent and current GAO studies of crosscutting problems in intergovernmental relations include:

- procurement practices and problems in spending federal grant funds in a sample of cities;
- lack of uniform treatment of people displaced from their homes and businesses by federally assisted projects;
- the effectiveness in federal grant programs of matching and maintenance of effort requirements on state and local governments;
- the role of state legislatures in controlling federal funds awarded to states;
- the lack of coordination among federally assisted area-wide planning bodies;
- the effectiveness of Federal Regional Councils;
- the federal role in improving state and local productivity;
- the federal government's organization for intergovernmental relations;
- a mechanism for facilitating the legislative consolidation of

grant programs;
- the effectiveness of federally assisted "seed money" in bringing about self-sustaining programs; and
- the continued monitoring of general revenue sharing.

The GAO's proper role with respect to federalism can hardly be defined apart from one's view of the proper role of the federal government in its relationships to state and local governments. These roles may be considered from the standpoint of three underlying questions. The first of these is the almost incredible and unfathomable complexity of the grant-in-aid system, especially as it has developed since the early 1960s. There were in November 1977 almost 1,100 domestic assistance programs, administered by fifty-six different federal agencies. The recipients and administrators of federally aided programs included 50 states, 38,000 general purpose local governments, 15,000 school districts, 24,000 special districts and authorities, 2,000 area-wide organizations including councils of governments, the District of Columbia, Puerto Rico, and several territories.[37] The purposes of these different programs differ from each other somewhat though there is a good deal of overlapping; there is a wide difference in their criteria, procedural requirements, and degrees of centralized control. In general, the GAO has consistently favored simplification, consolidation of related grant programs, and standardization of substantive and procedural requirements.

The second underlying question arises from the continuing tension between the demands for independence and autonomy of state and local units and for control and accountability in the application of federal funds on the part of the federal spending agencies and segments of the Congress. The GAO has generally favored strong systems of accountability, though not necessarily detailed controls over state and local spending of federal funds. On the other hand, it has taken steps to broaden and improve state and local auditing and to persuade federal agencies to accept the reports of state and local auditors.

The third underlying problem arises from the tension between specialized interests (in the society, the Congress, the executive branch, and the state, local, and subunits in particular programs) and the "generalists" in the executive and legislative branches at all levels. The GAO has sided predominantly with the "generalists."

Although there have been some differences on these and other problems in intergovernmental relations between the GAO and the Office of Management and Budget, they have been basically agreed on the main issues and have worked together cooperatively to achieve common goals. On most matters, the GAO has likewise collaborated with the Advisory Commission on Intergovernmental Relations and with the public interest groups of state and local officials despite differences in emphasis on the (second) issue of state/local autonomy versus federal accountability.

The International Scene

The development of the GAO's involvement in foreign affairs paralleled that in state and local governments though for quite different reasons. Following World War II, it became concerned with the establishment and operations of U.S. installations and forces overseas and with the administration of the Marshall Plan for the assistance of nations devastated by the war. It expanded its audit mission to examine the military supply and construction programs as well as those for economic assistance, including in both cases the problems attending offshore procurement. In 1952, it established its first overseas office, and later, in 1963, it established the International Division to superintend its overseas activities and to conduct reviews of the headquarters operations in Washington. During the Vietnam period, it established a suboffice in Saigon to conduct audits and reviews primarily concerned with the receipt, transfer, and use of American supplies and equipment. Some of its reports dealt with the control and use of American material and personnel by sovereign foreign nations, but its reports were directed toward the improvement of management systems and controls by the U.S. administering agencies.

Over the last three decades, the GAO has broadened its sights on foreign affairs to comprehend both broad and specific studies of international trade, international finance, assistance programs in developing nations, security programs of various sorts, arms controls and nonproliferation of nuclear materials and technology, and the conduct of foreign affairs generally. Its recent reports and/or testimony to Congress have dealt with such topics as:

- the financial and economic impact of the Panama Canal treaties (when under consideration in the Senate);
- economic sanctions against Rhodesia;
- measures with which to deal with the oil crisis;
- effects of changed tax policies on U.S. citizens abroad;
- the world population explosion;
- the administration of various economic development programs in the African Sahel region;
- U.S. forces in Korea;
- the F-16 fighter aircraft program, sponsored by the United States and four European nations.

Obviously, many topics such as these relate to the policies and administration of international organizations and sovereign foreign nations. The GAO's studies and recommendations, however, are directed to Congress and to concerned agencies of the American national government.

Since the closing months of World War II, the United States has helped to develop and has joined an increasing number of multilateral, international organizations that are governed by boards or assemblies of member nations of which the United States is but one. They include several categories: the United Nations (U.N.) and a variety of organizations immediately responsible to it; specialized agencies that are administratively independent of the U.N. such as the Food and Agriculture Organization (FAO), the World Health Organization (WHO), the World Bank and various development banks, the International Monetary Fund (IMF), the U.N. Educational, Scientific and Cultural Organization (UNESCO), and the International Labor Organization (ILO); regional political and military organizations such as the North Atlantic Treaty Organization (NATO), and the Organization of American States (OAS); and multilateral economic agencies such as the Organization for Economic Cooperation and Development (OECD).

Since about 1970, the United States has channeled an increasing amount (and proportion) of its assistance for overseas development through international organizations rather than on a bilateral basis. Total American contributions to international organizations were approaching $9 billion in 1976, not including cumulative contributions and commitments to the multinational development banks of about $17.5 billion.[38] The United States is the largest single contributor to most international organizations although Congress in 1972 limited its contribution to 25 percent of the total annual assessment of the United Nations or any affiliated agency.

In its relations with the international organizations, the federal government stands in a posture somewhat similar to its relations with state governments in respect to general purpose grants. Once its money is appropriated and transferred, it is mixed with the contributions of other members. The organization decides how and where to spend it. The United States has membership on the agency's governing council and may exercise political influence through other members.

Further, no member nation of an international organization may conduct an official audit of its programs and funds. A nation may withdraw from the organization, as the United States did in 1977 from the ILO; it may reduce its voluntary contributions and withhold its assessed contributions; it might place stipulations and restrictions on its contributions as some congressmen have repeatedly sought (e.g., no aid to Cuba or Vietnam), but this could result in rejection of the funds and, in effect, withdrawal from the organization. The international organizations are essentially self-governing, self-evaluating, and semisovereign, subject of course to the political representatives of the member nations that govern them. Nonetheless, the GAO has conducted and is conducting a number of studies on various aspects and problems of the international organizations. Mainly its reports are indirect in the sense that they are addressed to American participation in the government of the organizations while their ultimate goal is to improve the administration and effectiveness of the organizations themselves. It has made a variety of recommendations intended to upgrade, strengthen, and better coordinate the management of American participation in multi-lateral organizations; to coordinate planning and channeling of development assistance on a country basis rather than on separate bases for the agencies contributing to the assistance; and to restructure the U.N. system. It has repeatedly proposed that the United Nations establish an independent review and evaluation body to evaluate its programs and activities. It has supported the establishment of independent evaluation systems within individual international organizations.

Perhaps the clearest example of the problems of accountability in international operations is presented by the role of the GAO vis-à-vis the auditing of U.S. funds contributed to the World Bank Group. Any work issued by the GAO must be addressed to the U.S. Treasury Department and its representative to the bank, rather than to bank officials. Based on a 1973 amendment to the Foreign Assistance Act, the GAO did provide the Department of the Treasury with auditing and reporting standards for use by the banks in reviewing their projects. The World Bank set up its own evaluation system, and in 1978 the GAO issued its first report concerning the effectiveness of that system.[39] It included suggestions for improving the availability and utility of World Bank reports for the U.S. Congress. But the GAO was unable to report independently on the results achieved from the sizable U.S. investment in the World Bank, a situation that is representative of U.S. participation in other international organizations. As more specialized and ad hoc international agencies are created (to aid Sahel drought victims, to develop a "law of the sea," to assist Palestinian refugees, and so on), the GAO is forced into the difficult role of auditing the auditors but of being excluded from direct access to programs and application of funds.

One area that offers an opportunity to improve the accountability of international operations is the technical assistance that the GAO offers to the audit agencies of international organizations and individual countries. This work is accomplished through consultation with individual audit organizations and through the activities of the International Organization of Supreme Audit Institutions (INTOSAI). By developing standards, providing training, and encouraging an expanded flow of audit information, the GAO is able to promote audit coverage by the institutions closest to the expenditure of funds and to assure coverage of more programs than the GAO's own staff could ever examine singlehandedly. Through the improvement of auditing expertise and the expansion of audit availability, the GAO can achieve a greater degree of accountability for U.S.

funds worldwide than currently exists.

The Government and the Market Economy

From its beginnings, the GAO has been involved in the review and audits of federal contracts with private businesses, mainly for procurement and construction. Since the beginning of World War II, a very substantial part of its work and of its difficulties have concerned Defense procurement. It may be noted that prior to that war, the United States maintained minimal armed forces during peacetime, and a substantial share of its military supplies and equipment it produced in its own arsenals and shipyards. Since then, with the Cold War, the continuing arms race, and intermittent conflicts, it has depended heavily upon private industry to furnish ever more complex tools of warfare for purposes of deterrence, preparedness, and, periodically, actual combat. During the same period, there have been enormous increases in contractual procurement by civilian agencies, especially in the fields of energy (mainly nuclear), space exploration, health, transportation, and many others. Decisions made on federal procurement policy and on individual purchases have enormous impact upon the economy as a whole, on international trade, on regional or local growth and prosperity, and on inflation and unemployment. Indeed, though only rough approximations are available, it is very probable that more persons are employed and more goods bought and produced with federal dollars outside the government proper than within it.

It has long been federal practice and law to encourage advertising, submission of bids, and contracting with the lowest bidders for government equipment, supplies, construction, and services. The government could then rely upon competition in the market to keep the prices it had to pay within reasonable limits. Unfortunately, with the increasing sophistication of the equipment it requires and, in the case of many defense-related items, the need of security, competitive bidding for the largest part of federal procurement, both for defense and for other purposes, is impracticable. Less than one tenth of defense procurement and one sixth of other procurement is formally advertised.[40] The rest must be negotiated with one or more suppliers, and the bulk of that which is negotiated is with a single firm—that is, it is "sole-source" and not competitive procurement. The rules governing, and the audits seeking, a fair cost to the government on negotiated contracts where there is no competition are the most difficult of all.

The efforts to assure that the federal government gets its money's worth in its procurement—without excessive private profits, mismanagement, collusion, conflicts of interest, and outright fraud—have been a major source of political and administrative concern, dispute, and experimentation since the onset of World War II. They have given rise to a welter of legislation and regulations in what must now be one of the most complex fields of federal administration.[41] The problem is complicated by the fact that many of the most expensive federal contracts are in new and experimental areas on projects for which there is little guidance from past experience. It is further complicated by the practice, in the larger contracts, of subcontracting to a substantial number of other firms for parts of the main job. In addition, federal contracting in terms of "the most for the buck" must be conditioned by other considerations required by law or politics: preference where practicable for small as against big business; preference to areas of higher unemployment; balance in contracting among regions; equal employment opportunity and fair labor standards by the contractors; and many others.

Over the last several decades, the GAO has been a central party in the evolution of federal law and practice with respect to procurement. During some periods—World War II, the late 1950s, and the early 1960s—this topic, especially in the field of defense, has consumed half or more of its work effort. This proportion of GAO effort has considerably declined—in 1978, Comptroller General Staats estimated it at around 10 percent[42]—and although its role in this area has changed, it remains important. In the first place, the GAO continues to suggest revisions and additions to procurement law and regulations to both Congress and the responsible executive agencies —in reports, testimony, and sometimes drafts. As a principal member of the Procurement Commission, the Comptroller General contributed many of the ideas that became recommendations of the commission, and the GAO was subsequently called upon to monitor the implementation of its proposals. In the second place, the GAO's general counsel handles a great many legal questions in the procurement area—more than 2,100 in 1977—arising from a variety of sources (see chapter 7). In the vast majority of cases, GAO decisions are accepted without further argument, and many of them become the basis for new procurement regulations.[43]

For many years, the main "entrée" in the GAO's work menu was the audit of individual procurement contracts, particularly in the area of defense. This is no longer the case. Since the Defense Department established the Defense Contract Audit Agency (DCAA) in 1965, the bulk of defense auditing has been carried out by the Defense Department itself. The DCAA operates in some 240 different locations and has a staff nearly as large as the GAO itself. Somewhat comparable audit operations are carried on within the various civilian departments. The GAO audits a very limited sample of contracts annually, primarily to identify and evaluate the efficiency and effectiveness of procurement policy, pricing, controls, and auditing. Its focus is not upon individual contracts or contractors but upon the effectiveness of the systems and criteria whereby contracts are negotiated, carried out, and audited by the executive agencies. Its aims are primarily to develop and make recommendations for improvements in the process, not to seek out individual culprits.

In the last decade, the GAO has directed increasing attention to the acquisition of major systems for carrying out governmental programs, particularly weapons systems for defense.[44] The scope of this work is considerably broader and more substantive than the study of the contracting processes. It encompasses the definition of needs for each system; the cost and effectiveness of alternative systems; research, development, and testing; and production. Every year, the GAO reviews the status, progress, and problems of between twenty-five and thirty weapons systems and reports on them to Congress.[45] It also reports annually on the costs and cost overruns of major systems acquisitions in both the military and civilian realms.[46]

Though federal procurement has long been the principal channel for GAO activity in the market economy, in recent years emerging problems and new federal programs have led it into a great variety of studies involving the market economy in which federal procurement is only indirectly involved. Some of these stem from dissatisfaction with the many regulatory activities of federal agencies, which have themselves greatly expanded during the 1970s. A prominent example is its ambitious investigation of the regulation of banks by the three federal agencies charged with that responsibility, which inevitably involved looking into the practices of banks themselves.[47] Concern about the effectiveness and the effects of federal regulation have prompted studies in widely disparate realms of private industry: grain inspection, food, drugs, the insurance industry, safety of consumer products, protection of the environment, effects of regulation on competition and prices in the air transport industry, and many others. Congress has authorized and, for some purposes, mandated the GAO to make investigations and reports on almost every facet of the energy industries, most of which are carried out in the private sector, with or without federal financial support. There has grown up a steady succession of GAO studies and testimony in this area.[48]

For many years, Comptroller General Staats has been concerned about the relatively slow growth rate in productivity, both in the public and private sectors.[49] Following a pioneer study on industrial technology around the world in 1976,[50] the GAO initiated the first of what may become a series of studies of individual industries—in this instance, the shoe industry—to identify reasons for its slow improvement in productivity and to suggest steps that might be taken to make it more competitive with other producing nations to which it is losing its market. Finally, we would mention the massive study, begun by the GAO on its own initiative in 1976, of "metricality"—the process of moving the United States to a metric (decimal) system in its weights and measures. The metric system, which would apply to measures of length and distance, mass, liquids, temperature, and others, is now standard in most industrialized countries of the world and is voluntary in this country. The GAO's study, published during 1978, analyzes the advantages, the costs, the methods, and alternative courses of action for the United States.

The Not-for-profit Institutions

In the years following World War II, the federal government relied upon a plethora of not-for-profit organizations to carry out or assist in carrying out national purposes. Their variety in terms of objectives, modes of operating, degrees of federal control, and degrees of federal financial support defies systematic classification. Virtually all the missions of government have utilized them. Some represented the utilization, development, or conversion of existing institutions for federal purposes. Some were established by the national government outside the regular machinery of other federal agencies but are dependent exclusively, primarily, or partially upon federal financial support. Some lie in the twilight zone between public and private or national and state/local spheres, in which federal control ranges between zero or minimal to nearly total.

Under these circumstances, it is impossible to describe in common terms what standards are applied to the control of not-for-profit institutions or to prescribe what standards should apply to them. For the same reasons, the maintenance of accountability for the not-for-profit institutions is among the most difficult and subtle of all fields of federal activities. Their purposes are mixed, sometimes conflicting or contradictory, and seldom specific; the degrees of actual or proper federal involvement are seldom defined and often controversial; their modes of operating and the sophistication of their management often differ radically from those of federal bureaus, and the results of their efforts and programs are more often than not unmeasurable, especially over the short run. In no other area is the dispute between independence and accountability more spirited. The problems of evaluation and auditing apply similarly to the administering executive agencies and the GAO.

One category of activities in which these problems are both acute and important is the advancement and application for federal purposes of scientific knowledge: that is, research and development (R&D). More than half of the supporting funds for R&D in this country are supplied by the federal government, and nearly three quarters of these federal expenditures go to institutions outside the federal establishment. The largest share, about two thirds, of federal R&D funds, are spent for the development of specific pieces or specific systems of equipment, preparatory to production, and the bulk of this work is performed by industrial firms on a profit basis, as described in the preceding section. On the other hand, nonprofit institutions, particularly the universities, perform a large share of the research work funded by the government: *basic research,* generally directed to the enhancement of scientific knowledge, and to a somewhat lesser extent, *applied research,* which consists of studies directed to more specific problems, often precedent to development. Nearly two thirds of all federal funds for basic research are expended by universities and other nonprofit institutions.[51] In 1977, over seventy different federal agencies sponsored research grants and contracts to more than 2,000 educational institutions in a total amount approaching $4 billion.[52]

The GAO has conducted and is conducting reviews of research and development programs of the government, a considerable number of which are conducted by not-for-profit organizations: studies of health and biomedical research, deep ocean mining research, technology and international trade, the development of weapons, space, energy, and transportation systems, and others.[53] Examples include reviews of the progress and problems of "Landsat," a satellite system for remote sensing of earth resources, the fast breeder nuclear reactor program,[54] and a broad study on computer-aided manufacturing technology.

But a substantial part of the research that is conducted at universities and at other not-for-profit research organizations—centers, institutes, consulting organizations, and others—is not immediately tied to any federally defined program. This is true particularly of research described as basic. Many of the studies are conceived and proposed by the prospective researchers themselves, within fairly or indefinitely broad federal guidelines; many are complex and esoteric, beyond the comprehension of the educated layman and even, sometimes, of scientists in the same discipline. The selection of individual projects deserving of federal support is frequently made by groups of knowledgeable scientists in the field or subfield involved, many or all of whom are not employees of or otherwise accountable to the federal government. This selection process, generally known as peer review, means that the government has delegated to outside scientists not only the conduct of the research but the determination of what projects should be pursued with federal support.[55] The products of such research are often not "evaluable," even by the scientists concerned. Some may be totally worthless; others currently worthless but of enormous importance in future years; others trivial or repetitive; still others valid and useful but valuable mainly to other scientists in the same field.

Under such circumstances, it is difficult if not impossible for federal agencies and the GAO to assess the results of scientific research against its costs. They may and sometimes do examine and criticize the methods by which projects are selected and the research strategies employed. The GAO has generally accepted the practice of peer review in the selection of projects, but it has sometimes audited and questioned their design and execution, particularly where the findings are intended to contribute to public policy.[56] In the main, however, the concerns of the administering agencies and of the GAO have centered on the financing and managerial efficiency of out-of-house research: the legality, honesty, and accuracy of costs charged to the federal government (the inputs), rather than to the effectiveness of research outputs.

Even with this rather limited definition of accountability, the problems are substantial, particularly in universities. Few scientist-professors are accustomed to, skilled in, or patient with maintaining time and cost records of their own and their subordinates' efforts for research in one or several research projects, an activity many of them equate with red tape. The accounting practices of most universities, which are in some cases quite primitive, seldom jibe with the reporting requirements of the federal government, and, for state and local universities, must meet additional and different specifications.

The most contentious area of federal-university research relationships is the quagmire known as indirect costs, chargeable to the federal government. These include all the costs to the university that are not directly attributable to specific projects—building space, equipment, common services and supplies, utilities, and administrative overhead. The percentage of direct costs that may be added as indirect is governed by circulars from the Office of Management and Budget and specifically determined for each university, by a designated agency of the national government—most frequently the Department of Health, Education and Welfare.

The GAO has often been involved in reviews of the administration of research grants and contracts as parts of studies of larger programs, and it has made a few studies of individual institutions. In 1969, it issued a general report on indirect costs,[57] and others dealing with this subject are underway as this is written.

Federal involvement in institutions of higher education has grown far beyond the support of university research. In the postwar period, and particularly following the Russian *Sputnik* in the late 1950s, the government launched a number of programs to increase the scientific capacities of American universities in general. Later, such assistance was extended to the arts and humanities. During the 1960s and early 1970s, a number of efforts were begun to aid in the survival and strengthening of developing colleges and to assist disadvantaged students through direct grants, loans, work-study programs, and other devices. During the 1970s, the federal government has been increasingly involved in regulatory activities at the universities to assure equal opportunities for students and facilities, protection of privacy, assistance for the handicapped, and for other purposes. At the same time, there has been growing concern about the general health of higher education, particularly its financial health.

The GAO has made a number of studies dealing with the federal programs for higher education.[58] It has under way at the time of this writing a general study of the condition of the liberal arts colleges. But it cannot be said that the GAO has by any means "blanketed" the field of higher education. Partly this may reflect the absence of a clear definition of the proper role of the national government in a field traditionally governed by private or state institutions where federal involvement is suspect. It probably also reflects the inherent difficulty of evaluating educational programs, particularly where funds come from a variety of different sources and are mixed.

The federal government has utilized a wide variety of not-for-profit institutions other than universities for an almost unlimited array of purposes. They include organizations for research, for training, for health, for neighborhood development, for the aged, and for advice in many areas. The GAO has conducted a variety of studies of hospitals, nursing homes, health maintenance organizations (HMOs), consultants, scientific organizations like the Smithsonian Institution, and many others.

Transfer Payments and Income Support[59]

The largest category of federal expenditures consists of payments, mainly to individuals and their families, of cash or its equivalent for which no services or products are expected. In many cases it has no control whatever over how the money it dispenses is actually spent by the recipients. There are exceptions. Medicare and Medicaid are required to be spent for health purposes; student tuition grants are for education; food stamps are for food. But, in the main, federal controls and accountability are truncated at the point that the government delivers the checks. The largest of these payments in 1977 were:[60]

		Billions of Dollars
Social security (OASDI)		$ 81.2
Medicare		20.6
Unemployment benefits		14.1
Veterans benefits and services		13.3
Civil service retirement		9.4
Military retired pay		8.1
Supplemental security income		4.7
Food and nutrition		4.6
Railroad retirement		3.7
All other		6.8
	Total	$166.5

This may explain in part why the GAO directs a relatively small proportion of its professional resources to transfers and other income support programs, which account for about two fifths of the federal budget. It may also explain the frustrations of those who seek to decrease federal expenditures and taxation. Large parts of these federal expenditures stem from legislation and commitments that originated forty or more years ago for social security, retirement, and other purposes, to most of which citizens, federal employees, and other groups have made contributions. A very substantial portion of Americans and some who are not citizens receive and are to varying degrees dependent upon federal largesse. There is here no quid pro quo in the sense that the beneficiaries of federal payments will provide services or goods in return for them.[61]

The key questions of control and accountability for the federal administering agencies and for the GAO have to do with eligibility of the actual or prospective recipients of payments. Eligibility requirements vary widely among different programs, even those addressed to overlapping target groups. Some are fairly precise in the law and depend mainly upon the ascertainment of facts; others involve interpretation and discretion in the application of law to individual cases. Especially in those cases where discretion is involved and where authority to make decisions is delegated to the federal field offices or to state and local or private agency officials, there is always the danger of inequity, even when the facts are complete and correct. That is, individuals in identical circumstances may receive different amounts of benefits, or some may be declared eligible while others are declared ineligible. In no other area of federal outlays are the possibilities of honest mistakes, inconsistencies, misinformation, maladministration, and fraud more pronounced. The operation of many different programs, administered by a great many different agencies and subunits, each with its own labyrinth of eligibility requirements and with overlapping target groups, complicates the problems of overhead administration and control enormously.

In this as in other areas of federal endeavor, the GAO considers that primary responsibility rests with the administering agency. It makes spot checks on eligibility determinations for selected programs, assesses the management organization and systems for assuring that eligibility requirements are properly enforced and that excessive payments are not made, approves the efficiency of management procedures, and makes recommendations to the agencies concerned and to Congress. Because of the enormity and numbers of support programs, these studies and audits must be made on a highly selective basis. One of the basic thrusts of the GAO's efforts has been to simplify eligibility requirements and make their application more uniform.[62]

The GAO also has underway a number of longer-range studies that cross agency lines of the social and economic impact of federal income support programs. One of these is a general assessment of alternative designs for a more rational, economic, and effective system of income support. Another is an effort to assess the impact upon a target population of all federal programs, such as a study now underway of the effectiveness of many federal programs upon the elderly. A third is a study of the quality of legal services provided to the economically disadvantaged by federal, state, and local agencies. Finally, there are a number of studies dealing with the interrelationships between income support programs and the economy.

Accountability versus Competing Values

Earlier, we indicated our belief that one of the generally accepted values of the American polity is the principle of accountability: that persons who receive, hold, use, and expend public resources should be held accountable for their decisions and actions with respect to those resources. In this chapter, we have emphasized that for a large and growing proportion of federal expenditures the executive branch is in effect a pass-through point. A large part of these resources are in fact expended and used under the direction of institutions and individuals outside the federal government and presumably not subject to its immediate authority. Basic questions are how far, in what ways, in how much detail, and with what sanctions should the federal government, including the GAO, enforce accountability upon outsiders. The question is especially relevant for those whose primary responsibility is to other authorities like state and local governments, the shareholders of business, and the management of universities.

This situation accentuates problems of accountability, many of which apply also to personnel in direct federal employ. In the first place, accountability has its own *costs*. They include not alone the time and effort and other expenses of those who hold others accountable but also the costs to those who are held accountable, which are often far greater. These latter costs include the maintenance of records, the filling out of forms, and the preparation, submittal, and defense of reports—in short, red tape and paperwork. Excessive requirements for accountability may occasion interruptions and delays in ongoing work and have a damaging effect on morale. Where the auditors or evaluators are unfamiliar with the purposes and nature of the work they are examining, there are likely to be additional delays to educate, explain, and justify. This is particularly true when the examiners come in from outside the organization and are unfamiliar with its background, its modes of operating, and the reasons for them. It is at least one reason why, for the last thirty years, the GAO has insisted that the first responsibility for auditing and evaluating should lie in the agencies themselves, not in the GAO. It also explains the increasing reliance upon systems as against individual transactions, sampling techniques, and evaluating the evaluations made by those immediately responsible for programs.

Costs are only one of the more obvious conditioning factors affecting accountability. It must often compete or accommodate with other values widely held in American society. One of these is *personal privacy,* the guarantee of which sometimes requires extraordinary precautions in the review of agencies and programs that involve confidential information about individuals. The "name of the game" of accountability in a democratic state is information and its exposure; yet the foundation of the information about many programs concerns persons whose identity should not or cannot be revealed or even hinted. Examples include individual tax returns, census data, investigative and police files when criminal conduct has not been established in the courts, bank accounts, individual health data, social security information, and even the grade records of students in education. One of the most difficult areas for accountability is the review of social experimentation that depends upon specific information—especially longitudinal information—about individuals.

Added to the social value of privacy is that of *equity* or equal treatment as applied both to individuals and institutions. Where reviews of programs are made in the business or nonprofit realms, they usually involve only a small sample of organizations. Where faulty practices are uncovered in one or only a few institutions, the GAO usually refrains from revealing in its published reports which ones they are on the grounds of fairness since there may be many other comparable organizations with equally or more questionable practices that it did not investigate. This policy, which the GAO adopted following the Holifield hearings in 1965 (see chapter 5), has been the source of criticism from some representatives of the media since it weakens their stories or deprives them of "juicy" details for publication.

Another widely held value is the maintenance of a *free market economy.* The argument here is that the internal decisions and management of individual firms are and should be for the firms to determine without governmental intervention and that their operations should be secret to assure their competitiveness in the market system. Access to information about the amount, detail, and accuracy of the internal management and financial affairs of such firms to governmental contracting agencies, their auditors, and the GAO have been matters of contention for years. Questions involving industrial use of governmental facilities and equipment that is provided free or rented, of mixed costs for both federal and commercial purposes, and of allocation of overhead (indirect) costs are perennials. Some of these problems may be on the way to resolution through the standards enunciated by the Cost Accounting Standards Board. But the basic question continues: To what extent can, does, and should the federal government influence the direction and decisions of presumably autonomous industrial corporations through its contracting, pricing, and auditing practices?

Similar questions attend federal grants to universities and other nonprofit institutions for research and development, for training, and for strengthened educational programs in fields of particular interest to federal agencies. To the social value of institutional autonomy independent of federal control are here added two other widely held values: *academic freedom* and *freedom of inquiry.* To what extent should the federal government prescribe or otherwise influence (some would say *warp*) educational and research programs through its contract and grant mechanisms? And to what extent should evaluators review such programs on the criteria of their usefulness to federal objectives?

We have discussed earlier the challenges to federal accountability introduced by the growing dependence of state and local governments on federal grants-in-aid. In this area, the basic competing values are those associated with *local self-determination* and *state sovereignty.* The questions are not dissimilar from those outlined in preceding paragraphs. But here they concern the nature and viability of the federal system itself. There is the question of to whom state and local agency administrators are accountable when lines of authority are multiple and diffuse and when the sources of funds are mixed among several "donors." Should federal grantors—and their auditors and the GAO—rely upon local and state governmental systems to assure the propriety of their spending? Or should the "feds" assume responsibility to assure that federal moneys, which are often mixed with state and local appropriations, are spent wisely and efficiently for federally defined purposes?

Another cluster of values that can be at odds with accountability includes *creativity, innovation* and *experimentation.* If a manager expects to be called to account after the fact for the effectiveness of a program or the way it was carried out, he or she is likely to be wary of taking risks on new departures that may fail. Under such circumstances, it is not unlikely that the manager might call upon the reviewer to examine his proposal in advance or to even participate in preparing it. This may shield him or her from future criticism, but it at the same time clouds the objectivity and credibility of the reviewer after the fact.

A related value is that of *freedom of thought and expression* of administrators and their advisers during the period when problems are being studied and analyzed, recommendations are being suggested and debated, and decisions are being reached. If these intermediate deliberations and documents are recorded and the participants are aware that they may later be disclosed, they are likely to shroud or suppress their judgments lest they be criticized by an outsider later on. On the other hand, it is not uncommon for auditors and evaluators themselves to be criticized because of their lack of knowledge and understanding of the processes, the considerations, and the alternatives that entered into the ultimate decision. In this connection, it is interesting to note that the GAO itself denies access to its own working papers and also to its reports until they have been reviewed, revised, and officially issued.

Finally, we would mention the value associated with protecting the *national security* and the accompanying restriction of access to classified information. In general, security classifications apply to information deemed to be potentially useful to other nations, particularly potential enemies, against the interests of the United States. They are most relevant in connection with intelligence, foreign affairs, and national defense. The classifications are determined within the executive branch under authority of executive orders of the President. In general, Congress and its support agencies, including the GAO, respect them. But there is a widespread opinion that security classifications are sometimes used to suppress information of no particular importance to national security but potentially embarrassing to the management and operations of executive agencies. A number of GAO employees are "cleared" to see documents that are variously classified, but the usefulness of such information for purposes of accountability is limited if it cannot be reported or otherwise disclosed.

* * *

The "quest for accountability" is a difficult and complex one in a mixed society such as ours. Accountability must adjust to, compromise with, and sometimes yield to other values. Congress through its legislation and its other signals is seldom of great assistance in balancing and reconciling the competing values. The processes of compromise and mutual adaptation through which most significant bills must pass, if they do in fact pass, often produce vague and platitudinous prescriptions of limited guidance in application to specific programs, expenditures, and means of achieving accountability. With respect to federal grants, subsidies, and purchases, the stance of the administering agencies does not differ much from that of the GAO. Both seek accountability and feasible means of maximizing it. Both must take account of competing values.

The scope, depth, techniques, and timing of the instrumentation of accountability are subtle and hard questions, the ramifications of which go well beyond the principle of accountability itself. Perfect accountability is a will-o'-the-wisp. If it were possible it would be forbiddingly expensive and it would threaten many of the other values that Americans embrace most dearly.

Notes

1. These data are drawn from the national income accounts as reported in the *Economic Report of the President* (Washington, D.C.: U.S. Government Printing Office, 1978), appendix B, table B-1, p. 257. They do not include

total expenditures of the Postal Service and other governmental enterprises, only their surpluses or deficits that affect the federal budget.

2. *Special Analyses: Budget of the United States Government,* fiscal year 1979 (Washington, D.C.: U.S. Government Printing Office, 1978), p. 210.

3. For 1947, 1957, and 1967, U.S. Department of Commerce, Bureau of the Census, *Historical Statistics of the United States* (Washington, D.C.: U.S. Government Printing Office, 1975), p. 1141. For 1977, *Special Analyses,* Analysis I, tables I2 and I4, fiscal year 1979.

4. See National Science Foundation, *Federal Funds for Research, Development, and Other Scientific Activities,* fiscal years 1975, 1976, 1977, NSF 77-301, Vol. 25 (Washington, D.C.: U.S. Government Printing Office).

5. Some of these emerging problems of accountability, growing out of the changing nature of federal programs, were discussed a few years ago by Elmer B. Staats in a thoughtful article, "New Problems of Accountability for Federal Programs" in Bruce L. R. Smith, ed., *The New Political Economy: The Public Use of the Private Sector* (New York: Halsted Press, 1975), pp. 46-67.

6. In 1978, the GAO reported that its evaluations of internal audit operations resulted in more than thirty reports in the preceding three years. Comptroller General of the United States, *Financial Audits in Federal Executive Branch Agencies,* FGMSD-78-36, June 6, 1978, p. 3.

7. As a result of a congressional request, the GAO in 1978 conducted a questionnaire survey of 607 different units in the executive branch. Of the 418 units that responded, almost one third reported that they had not had a financial audit of their accounts and records in the three years, 1974-1976. Comptroller General, *Financial Audits,* p. 2.

8. See chapter 6.

9. See, for examples, the cases on the *Mayaguez,* FBI domestic intelligence, and bank examining in Erasmus H. Kloman, ed., *Cases in Accountability: The Work of the GAO* (Boulder, Colo.: Westview Press, 1979).

10. See, for example, the recent report of the Comptroller General, *Is the Air Force Inspection System Effective? GAO Was Denied Access to Pertinent Records,* FGMSD-78-24, June 29, 1978.

11. Except for congressional investigating committees, which command the attention of the electorate. See Arthur M. Schlesinger, Jr., and Roger Bruns, *Congress Investigates: A Documented History, 1792-1974* (New York: Chelsea House, 1975).

12. Letter from Comptroller General Staats to chairman, Joint Committee on Congressional Operations, August 8, 1974.

13. As stated by Comptroller General Staats in his speech on "A Case Study in Administrative Reform: Setting National Priorities," Lincoln, Nebraska, April 14, 1978.

14. See the case studies on the National Energy Plan and bank

examination in the companion volume, Kloman, ed., *Cases in Accountability*.

15. For example, *Section 236 Rental Housing—An Evaluation With Lessons For the Future*, PAD-78-13, January 10, 1978.

16. For example, *The Army's Test of One-Station Unit Training: Adequacy and Value*, FPCD-76-100, February 9, 1977.

17. *HUD's Evaluation System—An Assessment*, PAD-78-44, July 20, 1978.

18. This function, and the one that follows, are superintended within the GAO by the Program Analysis Division, which was created in response to the 1974 Act for overall coordination and leadership of the GAO's evaluation responsibilities.

19. A term that was coined and popularized by the Urban Institute, a nonprofit, Washington-based "think-tank" and government contractor.

20. P.L. 93-378, August 17, 1974.

21. PAD-76-9, September 1, 1976.

22. FGMSD-CS-7, July 1976.

23. Committee on Evaluation Research, Social Science Research Council, *Audits and Social Experiments*.

24. In general and unless invited, the GAO keeps its hands off the Executive Office of the President, of which the central personnel agency is not a part.

25. In fact, the deputy director of that new office transferred there from the staff of the GAO's general counsel.

26. P.L. 94-505, October 15, 1976.

27. Apparently the charges and suspicions were not misplaced. The HEW inspector general in his first *Annual Report* estimated that for fiscal year 1977 "fraud, abuse and waste—at a minimum—ranged between $6.3 and $7.4 billion." March 31, 1978, p. 1.

28. The first (and current) HEW inspector general is Thomas D. Morris, who had been an Assistant Comptroller General under Staats.

29. This bill passed as P.L. 95-452, October 12, 1978.

30. The organizations covered are the Departments of Agriculture, Commerce, Housing and Urban Development, Interior, Labor, and Transportation; and the Community Services Administration, the Environmental Protection Agency, the General Services Administration, the National Aeronautics and Space Administration, the Small Business Administration, and the Veterans' Administration.

31. Statement of D. L. Scantlebury of the GAO before the Senate Committee on Governmental Affairs, Subcommittee on Governmental Efficiency and the District of Columbia, June 15, 1978.

32. In his essay on "Centralization and Decentralization in the American Federal System," Robert A. Goldwin, ed., *A Nation of States: Essays on the American Federal System* (Chicago: Rand McNally and Co., 1961), pp. 1-23.

33. Speech by Comptroller General Elmer B. Staats on "Achieving

Better Cooperation: Washington, California, Los Angeles," delivered to the Town Hall of California, Los Angeles, March 7, 1972.

34. The State and Local Fiscal Assistance Act, P.L. 92-512 (October 20, 1972).

35. P.L. 94-488 (October 1976).

36. See the case study, "Financing the Big Apple—The GAO Review of New York City's Fiscal Crisis" in Kloman, ed., *Cases in Accountability.*

37. These data are drawn from the GAO's Program Plan on "Intergovernmental Policy and Fiscal Relations," processed, July 1978.

38. These data and some of the other information in these paragraphs are based upon the Comptroller General's *Report* on *U.S. Participation in International Organizations*, ID-77-36, June 24, 1977.

39. *Effectiveness of the World Bank's Independent Review and Evaluation System*, ID-78-14, June 5, 1978.

40. *Military Prime Contract Awards*, fiscal year 1977, Office of the Secretary of Defense (processed) and "Procurement by Civilian Executive Agencies for the Period October 1, 1976–September 30, 1977," General Services Administration, Office of Finance (processed table).

41. There has been a succession of legislation, rules, and rulings over the last forty years, some of which have been summarized in chapters 3 through 6 above. They include price fixed in advance, cost plus a fixed fee, renegotiation, incentive contracts, differing bases for computing profits, development of cost accounting standards, "should cost" rather than "historic" costing, value engineering, certified advance costs in negotiating, and many others.

42. In his address on "General Accounting Office Reviews of Department of Defense Procurement in the United States" to the Rigsrevisionen, Cophenhagen, Denmark, June 12, 1978 (processed).

43. See Paul A. Shnitzer, *Government Contract Bidding* (Washington, D.C.: Federal Publications Inc., 1976), pp. 30ff.

44. At the time of writing there were nearly 150 different major weapons systems in the Department of Defense, the eventual cost of which will exceed $250 billion. See Comptroller General Staats' address in Copenhagen.

45. See "Airborne Warning and Control System (AWACS)" in Kloman, ed., *Cases in Accountability.*

46. See "Financial Status of Major Weapon Systems," in ibid.

47. The three agencies involved were the Federal Reserve Board, the Federal Deposit Insurance Corporation, and the Comptroller of the Currency. See the case study on this project in Kloman, ed., *Cases in Accountability.*

48. See, for example, the cases on the liquid metal fast breeder reactor and the President's energy plan, in Kloman, ed., *Cases in Accountability.*

49. For example, the work of the Joint Financial Management

Improvement Program, described in chapter 7.

50. "Manufacturing Technology—A Changing Challenge to Improved Productivity," LCD-75-436, June 3, 1976.

51. These data are based upon National Science Foundation, "Federal Funds for Research, Development, and Other Scientific Activities," SF-77-301.

52. Report of the General Accounting Office, *Federally Sponsored Research at Educational Institutions—A Need for Improved Accountability*, PSAD-78-135, August 18, 1978, p. 1.

53. Paper by Elmer B. Staats, Comptroller General, on "The Role of the General Accounting Office in Appraising Science and Technology in the United States" (processed, undated).

54. See the case study on this program in Kloman, ed., *Cases in Accountability*.

55. Harold Seidman somewhat satirically described scientific research as "the only pork barrel for which the pigs determine who gets the pork." *Politics, Position, and Power: The Dynamics of Federal Organization* (New York, Oxford University Press, 2nd. ed., 1975), p. 15.

56. Among the best examples were GAO audits of two social research projects: its report to the Congress entitled "Preliminary Comments on the New Jersey Graduated Work Incentive Experiment," reprinted in *Hearings*, U.S. Senate Committee on Finance, August 18, 1970, 930-941; and its report to Congress, "Observations on Housing Allowances and the Experimental Housing Allowance Program," Washington, D.C., 1974.

57. *Study of Indirect Cost of Federally Sponsored Research Primarily by Educational Institutions*, Report B-117219, June 12, 1969.

58. These have included, for example, reports to the Congress on *Assessing the Federal Program for Strengthening Developing Institutions of Higher Education*, MWD-76-1, October 31, 1975; *Examination of Financial Operations for Fiscal Year 1975 Shows Need for Improvements in the Guaranteed Student Loan Program*, FOD-76-23, February 10, 1977; and *Office of Education's Basic Grant Program Can Be Improved*, HRD-77-91, September 21, 1977.

59. These terms are not exactly synonomous, and they are differently classified in different federal documents. In dollar amounts, the largest are made directly to individuals and families. But some are grants to state and local governments that administer them and make the transfers themselves, in some cases adding to them in varying amounts their own funds. Others pass through private or semipublic organizations on their way to the beneficiaries.

60. *Special Analyses: Budget of the United States Government*, 1979 (Washington, D.C.: U.S. Government Printing Office, 1978), table B-5, pp. 54-55. These figures do not include federal grants in aid to state and local governments for human resources programs, which in 1977 amounted to

$38.5 billion. The two largest elements of this total were public assistance in cash ($6.3 billion) and medicaid ($9.8 billion).

61. The quid pro quo may operate in reverse in the sense that the government is repaying for earlier contributions and sacrifices of the recipients, as in payroll taxes for social security and related purposes, and benefits to veterans.

62. Examples of recent and current work of this kind are studies on the need for more uniform application of the presumptive disability provision of the supplemental security income program; student participation in the food stamp program at six selected universities; comparison of criteria for food stamp, aid for dependent children, and supplemental security income programs; the need for the social security administration to provide more leadership in the management of the disability determination process; complexity and lack of uniformity in eligibility criteria in several selected programs, including social security disability benefits, black lung benefits, and veterans' pension programs.

11

THE GAO TODAY:
A VIEW FROM INSIDE

The development of the modern form of organization of corporate groups of all kinds is nothing less than identical with the growth and continually widening extent of bureaucratic administration.
—Max Weber, *The Theory of Social and Economic Organization*, 1924

The social structure of organizations of the future will have some unique characteristics. . . . There will be adaptive, rapidly changing temporary *systems. These will be task forces organized around problems to be solved by groups of relative strangers with diverse professional skills.*
—Warren G. Bennis, "Beyond Bureaucracy,"
in Bennis and Philip E. Slater, *The Temporary Society*, 1968

This chapter will describe some of the salient features of the GAO's operations at the time of writing, the nature of its internal culture, and its internal efforts to change. It is not an effort to evaluate either the current operations or the current proposals to change those operations. The GAO has been studied and to some extent emulated by some state and local agencies, by some foreign governments, and even by some public accounting firms. Its internal processes and problems are therefore of some consequence beyond the federal government itself.

The Basic Processes

Planning and Programming

The number and scope of possible topics for GAO study are almost limitless. If it were to respond to all requests from Congress and all suggestions from inside and outside its own organization, its staff would have to be multiplied many times. Obviously, the identification and selection of the subjects to be studied from the near infinity of possible topics are matters of crucial importance. Generally, top priority is given to requests of congressional committee and subcommittee chairmen and minority leaders. Beyond that, the GAO has developed a number of criteria and procedures for planning its work. The basic stated policy is very general:

to apply our available resources to the Government's programs, activities, and operations where they will be the most useful to the Congress and do the most good in bringing about greater efficiency, economy, and effectiveness. . . . The overriding factor is constructive contribution to improved conduct and management of Government operations.[1]

Beyond this broad mandate, the GAO considers other criteria in its decision making on whether or not to undertake an assignment:

- congressional and public interest;
- other work in the area (whether the GAO or any other congressional group has worked on the subject);
- program considerations (whether a program is a national issue, the extent of its impact, the growth of the program in the future, etc.);
- sensitivity considerations (will results be sensitive?);
- operational considerations (time to complete, nature of auditing techniques, need for special disciplines or consultants, cost of job, staff capability for job, etc.);
- management considerations (availability of desired staff, use of regional offices and relationships with Washington, etc.).

Obviously, within these guidelines, there is room for a great deal of discretion.

In fact, during the years following its turnabout after World War II, the origin as well as the conduct of most GAO studies rested within the divisions of the GAO. These and their subunits were themselves organized on the basis of the structures of the executive branch. Among other effects, this meant that most GAO studies would be conceived by officials of the operating divisions or on the many individual sites of federal organizations where GAO personnel were stationed or in the field. The integration of these varied efforts into a consistent overall plan was fortuitous and perhaps impossible. Further, the location of GAO audit sites within federal agencies and bureaus discouraged broader interagency perspectives.

The reorganizations of 1971 and 1972 on the basis of broad functional areas, crossing federal organizational lines, was an opening wedge toward more comprehensive and integrated approaches (see chapter 6). It was followed in the mid 1970s by the development of a planning and programming system that would assist in making the above guidelines more operational as well as insuring that government-wide priorities and emerging nationwide issues were addressed. The GAO's top management, including directors of the audit divisions and staff offices, developed a list of the most pressing national concerns—energy, food, criminal justice, and so on—and the most important management initiatives—automatic data processing, program evaluation, and so on—and assigned each one of these issue areas to a "lead" division. That division became responsible for developing a program plan for total GAO work in the issue area, even when the work crossed divisional lines in terms of organizational responsibility. For example, the Human Resources Division became responsible for developing and instituting a government-wide series of audits in the issue area of consumer protection, even though the actual work would include studies performed by the Community and Economic Development Division on meat inspection in the Department of Agriculture, since the latter division maintained audit sites at, and audit responsibility for, that department.

The GAO maintains a growing list of issue areas, a total of thirty-seven of them in mid 1978 (see Figure 8). For each, the lead division prepares a program plan to cover the work in that area for the following eighteen months. The preparation of each program plan is usually begun with extensive explorations of the nature of emerging problems, discussions and conferences, sometimes including experts and practitioners from outside the GAO. The program plan is then drawn up by the lead division with such assistance as may be necessary from site auditors, field offices, other divisions that are involved, and from staff members of congressional committees. This document usually begins with a general statement of the background, nature, and problems of the issue area. It then proceeds to identify and describe key topics within the area to which the GAO should address itself. Some of these "lines of effort" are assigned priorities, and the division states how much staff time (in staff years) it proposes to assign to each (see Figures 9 and 10). The projected programs are checked out with other research agencies, including the congressional support units, to avoid duplication. The program plan is then transmitted to the central staff office of program planning, which reviews it with care, raises questions it deems appropriate, and then convenes a meeting of a program planning committee for extended discussion and decision on the plan. That committee includes the Comptroller General, the Deputy Comptroller General, the heads of some of the staff offices, and of course the top officials of the divisions concerned. The head of the program planning office then writes a memo to the division officials stating in some detail the changes that should be made in the plan as directed from that meeting. The program plan then becomes the base for projecting most of the GAO's specific assignments.

A new "wrinkle" was added to the planning and programming process early in 1978, when the GAO—the agent of governmental accountability—introduced an accountability model into its own work system. When program plans are reviewed after eighteen months of work, the lead division must assess what has been accomplished as compared to what was planned. This accountability model generally follows the format of listing how—and

Figure 8

LIST OF GAO ISSUE AREAS
AND RESPONSIBLE LEAD DIVISIONS

	Percentage of Total GAO Resources During FY 1978
Community and Economic Development Division:	
Domestic housing and community development	2.8
Environmental protection	2.4
Food	2.2
Land use planning and control	1.2
Transportation systems and policies	3.0
Water and water-related programs	1.2
Energy and Minerals Division:	
Energy	5.6
Materials	0.9
Financial and General Management Studies Division:	
Accounting and financial reporting	6.2
Automatic data processing	2.5
Internal auditing systems	1.9
National productivity	1.6
Federal Personnel and Compensation Division:	
Federal personnel management and compensation	4.8
General Government Division:	
Data collected from nonfederal sources	1.0
Intergovernmental relations and revenue sharing	2.2
Law enforcement and crime prevention	3.9
Tax administration	2.5
Human Resources Division:	
Administration of nondiscrimination and equal opportunity programs	1.4
Consumer and worker protection	1.3
Education	2.9
Employment and training	2.5
Health	6.0
Income security	4.9
International Division:	
International economic and military programs	3.8
Logistics and Communications Division:	
Facilities and material management	5.4
Federal information management	1.3
Implementation of military preparedness plans	3.0
Procurement and Systems Acquisition Division:	
Federal procurement	9.0
Science and technology	2.3
Program Analysis Division:	
Alternative approaches to federal objectives	0.7
Budget information for Congress	1.3
Evaluation guidelines	0.7
Regional and national economic problems	0.5
Tax policy	0.3

Figure 9

SOME ILLUSTRATIONS OF THE GAO'S PROGRAM PLANNING SYSTEM: ISSUE AREAS, PRIORITY LINES OF EFFORT, AUDIT REPORTS

Issue Area: Law Enforcement and Crime Prevention

  Priority Line of Effort: How effective are efforts to control and eliminate organized crime?

    Audit Report: Survey of LEAA assistance to state and local governments to combat organized crime
    Audit Report: Review of the Justice Department's Organized Crime and Racketeering Section strike forces

  Priority Line of Effort: Is adequate protection provided persons and property in federally controlled areas?

    Audit Report: Review of law enforcement activities at national recreation areas and forests
    Audit Report: Practices in providing cleaning and guarding services in federal buildings

Issue Area: Implementation of Military Preparedness Plans

  Priority Line of Effort: Adequacy of programs to develop and maintain a defense industrial production base

    Audit Report: Stockpile objectives of strategic and critical materials should be reconsidered because of shortages
    Audit Report: Review of the U.S. Army's program for the procurement of ammunition and the modernization of ammunition plants

  Priority Line of Effort: Readiness of transportation systems to move troops, equipment, and supplies in emergency situations

    Audit Report: Evaluation of the airlift operations of the Military Airlift Command (MAC) during the 1973 Middle East War
    Audit Report: Survey to determine the capability of the National Reserve Defense Fleet to support sealift requirements in a mobilization or nonmobilization contingency

Issue Area: International Economic and Military Programs

  Priority Line of Effort: Assessing U.S. international security commitments abroad

    Audit Report: Review of U.S. participation in the Sinai early warning system
    Audit Report: Financial and legal aspects of the agreement on the availability of certain Indian Ocean islands for defense purposes

to what extent—major reports and ongoing assignments have accomplished the objectives stated in the issue area's program plan. In addition, two new elements were required of divisions during the review of their program plans. The divisions must present evidence that the revised program plan meets the needs of the cognizant congressional committees, with whom they have consulted in advance. Also, they must present a long-range perspective,

Figure 10

EXAMPLES OF ISSUE AREAS
AND LINES OF EFFORT

EDUCATION

ENERGY

P R I O R I T Y   L I N E S   O F   E F F O R T :

EDUCATION	ENERGY
Organization and management of federal education programs	Federal efforts in energy conservation
Federal programs to foster educational opportunity	Transition to inexhaustible energy resources
Specialized programs to prepare fully functioning students	Role of fossil fuels
Developmental services to improve quality of life	Nuclear fission potential and problems
	Government action (regulation, incentive) and energy supply
	Coordination of international policy with domestic requirements
	Federal trusteeship

O T H E R   L I N E S   O F   E F F O R T

EDUCATION	ENERGY
Educational innovation and research	Public and private energy decision making

including possible future trends and likely long-term interest in the subject matter, as well as what is left for the GAO to do in the area.

The program planning and accountability systems provide a mechanism whereby the Comptroller General and his top staff assistants, as well as the division directors, may intervene more directly in charting and controlling the nature and emphasis of GAO work. They are steps in the direction of centralization of basic decision making and hopefully of a better coordinated and integrated work program for the organization as a whole.

The majority of individual projects, however, continue to originate in the site offices, or from intermediate officials in the divisions and in the field. They are supposed to fit into approved lines of effort of issue areas. The project proposals flow up through channels, with amendments along the way, to the division director for approval. After that, if the program planning staff—which looks at all approved jobs on behalf of the Comptroller General—has significant questions, it refers them to a top-level assignment review group that meets weekly and consists principally of top GAO staff officers. Major or critical problems may be carried up to the Comptroller General or his deputy for resolution.

Congressional requests of course are the basis of a good many projects, and some of them do not fit within the framework of any issue area. Likewise, a very few projects are initiated by the Comptroller General, his deputy, or other senior personnel. But the vast majority of GAO-initiated projects still come up from the divisions, not down from the top. The program planning system provides a tool for evaluating these proposals against a carefully thought out and centrally approved general statement of directions.

Conduct and Review of the Work

For its general studies—that is, studies that are not in response to a very specific problem or congressional request—the GAO usually divides its work into two parts. The first of these is referred to as a *survey,* which is a quick overall review of the activity or program as a whole, primarily for the purpose of identifying issues, problems, and probable deficiencies that should be explored in more depth. It involves gathering background information about the program or activity, examining pertinent legislation and legislative histories, and limited testing of management controls. For the most part, the survey work is developed and planned at the audit site (or headquarters group) of the relevant program, and is carried out by two or three field offices under headquarters direction. In recent years, regional personnel also have developed a good deal of program expertise and may be consulted on the design of the survey and selected by the division on the basis of prior work in the subject area.

On the basis of the findings of the survey, a decision is made on which phases promise to yield the most positive results, and plans are laid out for detailed inquiry and analysis; this is known as the *review*. The review normally results in one or more reports. The headquarters division decides what additional fieldwork is needed and what form the report will take, with increasing input from the regional staff. If one regional office is assigned responsibility for supervising work done by other regions (as lead region) or is the sole field office working on the review, it drafts the report in the field. For most GAO studies the time required to conduct the study and prepare a draft report constitutes about one half of the total time necessary to complete the job.

One element of the review of the report that deserves special mention is the auditor's tool known as "referencing." As the auditors obtain information and develop findings, they are responsible for maintaining work papers. To insure uniformity and accuracy, these work papers are kept in a rather complex system of indexing, format, and style. After the report is drafted, each line of the report is referenced to information from the work papers. This task must be performed by an auditor of sufficiently high rank (usually at least GS-12) who did not work on the project itself. For example, every numerical figure in the body of the report must be referenced back to source material in the work papers and any arithmetical calculation performed must be documented and rechecked. Most of the review in the field is necessarily concerned with the accuracy of information.

After reviewing the field input, the headquarters division begins to analyze, redraft, and process the report for release. Washington staff is especially concerned about the general significance of and the current interest in the program under study. When a draft report is completed by the division, the report is usually sent to the agency or agencies responsible for the program under study for comment and criticism. The GAO generally asks that the agency comments on the draft be sent within sixty days, but not infrequently they take longer. Although most studies have been discussed informally with program officials in the field and headquarters, agency comments allow top departmental officials to examine the GAO's findings and to point out any inaccuracies, misinterpretations, or disagreements, and to advise the GAO what they plan to do about its recommendations. Upon receipt of the comments, the divisions review the points raised by the agencies in order to make changes that appear appropriate and to append any comments on which there is continuing disagreement. Before the report is released, the staff offices review the draft on substantive, legal, and editorial matters and assess the timeliness and proper disposition of the report. They may call to the attention of the Comptroller General any particularly questionable or sensitive material.

The process described above is the one used for the bulk of the GAO's work: reports to Congress over the signature of the Comptroller General. Much less time is involved when the product is a report to a specific congressman from the Comptroller General or when the product is testimony by the Comptroller General or other officials before a congressional committee (in these instances, the congressional requester may not wish the GAO to obtain agency comments). Reports without significant recommendations on national programs are generally sent to lower agency officials or to congressional committees by a division director and are usually less time consuming because Washington headquarters staff spends less time on redrafting and processing.

The Organizational Culture

This study has stressed the uniqueness of the GAO as an institution of the federal government. Indeed it is unique in some ways as are all organizations. On the other hand, it bears resemblances to many stable and sizable public agencies; its fifty-seven-year history, as described in the preceding chapters of this work, parallels that of a good many others that went through a process of professionalization in a single field followed by a process of "scatteration" among other professional fields as the nature of its work changed. Like them, it is essentially an administrative organization, though not within the executive branch, and it probably approaches the Weberian model of a bureaucracy as closely as most other administrative agencies. It has a well-established hierarchical structure with clearly understood authorities and delegations up and down the line. Entry has been largely at the bottom of a professional ladder on the basis of merit, and steady advancement up that ladder to journeyman grades is reasonably assured if performance is satisfactory. The modes of operating are largely standardized and set forth in considerable detail in manuals and other instructions. There is a rigorous process of checking and review before the organization's products are released; when they are released (with a few exceptions) they are products of an institution, not of their initial authors.

Status attached to position and level receives as much recognition and deference as in other organizations, probably more than most. Turnover among most of the professional staff has been relatively low, evidence perhaps of job satisfaction, perhaps because the work has not qualified the staff for more rewarding employment elsewhere, perhaps of both. One of the effects has been the occupation of the bulk of senior posts by persons with long experience within the organization. Relatively few of them are tempted by the "revolving door" to positions in business and industry.

The extended and secure tenure of the GAO's professional staff, coupled with their orderly progression up the ladder of responsibility, has contributed to the virility of its internal career system. There have been other contributing factors. One is the fact that for two decades—from about 1945 to 1966—virtually all its professional recruits came from similar educational backgrounds: degrees in accounting. Those recruited more recently are, for the most part, still relatively junior in the hierarchy. Another is that all have weathered an intensive program of training, indoctrination, and experience in the ways and techniques of GAO operations, in the goals they perceive for the GAO, and in their view of the world.

Mention should be made too of the policy, instituted in the 1950s, of relatively rapid transfer of younger employees from job to job, from supervisor to supervisor, and from one area of activity to another. Journeyman auditors in the GAO were expected to become generalists, capable of handling responsibilities in any area. Specialization was encouraged only after one gained a post of at least intermediate executive responsibility. This policy was designed both to broaden the capabilities of the individual auditors and to imbue them with a consistent, overall view of the GAO and its mission.

Some of the policies cited above have been considerably modified in recent years, but changes in culture take time. All generalizations sweep too broadly, but on balance the characteristics of the GAO's organization would appear to include stability, continuity, orderliness, self-containment, and self-governance. Differences in views as to objectives and methods exist, but on the whole, they rest on a fairly solid core of agreement on the value and role of the GAO. Particularly among the older and higher-level officers, one is impressed by the pride and faith in the organization and the feeling of identification with and loyalty to the GAO. Some have expressed a sense of insularity from the outside world, particularly from the executive agencies with which they deal. In most of these regards, the GAO is not unlike well-established agencies in the executive branch, like the arms, services, and bureaus of the military departments, the Foreign Service, the Forest Service, the National Bureau of Standards, and many others.

Yet it differs sharply from many executive agencies in significant respects. Some of these derive from its unusual political posture. It is a servant of one of the most "political" bodies in the world, the U.S. Congress. But, as we have noted earlier, Congress obviously is not a "body" in any strict sense. Those at and near the top of the GAO must obviously be politically astute, sensitive, responsive, selective, and anticipatory if they are to be effective. Yet the organization itself is nonpolitical. Like other complex organizations, the GAO has its own internal politics. But it is not the politics of parties or of interest groups or even of program, as it is in many other government agencies. Its career personnel system seems to be immune from political pressures in hiring, promoting, placing, and firing. While most of the Comptrollers General have been of the same political party as the President who appointed them, none, except perhaps the first one, has been widely accused of partisanship in the performance of his duties. The present

Comptroller General, who served as deputy director of the budget under four presidents of both parties, deals evenhandedly with executive and legislative leaders of both parties. His own political affiliation, if it is known, seems quite irrelevant, as do those of the Deputy Comptroller General and his predecessors. With very few exceptions, the office and division directors and the regional directors came up through the GAO ranks; and all of them were designated by the Comptroller General without any formal outside clearance other than that of the Civil Service Commission.

This means, among other things, that the GAO contains no "mélange" at the top of political "strangers" and career officers.[2] It serenely pursued its steady path through the Watergate crisis, the election campaign of 1976, and the transition to President Carter in 1976-1977.[3] It was unsullied by the taint of scandal growing out of the political "commissars" and the invasion of the civil service in the Nixon era. In fact, there is no evidence that the White House brought any personnel pressure whatever on the GAO.

Leadership from the Top

The Comptroller General is unique in the powers, prestige, and influence that he enjoys within the GAO organization. The evaluation of his aspirations for the GAO program and organization, his views, and his wishes is a continuously conditioning element in the efforts and decisions that are made at subordinate levels. This appears to have been true from the beginning among the four Comptrollers General who served any substantial part of their terms, regardless of their ideologies, managerial styles, or forcefulness—though all of them from McCarl to Staats have been forceful personalities. It probably derives in part from his extensive powers (described in chapter 3) to shape the GAO organization and to guide the destinies of its personnel—within the limits of civil service regulations. But more important is the legal fact of the fifteen-year term that is virtually assured if the incumbent is able and willing to fill it out, barring such excessive abuses as might warrant impeachment. No other federal administrative officer is legally assured such longevity in office though a very few, like J. Edgar Hoover, gained it de facto through the cultivation of a political power base.

Students of public administration may ponder the effect of virtually assured long terms on the nature and extent of executive influence and upon the culture of the organizations the executives superintend. This writer has sensed in the GAO little of the attitude common within many executive agencies that their political boss will be around only two or four or, at the outside, eight years, and that subordinates can wait him out before their programs can be seriously modified or damaged. In the GAO, there is more of an inclination to understand and respond to the boss; where there are differences, to search for acceptable compromises; but certainly to satisfy him in his perceptions of purpose, even when they are not in full agreement. The impact is considerable. The Comptroller General's subordinates read and study his directives and other internal announcements, his testimony, his speeches, and his articles with care. It is at least probable that, over time, these considerably influence the nature and content of GAO work. To those within the GAO, as to those outside it, the office and person of Comptroller General are interchangeable and virtually synonymous with the organization that is itself known as the General Accounting Office.

Line and Staff

This is not, however, to suggest that the supervision of the GAO's operations is highly centralized in the Comptroller General's office. At least since World War II, there have been strong centrifugal forces from the center to the line divisions, and it is probably still true that the day-to-day work of the GAO is most heavily influenced by the views, the methods, and the managerial styles of the leaders of those divisions. Four of the twelve divisions (claims, financial and general management studies, program analysis, and field operations) have distinct kinds of responsibilities, different from the other eight and from each other.[4] But among the eight with general evaluating and auditing responsibilities for different governmental programs, there is a considerable variety in approach and emphasis in their relationships with the executive branch and with Congress, and the ways and degrees to which they have responded to the wishes, implicit as well as explicit, of the Comptroller General. Some GAO personnel have referred to the divisions as "fiefdoms" under the command of their directors and their immediate aides. The term is probably too strong, for there are in fact a good many constraints on the freedom of divisional action.

Many of the GAO's administrative changes over the past two decades have been in the direction of reducing the autonomy and independence of the divisions and assuring that the whole organization operates as a unit and speaks more nearly with one voice—the voice of the Comptroller General. This was probably the case in the reorganizations instituted by both Campbell and Staats. It has been reflected in the detailed manuals on auditing standards, methods, and reports; the identification of issue areas and priorities, many of which cross divisional lines; the institution of the program planning system; the development of a centralized, or centrally directed, training program; the central review of most reports for the Comptroller General's signature; the recent institution of a competitive placement and promotion system whereby all candidates for a given professional vacancy, from whatever division or office, are reviewed and rated by a centrally designated panel.

All of these activities, and a good many others, are carried on by or under the direction of staff offices. In fact, apart from the general counsel, the beginnings of formal staff units, other than strictly service organizations, may largely be attributed to Comptroller General Campbell. They grew, and their responsibilities grew, under Staats. They provide a considerable influence toward the development and enforcement of common policies and standards and the coordination of plans and operations of the various line units, to some extent countervailing the centrifugal tendencies of the divisions. As in other sizable organizations there is built in a certain degree of tension between staff and line.

Like other administrative organizations that have a dominant career service, the great bulk of the heads of the staff offices and a substantial proportion of their professional staffs are drawn from "the career."[5] They are, or were, line auditors, and most of them expect to return to operating divisions after a brief period of years. In fact, under current policy, career personnel below the top who are assigned to staff offices cannot be promoted while in that capacity and must have "home" divisions to which they can return.[6] Assignments to staff offices are therefore regarded by a good many as diversions from, if not impediments to, career progression.

Headquarters and Field

The main building on G Street, N.W., in Washington, D.C., is the GAO's headquarters. Most of its operative work is carried on elsewhere. Some of it is located at about ninety audit sites in and around Washington, most of which are housed in office space provided by the various agencies with which they deal. These are extensions and parts of the various operating divisions of the headquarters.[7] About half of the professional officers are located in the field. There are fifteen regional offices, each located in a major city—from Boston to Atlanta to Los Angeles to Seattle. Most of them have "sublocations" that allow for full coverage of large geographic areas—Dallas, Denver, Seattle— or for special concentration on large federal and/or military installations— Cape Kennedy, Wright Patterson Air Force Base, the military finance centers, and so on. Each regional office is headed by a manager, and their operations are administratively supervised by the director of the Field Operations Division in Washington. But they receive their substantive assignments from—or work them out with—the appropriate subject matter line divisions.

Finally, there are three overseas branches, all under the administrative jurisdiction of the International Division, but all of which conduct studies for other divisions as directed. The oldest of these is the European Branch, now located in Frankfurt but with jurisdiction over activities in Africa and the Near East as well as Europe; the second is the Far East Branch, now located in Honolulu but with a suboffice in Bangkok; and the third, the Latin American Branch, is stationed in Panama City. The overseas branches are staffed by professionals assigned from Washington or regional offices in the

United States for temporary periods—usually two years, often extended to four years. There is thus a pretty continuous turnover and rotation in their personnel, unlike most of the rest of the GAO.

Regional managers are moved about with increasing frequency—from one region to another and sometimes to a high post in Washington. Likewise, a number of the top Washington officials have had experience in one or more of the regions. But below them, and despite sporadic efforts from Washington to encourage rotation of personnel between regions and between them and Washington, most of the professional personnel are homegrown, initially recruited in their region and spending their working lives in the same office. Each regional manager has a good deal of freedom in the way he deploys his resources, and practices vary quite widely from region to region. However, since each regional office serves most of the specialized divisions in Washington, there must necessarily be flexibility among the personnel so that they may be able to move from one kind of job to another without great difficulty. There are individuals who have concentrated their work in one subject matter like weapons, taxes, or pensions; and there is a suboffice in the field (Houston) that is almost entirely concentrated in one functional area, energy. But in the main, the field personnel are less specialized than those in Washington. Washington project managers are likely to steer their projects to regions, and individuals within those regions, that have already had experience and demonstrated their capability in subject matter fields. And they are likely to be impatient with what they consider amateurism in reports from field generalists. There is thus a certain amount of built-in pressure from headquarters toward more specialization in the field. The difference in perspective and approach undoubtedly varies widely in degree but overall is of some significance. It lies between those who give primary emphasis to understanding in some depth the substantive issue under consideration and those who feel that the fact-finding and analytic skills possessed by competent professionals can be utilized effectively in almost any subject matter.

Those in the field are sometimes impatient with the frequently long delays involved in headquarters reviews of their work and reports. They are unhappy when their reports are heavily criticized, largely or totally rewritten, or occasionally buried in the headquarters. The temporal and procedural distance between the work itself and the evidence of it in a published report, coupled with the absence of personal credit to those who did the actual work, is a source of dissatisfaction.

In comparison with other organizations with large field components, the dissension between headquarters and the regions has not been unusually serious. According to some of the old-timers in the GAO, it has tended to grow over the years as the field personnel have grown in capability, experience, and confidence. The regional offices and their managers are less submissive and more willing to state and argue their points of view when they are at odds with the central office than they were two decades ago. The headquarters-field relationship, like that between staff and line, may involve built-in situations that produce what Mary Parker Follett described years ago as "constructive conflict." But not all conflict is constructive, and the GAO in recent years has gone to considerable lengths to enhance the openness, the dialogue, and the understanding whereby its internal disagreements may be made more truly constructive (as discussed in subsequent paragraphs).

The Reward System

Students of administration have long recognized the impact upon performance and behavior of the systems whereby offices and individual employees are rewarded or penalized. Organizational rewards take varying forms—approval and esteem by superiors and peers, honors and other forms of special recognition, more rapid advancement in income and responsibility, more interesting assignments, and others. Penalties are approximately the reverse of these. For many years, the rewards for GAO professionals, units, and even the agency itself were primarily based upon deficiencies discovered in the financial management of executive agencies. If, following a careful investigation, an auditor reported that everything was just fine, he was not likely to score many points—nor was the GAO itself, whose support in Congress has long depended in considerable part on the deficiencies it could report in the executive branch and the amount of savings its revelations brought about beyond the cost of its own budget.

Comptroller General Staats has stated the GAO's objectives in more positive terms: to improve the effectiveness of government. Deficiencies are still searched for and reported, but the accent in the GAO's reward criteria has broadened to the production of reports about agencies, their problems, and recommendations for improvement. Preferably, they are reports that will be signed by the Comptroller General, reported officially to Congress, and encased in blue covers. The basic element of the GAO's reward system has become the production of blue cover reports. This practice is widely referred to and deplored by some GAO leaders as the "blue cover syndrome." The emphasis upon the blue covers has, according to the GAO's own leaders, had dysfunctional effects. It has discouraged initiative and originality, speed in the revelation of significant findings, timeliness in relation to the decision-making demands of Congress, and relevance in relation to immediate problems. Normally, the blue cover reports take a long time in referencing (to assure accuracy), reviewing, editing, and rewriting. Other means of communication like testimony, informal letters and memoranda, and even informal conversations are often quicker and more useful. But these are less safe and have been less recognized in the reward system.

The People

It will be recalled that during its first quarter century, lawyers were the elite group of the GAO. All the Comptrollers General, Assistant Comptrollers General, and of course general counsels were attorneys, and almost all of the staff with the distinction of being considered professional were likewise lawyers. The legal group is said to have been the principal counselors if not decision makers on policy questions. The closing years of Warren and the entire tenure of Campbell witnessed the rise to preeminence of the accounting profession. Campbell was of course himself a CPA, and most of the professionals hired between 1945 and 1966 were likewise trained as accountants. The legal profession remains influential; the Deputy Comptroller General and the general counsel and his entire professional staff are lawyers. But the principal activities of the legal staff are fairly clearly defined although it contributes to and abets the main line work of research and auditing. The leadership in the latter type of activities as well as the majority of the operative personnel were initially employed as auditors, trained in accounting.

Some aspects of the GAO's reward system are heritages from its own past—a bequest from the second GAO to the third.GAO. They include the value systems, approaches, techniques, and vocabulary still maintained, though modified, in the minds of the majority of its professional people and in the processes through which they work. Among the traditional values of GAO auditing are:

- independence—nonpartisan, unbiased;
- dependability—provable facts, uncolored by ideology, preference, or parochialism;
- accuracy and specificity;
- reliance on hard, countable data;
- emphasis on financial aspects and data, even (though not universally) in projects not classified as financial;
- care, rigor, and discipline in the work itself and the processes whereby its products are reviewed; and
- temporal orientation to the past and present, not the future.

The strength of these values varies a good deal among the divisions and field offices, and within some of them. But their importance is attested by many of the admonitions in the GAO's various operating manuals, the processes mentioned earlier (such as working papers, referencing, multiple internal reviews, and so on), and many of the published reports themselves. An error in a draft of a report, even if it is inconsequential, is often perceived by its author to be more damaging than the fact that it is six months late.

But the GAO has been for a decade or more in transition. The content of much of its work has changed and with it have changed the capabilities, perspectives, and orientations of its professional personnel. The changes in the nature of GAO projects have been propelled by a number of factors; the consequences of these changes on GAO values have been gradual, not spectacular, and partial, not universal. Among them have been increasing concern about the future rather than the past or, perhaps more accurately, the understanding of past experience as a tool for the future; increasing concern about externalities and nonmeasurable effects of federal programs; greater emphasis upon systems rather than individual transactions; and interest in the general effects and effectiveness of federal programs and policies in addition to, or instead of, the legality and propriety of how the moneys were expended.

On the basis of a limited number of interviews, this author's impression is that the shifts in values away from those traditionally associated with auditing have been more pronounced among the senior leaders of the GAO and its junior personnel than among the intermediate supervisors. They seem to be more prevalent in the headquarters than in the field, and far more pervasive among certain of the newer divisions than the older ones. But most of these newer directions of GAO activities were approved and encouraged by all of the directors of operating divisions. The degree to which they have moved the work of their organizations away from the traditional methods and goals of auditing varies a great deal. Fifteen years ago, it might have been accurate to describe the GAO as a homogeneous organization, but this is no longer the case. There are today wide disparities of perspectives and of values among the various divisions and, to a lesser extent, within them.

The changing values of GAO professional personnel have arisen from a number of processes and internal policies. First among them is socialization on the job, augmented by a wide variety of training programs. The influence of this factor can hardly be more pronounced in any organization. Some of those who came in as accountant-auditors volunteered to this writer that they could not today examine with any confidence the balance sheets of a private business, and that, if they could, they would be bored to death. Accounting to many of them had become secondary to the problems of governmental programs and policy. Second was the practice, instituted by Comptroller General Staats in 1967, of hiring personnel educated in fields other than accounting. About two fifths of the GAO's professional personnel today are from other fields, such as business and public administration, economics and other social sciences, computer technology, engineering, and others. Most of these are at intermediate and lower professional levels, but their influence is certain to rise. A third factor is the increasing use of consultants from a great variety of specialized fields. And finally, the GAO is undertaking to utilize interdisciplinary teams on its projects whereby the knowledge and perspectives of a variety of sciences, from both within and outside its own organization, may be brought to bear upon governmental problems.

Efforts at Self-improvement

During the mid and later 1970s the GAO has undertaken a variety of programs to improve its overall effectiveness, to better develop the capabilities of its personnel, and to make it a happier and more rewarding place to work. Some of these are adaptations to the GAO of tools and techniques of organizational improvement currently used in many other federal and nonfederal agencies. Some are responses to criticisms from the outside, particularly Congress. Some are responsive to self-criticisms and internal complaints. These efforts are particularly important, and probably also difficult, because the GAO is not growing rapidly, a situation that may continue for the indefinite future. The problem is aggravated among its professional personnel because of the rather low rate of turnover and the relative youth of most of its top officials; relatively few of the latter are expected to resign or retire within the next several years. The GAO feels that it must do better principally with the people who are already in the organization.

Personnel Management

One of the problems and programs that the GAO shares with a great many other organizations is equal employment opportunity. The extent to which there has been in the past, or even is today, intentional discrimination against women and against minorities is a matter of conjecture. At the time of this writing, there are very few women and very few blacks in the upper echelons of the hierarchy—none at the levels of regional managers, division and staff directors, and higher offices. An explanation of this situation is that most of the incumbents in these posts were hired more than a decade ago from college majors in accounting, and very few women or minorities opted for accounting careers. More recently, as GAO recruiters broadened their net to include other specialties, a rising proportion of women and minorities have been hired to professional posts. But few of them have had time to advance very far up the hierarchy, and opportunities for promotions beyond journeyman levels are rather limited. The GAO has an active equal employment opportunity program, comparable to those in other agencies. And it has developed a two-day program against "functional racism" that all employees are required to attend. But the problem is not one that will be resolved overnight.

Like many other agencies, the GAO a few years ago launched a program of what is commonly known as "organization development." It is intended to foster better interpersonal relations within the organization, more openness and frankness in dialogue, reduction of the barriers and distances induced by hierarchy, encouragement of participative management, and resolution of problems and controversies through joint meetings and discussions. Private consultants and a consulting firm have participated in this effort for some time, and the GAO has created its own staff to continue it on a permanent basis.

Partially prompted by what GAO leaders felt to be an inflexible approach of the Civil Service Commission to its special mission and needs, the GAO undertook several initiatives. It engaged a private consulting firm to develop a single-agency series of professional positions that would encompass the GAO's auditing and analysis jobs and that would be exclusive to the GAO. The firm proposed that a new single series to be known as "GAO Evaluators" replace the two existing job series within which most of the line personnel are now classified: accountants and management analysts. The recommendation was based on the premises that the GAO's work is unique to that organization and that it was best described as evaluating, not auditing or analyzing. The Comptroller General approved the proposal in principle and sent it to the Civil Service Commission. Its ultimate fate had not been determined at the time of this writing. The Comptroller General also proposed to Congress that the GAO be exempted from civil service jurisdiction with regard to major personnel management functions.[8] And serious consideration was begun of the desirability of going on a "rank in person" rather than "rank in position" basis.[9] The latter two changes would require fundamental amendments in law.

Productivity and the Timeliness of Reports

The GAO has been sensitive to criticisms, both from within and without, that its reports take too much time, are often released too late to be maximally useful to their users—mainly in Congress—and are too expensive in relation to their value. The criticisms of the two congressional groups cited earlier[10] were not a surprise to the GAO's leaders, and they did not contest them. Many months before the House Committee's report was published, the GAO's top leadership, including its division directors, in June 1977 dedicated its semiannual meeting to the problems of timeliness and productivity. Growing out of that meeting was the creation of a task force by the Comptroller General to make corrective recommendations on these problems. The task force of eleven members consisted principally of directors of headquarters divisions and staff offices. It met frequently during the summer and fall of 1977 and convened on its problems with many others in the headquarters and field. But the main thrust of its thinking was evident early in its deliberations. Its report, issued in November 1977, proposed basic changes in the modes of operating and in the nature of the products of the GAO.[11]

The 1977 task force proceeded from the central premise that: "The work of GAO takes too long and costs too much." The discussions that preceded and followed issuance of the November report contained a wide range of disagreement about its recommendations, but there seemed to be little argument on the premise. The task force attributed the central problems to a variety of factors:

- overkill of subject at hand—more information than necessary to meet need;
- too many people involved in jobs;
- too many jobs at one time;
- overemphasis on completeness, accuracy, and literary quality, and underemphasis on use and timeliness;
- the "blue book syndrome";
- inadequate system of internal accountability for the use of resources;
- the reward system.[12]

Later in its report the task force criticized the hierarchical structure and its multiple levels of review, "pinballing" of draft reports back and forth between levels of management, and field-headquarters relationships.

The task force made a great variety of proposals to counteract these difficulties. They included closer day-to-day relationships with the pertinent elements of Congress on their needs and on the timing and usefulness of GAO reports; greater emphasis on communications, oral and written, to the users, and less emphasis on blue cover reports; delegations to the division chiefs and other officers below them to sign communications other than the blue cover reports; revision of the internal reward system to give appropriate recognition to new ideas, staff development, staff work, planning, and the like; and relaxation of the requirements for multiple reviews, referencing, and so on.

But by far the most important and controversial recommendation was that the GAO's divisions adopt a "project team approach as a normal way of doing business."[13] The task force envisioned that for each major and finite project a team leader, drawn from either headquarters or the field, be designated; that the members of the team, from any sources, be assigned to him and work under his leadership (regardless of their permanent organizational affiliation) until the project is completed; and that the normal hierarchical review processes be minimized. This project system of management had already been used on a few occasions;[14] the task force proposal would make it common practice. Its potential impact upon the existing hierarchy of directors and regional managers and their various deputies, associates, and assistants is great, and to some, threatening. The same is true with respect to the personnel system, which would certainly have to be modified substantially, very possibly to the point of converting to a personal rank (as distinguished from a position-classification) base.

The Comptroller General approved the bulk of the recommendations of the task force, and on January 9, 1978,[15] directed that most of them be put into effect as rapidly as feasible. Basic responsibility for implementation was placed upon the division directors, and it is likely if not indeed inevitable that they will move ahead on the proposals—particularly on the team approach for handling GAO projects—with varying degrees of speed, forcefulness, and enthusiasm.

*   *   *

It is not within the province of this book to evaluate these various problems and proposals. But a few general observations seem appropriate. One is that the GAO continues to be in transition as it has been for the past dozen years. The basic thrusts of this transition have been fairly consistent. The effort to establish a team approach and to relax the requirements of internal and external review of GAO products, which has now begun, seems a logical next step to the reorganizations of 1971 and 1972 and the subsequent program planning system, which is still being developed. As other organizations particularly in research undertakings, have found, the administration of team organizations within or alongside of the more traditional hierarchical structures is difficult; this will be a major challenge for the GAO's management in the future.

Notes

1. U.S. General Accounting Office, *Comprehensive Audit Manual*, part 1, p. 6.

2. These apt expressions are borrowed from Hugh Heclo in his recent book describing the political-bureaucratic leadership of most executive departments, bureaus, and other agencies: *Government of Strangers: Executive Politics in Washington* (Washington, D.C.: Brookings Institution, 1977).

3. The GAO was of course involved in Watergate because of its responsibilities at that time in connection with campaign financing. But those activities proved to be temporary and apparently had little impact upon its political stance.

4. The Office of the General Counsel is generally considered a staff office in the GAO, but it performs a number of functions having the characteristics of "line." Thus, while it is legal adviser to the Comptroller General and Deputy Comptroller General and provides legal assistance to the operating

divisions, and reviews their reports in draft, it also renders decisions and opinions on a great variety of federal questions in response to requests from Congress, the executive agencies, contract bidders, and others.

5. This is true of the two assistants to the Comptroller General, the director of organization and management planning, and the directors of internal review, of policy, and of program planning.

6. There are, however, certain occupational fields other than auditing employed in staff offices that offer careers and advancement opportunities. They include specialists in budget, personnel, libraries, and others.

7. A conspicuous exception to this practice is the Department of Defense, for which a large part of the Washington work is conducted in the GAO building itself.

8. See chapter 9.

9. "Rank-in-person" means that personnel could be freely assigned above or below their class, without threat to their rank or pay. Such a system has long been common among the "excepted" personnel systems like the military and the Foreign Service.

10. These criticisms were among the major points in the reports of the Commission on the Operation of the Senate in 1976 and of the House Select Committee on Congressional Operations in 1978 (see chapter 9).

11. Memorandum to the Comptroller General from the Task Force on Improving GAO Effectiveness, "Report of Findings, Conclusions and Recommendations" (processsed), November 9, 1977.

12. Ibid., p. 3 (synthesized).

13. Ibid., p. 6.

14. See, for example, the bank examining and grain inspection cases in Kloman, ed., *Cases in Accountability: The Work of the GAO* (Boulder, Colo.: Westview Press, 1979).

15. General Accounting Office *Management News*.

CONCLUSION:
CONTINUITY AND CHANGE,
PAST AND FUTURE

The history of the GAO's predecessors in the Treasury Department and of the GAO itself offers a striking contrast between permanence and continuity on the one hand and profound change on the other. Elements of the financial system that were set up by Alexander Hamilton under the authority of the Treasury Act of 1789 survived more than 150 years; a few vestiges remain today. The basic organization and procedures mandated in the Dockery Act of 1884 continued for more than 60 years without substantial change, and significant parts of it too remain. Some of the powers provided the comptroller and auditors of the treasury by that act and earlier ones continue as principal weapons in the artillery of the Comptroller General.

In 1921, the organization underwent what would appear to be a wrenching change. It was removed from an executive department and given a vaguely quasi-independent, quasi-legislative status. The titles and some of the incumbents at the very top changed, and the organization apparently assumed a more aggressive—or aggressively negative—posture. But the underlying philosophy, the self-perceived view of mission, and the modes of operating of the first GAO continued pretty much as before—as did the people who carried on its activities. Indeed, most of these—the view of mission and the modes of operating—persisted through the most tumultuous period of change in the peacetime history of the federal government, the New Deal, and through the greatest war in the history of the world.

The GAO was conceived by its founders to become the leading and central accounting and auditing organization in the United States government. Yet it effectively, if unintentionally, resisted the development of real expertise in accounting. That profession was on its feet and running well before the GAO was founded, and before World War II it had made significant inroads and contributions in both state and local governments. During its first quarter century, and especially in the later years of that period, the GAO made some sporadic efforts to improve federal accounting. But the concept that accounting systems should be designed and operated as an instrument of management as well as a basis for checking up on management did not then take hold in the GAO.

It is paradoxical that one of the probable reasons for the long period of stability and nonchange was the long, virtually guaranteed term of the Comptroller General. The paradox arises from the fact that one of the factors that made possible the massive changes that were to follow was also the long term of the Comptroller General. The perspectives and activities of the GAO were not inappropriate during the 1920s when economy and detailed controls were the watchwords. Neither Comptroller General McCarl nor his organization, which he had largely inherited, was able or willing to adjust when the new, and totally different, demands of the depression arrived.

Another explanation for the continuing obdurateness of the first GAO was the desire of the first Comptroller General to establish, maintain, and make conspicuously clear that he and his organization were completely independent of the executive branch, that he would bow to no executive influence, and that, on specific financial questions, he would rule it. Criticisms from the administration, the occasional presidential recommendations that the GAO be abolished or that its powers be sheared, very likely contributed to a stubborn determination to carry on its affairs as they were.

In the major wave of change begun at the close of World War II, the first bridge that the GAO had to cross was this one: the resolution that it could work with—as well as against—the executive branch. This probably did not come easily to Comptroller General Warren, a long-term, highly respected congressman who took pride in proclaiming that the GAO was a legislative agency. But even before the war, he superintended a peace agreement with the TVA, one of the GAO's most vigorous foes; during and immediately following the war, GAO staff had contact and to some extent collaborated with staff of the Bureau of the Budget on the problem of government corporations; and following the war Warren was induced, under the forceful persuasion of his longtime friend, James E. Webb, then director of the budget, to enter upon the joint program with the Bureau of the Budget and the Treasury Department that continues to the time of this writing.

It is hard to say whether the sources of the massive changes of the late 1940s and 1950s were internal or external to the GAO itself. The seeds of the second GAO were planted during the war when some of the GAO staff worked with a committee of Congress on government corporations, their efforts culminating in the Corporation Control Act of 1945. Congress subsequently gave assent to GAO changes in a variety of legislation, but Congress was not the driving force. The changes began with the hiring of trained accountants for corporation auditing and later of more accountants to lead and implement the pact between the GAO, the BoB, and the Treasury Department. Thereafter, it was a self-propelled revolution, engineered principally by newly acquired accountants who perceived the role of the GAO in entirely different terms than had most of those who were already there and who did then or would soon depart. Comptroller General Campbell not only permitted, but encouraged, this development with his auditor's views of a professional accounting organization.

The changes in the GAO during the first dozen years of the term of Comptroller General Staats have been more gradual, less turbulent, and less painful to the incumbents than those in the postwar years. Some say that they have been too slow, others that they have been too fast for the organization to digest them. But they have been basically consistent and persistent, and overall their effects have been profound. In the first place, the organization has become more aware of, and sensitive and responsive to, the environment around it. The third GAO has, to a greater extent than any of its predecessors, adapted and also contributed to changes in the Congress—its assertiveness, structure, modes of operating, and interests. GAO relationships with the various elements of Congress are multifarious and continuous (see chapter 9). The GAO has been involved in the field of contract auditing since the start of World War II. But its concern with the developments and problems of the society beyond the federal government and beyond government contracts is relatively new and growing: international affairs, state and local governments and intergovernmental relations, the shape and problems of business, the universities, the environment, energy, and many others.

The third GAO has stretched its meaning of the word "audits" beyond anything contemplated twenty years ago, and some of its work—an increasing share—can hardly fit within that rubric, however it is defined. It has oriented a great deal of its work to problems of the future, far more so than in previous years. Audits of actions of the past are perceived less as simply informative, deterrent, or potentially punitive expeditions, and more as the identification of problems that will challenge the government in the future. The third GAO has broadened its professional base to include a variety of professions and specialties other than accounting and law. Many of those who came in as auditors have long departed that field as it was traditionally defined.

The sources of the changes in the GAO in the last several years have been several, and it would be hazardous to attribute their relative degrees of importance. The person, the experience, the interests, and the reputation of Comptroller General Staats, most would agree, were significant. He initiated internal studies leading to reorganization, to a central program planning system based upon a listing of issue areas, most recently a project (or team) management system—all directed in part to focus GAO efforts on broader problems of the government than audits of individual components and their financing. He prescribed that governmental auditing should comprehend not alone financial integrity, legality, and managerial efficiency but also the evaluation of program results.

But Staats was not alone in all of this. Studies of efficiency in management had begun under the rubric of comprehensive auditing long before he arrived in the second GAO; scattered studies of program results and effectiveness had likewise been performed. One longtime GAO official suggested to the author that the main thrust toward management auditing and then to reviews of program results came from the people on the job, not from top leadership. Such studies seemed more important or more interesting, or both, then auditing the books. For many, financial auditing had become a bore. It is true today that the large majority of GAO-initiated projects are suggested by the staffs of the operating divisions and the regional offices, not by the division and office directors and their superiors at the top.

Congress also propelled, prodded, and otherwise encouraged the GAO to move in the directions associated with the Staats term. The GAO's first sweeping effort at program evaluation was its study in the late 1960s of the poverty program, a study initiated and directed by Congress in the Prouty Amendment (see chapter 6). As Congress became more restive and assertive during the following years, it called more and more upon the GAO and its other support agencies for data, analyses, and evaluations. Through legislation, it thrust the GAO into new areas and new responsibilities, not all of which were sought by GAO.

A Fourth GAO?

During the course of this study, the writer has been exposed to a great variety of different views, both within and outside the organization, as to where the GAO should go in the future. One, probably the most frequent, is that it should continue doing about what it is doing today but should equip itself to do it better. A second is that it should shed, or be shed of, most or all of its executive-type functions, exercise less discretion in its choice of projects, and become more subservient to Congress in most or all of its work. A third view is approximately opposite: that GAO be freer of congressional and political influence, report the "shots" as it sees them without regard to who in Congress might not like them, and give as much emphasis in its public reports to favorable findings as to deficiencies.

Along a somewhat different dimension, quite a number of both GAO employees and outside observers foresaw, and generally thought it desirable, that the GAO give more and more emphasis to program evaluation and policy studies. Some took exactly the opposite view and argued that the GAO should return to what it had done and could do best: auditing hard financial facts and figures to identify and minimize fraud, misuse of funds, and inefficiency. Some of these questioned the capabilities of the GAO's staff to perform in-depth evaluations of programs and doubted that, even with better qualified staff, it was in a position to perform such work effectively because it is outside the executive branch where most decisions are made and most programs are run.

In the light of the GAO's stormy early history, when it was the butt of frequent attacks from Presidents and study groups, it is interesting that no one suggested (to this writer) that it be abolished or that the bulk of its functions be transferred to the executive branch (although it is perfectly possible that some thought this but would not say it). It may be recalled that one repeated part of the argument was that accounting and the direction of accounting systems was properly an executive function and should be within the executive branch. Another was that the audit of financial transactions should be conducted by an agency responsible and reporting to the legislative branch. It is therefore somewhat ironic that today, while the accounts are kept in the executive agencies, the GAO prescribes the ground rules for agency accounting systems, and it reviews and approves or disapproves them; and that most financial auditing of executive transactions is in fact done within the executive agencies—with the encouragement of the GAO. And there seems to be little criticism of either situation. Furthermore, none of the participants on either side of the warm debates of the 1930s and 1940s suggested that the GAO would or should devote a substantial part of its efforts to the evaluation of the effects of federal programs or the analysis of policies, in place or proposed.

Times change, and with them problems and perspectives. This writer, no prophet, refrains from predicting what the GAO will look like two decades hence or prescribing what it should look like. But attention should be called to some of the factors, largely growing out of history, that are relevant to those who will have a hand in shaping its future. One is that the GAO has sought to relate its work more and more to the problems of society as they impinge upon governments and to the federal undertakings in response to them, their purposes, content, and processes. This has involved the increased use of, and dependence upon, other levels of government as well as other institutions of society in the pursuit of national goals. The GAO could not long serve much useful purpose if it divorced itself effectively from its society and the rest of the government as it very nearly did during the 1920s and 1930s.

A second factor is that the separation of powers in the national government remains alive and, if not perfectly well, is at least not critically ill. Despite recent concerns about the "imperial presidency," the alleged aggrandizement by Congress of presidential powers, or about unholy alliances between pockets of Congress and pockets in the executive branch, there continues a general recognition that these two branches have somewhat different powers (though some are shared), different constituencies, and different responsibilities. Conflicts between the two are endemic, built into the Constitution and supported through the development of a loose, relatively undisciplined two-party system. The GAO could hardly operate as it does without the separation of powers. There are few if any other nations in the world, free or totalitarian, wherein an official agency would, as a matter of normal operating procedure, publish reports critical of the policies and programs of another official agency—even when the two agencies are ultimately responsible to branches controlled by the same political party.[1] This is routine for the GAO, some of the other congressional support units, committees of the Congress, and sometimes the Congress as a whole.

Another factor is the continuing confidence and faith in the United States on facts and figures, on objective analysis as the proper bases for determining public policy. True, there is widespread suspicion of "intellectuals" and of scientists in general. But much of this distrust derives from the fear, even the expectation, that they warp their data and their interpretations to suit ideological or political purposes. Yet, there remains a substantial trust in the value of factual, scientific appraisal when there is confidence that it is not self-serving, not partisan or otherwise political, and not colored by ideological prejudices.

This is to suggest that the GAO's strength and influence depend ultimately on its credibility—in the Congress, in the media, and among the public. To the extent that its findings and recommendations are perceived to be biased for personal, institutional, ideological, or political reasons, to that extent is the esteem and reliability of the organization itself damaged. The concern about credibility is one justification for the careful reviews of GAO reports and of the alleged timidity of some of its findings and recommendations—alleged both by outsiders and by some GAO staff. On the other side, incisive reports on matters that cannot be established through quantitative data threaten the organization's credibility if they are challenged and disproved. Most of the findings and recommendations of the GAO are issued as products of the institution, not the authors. There are no disavowal or saving clauses in the GAO's major reports, and they are signed by the Comptroller General. The credibility of the institution rides with each one.

Over the years, the GAO has built its reputation for credibility largely through its financial analyses and audits, matters that are usually quantifiable and provable. Its continuing emphasis upon the financial and cost aspects of its studies may be explained and also justified on this basis in addition to their intrinsic value. On the other hand, even those with whom we discussed the matter within the GAO—and they were a majority—who predicted and endorsed the extension of the GAO's pursuits in more general program and policy matters, stressed that there were hazards in this kind of activity. Questions of policy and program are almost by definition political or potentially political; in social areas particularly, few propositions can be proven by quantitative data. Most involve judgments and unprovable predictions. If the GAO is to proceed in this direction, it must do so with care and caution.

One of the pervasive problems of American national government is the fragmentation of programs, functions, appropriations, and organizations within relatively narrow compartments though their purposes overlap, complement, and sometimes compete with one another. Such fragmentation has long been the object of complaint and of efforts to reform in the executive branch. In recent years, with the development of a multitude of strong subcommittees, it has become a problem of roughly comparable magnitude in Congress. The GAO with its almost unlimited scope of jurisdiction, its resources scattered among the various headquarters offices in Washington and in the field, is uniquely positioned to attack problems that cross both organizational lines in the executive branch and committee lines in the Congress. In its reorganization of 1971-1972 on the basis of broad functional areas rather than executive branch structure and its more recent development of a program system built around issue areas, it has facilitated such an approach. The potential of the GAO for a unifying, integrating, coordinating contribution is great.

Finally, we would mention another potential of the GAO that has so far been only partially realized. It relates to time and timing and applies to the other congressional support agencies as well. During recent years and particularly at present, the GAO has been increasingly pressed by Congress, and has pressed itself, to gear its work schedule to congressional interests in terms of current and upcoming legislation and to the rhythm of the budget cycle. This has undoubtedly been necessary and desirable from the standpoint of the relevance and usefulness of its work products for immediate congressional needs. But there are also public problems of great future importance to which the GAO, through longer-range studies, can make significant contributions. A problem for GAO management, now and in the future, is to assure that long-range opportunities not be too greatly sacrificed to, but rather balanced with, short-range demands.

Shortly after the appointment of Comptroller General Staats in 1966, Harlan Cleveland, a distinguished government official, ambassador, scholar, and writer, wrote that the Staats appointment could be the most important in the Johnson presidency.[2] The appointments of earlier Comptrollers General McCarl, Warren, and Campbell all proved to be important. The unique powers, resources, and potential of the GAO (for better or worse) contribute to that importance. The term and security of the office together with its authority over the organization add to it. Barring basic changes in the law, the selection of the successor to Elmer Staats by whoever is President in 1981 may be crucial; that successor will very likely continue in the office until the nation is within shouting distance of the twenty-first century.

Notes

1. Following a visit to Western Europe in 1978, Comptroller General Staats described the dismay of many European officials with whom he talked about the published reports, widely headlined in Europe, of the GAO's criticisms of the F-16 airplane program, a program jointly sponsored by the United States and several NATO countries.

2. In a letter to John W. Macy, Jr., then chairman of the Civil Service Commission and adviser to the President on political appointments. The letter itself has been lost, but both its author and its recipient confirmed it to the writer.

APPENDIX

ORGANIZATION OF THE
UNITED STATES GENERAL ACCOUNTING OFFICE

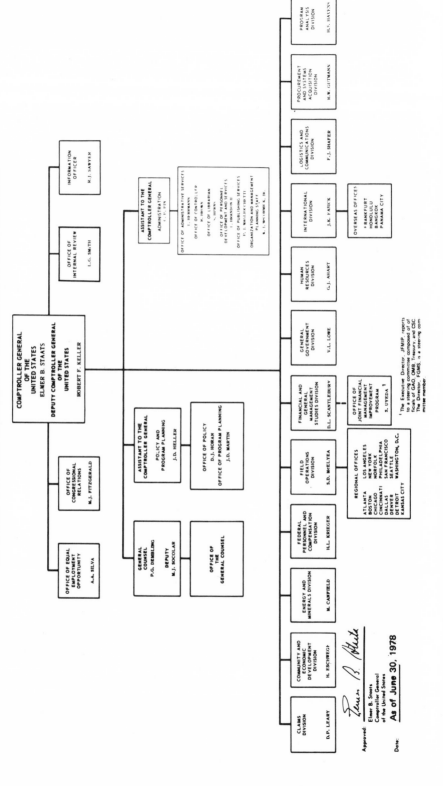

Approved: _Elmer B. Staats_

Elmer B. Staats
Comptroller General
of the United States

Date: **As of June 30, 1978**

SELECTED BIBLIOGRAPHY

Books

Anthony, Robert N., and Regina Herzlinger. *Management Control in Nonprofit Organizations*. Homewood, Ill.: Richard D. Irwin, 1975.

Bartelt, E. F. *Accounting Procedures of the U.S. Government*. Chicago: Public Administration Service, 1940.

Bolling, Richard. *House Out of Order*. New York: Dutton, 1965.

———. *Power in the House*. New York: Dutton, 1968.

Brown, Jewel D. *The U.S. General Accounting Office's Changing Focus As The Federal Government's Auditor, 1921-1972*. Washington, D.C.: George Washington University (unpublished dissertation), 1973.

Brown, Richard E. *The GAO: Untapped Source of Congressional Power*. Knoxville: University of Tennessee Press, 1970.

Carey, John L. *The Rise of the Accounting Profession*. 2 vols. New York: American Institute of Certified Public Accountants, 1969.

Chubb, Basil. *The Control of Public Expenditure: Financial Committees of the House of Commons*. Oxford: Clarendon Press, 1952.

Clark, Joseph S. *Congress: The Sapless Branch*. New York: Harper and Row, 1964.

Cleveland, Frederick A., and Arthur E. Buck. *The Budget and Responsible Government*. New York: Macmillan, 1920.

Cooper, William W., and Yuji Ijiri, eds. *Eric Louis Kohler—Accounting's Man of Principles*. Reston, Va.: Reston Publishers, 1978.

Dodd, Lawrence C., and Bruce I. Oppenheimer, eds. *Congress Reconsidered*. New York: Praeger, 1977.

Emmerich, Herbert. *Federal Organization and Administrative Management*. University, Ala.: University of Alabama Press, 1971.

Fairfield, Roy P., ed. *The Federalist: A Collection of Essays Written in Support of the Constitution of the United States*. New York: Mentor, 1961.

Fisher, Louis. *Presidential Spending Power*. Princeton, N.J.: Princeton University Press, 1975.

Fox, Harrison W., Jr., and Susan Webb Hammond. *Congressional Staffs:*

The Invisible Force in American Lawmaking. New York: Free Press, 1977.

Gordon, Lawrence A., ed. *Accounting and Corporate Social Responsibility,* Lawrence: University of Kansas, 1978.

Harris, Joseph P. *Congressional Control of Administration.* Washington, D.C.: The Brookings Institution, 1964.

Hart, James. *The American Presidency in Action, 1789: A Study in Constitutional History.* New York: Macmillan, 1948.

Heclo, Hugh. *A Government of Strangers: Executive Politics in Washington.* Washington, D.C.: The Brookings Institution, 1977.

Heclo, Hugh, and Aaron Wildavsky. *The Private Government of Public Money: Community and Policy Inside British Politics.* New York: Macmillan, 1974.

Karl, Barry D. *Executive Reorganization and Reform in the New Deal.* Cambridge, Mass.: Harvard University Press, 1963.

Kaufman, Richard F. *The War Profiteers.* New York: Bobbs-Merrill, 1970.

Machinery and Allied Products Institute and Council for Technological Advancement. *The Government Contractor and the General Accounting Office.* Washington, D.C.: MAPI, 1966.

Mansfield, Harvey C., Sr. *The Comptroller General: A Study in the Law and Practice of Financial Administration.* New Haven, Conn.: Yale University Press, 1939.

———, ed. *Congress Against the President.* New York: Praeger, 1975.

Mautz, Robert K., and Hussein A. Sharaf. *The Philosophy of Auditing.* Chicago: American Accounting Association, 1961.

Mosher, Frederick C., ed. *American Public Administration: Past, Present, and Future.* University, Ala.: University of Alabama Press, 1975.

Normanton, E. L. *The Accountability and Audit of Governments.* New York: Praeger, 1966.

Ornstein, Norman J., ed. *Changing Congress: The Committee System,* Vol. 411. Philadelphia: American Academy of Political and Social Science, 1974.

Pois, Joseph. *Watchdog on the Potomac: A Study of the Comptroller General of the United States.* Pittsburgh: University of Pittsburgh (unpublished manuscript), 1971.

Powell, Fred Wilbur. *Control of Federal Expenditures: A Documentary History 1775-1894.* Washington, D.C.: The Brookings Institution, 1939.

Price, Don K. *The Scientific Estate.* Cambridge: Belknap Press, 1965.

Saunders, Charles B., Jr. *The Brookings Institution: A Fifty-Year History.* Washington, D.C.:The Brookings Institution, 1966.

Seidman, Harold. *Politics, Position, and Power: The Dynamics of Federal Organization.* 2nd ed. New York: Oxford University Press, 1975.

Shnitzer, Paul A. *Government Contract Bidding.* Washington, D.C.: Federal Publications, 1976.

Smith, Bruce L. R., ed. *The New Political Economy: Public Use of the Private Sector.* New York: Halsted, 1975.

Smith, Bruce L. R. and D. C. Hague, eds. *The Dilemma of Accountability in Modern Government: Independence versus Control.* New York: St. Martin's Press, 1971.

Smith, Bruce L. R. and Joseph J. Karlesky. *The Universities in the Nation's Research Effort.* New York: Change Magazine Press, 1977.

Smith, Darrell Hevenor. *The General Accounting Office: Its History, Activities, and Organization.* Baltimore: Johns Hopkins Press, 1927.

Stourm, René. *The Budget.* Translation of *Le Budget: A Cours de Finances,* 1913. New York: D. Appleton, 1917.

White, Leonard D. *The Federalists: A Study in Administrative History.* New York: Macmillan, 1948.

Willoughby, William F. *The Legal System and Functions of the General Accounting Office of the National Government.* Baltimore: Johns Hopkins Press, 1927.

Wilmerding, Lucius, Jr. *The Spending Power.* New Haven: Yale University Press, 1943.

Official Documents

(Note: Except where otherwise noted, all documents listed here are published in Washington, D.C., by the U.S. Government Printing Office.)

Advisory Commission on Intergovernmental Relations. *Auditing Federalism: GAO's New Intergovernmental Units.* Bulletin 74-9. September 1974.

Budget and Accounting Act of 1921. 67th Congress, Public Law 13. June 10, 1921.

Budget and Accounting Procedures Act of 1950. 81st Congress, Public Law 784. September 12, 1950.

Comptroller General of the United States. *Annual Report of the Comptroller General of the United States.* 1921-1977. Annual.

———. *Decisions of the Comptroller General of the United States,* Vols. 1-57. Annual.

———. *Reports to the Congress by the Comptroller General of the United States.* Various issuances.

Congressional Budget and Impoundment Control Act of 1974. 93rd Congress, Public Law 344. July 12, 1974.

Dockery Act. 53rd Congress, Public Law 174. July 31, 1894.

Federal Election Campaign Act of 1971. 92nd Congress, Public Law 225. February 7, 1972.

Federal Property and Administrative Services Act. 81st Congress, Public Law 151. June 30, 1949.

Fessenden Act. 40th Congress, Public Law 36. March 30, 1868.

General Accounting Office Act of 1974. 93rd Congress, Public Law 604. January 2, 1975.

George Act. 79th Congress, Public Law 4. February 24, 1945.

Government Corporation Control Act. 79th Congress, Public Law 248. December 6, 1945.

Hewlett-Packard Co. v. *United States,* 385 F. (2d) 1013 (1967).

Humphrey's Executor v. *United States,* 295 U.S. 602 (1935).

Improve Governmental Budgeting and Accounting Methods Act. 84th Congress, Public Law 863. August 1, 1956.

Intergovernmental Cooperation Act of 1968. 90th Congress, Public Law 577. October 16, 1968.

Legislative Reorganization Act of 1946. 79th Congress, Public Law 601. August 2, 1946.

Legislative Reorganization Act of 1970. 91st Congress, Public Law 510. October 26, 1970.

Myers v. *United States,* 272 U.S. 52 (1926).

National Security Act Amendments. 81st Congress, Public Law 216. August 10, 1949.

"Need for a National Budget." Message by President W. H. Taft on the Report of the Commission on Economy and Efficiency. 62d Congress. House Document No. 854. 1912.

Post Office Department Financial Control Act. 81st Congress, Public Law 712. August 17, 1950.

President's Commission on Budget Concepts. *Report.* October 1967.

President's Committee on Administrative Management. *Report of the Committee with Studies of Administrative Management in the Federal Government.* 1937.

Prompt Settlement of Public Accounts Act. 14th Congress, Public Law 45. March 3, 1817.

Reorganization Act of 1939. 76th Congress, Public Law 19. April 3, 1939.

Reorganization Act of 1945. 79th Congress, Public Law 263. December 20, 1945.

Treasury Department Act. 1st Congress, Public Law 12. September 2, 1789.

Truth in Negotiations Act. 87th Congress, Public Law 653. September 10, 1962.

U.S. Commission on Federal Paperwork. *Final Summary Report.* October 1977.

U.S. Commission on Government Procurement. *Report.* 4 vols. December 1972.

U.S. Commission on Organization of the Executive Branch of Government (1953-1955). *Budgeting and Accounting.* February 1949.

———. *Concluding Report.* May 1949.

U.S. Commission on Organization of the Executive Branch of Government (1953-1955). *Budget and Accounting.* June 1955.

———. *Final Report to the Congress.* May 1955.

U.S. Congress, Joint Committee on the Organization of the Congress. 89th

Congress. *Final Report to the Congress.* 1966.

U.S. Executive Office of the President. Council of Economic Advisers. *Economic Report of the President.* Annual.

———. Office of Management and Budget. *The Budget of the U.S. Government.* Annual.

U.S. General Accounting Office. *Comprehensive Audit Manual.* Processed, 1952, periodic revisions.

———. *Evaluating Governmental Performance: Changes and Challenges for GAO.* 1975.

———. *GAO Review.* Quarterly, 1966-1978. Of particular interest, summer 1971 issue devoted to the fiftieth anniversary of the GAO.

———. *Improving Management for More Effective Government.* 1971.

———. *Intergovernmental Administration and Grants Management.* Donald C. Stone, ed. Processed, 1977.

———. *Report Manual.* Processed, 1958, periodic revisions.

———. Standards for Audit of Governmental Organizations, Programs, Activities and Functions. 2d ed. 1974.

U.S. House of Representatives, Committee on Government Operations. 89th Congress. *Comptroller General Reports to Congress on Audits of Defense Contracts.* Hearings, 1965.

———. 90th Congress. *Defense Contract Audits.* House Report no. 1132. March 23, 1966.

———. 84th Congress. *The General Accounting Office: A Study of its Organization and Administration with Recommendations for Increasing its Effectiveness.* House Report no. 2264. November 1, 1956.

U.S. House of Representatives, Select Committee on Congressional Operations. 95th Congress. *General Accounting Office Services to Congress: An Assessment.* House Report no. 1317. June 22, 1978.

U.S. House of Representatives, Select Committee on the Budget. 66th Congress. *National Budget System.* Hearings, 1919.

U.S. Privacy Protection Study Commission. *Personal Privacy in an Information Society.* 1977.

U.S. Senate, Commission on the Operation of the Senate. 94th Congress. *Congressional Support Agencies: A Staff Study.* Ernest S. Griffith, ed. 1976.

———. 94th Congress. *Toward a Modern Senate.* Senate Document no. 278. December 1976.

U.S. Senate, Committee on Government Operations. 94th Congress. *The Accounting Establishment: A Staff Study.* December 1976.

———. 91st Congress. *Capability of GAO to Analyze and Audit Defense Expenditures.* Hearings, 1969.

———. 92nd Congress. *Financial Management in the Federal Government.* 2 vol. Senate Report no. 50. 1971.

———. 94th Congress. *GAO Legislation.* Hearings, 1975.

U.S. Senate, Committee on Government Operations. 84th Congress, *Nomination of Joseph Campbell to Become Comptroller General of the United States.* Hearings, 1955.

Articles and Other Materials

It would be impracticable to list all of the articles, speeches, oral histories, interview notes, and other reference materials on which we have relied. Among the journals that were particularly helpful are: *Public Administration Review, American Political Science Review, Journal of Accountancy, Federal Accountant, National Journal, Congressional Quarterly,* and *International Journal of Government Auditing.*

INDEXES

NAME INDEX

379

SUBJECT INDEX